The Performing Arts

Reference Sources in the Humanities Series
James Rettig, Series Editor

Communication and the Mass Media: A Guide to the Reference Literature. By Eleanor S. Block and James K. Bracken.

Journalism: A Guide to the Reference Literature. By Jo A. Cates.

Judiasm and Christianity: A Guide to the Reference Literature. By Edward D. Starkey.

Linguistics: A Guide to the Reference Literature. By Anna L. DeMiller.

Music: A Guide to the Reference Literature. By William S. Brockman.

On the Screen: A Film, Television, and Video Research Guide. By Kim N. Fisher.

The Performing Arts: A Guide to the Reference Literature. By Linda Keir Simons.

Philosophy: A Guide to the Reference Literature. By Hans E. Bynagle.

Reference Guide to Science Fiction, Fantasy, and Horror. By Michael Burgess.

Reference Works in British and American Literature: Volume I, English and American Literature. By James K. Bracken.

Reference Works in British and American Literature: Volume II, English and American Writers. By James K. Bracken.

The Performing Arts
A Guide to the Reference Literature

Linda Keir Simons

1994
Libraries Unlimited, Inc.
Englewood, Colorado

For Bob

"The best is yet to be!"

Copyright © 1994 Linda Keir Simons
All Rights Reserved
Printed in the United States of America

No part of this publication may be reproduced, stored in a retrieval system, or transmitted, in any form or by any means, electronic, mechanical, photocopying, recording, or otherwise, without the prior written permission of the publisher.

LIBRARIES UNLIMITED, INC.
P.O. Box 6633
Englewood, CO 80155-6633
1-800-237-6124

Library of Congress Cataloging-in-Publication Data

Simons, Linda Keir
   The performing arts : a guide to the reference literature / Linda Keir Simons.
     ix, 244 p. 17x25 cm. -- (Reference sources in the humanities series)
     ISBN 0-87287-982-8
   1. Reference books--Performing arts--Bibliography. 2. Performing arts--Bibliography. I. Title. II. Series.
Z6935.S56 1993
[PN1584]
016.791--dc20
                                              93-31465
                                                 CIP

Contents

Preface vii

Chapter 1—Bibliographic Guides 1
    Theatre Guides 1
    Dance Guides 4

Chapter 2—Bibliographies 6
    Theatre Bibliographies 6
    Dance Bibliographies 32
    Play Bibliographies 37
    Discographies 45

Chapter 3—Catalogs 49
    Theatre and Related Arts Catalogs 49
    Commercial Catalogs of Plays 60
    Dance Catalogs 61

Chapter 4—Indexes 64
    Theatre and General Indexes Covering the Performing Arts . 64
    Dance Indexes 71
    Indexes to Plays, Monologues, and Dances 72
    A Costume Index 80

Chapter 5—Dictionaries, Encyclopedias, and Companions . . . 81
    Theatre and the Related Arts 81
    Dance 96

Chapter 6—Biographical Sources 99
    Dance Biographies 114

Chapter 7—Handbooks and Yearbooks 115
    Dance Handbooks 141

Chapter 8—Directories 147
    Dance Directories 158

Chapter 9—Review Sources 160

Chapter 10—Chronologies and Histories 165
        Dance Chronologies 174

Chapter 11—Electronic Discussion Groups 175
        Theatre Discussion Groups 175
        Dance Discussion Groups 177

Chapter 12—Core Periodicals 178
        Theatre and Related Arts 178
        Dance Periodicals 192

Chapter 13—Libraries and Archives 197
        Dance Collections 207

Chapter 14—Professional Organizations and Societies 209
        Dance Associations 213

        Author/Title Index 217
        Subject Index 237

Preface

*"Behind the curtain's mystic fold
The glowing future lies unrolled."*

So Bret Harte described the magic moment we in the audience feel just before the curtain rises on a live performance. For better or worse, we are about to experience the playwright's words or the choreographer's steps as interpreted by these performers on this evening in this theatre. This particular performance will never happen exactly the same way again. And yet, some experiences in the theatre can be vivid enough to last a lifetime. Books about these most ephemeral of the arts are rather more solid, and reading about the theatre or dance can add to one's enjoyment of a performance. An informed audience brings its own dimension to the event.

This book describes, evaluates, and compares reference sources in the performing arts. In defining the scope of the work I have concentrated on theatre and dance along with the minor arts of puppetry, mime, magic, and the circus. Because other guides in this series have dealt with music, film, and television, I have excluded them here. I have included musical comedy, however, which seems more closely related to the commercial theatre of Broadway and the West End than to its distant cousin opera. When evaluating books, I have considered the busy reference librarian who needs to find an answer quickly; the student who requires guidance through an unfamiliar subject; and the scholar who may need help in a field other than her specialty. I emphasize works in English, primarily from the last 30 years, but I have described some older works and some foreign-language works if they have particular value. My standards have differed from chapter to chapter; older bibliographies are included because they contain useful information, but all directories listed are up-to-date.

I have emphasized performance above all, and this guide does not look at books that are primarily interested in drama as literature. Separating performance from text is a risky venture, but if I had included all the drama reference books, I would have written a much longer book with a looser focus. When I examined a work, I considered primarily its value to a reader who was interested in how works are performed on stage. I have, however, included bibliographies of and indexes to plays for the convenience of performing groups who are looking for plays to present. I have tried to represent all aspects of the theatre including a representative group of works dealing with costuming, lighting, makeup, and stage design. For the subjects of puppetry, magic, mime, and the circus, I have described the relatively few works which cover these topics.

Dance presented a unique problem. Unlike other performers, dancers do not need an audience. People have danced since before recorded history to celebrate, to mourn, to pray, and for reasons other than to perform. Today, many people dance purely for recreation. I have included works that deal with dance as performance, that is, classical ballet, modern dance, and show dancing, and a selection of works on traditional and folk dancing. Folk dance is increasingly presented as performance dance by such groups as the Los Angeles based AMAN International Folk Ensemble. I have excluded ballroom and square dancing, which remain primarily recreational and competitive activities.

Like books in this series, this work is arranged by reference-book type—indexes, encyclopedias, bibliographies, directories, and so forth. During the reference interview, librarians must consider not only the subject but the type of source most likely to answer the question. It is hoped that this arrangement will help the librarian choose the best source for the inquiry. The subject index pulls together all books on a single topic, and the author-title index allows one to find the description of a particular work.

Works that relate only to dance have been placed in a separate section in each chapter, but readers should be aware that many of the books in the theatre and related arts sections also discuss dance. The chapter on library and archival collections, especially, contains a number of repositories whose collections, while emphasizing theatre, contain materials relating to dance and other performing arts.

Because not all information needs can be met through reference books, the final chapters describe periodicals, libraries, archives, associations, and electronic discussion groups to which readers may go for additional information. In compiling this information, I have found association representatives, archivists, and librarians to be unfailingly enthusiastic and willing to share information with other librarians and the public. They represent a source that is not used as often as it might be.

Researching this book brought to light a few areas that seem to be in need of further work. The field of dance eagerly awaits the publication by the University of California of *The Encyclopedia of Dance* under the able editorship of dance historian Selma Jean Cohen. The field currently has no equivalent to the *McGraw-Hill Encyclopedia of World Drama* or *The Cambridge Guide to World Theatre*. St. James Press has also promised an international dictionary of ballet that will update the aging guides of Raffe and Koegler. In the area of theatre, American theatre history still awaits a good bibliography on the order of Arnott and Robinson's and Cavanaugh's works. While Odell's *Annals of the New York Stage* and Leiter's chronologies have given scholars a list of productions in New York, the records of the stage in other major cities remain, for the most part, undocumented. Finally, a good periodical index for the performing arts would bring together material that currently is found in the *Humanities Index*, the *Physical Education Index*, the *Modern Language Association Annual*

Bibliography and several others. Although S. Yancey Belknap attempted such an index with her *Guide to the Performing Arts*, no volumes have been published since 1968. The new *Index to Dance Periodicals* promises thorough coverage of that art, but references to theatre and the other performance areas remain scattered in many indexes.

Many people helped transform this book from an idea to a reality. My editor, Jim Rettig, first suggested this project to me, and his sharp eye and pencil have greatly improved my prose. I thank him for his guidance, his patience, and his friendship.

At the University of Dayton, Fr. James Heft, S.M., provost, and Dr. John Geiger, Associate Provost, granted me a sabbatical leave during which I was able to start the research for the book. Dr. Edward Garten, director of libraries, encouraged my efforts and assisted me with my sabbatical application. Everyone in the information services department of Roesch Library shouldered extra burdens during my sabbatical, and I remain grateful for the support of my colleagues. The interlibrary loan department, especially Robert Leach, Mary Ann Middendorp, and Terry Graham, cheerfully ordered and returned dozens of titles for me.

Thanks to the Research and Publications Committee of the Academic Library Association of Ohio for a grant which helped with travel expenses. Librarians at many institutions helped me, especially those at Butler University in Indianapolis who allowed me to use their collection while they were officially closed for renovation. I also received help from the librarians at the Library of Congress/John F. Kennedy Center for the Performing Arts Library in Washington, D.C. and at my alma mater, the University of Illinois/Urbana library.

This book would never have been written without my father and mother, Arthur and Margaret Keir, who instilled in their children a love of books and of the performing arts. Besides the weekly trips to the library and the piano and dance lessons, my parents provided me the opportunity to see the Bolshoi Ballet, touring versions of Broadway musicals, plays produced by the local community theatre, and many other performances. I owe much more than this book to my parents, and I am pleased that they will see its publication.

Finally, I dedicate this work to my husband, Bob Simons. Despite his preoccupation with obtaining a second university degree and changing careers at midlife, he has unhesitatingly supported my work on this book. I truly appreciated his unwavering enthusiasm and optimism, especially when I needed large doses of both.

The mistakes in this work, of course, are mine alone.

Chapter 1

Bibliographic Guides

The guides in this chapter list materials useful for research in one or more of the performing arts. Besides a list of reference sources and a bibliography of important books, a guide often includes a bibliography of journals, a listing of organizations, a directory of libraries, or other supplementary materials useful to a researcher.

Theatre Guides

1. Bailey, Claudia Jean. **A Guide to Reference and Bibliography for Theatre Research**. 2d ed. Columbus: The Ohio State University Libraries Publications Committee, 1983. 149p. LC 83-61581. ISBN 0-88215-049-9.

   A revision of a 1971 edition, this book is divided into two parts reflecting its original purpose as a resource for a theatre research course. The first half is an annotated guide to general reference works; the second half annotates reference sources for theatre, drama, speech, and literature. Arranged by author within subject sections, about two-thirds of the 654 entries are related directly to theatre and drama. An author-title index refers readers to entry numbers. Bailey includes many works on the literary aspects of plays and dramatic criticism. Because her bibliography includes most items in Brockett, Becker, and Bryant's *A Bibliographical Guide to Research in Speech and Dramatic Arts* (Glenview, Ill.: Scott, Foresman, 1963) readers need not consult the older work. Annotations are short and descriptive, but not evaluative. The work's arrangement and the selection of items make it well suited to textbook use, but less useful to librarians who can access the general materials elsewhere.

2. Blazek, Ron, and Elizabeth Aversa. **The Humanities: A Selective Guide to Information Sources**. 3d ed. Englewood, Colo.: Libraries Unlimited, 1988. 383p. LC 87-33907. ISBN 0-87287-558-X.

   Written for library science students, this work deals with each discipline in the humanities in two ways. An "Access" chapter defines the field, describes useful material in general reference books, looks at the use of computers in the field, and lists major institutions (libraries, associations, publishers) associated with it. The "Sources" chapter consists of annotated citations for the most important reference titles. Informative annotations describe and evaluate each work. The authors deal with about 300 items in the performing arts chapter, 100 of which relate to theatre or dance. Other subjects covered include music, film, and television. Author-title and subject indexes provide additional points of access. Both of the authors teach advanced-level reference courses in graduate library schools, and their expertise is apparent in this well-written work.

3. Cheshire, David F. **Theatre: History, Criticism and Reference**. London: Bingley, 1967. 131p. LC 67-92149.

Cheshire's book, a series of bibliographical essays on various types of books about the theatre, discusses reference works, histories, criticism, biographies, theoretical works, and periodicals. Although now dated, it is valuable for excellent critical comments on the works included. Cheshire exhibits a British slant, particularly in the chapters on periodicals and biography.

4. Coleman, Earle J. **Magic: A Reference Guide**. (American Popular Culture series). Westport, Conn.: Greenwood, 1987. 198p. LC 86-29611. ISBN 0-313-23397-7.

More recent and broader in scope than Gill's bibliography (entry 38) Coleman's work is written as a series of bibliographical essays arranged by broad subject areas. Each essay is followed by bibliographical listings for books and periodical articles. Particularly interesting are the chapters on the principles of psychology and showmanship underlying the performance of magic and on magic in relation to other arts. Most of the books listed in the chapter on magic manuals are also found in Gill's list. An appendix lists major periodicals, directories, and research collections. Coleman also lists magic book dealers, an important list since magic books are often difficult to find. The book concludes with author and subject indexes. This work is the most recent and complete guide to magic.

5. Hatch, James V., and Abdullah Omanii, comps. **Black Playwrights, 1823-1977: An Annotated Bibliography of Plays**. New York: R. R. Bowker, 1977. 319p. LC 77-11890. ISBN 0-8352-1032-4.

In an effort to make this book useful both to play producers and to scholars, the authors have included as much information as practical about 2,700 plays written by African-Americans. This work is more comprehensive in numbers of writers covered and in information about each play than Arata and Rotoli's *Black American Playwrights* (entry 18) and its sequel (entry 17), although it does not include any references to reviews or criticism. The main body of the work is an alphabetical list of 900 playwrights with each of the author's plays listed. Producers will be interested in the plot summary, cast information, number of acts, and permissions information. Scholars will be happy to note the date and place of the first production. They will also use the separate bibliographies of books and dissertations on African-American drama and theatre, the list of oral history interviews in the Hatch-Billops Archives in New York City, and the list of theatrical awards presented to Black Americans. Both groups will find the title index useful. Because this book stops at 1977, readers should consult Peterson's *Contemporary Black American Playwrights* (entry 354) for more recent information.

6. Inge, M. Thomas, ed. **Handbook of American Popular Culture**. 2d ed., rev. and enlarged. Westport, Conn.: Greenwood, 1989. 3v. LC 88-39092. ISBN 0-313-25406-0.

Designed to guide readers through the bibliographic maze of American popular culture, the *Handbook* presents a chronological survey of the development of each topic it covers; critical bibliographic essays; descriptions of research centers and collections of materials; and bibliographies of works cited in the text. Of special interest are chapters on the circus, musical theatre, and stage entertainment, all written by Don B. Wilmeth (see entries 12, 97, 98, and 306); on dance; and on magic. Librarians should remember this work, whose bibliographies may suffice in place of more specialized guides they do not own.

7. Mikhail, E. H. **An Annotated Bibliography of Modern Anglo-Irish Drama**. Troy, N.Y.: Whitston, 1981. 300p. LC 80-51874. ISBN 0-87875-201-3.

Written by a prolific bibliographer of Anglo-Irish drama and theatre, this volume lists and describes 1,775 works that present "general criticism on Anglo-Irish drama from 1895 ... to the end of 1977" (preface). Mikhail arranges his guide by type of work, such as bibliographies, reference works, books, periodical articles, and dissertations. Short annotations describe but do not evaluate the works. He also describes library collections that contain information on Anglo-Irish theatre. Although two indexes provide access by name and by subject, neither is very useful because of their general nature. This is a supplementary source.

8. Pronko, Leonard C. **Guide to Japanese Drama**. 2d ed. (Asian Literature Bibliography series). Boston: G. K. Hall, 1984. 149p. LC 84-9026. ISBN 0-8161-8631-6.

As the first Westerner admitted to the kabuki training program of the National Theatre of Japan, Pronko brings both acting and academic credentials to his work, which includes 105 citations arranged by subject. Designed to guide the nonspecialist through the English literature on the Japanese drama and theatre, the long annotations describe and evaluate each work. Of special interest are the chapters on texts of Japanese plays and on the history and culture of Japanese theatre.

9. Rachow, Louis A., ed. **Theatre and Performing Arts Collections**. (Special Collections, vol. 1, no. 1). New York: Haworth Press, 1981. 166p. LC 81-6567. ISBN 0-917724-47-X.

The first of Lee Ash's Special Collections series, this work gains from having as its editor the distinguished theatre librarian Louis Rachow. Besides writing an informative historical introduction and a bibliographic essay that notes important catalogs and bibliographies, Rachow has chosen eight important American theatre collections to profile. The curators or librarians of the collections at the Library of Congress, the New York Public Library's Billy Rose Theatre Collection, The Players Club, Princeton University, the Universities of Texas and Wisconsin, and the Metropolitan Toronto Library, and the now defunct Theatre Museum in Boothbay, Maine describe their holdings and note finding aids. In his introduction Rachow names and describes several other important theatre repositories including the collections at Harvard University, Boston University, and the University of California at Davis. He also profiles the Shubert Archives in New York City. Additional chapters list booksellers with strong theatre inventories, significant performing arts collections by state, and major theatre and drama awards. Although not comprehensive, this book's well written descriptions of major collections will help guide readers to significant manuscript and archival materials. It can be used with Young's *American Theatrical Arts* (entry 522).

10. Shaland, Irene. **American Theater and Drama Research: An Annotated Guide to Information Sources, 1945-1990**. Jefferson, N.C.: McFarland, 1991. 157p. LC 91-52741. ISBN 0-89950-626-7.

Concentrating on works about American theatre and drama since World War II, Shaland annotates 451 books, periodicals, and databases arranged by subject and type of source. She also describes eighty-five organizations and research centers that provide information about American theatre. With an emphasis on works published since 1965, Shaland has selected only books written in English and published in the United States. Her narrow focus allows her to include a number of books that may contain useful information but are not strictly reference works. She has annotated many monographs and collections of essays, especially in the area of theatre history. For this reason her work may be more useful to readers looking for extensive information than to reference librarians trying to answer specific questions.

11. Whalon, Marion K. **Performing Arts Research: A Guide to Information Sources**. Detroit: Gale Research, 1976. 280p. LC 75-13828. ISBN 0-8103-1364-2.

Although it is now aging, this well-written work remains a valuable guide to the field. Arranged by type of reference tool and then by subject area, the citations describe each work. Some annotations include evaluative comments as well. Whalon defines her subject broadly and includes works on drama, film, opera, music, aesthetics, and television as well as theatre, dance, and mime. Her chapter on sources of illustrations and audiovisual materials is especially helpful and not duplicated in other guides. A useful author, title, and subject index provides access. Cross-references in the text are ample but difficult to use since items are not numbered.

12. Wilmeth, Don B. **Variety Entertainment and Outdoor Amusements: A Reference Guide**. (American Popular Culture series). Westport, Conn.: Greenwood, 1982. 242p. LC 81-13417. ISBN 0-313-21455-7.

This guide aims to "provide brief historical overviews of major forms of American variety entertainment and outdoor amusements," to present a short description and evaluation of the literature, and to list major sources (preface). Wilmeth organizes his material into chapters on the circus, wild west exhibits, dime museums, medicine shows, minstrel shows, vaudeville, burlesque and striptease, musicals, magic, floating palaces and tent theatres, fairs, carnivals, and theme parks. Each chapter begins with a short history of the amusement, concentrating on its American form but mentioning European antecedents if appropriate. A bibliographic essay follows in which Wilmeth evaluates major books and articles on the topic. He also notes significant periodicals, collections, and organizations. Each chapter concludes with a bibliography arranged by author and containing standard bibliographic data for each entry. The alphabetical index of authors and subjects refers only to the historical and bibliographical essays, not to the final bibliographies in each chapter. See also Wilmeth's *American and English Popular Entertainment* (entry 97).

Dance Guides

13. **Dance Resource Guide**. Reston, Va.: National Dance Association, 1990. 65lp. LC 91-662244. ISBN 0-88314-484-0.

Although this guide is aimed at dance teachers in elementary and secondary schools, much of its information will interest anyone involved in dance. Arranged by type of material and then by topic, the entries list names and addresses of professional organizations, journals, and book publishers and distributors. This directory information precedes annotated lists of recordings, reference books, and books and films on various dance topics such as ballet, jazz dance, multiculturalism and dance, and health concerns of dancers. Appendices list additional art and dance organizations and additional periodicals. Although it suffers from inadequate organization (all organizations should be merged into one list, for example), this guide helps beginners find their way through the literature of the dance world today. One hopes the National Dance Association will publish revised and improved editions at regular intervals.

14. Drewal, Margaret and Glorianne Jackson Thompson, comps. **Sources on African and African-Related Dance**. New York: American Dance Guild, 1974. 38p. LC 78-313651.

Compiled by two teachers of dance, this bibliography lists books and articles "useful in the reconstruction and understanding of traditional dance forms as well as in the evaluation of approaches to the study of dance" (introduction). It also lists organizations and archives that might be helpful to the researcher as well as bibliographies and filmographies. Unfortunately, the citations are not annotated, and no explanation is given of the sources or methods used to compile this work. It should be supplemented by consulting the New York Public Library's *Dance Catalog* (entry 195), its annual bibliographies (entry 193), and standard periodical indexes.

Chapter 2

Bibliographies

This chapter is divided into four parts: listings for theatre and related performing arts, dance bibliographies, bibliographies of plays, and discographies. Readers may wish to check the annotations of catalogs in the next chapter as well, because catalogs are simply bibliographies of particular collections.

Theatre Bibliographies

15. **Afro-American Poetry and Drama, 1760-1975: A Guide to Information Sources.** (American Literature, English Literature, and World Literatures in English, vol. 17; Gale Information Guide Library). Detroit: Gale Research, 1979. 493p. LC 74-11518. ISBN 0-8103-1208-5.

The second half of this book, written by G. E. Fabre, lists resources that aid the student of African-American drama and theatre. The majority of citations are to published plays and criticism of Black American playwrights. Unpublished plays are also cited if the playwright has published at least one play. Only published plays are annotated. Fabre includes chapters on major library collections, periodicals, and anthologies that deal with Black drama as well as general bibliographies of secondary works on Black theatre.

16. Alfredson, James B., and George L. Daily. **A Bibliography of Conjuring Periodicals in English: 1791-1983**. York, Pa.: Magicana for Collectors, 1986. 395p. LC 76-377483. ISBN 0-916638-37-5.

Alfredson, a longtime collector of magic periodicals, and Daily, a mail order bookseller specializing in out-of-print magic periodicals and books, have collaborated on an extensive list of conjuring periodicals published during the last two hundred years. Confining themselves to titles in English, the authors list publishing information (title, editor, place of publication, publisher or sponsoring organization, frequency) as well as reproduction method (printed, mimeographed, and so forth), size, and dates of first and last issues. Of interest to collectors is the information on the number of issues comprising a complete file and the estimated scarcity of the title. Alfredson and Daily list each issue of the periodical so that readers can note incomplete volumes and unpublished issues. This work supersedes the authors' earlier book, *A Short Title Check List of Conjuring Periodicals in English*, which is virtually unobtainable.

17. Arata, Esther Spring. **More Black American Playwrights: A Bibliography**. Metuchen, N.J.: Scarecrow, 1978. 321p. LC 78-15231. ISBN 0-8108-1158-8.

18. Arata, Esther Spring, and Nicholas John Rotoli. **Black American Playwrights, 1800 to the Present: A Bibliography**. Metuchen, N.J.: Scarecrow, 1976. 295p. LC 76-2376. ISBN 0-8108-0912-5.

These guides, while uneven in coverage, supplement Hatch and Omanii's *Black Playwrights, 1823-1977* (entry 5). Unlike that work, these two books do not provide annotations for plays. Rather, they list plays, filmscripts, criticism, and play reviews for Black American playwrights. Well-known authors such as Ossie Davis have long, relatively complete entries, while some lesser-known writers have only the title of their play(s) listed. The first volume includes 530 playwrights while the second volume covers 480 writers, 190 of whom overlap the first volume. For those who appear in both volumes, Arata has provided new primary and critical material in the second volume. Entries appear in alphabetical arrangement by playwright's name. Each volume also presents a fairly substantial, though now outdated, general bibliography on African-Americans and the American theatre. An index of play titles completes each volume. Few reviews from major African-American newspapers appear, a regrettable oversight. This work is not as complete as Hatch and Omanii or as recent as Peterson (entry 354). Because of the lack of information about many Black playwrights, however, it should be used as a supplemental source to these other bibliographies.

19. Archer, Stephen M. **American Actors and Actresses: A Guide to Information Sources**. (Performing Arts Information Guide Series, vol. 8; Gale Information Guide Library). Detroit: Gale Research, 1983. 710p. LC 82-15685. ISBN 0-8103-1495-9.

Archer focuses on books and periodical articles "about American actors and actresses from the beginning of professional theatre in this country to the present" (introduction). He lists and describes over 2,600 books and articles that discuss the lives and careers of 226 actors. About 600 additional entries cite sources such as biographical dictionaries, group biographies, and nontheatrical memoirs that contain information on actors. Newspaper articles and manuscript materials are omitted, as are dissertations. Archer's short annotations describe and sometimes evaluate the materials cited. Author, title, and subject indexes augment the many cross-references in the text. Use this bibliography with Wearing's index (entry 364), Johnson (entry 53), and Moyer (entry 76).

20. Arnott, James Fullarton, and John William Robinson. **English Theatrical Literature, 1559-1900: A Bibliography; Incorporating Robert W. Lowe's A Bibliographical Account of English Theatrical Literature Published in 1888**. London: Society for Theatre Research, 1970. 486p. LC 76-552584. ISBN 0-85430-000-7.

A "recension" of Robert Lowe's *Bibliographical Account of English Theatrical Literature* (1888), this work corrects and adds to the original. Arnott and Robinson have kept all of Lowe's notes and comments, many of which have a distinct nineteenth-century character. (Lowe wrote of the eighteenth-century actress Sophia Baddeley, "A very beautiful woman with a very bad character.") The present authors have added their own notes when necessary to clarify or correct the earlier work. Broad in scope, this work includes opera, pantomime, and the music hall, although it excludes ballet and the circus. It includes all printed materials except playbills and programs of plays. The book's scope extends to Irish and Scottish theatre as well as English, and includes American and other overseas editions and translations, listed as notes to the British edition. Although the authors examined the great majority of works listed, they have included a few items not seen. The work is arranged by broad subject categories such as "Government Regulation of the Theatre," "Amateur Theatre," and so on. Many subheadings are used, and within these classifications, entries are arranged chronologically. One location, usually a British library, is listed for each book. Cross references at the beginning of each section and three indexes guide the reader to the appropriate entries. These indexes are an author index, a short title index, and an index of places of publication, the last useful for locating books of local theatrical history. Scholarly, yet entertainingly written, this is a model of a good bibliography. It is an essential work for anyone researching pre-1900 English theatre and should be used with John Cavanagh's *British Theatre: A Bibliography 1901 to 1985* (entry 28), which continues it.

21. Babula, William. **Shakespeare in Production, 1935-1978: A Selective Catalogue**. (Garland Reference Library of the Humanities, vol. 133). New York: Garland, 1981. 383p. LC 78-68244. ISBN 0-8240-9814-5.

Babula has selected from among the many productions of Shakespeare's plays staged in the United States, Canada, and England between 1935 and 1978 those that he deems important because of their unusual or influential staging, setting, stage business, or interpretation. He arranges his choices by play, starting with *All's Well That Ends Well* and ending with *The Winter's Tale*, and lists company, theatre, location, director, and year of the production. In separate paragraphs, he cites and summarizes two or three reviews. Many readers will find Babula's purpose unclear and his execution unsatisfactory. With the assurance that both the list of productions and the review summaries are incomplete, readers may wonder what they have missed. At best, this work is a starting point for those who want to know more about Shakespearean production.

22. Baker, Blanche M. **Theatre and Allied Arts: A Guide to Books Dealing with the History, Criticism, and Technic of the Drama and Theatre and Related Arts and Crafts**. New York: B. Blom, 1967 (c. 1952). 536p. LC 66-12284.

Baker records and describes about 6,000 works on drama, theatre, and related fields, including dance, published between 1885 and 1948 (plus a few printed earlier). Geographical scope is worldwide, but the books cited are written in English except for some works on costume. Baker uses a broad subject arrangement with indexes to authors and more specific subjects. A special section lists indexes, bibliographies, directories, periodicals, and other reference sources. The short annotations are descriptive and sometimes evaluative. Many of the works discussed have been updated or superseded, but Baker's book is the most comprehensive for the time period she covers. This largely supersedes Baker's earlier book, *A Dramatic Bibliography*.

23. Ball, John, and Richard Plant. **A Bibliography of Canadian Theatre History 1583-1975**. Toronto: The Playwrights Co-op, 1976. 160p. Supplement, 1979. 75p. LC 76-383197; 80-472623. ISBN 0-919834-02-7; 0-919834-03-5 pa. Supplement. ISBN 0-88754-170-4; 0-88754-136-4 pa.

Designed to accompany McCallum (entry 497) and the *Brock Bibliography* (entry 140), this records 2,000 works spanning 400 years of Canadian theatrical history. The compilers have chosen to concentrate on English-speaking Canada, and they warn readers that the chapter on French-Canadian theatre is not exhaustive. They arrange their unannotated citations by topic with special sections for the Stratford Festival, the Canadian community theatre movement, theatre education, and so on. Within each chapter items fall in chronological order. Both the original volume and the supplement, which brings the bibliography up to 1976, contain an alphabetical index to authors, titles, and subjects. This work, together with McCallum and the *Brock Bibliography*, is essential to the researcher of Canadian theatrical history.

24. Benedict, Stephen, and Linda C. Coe. **Arts Management: An Annotated Bibliography**. rev. ed. New York: Center for Arts Information, 1980. 1v. LC 80-25918. ISBN 0-89062-049-0.

Benedict and Coe access books, periodical articles, and reports, most published in the 1970s, about arts management. Arranged by broad subject headings, the work is indexed by author and title. Entries consist of a citation and an annotation. Because of its age, this work should be used only as a supplement to the bibliography in Langley's handbook (entry 417).

25. Bergeron, David M. **Twentieth-Century Criticism of English Masques, Pageants, and Entertainments: 1558-1642; With a Supplement on the Folk-Play and Related Forms by Harry B. Caldwell**. San Antonio, Tex.: Trinity University Press, 1972. 67p. LC 71-190310. ISBN 0-911536-46-9.

Bergeron concentrates on British and American criticism of civic pageants and court masques that flourished during the reigns of Elizabeth I and the first two Stuart kings. The unannotated citations are listed alphabetically by author of the criticism. Special chapters deal with Ben Jonson and John Milton. Bergeron identifies 416 items on court entertainments, and Caldwell lists 103 items on folk and mummers plays of the period. The book is indexed by author and subject.

26. Brandon, James R., ed. Elizabeth Wichmann, associate ed. **Asian Theatre: A Study Guide and Annotated Bibliography**. (Theatre Perspectives, no. 1). Washington, D.C.: American Theatre Association, 1979. 197p. LC 81-173303. ISBN 0-940528-16-9.

Brandon has based his bibliography on twenty-four years of research on the Asian theatre, and he believes it to be the most comprehensive list of materials on that subject. Its purpose is "to help the general English-language reader find materials for the study of Asian theatre" (introduction). Brandon lists all major books and dissertations and many secondary or specialized works as well. He also includes references to significant journal articles and book chapters, recent translations of plays, some recordings, film and videotapes available in the United States, and important reference books. Organized by geographic area, the book's coverage is more complete for the smaller Asian countries than for Japan and China. Each chapter consists of an introductory essay on the theatre of that country and a listing of bibliographic entries. A short annotation follows the bibliographic citation for each entry. Because Asian theatre incorporates dance, music, and puppetry, readers will find references to those arts here as well. This is a well-executed bibliography especially helpful to readers who lack Asian language skills.

27. Carpenter, Charles A. **Modern Drama Scholarship and Criticism 1966-1980: An International Bibliography**. Toronto: University of Toronto Press, 1986. 587p. LC 86-218913. ISBN 0-8020-2549-8.

Though primarily a bibliography of drama, this work includes material on the theatre. Its strength lies in its coverage of many countries including those in North America, Western and Eastern Europe, Africa, Australasia, and Asia. Carpenter examined 1,600 journals and thousands of books in many languages to compile 27,300 entries. Arranged by country, unannotated citations for works about theatre are usually found in a separate subsection labeled "theatre." A name index locates authors and subjects by name. To understand the compiler's selection policy and to interpret the citations correctly, users should read Carpenter's lengthy introduction.

28. Cavanagh, John. **British Theatre: A Bibliography, 1901-1985**. Romsey, England: Motley Press, 1989. 510p. LC 90-139675. ISBN 0-900281-01-4.

A continuation of Arnott and Robinson (entry 20), this equally scholarly bibliography uses a similar classified arrangement and chronological approach. Cavanagh broadens his scope to include theses, dissertations, and foreign works (not just foreign editions of British titles). More importantly, he extends coverage to works on dance, music, and drama as well as theatre. On the other hand, he has omitted some works because they are included in other standard bibliographies such as Stratman's *Bibliography of Medieval Drama* (entry 136). It is imperative that a user read Cavanagh's preface to understand both the scope and the arrangement of the work. Cavanagh arranges the bibliography by three major divisions: theatre, drama, and music. Theatre emphasizes performance while drama "covers the history of dramatic genres and influences, and the lives and work of dramatists" (preface). Music is treated as an adjunct to dramatic theatre and as musical theatre. Within these divisions a classified subject arrangement is used. Entries give standard bibliographic information and one location, usually a British library. Some entries have short, factual annotations. A subject index (mainly names) and an author index complete the volume. This well-organized bibliography, indispensable to anyone researching British theatre or drama, is a superb place to find biographies of actors, directors, designers, critics, and others related to the British stage. It should be used with Arnott and Robinson for a complete search.

29. Conolly, L. W., and J. P. Wearing. **English Drama and Theatre, 1800-1900: A Guide to the Information Sources**. (American Literature, English Literature, and World Literatures in English, vol. 12; Gale Information Guide Library). Detroit: Gale Research, 1978. 508p. LC 73-16975. ISBN 0-8103-1225-5.

The authors, founders of the journal *Nineteenth Century Theatre* (entry 624), have tried "to provide comprehensive, though not exhaustive, coverage of all important aspects of nineteenth-century English drama and theatre" (introduction). The largest part of this bibliography consists of entries for nineteenth-century dramatists, listing their works, biographies and critical studies. Nevertheless, there is much in this volume of interest to the theatre researcher. Chapters on British theatres, actors and managers, critics, and stage design list books, journal articles, and dissertations. Within each section, entries are arranged chronologically and are often given short annotations. The chapter on bibliographies and reference books cites the standard works as well as a number of important periodical articles. A chapter on periodicals includes both contemporary (nineteenth century) and modern titles and refers readers to Arnott and Robinson (entry 20) and Stratman's *Britain's Theatrical Periodicals* (entry 90) for more complete coverage. An index provides access by author and subject. This guide should be a first stop for anyone interested in nineteenth-century British theatre.

30. Coven, Brenda. **American Women Dramatists of the Twentieth Century: A Bibliography**. Metuchen, N.J.: Scarecrow, 1982. 237p. LC 82-5942. ISBN 0-8108-1562-1.

The women profiled in this work run the gamut from famous (Lillian Helman, Carson McCullers) to obscure (Gertrude Tonkonogy, a collaborator with George Kaufman on *Town House*). Some are associated more closely with other genres, for example, Edna St. Vincent Millay and Mary Roberts Rinehart. Each of the 133 women, however, has written at least one successfully produced play for Broadway or off-Broadway. Coven cites each author's plays, complete with bibliographic citations and details of the first production, play reviews, and criticism. Perhaps because of a lack of sources, the citations to critical works are the weakest part of the entries. Coven includes a short bibliography of works about American women dramatists in general and an index of play titles.

31. Crothers, J. Frances. **The Puppeteer's Library Guide: The Bibliographic Index to the Literature of the World Puppet Theatre.** Vol. 1, **The Historical Background of Puppetry and Its Related Fields.** Metuchen, N.J.: Scarecrow, 1971. 474p. LC 71-149991. ISBN 0-8108-0319-4.

Intended to be one of a six-volume bibliography on puppetry, this book and its companion, *The Puppet as an Educator* (entry 32), were the only two published. This volume concerns the history of puppetry worldwide and demonstrates the universal appeal of puppets and marionettes. Crothers notes that her bibliography is selective rather than comprehensive. She includes materials published in America between 1639 and 1970 and foreign publications starting somewhat earlier. The largely unannotated entries include works in English, French, German, Italian, and other languages. Crothers arranges the materials into two sections, "Historical Background of World Puppetry" and "The Organizations, Guilds, and Periodicals of Puppetry." The first section is further divided into subject areas. There is an excellent chapter on Punch and Judy materials, and a long chapter on puppetry in various countries. Crothers has enhanced the international chapter by listing and defining important words and phrases from each country's puppet tradition. She encourages the reader to use these terms in other bibliographies and indexes to search for additional sources. The second section lists puppet groups, periodicals devoted to puppetry, and articles about festivals, exhibits, and other gatherings of puppeteers. An author index is an additional help.

32. Crothers, J. Frances. **The Puppeteer's Library Guide: The Bibliographic Index to the Literature of the World Puppet Theatre.** Vol. 2, **The Puppet as an Educator.** Metuchen, N.J.: Scarecrow, 1983. 349p. LC 71-149991. ISBN 0-8108-1611-3.

The second volume of Crothers' puppet bibliography concentrates on puppetry in education. Including English-language books, journal articles, dissertations, and theses, Crothers arranges the book into chapters on broad subjects such as puppetry by age and grade level, puppets in special subjects like history or mathematics, puppets in higher education, and so forth. The compiler documents the twentieth century (materials date from 1903), the time when puppets as educational tools came into their own. Some citations are briefly annotated. This volume is not as important for the performing arts as volume 1 (entry 31), but it is useful to teachers and librarians who use puppets as a teaching tool.

33. Dillard, Philip H. **How Quaint the Ways of Paradox!: An Annotated Gilbert & Sullivan Bibliography.** Metuchen, N.J.: Scarecrow, 1991. 208p. LC 91-3763. ISBN 0-8108-2445-0.

Dillard lists and describes more than 1,000 books and journal articles written about the famous composer and librettist. The work includes not just materials about the Gilbert and Sullivan partnership, but also about each man himself. Dillard organizes his work by subject, and the largest chapters deal with biography and history of Gilbert and Sullivan (214 items) and analysis and criticism of their works (216 items). Other chapters contain references to books and articles describing productions; collected librettos, plays, and poems of Gilbert; and reference works. The work is indexed by title and by name of authors, editors, compilers, and translators of the books and articles. A short chronology provides important dates in the lives of Gilbert and Sullivan. Dillard's work is the most recent and complete bibliography on the creators of the Savoyard operas.

33a. Duffy, Susan, comp. **The Political Left in the American Theatre of the 1930's: A Bibliographic Sourcebook**. Metuchen, N.J.: Scarecrow, 1992. 213p. LC 92-10822. ISBN 0-8108-2577-5.

With the aim of encouraging research into the American political theatre of the 1930s, Duffy lists 1,300 books, book chapters, articles, plays, and dissertations, some with annotations. The book is divided into chapters according to type of material listed, and Duffy's introductory essays discuss the most important works and suggest additional avenues to explore. Entries list works published between the 1930s and the 1990s, both primary and secondary sources. Duffy includes names and addresses of archives that contain significant collections on political theatre. An index locates playwrights, book and journal titles, names, but not play titles. For additional material on the Federal Theatre Project of the 1930s, see *The Federal Theatre Project: A Catalog-Calendar of Productions* (entry 550).

34. Fleshman, Bob, ed. **Theatrical Movement: A Bibliographical Anthology**. Metuchen, N.J.: Scarecrow, 1986. 742p. LC 85-1795. ISBN 0-8108-1789-6.

Aimed at those who work or teach in the fields of theatre or dance, Fleshman's book features a series of bibliographic essays, each followed by a bibliography on a variety of movement topics. Written by academic specialists, chapters cover mime; dance notation; body language and nonverbal communication; and theatrical movement in a number of cultures including Japan, Korea, Turkey, Africa, and Eskimo society. Generally, the essays complement Barba's *Dictionary of Theatre Anthropology* (entry 259), which defines and illustrates movement patterns in other cultures. Those who want to go beyond Barba can be guided to additional sources by using Fleshman.

35. Fordyce, Rachel. **Children's Theatre and Creative Dramatics: An Annotated Bibliography of Critical Works**. Boston: G. K. Hall, 1975. 275p. LC 75-11868. ISBN 0-8161-1161-8.

Fordyce collects and annotates "2,269 source materials related to drama with and for children, and available in the United States" (preface). Directed to the academic rather than the practitioner, the book concentrates on works of a critical, instructional, historical, or evaluative nature. The first section describes articles, books, and dissertations that cover both children's theatre and creative dramatics. The next sections deal with works on children's theatre and materials about creative dramatics, respectively. About 90 percent of the entries are annotated, and they are arranged within each section by subject. An author index completes the book. Of special interest are the many references to works about specific children's theatre groups. Carol Jean Kennedy's bibliography (entry 55) updates this work through 1979.

36. Fuld, James J. **The Book of World-Famous Libretti: The Musical Theater from 1598 to Today**. New York: Pendragon Press, 1984. 365p. LC 83-17438. ISBN 0-918728-27-4.

Fuld provides a facsimile of the title page and bibliographic and physical descriptions of the original librettos of 168 operas, operettas, and musical comedies. He also lists the date of the work's first performance and locates at least one copy of the original libretto.

Although most of the works are operas, Fuld describes the works of Gilbert and Sullivan and musical comedies such as *Carousel, West Side Story, My Fair Lady,* and *Annie Get Your Gun.* He indexes the work by librettist and composer and provides a chronology. This is a specialized work of interest to those enamored of bibliographic minutiae.

37. Gamble, William Burt. **Development of Scenic Art and Stage Machinery; A List of References in the New York Public Library**. rev., with additions. New York: New York Public Library, 1928. 231p. LC 30-23639.

An old but well-written work, Gamble's bibliography lists books and magazine articles on stage technique during every historical period from the ancient Greeks to the early twentieth century. He includes references to works in several languages that describe practices of the Russian and Asian stage as well as the European and American theatres. Other subjects that Gamble treats are scenery, lighting, machinery, open air theatres, little theatres, and marionettes. Altogether, 4,766 items are cited with one- or two-line annotations. This book is helpful when looking for historical material on the technical aspects of theatre.

38. Gill, Robert. **Magic as a Performing Art: A Bibliography of Conjuring**. (College of Librarianship, Wales Bibliographies). New York: R. R. Bowker, 1976. 252p. LC 77-36982. ISBN 0-85935-038-X.

Called the most useful bibliography on magic by Coleman (entry 4), this work describes almost 1,100 books and booklets on magic published in English between 1935 and 1975. Meant to be a practical guide for the practicing magician, the book is divided into a chapter on the bibliography of magic and a chapter listing biographies of magicians and manuals of tricks. Both chapters are arranged alphabetically by author. One can find Robert Alan Nelson's "How to Read Sealed Messages" and Ian H. Adair's many published works on "dove magic"(using doves in a magic act). Subject, title, and name indexes provide good access to the bibliography. Himself a magician, Gill acknowledges the difficulty non-magicians will have in obtaining much of this material. Most of it is published in limited editions and sold only to magicians. He suggests joining a magician's society to gain access. Most organizations will require a demonstration of some proficiency in performing magic before admitting a newcomer, however. Many of the works listed here are also listed in Coleman's chapter on manuals.

39. Gohdes, Clarence. **Literature and Theater of the States and Regions of the U.S.A.: An Historical Bibliography**. Durham, N.C.: Duke University Press, 1967. 276p. LC 66-30584.

Gohdes' interest lies in local literary and theatrical activities in the United States from its beginnings to 1964. He provides an unannotated list of works on theatre in every state and region of this country. The majority of citations are to periodical articles, but books and pamphlets are also included. Gohdes concentrates on legitimate theatre, and this work is more limited in scope than Carl Stratman's *A Bibliography of the American Theatre, Excluding New York City* (entry 89). Larson (entry 64) has updated and corrected Gohdes, but stops at 1900. Gohdes, moreover, contains a section on New York City theatrical history, the only book of these three to do so. The work is arranged by state and region (e.g. Middle West, New England), and entries dealing with the theater (more than 2,000) are separated from those referring to literature. There are no indexes. Gohdes should be consulted along with Stratman for twentieth-century regional theatrical history.

40. Gray, John, comp. **Black Theatre and Performance: A Pan-African Bibliography**. (Bibliographies and Indexes in Afro-American and African Studies). Westport, Conn.: Greenwood, 1990. 414p. LC 89-25836. ISBN 0-313-26875-4.

Gray admits to a didactic reason for compiling this bibliography. Wanting to provide resources for educators who are pursuing multiculturalism in the classroom, he locates a great many books, articles, dissertations, films and other materials about Black theatre both in Africa and elsewhere. This book does not cover Black theatre in the United States, however. Readers who need African-American materials should consult Hatch (entries 5, 126), Arata (entries 17, 18) and Peterson (entries 354, 355). This unannotated bibliography divides into two parts: Africa and what Gray calls The Diaspora. Within each section studies of theatre in individual countries are followed by studies of individual playwrights and their works. Gray has included references to as much biographical and critical work as he can find about each playwright and has listed all plays. He has managed to find at least a few studies of theatre for even the smallest, poorest African countries such as Malawi, and for Canada, Europe, and the West Indies nations. A large amount of this material is written in English although many European and African languages are also represented. The book is indexed well, with an index of playwrights, as well as author, title, and subject indexes.

41. Hainaux, René. **Les arts du spectacle: bibliographie; ouvrages en langue française concernant théâtre, musique, mime, marionettes, variétés, cirque, radio, télévision, cinéma, publiés dans le monde entre 1960 et 1985**. Brussels: Editions Labor, 1989. 268p. LC 89-190114. ISBN 2-8040-0394-9.

With a table of contents, introduction, and foreword written in English as well as French, this bibliography concentrates on French-language books written on the performing arts worldwide. As the title indicates, it covers not just theatre and dance, but also circus, music, pantomime, puppetry, the electronic media, and variety entertainment. Arranged by these types of performance, then by further subject subdivisions, then by author, entries list author, title, place of publication, publisher, date of publication, and number of pages. Neither plays nor periodical articles are included. The large theatre section encompasses staging; technical theatre topics; theatre as a social phenomenon (vis-à-vis politics, religion, and so forth); theatre history; and theatre activity in various countries. This should be useful to the advanced student or scholar seeking recent books in French on the performing arts.

42. Hall, Trevor H. **A Bibliography of Books on Conjuring in English from 1580 to 1850**. Minneapolis, Minn.: Carl Wring Jones, 1957. 96p. LC 57-49046.

Intended for the collector of rare magic books, Hall's bibliography describes 319 conjuring books written during the late sixteenth through the mid-nineteenth centuries. Arranged by author, the entries provide title, place of publication, publisher, date, and pagination. The name index lists authors, publishers, and other people mentioned in the text. Hall's *Old Conjuring Books* (entry 43) contains a supplementary checklist that updates this specialized bibliography.

43. Hall, Trevor H. **Old Conjuring Books: A Bibliographical and Historical Study with a Supplementary Check-list**. New York: St. Martin's Press, 1973. 228p. LC 72-93469.

Although mainly a historical study of a small number of conjuring books, Hall's work includes a checklist that supplements his earlier bibliography (entry 42); a critical assessment of conjuring and magic bibliographies; and a chapter on collectors and libraries that is now outdated but useful for historical purposes.

44. Harris, Richard H. **Modern Drama in America and England, 1950-1970: A Guide to Information Sources**. (American Literature, English Literature, and World Literatures in English, vol. 34; Gale Information Guide Library). Detroit: Gale Research, 1982. 606p. LC 74-11524. ISBN 0-8103-1218-2.

Harris cites and annotates the works of and criticism of 255 British and American playwrights who published plays between 1950 and 1975. The introductory chapters refer to materials that describe the theatre during that period. For each playwright Harris lists plays, selected nondramatic writing, and criticism. Author, title, and subject indexes provide good access to the citations. Although not comprehensive by any means, this is a good starting point for information about modern playwrights, especially for undergraduate students.

45. Hebblethwaite, Frank P. **A Bibliographical Guide to the Spanish American Theater**. (Pan American Union, Division of Philosophy and Letters, Basic Bibliographies, 6). Washington, D.C.: Pan American Union, 1969. 84p. LC 70-604133.

Drawing from the holdings of the Library of Congress and the Pan American Union Library, Hebblethwaite has compiled "an extensive listing of materials on the history and criticism of the Spanish American theatre in its entirety, from the colonial period to the present" (introduction). Most of the works cited are written in Spanish with a few written in English. The bibliography is divided into three sections: books, journal articles, and bibliographies. Each section is further divided into general sources that treat Spanish American theatre in its entirety and sources by country. The author annotates books and some periodical articles. An author index provides additional access. Readers should also check Lyday and Woodyard (entry 70).

46. Heck, Thomas F. **Commedia Dell'Arte: A Guide to the Primary and Secondary Literature**. (Garland Reference Library of the Humanities, vol. 786). New York: Garland, 1988. 450p. LC 87-29210. ISBN 0-8240-6644-8.

The most current and comprehensive bibliography on the subject of commedia dell'arte, its history and its influence on later theatrical forms, this book will appeal to the advanced researcher. Only 29 percent of the 1,000 works it lists are in English, and one half of the total are in Italian or French. The book is arranged in chapters by subject (for example, the influence of commedia dell'arte on later forms such as vaudeville, minstrel shows, and comedians like the Marx Brothers and Charlie Chaplin). Within each chapter the alphabetical entries include annotations. Heck includes a subject index and a title list of scenarios. The casual reader may be better served by the bibliographies in the *New Encyclopedia Britannica* (1979) or in the *Readers Encyclopedia of World Drama* (Crowell, 1965), both cited by Heck.

47. Hiler, Hilaire, and Meyer Hiler. **Bibliography of Costume: A Dictionary Catalog of About Eight Thousand Books and Periodicals**. Bronx, N.Y.: H. W. Wilson, 1939. Reprint New York: B. Blom, 1967. 911p. LC 66-12285.

16 / 2—Bibliographies

This scholarly bibliography is an old but still useful standard work in the field of costume. It provides bibliographic information on 8,400 works in many languages on all aspects of costume, not just theatrical costume. In this respect it is more comprehensive than Kesler's work (entry 56), which concentrates on costume for the theatre and dance. Readers can use this bibliography to find information on very specific subjects such as handkerchiefs or fans, for instance. Each work is listed by author, title and subject(s), and full information is stated under the author listing. The Hilers sometimes include a brief annotation to clarify the subject matter of an entry. This book should be consulted for historical treatments of various aspects of costume. For more recent works and for technical works on costume, consult Kessler.

48. Hotaling, Edward R. **Shakespeare and the Musical Stage: A Guide to Sources, Studies, and First Performances**. Boston: G. K. Hall, 1990. 517p. LC 89-26776. ISBN 0-8161-9070-4.

What do *The Boys from Syracuse* and *Kiss Me, Kate* have in common? Both musicals are based, more or less loosely, on Shakespearean plays. Hotaling lists operas and musical plays believed to be based on Shakespeare's works. Organized by composer's name, the book's entries contain the title of the work; author of the text; the date of its premiere; the number of acts; the type of work; its language; the publisher of the vocal score; and a list of sources which confirm or deny the Shakespearean origins of the work. If possible, the author provides information on the characters and on the cast of the first performance. Indexes or "sortings" access entries by title, city of premiere, date of premiere, and title of source play. Because Hotaling uses many abbreviations, some of which are not immediately comprehensible, one should read the introductory material before using the book.

49. Howard, John T., Jr. **A Bibliography of Theatre Technology: Acoustics and Sound, Lighting, Properties, and Scenery**. Westport, Conn.: Greenwood, 1982. 345p. LC 81-7204. ISBN 0-313-22839-6.

Howard used a computer to prepare his bibliography of materials related to theatre technology. Unfortunately, his failure to properly edit the work makes it difficult to use. He arranges his unannotated citations into four very broad subject areas: acoustics and sound, lighting, properties, and scenery. A fifth chapter includes reference sources and collections of materials on theatre technology. Within chapters entries are arranged alphabetically by title with no further subject divisions. "Scenery" alone contains 2,732 citations. Howard claims to have indexed twenty-five periodicals but does not list their titles or dates indexed. He provides an author index and five subject indexes (one for each chapter). For a comprehensive search one must look in five separate places. Unfortunately, the field of theatre technology is still waiting for a better bibliography with which to replace this one.

50. Hunter, Frederick J., comp. **Drama Bibliography: A Short-Title Guide to Extended Reading in Dramatic Art for the English-Speaking Audience and Students in Theatre**. Boston: G. K. Hall, 1971. 239p. LC 74-166465.

Supplementing Blanche Baker's bibliography (entry 22) up to 1970, Hunter's work cites materials about "the total process of creating dramatic art out of the materials of the printed play and of the theatre" (introduction). The book includes theatrical history and biography, dance, techniques of theatre, and drama criticism. Additional chapters list reference works and periodicals. Although the lack of annotations weakens the work, it is nevertheless a good attempt at a general bibliography of drama and theatre.

51. **International Bibliography of Theatre**. Sponsored by the American Society for Theatre Research and The International Association of Libraries and Museums of the Performing Arts in cooperation with the International Federation for Theatre Research. New York: Theatre Research Data Center; Distr., Publishing Center for Cultural Resources, 1985- . Annual. ISSN 0882-9446.

An ambitious undertaking by several theatre research groups, this annual bibliography "lists theatre books, book articles, dissertations, journal articles and miscellaneous other theatre documents" in any language on "any aspect of theatre significant to research" (Guide for Users, 1987). The classified arrangement includes chapters for theatre in general, dance, mime, puppetry, and music drama (that is, opera and operetta). Note that dance is covered only if it is related to theatre or if an article about dance appears in a journal which the editors index in full. The list of journals indexed marks each title as receiving full or partial indexing treatment. Each chapter of the bibliography is further divided by numerous subtopics. To find the structure of the classification system, consult the inside front cover. Standard bibliographical citations with foreign titles translated into English are accompanied by brief abstracts and indications of the time and place to which the document pertains. Each volume is indexed by author, subject and country, subdivided by date. This is an important ongoing source for theatre research.

52. **International Mimes & Pantomimists Directory 1974/1975**. New York: International Mimes & Pantomimists, 1974. 97p.

Despite its title, the major part of this book is a bibliography of books, articles, scripts, and films relating to mime. Arranged by type of material, citations are accompanied by one-line annotations and location symbols for New York City libraries. Given the lack of bibliographic information on mime, this is still a valuable source. One wishes it would be updated, enlarged, and given an appropriate title.

53. Johnson, Claudia D., and Vernon E. Johnson. **Nineteenth-Century Theatrical Memoirs**. Westport, Conn.: Greenwood, 1982. 269p. LC 82-15576. ISBN 0-313-23644-5.

The compilers assert that the theatrical memoir as a genre flourished in nineteenth-century America and England, and they have located 427 published memoirs of actors, minstrel show entertainers, circus folk, and other show people. Their intent is to provide access to materials for researchers in theatrical and cultural history. Certainly, some of these memoirs show the ugly side of Victorian show business—uncertain wages, social ostracism, and great opportunity for failure. Each entry includes a good annotation that describes the author and summarizes the work. The bibliography is arranged alphabetically by author. The subject index allows one to find actors who are mentioned in other people's memoirs and to look up subjects such as accidents on stage and income of actors. Moyer's *American Actors, 1861-1910* (entry 76) supplements in part this well-written bibliography.

54. Karpel, Bernard, ed. **Arts in America: A Bibliography**. Washington, D.C.: Smithsonian Institution, 1979. 4v. LC 79-15321. ISBN 0-87474-578-0.

Conceived as a Bicentennial project, *Arts in America* aims to summarize the bibliography of both the visual and the performing arts in the United States. Karpel recruited bibliographic authorities in each field and gave them considerable independence

18 / 2—Bibliographies

in their selection of materials and in organizing their chapters. Genevieve Oswald, former curator of the Dance Collection of the New York Public Library, wrote the chapter on dance, while Paul Myers, her counterpart at the New York Public Library's Theatre Collection, contributed the chapter on theatre. Both chapters (found in volume 3) begin with an introduction and table of contents followed by entries arranged by topic. Oswald's well organized chapter provides descriptive annotations for 1,501 books, serials, collections, and reference works on all types of American dance. Myers' chapter is especially strong on biography and history. Of his 811 citations, 311 refer to individual biographies. He also covers community and regional theatre, theatre technology, musical theatre, and acting. Because these two bibliographies appear in a larger work, librarians will have to make a special effort to remember their existence. They are worth remembering.

55. Kennedy, Carol Jean. **Child Drama: A Selected and Annotated Bibliography 1974-1979**. Washington, D.C.: Children's Theatre Association of America, 1981. 51p. LC 81-209869.

Designed to update Rachel Fordyce's bibliography (entry 35), this work annotates 219 books, articles, and dissertations related to theatre and children from preschoolers to ninth-graders. Emphasizing connecting children "with their own creative process" rather than performance, Kennedy surveys works in creative drama and children's theatre; theatre and the handicapped; child drama in religious education; drama with children and senior adults; and puppetry. Within these subject categories she divides her citations by type of material and then by author's name. Annotations provide full descriptions of the materials, making this a still-useful addition to the literature of children's theatre.

56. Kesler, Jackson. **Theatrical Costume: A Guide to Information Sources**. (Performing Arts Information Guide series, vol. 6; Gale Information Guide Library). Detroit: Gale Research, 1979. 308p. LC 79-22881. ISBN 0-8103-1455-X.

This work is the most recent and best costume bibliography now available. Unlike the Hilers' more scholarly *Bibliography of Costume* (entry 47) this title is intended to be a selective list useful to the working costumer. Only books are included, and most of them were published after 1957, although important older books are included. Especially in the chapter on reference books, Kesler has listed many older and more specialized works. The bibliography is arranged by broad subject areas with author, title, and subject indexes. Kesler's scope is broad enough to include not only works on theatrical and dance costume and historical costume, but also books about the technical aspects of costume construction and textiles as well as customs, manners, stage movement, and the psychology of fashion. Special categories of costume such as military uniforms, children's wear, and accessories receive their own chapters. Each entry features a short description of the work and, occasionally, an evaluation of its worth. Kesler is not as comprehensive as Hiler and Hiler, but his book is more easily used and more current.

57. King, Christine E., and Brenda Coven. **Joseph Papp and the New York Shakespeare Festival: An Annotated Bibliography**. (Garland Reference Library of the Humanities, vol. 793). New York: Garland, 1988. 369p. LC 87-25921. ISBN 0-8240-6609-X.

Almost singlehandedly Joseph Papp brought Shakespeare and theatre back to "the people." He produced plays in church basements, on "playmobiles," and, finally, in New York's Central Park where thousands gathered to see and hear Shakespeare. He brought to the stage *A Chorus Line, The Pirates of Penzance, Streamers, True West,* and many other plays. A controversial figure and often in the limelight, Papp has not yet been the focus of scholarly biographies or articles. Most of this bibliography refers to articles from newspapers, especially the *New York Times,* the *Wall Street Journal,* and the *Christian Science Monitor.* It also contains annotations of Papp's writings, mostly letters to newspapers, interviews, and testimony at Congressional hearings; and periodical articles and books that contain references to Papp. Each entry has a lengthy annotation, longer than one would find in the *New York Times Index.* Appendices list major events and productions of Papp's life. The book also contains author and subject indexes. This is a useful work for anyone researching Papp or the New York theatre world of the last four decades. Now that Papp has died, the expected outpouring of books and articles will doubtless necessitate an update of this book in the near future.

58. King, Kimball. **Ten Modern American Playwrights: An Annotated Bibliography.** New York: Garland, 1982. 251p. LC 80-8498. ISBN 0-8240-9489-1.

The ten playwrights included in this work are Edward Albee, Amiri Baraka, Ed Bullins, Jack Gelber, Arthur Kopit, David Mamet, David Rabe, Sam Shepherd, Neil Simon, and Lanford Wilson. After providing basic biographical information on each writer, King divides his bibliographies into primary sources: stage plays, filmscripts, and other writings; and secondary sources, most of which are annotated. Indexed by author of secondary works, this book should help students start research on any of these writers.

59. King, Kimball. **Ten Modern Irish Playwrights: A Comprehensive Annotated Bibliography**. (Garland Reference Library of the Humanities, vol. 153). New York: Garland, 1979. 111p. LC 78-68289. ISBN 0-8240-9789-0.

King has chosen ten Irish writers whose work he feels represents the best Irish drama since the 1950s. For each playwright, who range from Brendan Behan to Brian Friel to Hugh Leonard, King presents a short biography, a list of works, an annotated bibliography of criticism, and a selected list of reviews of individual plays. An index guides readers to authors of criticism and other secondary sources. This work complements King's *Twenty Modern British Playwrights* (entry 60).

60. King, Kimball. **Twenty Modern British Playwrights: A Bibliography, 1956 to 1976**. (Garland Reference Library of the Humanities, vol. 96). New York: Garland, 1977. 289p. LC 77-83353. ISBN 0-8240-9853-6.

Concentrating on British authors writing after John Osborne's *Look Back in Anger* opened in 1956, King provides a biographical sketch and cites works, interviews, play reviews, and criticism. He annotates the citations to critical articles. A glance through the names of dramatists included here reminds one how fruitful this period of English drama has been: Alan Ayckbourn, Peter and Anthony Shaffer, Harold Pinter, Tom Stoppard, and Ann Jellicoe are a few of the playwrights who are profiled. See also King's *Ten Modern Irish Playwrights* (entry 59).

61. Krasker, Tommy, and Robert Kimball. **Catalog of the American Musical**. Washington, D.C.: National Institute for Opera and Musical Theater, 1988. 442p. LC 87-061421. ISBN 0-9618575-0-1.

Krasker and Kimball concentrate on six giants in American musical theatre: Irving Berlin, George and Ira Gershwin, Cole Porter, and Richard Rodgers and Lorenz Hart. For seventy-five musicals composed by these men, the authors have tracked down "surviving performance materials for each musical number" (How to Use This Book). Their goal is to help preserve the authenticity of the musicals for future performers. Each composer's work is grouped together in chronological order. After providing basic information such as opening date, length of run, and the names of the librettist, producer, and others involved with the production, the authors summarize the plot and describe the orchestration required for the score. They list the locations of various materials such as the original scripts, piano-vocal scores, full scores, and parts of scores. Some items are in the Library of Congress and the New York Public Library Theatre Collection while others can be found at Yale, Amherst, and other libraries. Still more materials are owned by estates and trusts of the composers. Readers will find a list of location symbols at the end of the book. Krasker and Kimball name the publisher of the score and identify sources to contact for further information about renting or using performance materials. Entries also locate music for individual songs in each show. The song title index leads one to the correct entry. With its emphasis on printed and manuscript materials, this work complements discographies of the musical such as Raymond (entry 146) and Harris (entry 144).

62. Lancashire, Ian. **Dramatic Texts and Records of Britain: A Chronological Topography to 1558**. (Studies in Early English Drama, vol. 1). Toronto: University of Toronto Press, 1984. 633p. LC 84-614. ISBN 0-8020-5592-3.

Lancashire describes 1,800 texts and records of dramatic activity in 400 areas of Great Britain between Roman times and 1558. His work complements but does not duplicate the Records of Early English Drama (REED) series (entries 568-576a), which actually reprints the documents themselves. Further, REED deals with records of dramatic activity up to 1642 while Lancashire focuses on texts of plays and of speeches given at pageants. The first part of the volume chronologically lists plays, play fragments, and pageants with speeches, both published and unpublished which are not associated with any particular location in Britain. In some cases the compiler gives a reference to editions, translations, and facsimiles, bibliographic information available in reference works, and important secondary sources. If a play is associated with one town, its main entry is listed under that place name in the second section, "The Topographical Lists of Dramatic Records." These lists are arranged by country—England, Wales, Scotland, Ireland, and France (during English occupation)—and then by town. Lancashire describes plays as completely as the existing documentation permits and provides a reference to the best printed edition available. Doubtful texts are put into a third section. Appendices provide a considerable amount of information including a list of acting troupes identified by place of origin, by patron, or by chief actor; a list of playwrights with references to biographies; a list of play venues with bibliographic references and an indication of whether the building is destroyed or extant; and a list of "salient dates" in English history with entry numbers of associated plays. Read the introduction to the index before using it because the index is rather complicated. This book will interest advanced researchers in early British theatre history.

63. Langhans, Edward A. **Eighteenth Century British and Irish Promptbooks: A Descriptive Bibliography**. (Bibliographies and Indexes in the Performing Arts, vol. 6). Westport, Conn.: Greenwood, 1987. 286p. LC 87-23638. ISBN 0-313-24029-9.

In his absorbing introduction Langhans explains the significance of promptbooks to the study of theatre history; provides an excellent introduction to eighteenth-century theatre architecture, scenery, and lighting; and illustrates his essay with drawings of London's Drury Lane and Covent Garden theatres. He then describes 380 promptbooks, arranged by playwright and play title. Each entry features a "headnote" or bibliographic citation, location, and call number plus a narrative description of the markings or annotations on the copy. The excellent descriptions indicate Langhans has researched his topic thoroughly, checking sources, comparing various copies, and generally applying his knowledge of eighteenth-century theatre practices to these materials. An appendix lists names of prompters and annotators. A bibliography of works about eighteenth-century theatre precedes a general index.

64. Larson, Carl F. W., comp. **American Regional Theatre History to 1900: A Bibliography**. Metuchen, N.J.: Scarecrow, 1979. 187p. LC 79-11282. ISBN 0-8108-1216-9.

Larson's aim is "to provide access to research on the history of American regional theatre up to 1900, excluding New York City" (preface). The bibliography shows the enormous vitality of nineteenth-century American theatre before radio and television destroyed much of it. Larson has listed works about theatres in Bismarck, North Dakota, and Fayetteville, Arkansas, as well as Boston, Chicago, Philadelphia, and other cultural centers. He includes books, periodical and magazine articles, dissertations, theses, and some manuscripts—1,491 items in all. He arranges the material by state and city where the theatrical activity took place, then chronologically. Three indexes provide access by author, names of persons who are subjects of works cited, and names of foreign-language theatres that existed in many American cities during the nineteenth century. Larsons's work is based on Carl Stratman's *Bibliography of American Theatre, Excluding New York City* (entry 89) and Clarence Gohdes' *Literature and Theater of the States and Regions of the U.S.A.* (entry 39). Because Larson ends his coverage at 1900, however, the other two books should be consulted for materials on the twentieth century.

65. Levine, Robert. **Guide to Opera & Dance on Videocassette**. Mount Vernon, N.Y.: Consumers Union, 1989. 213p. LC 88-71036. ISBN 0-89043-261-9.

Not a comprehensive work, Levine's videography lists selected videocassettes and a few feature films that record opera and dance performances. About one-fourth of the entries describe dance videos, arranged in three chapters: ballet and modern dance, dance documentaries, and special dance films. Entries list principal dancers, conductor, choreographer, composer, cassette producer, date, and running time. Most valuable is the lengthy detailed evaluation of the cassette. Levine, opera critic for the *San Francisco Chronicle*, expresses strong opinions about both the dancing and the technical qualities of each video. An appendix lists names and addresses of cassette producers and distributors, and a general index allows one to look for a favorite dancer in a video performance. Although it makes some curious omissions such as the Academy Award-winning *He Makes Me Feel Like Dancin'* and *The Turning Point*, this guide will help consumers choose videocassettes to buy or rent, just what one expects of a book published by Consumers Union.

66. Link, Frederick M. **English Drama, 1660-1800: A Guide to Information Sources**. (American Literature, English Literature, and World Literatures in English, vol. 9; Gale Information Guide Library). Detroit: Gale Research, 1976. 374p. LC 73-16984. ISBN 0-8103-1224-7.

The author's purpose is "to list every substantial book and article dealing with English drama 1660-1800 published through 1973." About 75 percent of the work contains bibliographical essays about playwrights of the period. In the first quarter of the book, however, Link has retained the bibliographical essay form to deal with a variety of theatre and drama topics. Among these are playhouses and theatres, acting, theatrical biography, and play collections. Link evaluates sources as well as describing them, and, for this reason, his work is more valuable than Stratman and others (entry 92) on which it builds. However, Link's book is not as comprehensive, omitting many older works and many subject areas. A name index includes authors of works listed and names of subjects. There is also an index of play titles. This book includes much that is drama, not theatre, but it also includes much that is useful on topics such as playhouses, theatres, and theatrical biography.

67. Litto, Fredric M. **American Dissertations on the Drama and the Theatre: A Bibliography**. Kent, Ohio: Kent State University Press, 1969. 519p. LC 71-76761. SBN 87338-036-3.

Lotto used a computer to compile this list of 4,565 dissertations containing information about the theatrical arts. Although access is provided by author, subject, and keyword-in-context indexes, the actual bibliography is arranged by a computer-generated reference code. Each entry lists the author and title of the dissertation along with university and department names, degree granted, and date. Since this work stops at 1965, one must use *Dissertation Abstracts International* and the lists published annually in *Theatre Journal* (formerly *Educational Theatre Journal*) (entry 648) to find more recent theses.

68. Loewenberg, Alfred, comp. **The Theatre of the British Isles, Excluding London: A Bibliography**. London: Society for Theatre Research, 1950. LC 51-34078.

This work, a first attempt to locate printed material and local manuscript collections on regional British theatre, remains valuable for its descriptions of local manuscript collections. Readers seeking printed materials should consult Arnott and Robinson's *English Theatrical Literature* (entry 20) and Cavanagh's *British Theatre* (entry 28) as they are more complete. The bulk of this work is arranged alphabetically by name of British city or county, with an author index. An introductory general chapter has an index of places as well.

69. Lopez, Manuel D. **Chinese Drama: An Annotated Bibliography of Commentary, Criticism, and Plays in English Translation**. Metuchen, N.J.: Scarecrow, 1991. 525p. LC 91-15902. ISBN 0-8108-2347-0.

Lopez divides his work into two parts. The first cites books, articles, and dissertations written in English on Chinese drama and theatre from its origins to 1985. Arranged by topic, the 1,395 unannotated entries contain references to many works written within the last thirty years as well as some earlier publications. Subjects covered include puppets, children's theatre, costumes, theatre buildings, and acting. Lopez also cites publications about foreign theatre in China and Chinese theatre abroad. The index to part one follows immediately after the last citation and provides access by author. The second part of this work cites Chinese plays in translation and commentaries on them. Arranged by play title, the 1,929 unannotated citations are indexed by author. More comprehensive than Lynn's *Guide to Chinese Poetry and Drama* (entry 71) but without Lynn's helpful annotations,

Lopez's bibliography should be useful to students and others who do not read Chinese but wish to know something about Chinese drama and theatre.

70. Lyday, Leon F., and George F. Woodyard. **A Bibliography of Latin American Theater Criticism 1940-1974**. (Guides and Bibliographies series, no. 10). Austin: Institute of Latin American Studies, University of Texas at Austin, 1977. 243p. LC 76-45126. ISBN 0-292-70717-7.

More than 2,300 entries refer the reader to books and journal articles about theatre and playwrights in Latin America during the "establishment and development of a truly national theatre movement in most areas of Latin America" (introduction). Most of the materials cited are written in Spanish. The book is arranged by author with an index of playwright names and general subjects (censorship, puppet theatre, women, and so forth). A special section lists bibliographies about theatre in Latin America and in specific countries. Use this work with the *Handbook of Latin American Studies* (Gainesville: University of Florida Press, 1935-) and with Hebblethwaite (entry 45).

71. Lynn, Richard John. **Guide to Chinese Poetry and Drama**. 2d ed. Boston: G. K. Hall, 1984. 200p. LC 84-714. ISBN 0-8161-8633-2.

Although Lynn, who has taught Chinese language and literature, devotes most of his bibliography to poetry, he does include thirty references to traditional Chinese drama and an additional thirty to modern drama. Both translations of famous plays and works of history and criticism are included. Choosing titles in English for the nonspecialist, he describes and evaluates each work in a long annotation. Indexes allow access by author, title, and subject. Lynn's work is much shorter than Lopez's *Chinese Drama* (entry 69), but his evaluations make his book worthwhile, especially to the novice.

72. Mikhail, E. H. **A Bibliography of Modern Irish Drama, 1899-1970**. Seattle: University of Washington Press, 1972. 51p. LC 72-1373. ISBN 0-295-95229-6.

Mikhail lists books, periodical articles, and unpublished material on twentieth-century Irish drama and theatre in this small unannotated bibliography. He also includes a short list of additional bibliographies to consult. Organized by type of material, then by author, entries are not accessible by subject. Readers interested in the history of Dublin's Abbey Theatre, however, will find numerous references to articles and books written during the first 70 years of its existence.

73. Mikhail, E. H. **Contemporary British Drama 1950-1976: An Annotated Critical Bibliography**. Totowa, N.J.: Rowman & Littlefield, 1977. 147p. LC 76-16487. ISBN 0-87471-854-6.

Of some use to those who are studying postwar British theatre, Mikhail's bibliography suffers from a lack of subject indexing. Briefly annotated citations are arranged by type of material: bibliographies, reference works, books, and periodical articles. Within each section, an author arrangement allows the reader to find the works of writers and critics such as Kenneth Tynan and Harold Clurman. Yet, locating books and articles about topics such as the abolition of official censorship of plays or the formation of the National Theatre is difficult. Furthermore, Mikhail cites many reference books that are general works not specifically related to postwar British drama and theatre. The listing of periodical articles from English, American, and European journals and magazines is the most useful part of this book.

74. Mikhail, E. H. **English Drama, 1900-1950: A Guide to Information Sources**. (American Literature, English Literature, and World Literatures in English, vol. 11; Gale Information Guide Library). Detroit: Gale Research, 1977. 328p. LC 74-11523. ISBN 0-8103-1216-6.

Although Mikhail's emphasis on the literary aspects of drama makes this book of limited use to students of theatre and performance, it does cover some topics of interest. In particular, it cites many articles which deal with the Abbey Theatre and the Irish National Theatre. The many bibliographies for individual playwrights will help readers locate plays and criticism. Although the work is arranged by types of material, author, title, and subject indexes provide ample access to its contents.

75. Milhous, Judith, and Robert D. Hume. **A Register of English Theatrical Documents 1660-1737**. Carbondale: Southern Illinois University Press, 1991. 2v. LC 90-42095. ISBN 0-8093-1270-0 (set).

The result of fifteen years of work, this checklist describes "all documents related to the management and regulation of the theatre in England from the reopening of the playhouses in 1660 to the passage of the Licensing Act in 1737" (preface). Its purpose is to help scholars find needed material and to identify and publish new documents, both manuscripts and printed documents. However, the compilers omit works that only comment about the theatre, instead of focusing on its management, as those are cited in *The London Stage* (entry 563) and Arnott and Robinson (entry 20). Most of the records listed here are from the Lord Chamberlain's office, the governmental body that regulated the theatres during this period. Entries, arranged chronologically and numbered, give day, month, and year; bibliographic information, including a location code; an annotation; references to other copies; and citations to published commentaries or transcriptions. The authors include a list of abbreviations for document locations. Volume 1 covers the years 1660 to 1714 while volume 2 describes documents written or published between 1714 and 1737. Although Milhous and Hume disavow any claim to completeness, they have located many previously unknown documents and thus furthered British theatre history research.

76. Moyer, Ronald Lee. **American Actors, 1861-1910: An Annotated Bibliography of Books Published in the United States in English from 1861 through 1976**. Troy, N.Y.: Whitston, 1979. 268p. LC 79-64229. ISBN 0-87875-167-X.

Moyer has located more than 350 books that are biographies or biographical dictionaries of late nineteenth-century American actors. He defines American actors as those who resided and performed in the United States for at least part of their adult acting careers between 1861 and 1910. Arranged alphabetically by author, the work consists of full bibliographic data and a description of each book. In the annotation Moyer lists names of actors who are profiled in it as well as any special features such as illustrations, indexes, and so on. Readers can locate actors by name as well as book titles by using the indexes. This book should be used with *Nineteenth-Century Theatrical Memoirs* (entry 53), which it supplements.

77. Penninger, Frieda Elaine. **English Drama to 1660, Excluding Shakespeare: A Guide to Information Sources**. (American Literature, English Literature, and World Literatures in English, vol. 5; Gale Information Guide Library). Detroit: Gale Research, 1976. 370p. LC 73-16988. ISBN 0-8103-1223-9.

Aimed at undergraduate and graduate students looking for editions of plays and for criticism, this book selects and annotates recent English books on English drama and theatre prior to the Restoration. Penninger includes periodical articles, older books, and foreign works where they cover the subject best, and she arranges her bibliography by subject. Chapters of particular interest include one on theatre and stagecraft; one on playlists; and one on contemporary and other early records of the Renaissance stage. The last third of the book consists of entries for thirty-four playwrights, listing bibliographies, biographical references, editions of works, and secondary criticism. The index provides access by author and some titles. Subject access is severely limited, however.

78. **Performing Arts Books, 1876-1981: Including an International Index of Current Serial Publications**. New York: R. R. Bowker, 1981. 1,656p. LC 81-187862. ISBN 0-8352-1372-2.

Using records from its *American Book Publishing Record* database, publisher R. R. Bowker created this monumental work that lists 50,000 titles in the performing arts. The books, which were published or distributed in the United States, are arranged by 12,000 Library of Congress subject headings. Bowker also provides author and title indexes. A special chapter contains references to serials that were taken from the *Bowker Serials Bibliography* database. Entries include bibliographic citation and Dewey Decimal call numbers. This largely supersedes *Theatre Books in Print* although the latter work does contain some references, particularly to books about drama, that do not appear in the former.

79. Salem, James M. **Drury's Guide to Best Plays**. 4th ed. Metuchen, N.J.: Scarecrow, 1987. 480p. LC 87-380. ISBN 0-8108-1980-5.

Now in its fourth edition, *Drury's Guide* provides information on "1500 selected, non-musical, full-length plays in English, covering all dramatic periods ... and places." These plays are not just the critically successful but are also the commercial successes. Arrangement is alphabetical by playwright's name. Much of the information listed for each play is similar to that given in *Play Index* (entry 248), but this one-volume format is more convenient to use. For each play *Drury's* lists the publisher of the acting edition (if one exists) or a collection in which the play can be found; a plot summary; the number of acts; the number of sets required; the number of men and women actors necessary; and the royalty cost (as of 1986). The plays are indexed by title, subject, and cast requirements. Several appendices list award-winning plays, plays popular with high school groups, and popular plays for amateur productions.

80. Schoolcraft, Ralph Newman. **Performing Arts/Books in Print: An Annotated Bibliography**. New York: Drama Book Specialists, 1973. 761p. LC 72-78909. ISBN 0-910482-27-6.

A snapshot of performing arts books available for sale in the United States in 1973, this bibliography is still useful. Schoolcraft lists and annotates about 12,000 books under the subject headings theatre and drama; technical arts of the theatre; motion pictures; television; and mass media and popular arts. These broad headings are further subdivided by subject. Plays and collections of plays are excluded except for those of Shakespeare. Standard bibliographical information, price, and a short annotation comprise the entries, which can be accessed by author and title indexes. Because many of the books listed still stand on library shelves, Schoolcraft's bibliography will be useful to some looking for a

26 / 2—Bibliographies

book on a specific subject, particularly theatre history and biography. The technical theatre section, however, should be ignored except by those researching the history of stage technology.

81. Sedgwick, Dorothy. **A Bibliography of English-Language Theatre and Drama in Canada 1800-1914**. (19th Century Theatre Research. Occasional Publications, no. 1). Edmonton, Alta.: 1976. 48p. LC 76-377688.

Intended as a reference tool for theatre and Canadian studies courses, this bibliography arranges 525 citations according to subject: Canadian drama, dramatists, and dramatic criticism; theatres and theatre history; stage-tours and visits to Canada by famous actors; reference books and bibliography. Entries give bibliographic information and Canadian location codes for books, theses, and articles. Sedgwick includes plays published in Canada during this time period. For later works see the *Brock Bibliography* (entry 140). Sedgwick concludes with a short-title index to plays and a general index. This is necessary for anyone interested in early Canadian theatre.

82. Senelick, Laurence, David F. Cheshire, and Ulrich Schneider. **British Music Hall, 1840-1923: A Bibliography and Guide to Sources, with a Supplement on European Music-Hall**. (An Archon Book on Popular Entertainments). Hamden, Conn.: Archon Books, 1981. 361p. LC 81-4996. ISBN 0-208-01840-9.

The British music hall was a phenomenon that flourished in the latter half of Queen Victoria's reign and, especially, during Edward VII's time. It remained largely an urban working-class form of entertainment. This comprehensive bibliography lists all types of works, including phonograph records, that deal with music halls in Britain. A small supplement treats similar entertainments in Europe. Information on collections of material housed in British and U.S. repositories is an important part of the work. The authors have chosen a subject arrangement (music hall architecture, regulations governing the halls, operation of music halls, and so forth). The "Performance Materials" chapter lists song books, joke books, and recordings of music hall performers. Each chapter is provided with a well written introduction, but the entries are largely unannotated. An author index and a cross-reference index of music hall names further aid the reader. This is the standard work on British music halls.

83. Shattuck, Charles H. **The Shakespeare Promptbooks: A Descriptive Catalogue**. Urbana, Ill. and London: University of Illinois Press, 1965. 553p. LC 65-11737.

Shattuck tried to list and describe all known marked copies of Shakespeare's plays used in professional English-language theatre productions from the 1620s to 1961. These books, often associated with famous actors or directors, provide clues to the way a play was staged. Organized by play title and then chronologically, entries give the name of the person associated with the book, the theatre name, and the date of the book's first use. Shattuck names the collection now housing the promptbook and describes both the physical book and its markings. These consist of cues for lights and sound effects, scenic indications ("Gothic Hall;" "Woods"), stage business ("Benedick leads her forward by the hand"), and so forth. Shattuck published a supplement to his work in *Theatre Notebook* 24(1969-70): 5-17. For other promptbooks see Dubois (entry 163).

84. Steadman, Susan M. **Dramatic Re-Visions: An Annotated Bibliography of Feminism and Theatre 1972-1988**. Chicago: American Library Association, 1991. 367p. LC 91-16333. ISBN 0-8389-0577-3.

Steadman concerns herself with the burgeoning interest in women and the theatre, particularly the growing empowerment of women both in playwriting and in performance. Her sixty-page introduction discusses the history of feminist dramatic and theatrical theory and describes the arrangement of her bibliography. The 850 entries, organized into chapters by topic, cover works on feminist theories and overviews of theatre; feminist theatres and theatre groups; women playwrights; feminist reassessment of male playwriting; and performance issues. The author also lists selected play collections; reports of conferences; festivals; and organizations involved in feminist theatre. Within chapters, descriptive annotations are arranged by type of material: books and monographs followed by periodicals, serials, and annuals. Unannotated entries for works published in 1989 and 1990 appear in an appendix. Steadman indexes her work by name, title, and subject categories such as country and ethnic group. The bibliography will aid those researching in the fields of women's studies, performance studies, and dramatic criticism.

85. Stevens, David. **English Renaissance Theatre History: A Reference Guide**. (A Reference Guide to Literature). Boston: G. K. Hall, 1982. 342p. LC 82-2965. ISBN 0-8161-8361-9.

Stevens has annotated more than 1,600 items to fulfill his aim of presenting a comprehensive guide to Elizabethan theatrical history. Works cited and described briefly include books, dissertations, and journal articles. Citations are arranged chronologically by publication date (1664 to 1979), which makes the index essential. Unfortunately, the index is not as detailed as it could be; for instance "Court Performances" is followed by thirty-eight entry numbers with no individual descriptions for entries. The index includes authors and editors of works as well as subjects. An excellent introduction describes landmark works in Renaissance theatre history. Despite the difficulties posed by its arrangement, this book is the best bibliography available for this period of English theatrical history.

86. Stoddard, Richard. **Stage Scenery, Machinery, and Lighting: A Guide to Information Sources**. (Performing Arts Information Guide series, vol. 2; Gale Information Guide Library). Detroit: Gale Research, 1977. 274p. LC 76-13574. ISBN 0-8103-1374-X.

The reader seeking historical information on stage technicalities will find this book useful. The technician looking for advice on contemporary practice should look in periodical indexes instead of this book. Stoddard has annotated over 1,600 works about stage scenery in theatres from ancient times through the 1970s. After a general reference section, he divides the book into a section on scenery and machinery and one on lighting. Within each section entries are arranged by historical time period with works on today's practice listed at the end of the section. Unfortunately, the contemporary sections are weak. This weakness is aggravated by the deliberate omission of many articles from *Theatre Crafts* (entry 639), *Theatre Design & Technology*, and *TABS*, the British theatre lighting magazine that was published between 1937 and 1978. Stoddard chose to include only historical and biographical articles from these three journals.

87. Stoddard, Richard. **Theatre and Cinema Architecture: A Guide to Information Sources**. (Performing Arts Information Guide series, vol. 5; Gale Information Guide Library). Detroit: Gale Research, 1978. 368p. LC 78-14820. ISBN 0-8103-1426-6.

Claiming to be the first full-length bibliography of theatre and cinema architecture, this volume lists and describes books, journal articles, and dissertations, mostly written in English. About 80 percent of the 1,800 entries concern legitimate theatres, opera houses, and dance facilities located worldwide. The remainder of the entries concern motion picture theatres. After chapters on reference works and general studies, the book lists works on individual theatres, arranged by location. Although full-length biographies of architects have been excluded, one can locate articles about them in the index of architects and designers. Stoddard also provides indexes by author, subject, and theatre name. Because the index by theatre name is arranged geographically, the reader cannot find information on an individual theatre unless its location is known. Despite this serious flaw, researchers will want to consult this book as a starting place for their research.

88. Stratman, Carl J. **American Theatrical Periodicals, 1798-1967: A Bibliographical Guide**. Durham, N.C.: Duke University Press, 1970. 133p. LC 72-110577. ISBN 0-8223-0228-4.

Stratman has listed in chronological order all known theatrical periodicals published in the United States to 1967. Although he found 685 titles, he warned that this first effort was likely incomplete. Entries list bibliographic citations and holdings in several American libraries. Using the index readers can locate periodical titles, editors, cities of publication, organizations sponsoring periodicals, and some keyword-in-title terms such as "ballet," "dance," or "repertory." Stratman explains the use of the bibliography and index in a clearly written introduction. Although now in need of an update, this work will help those looking for older periodicals.

89. Stratman, Carl J. **A Bibliography of the American Theatre, Excluding New York City**. Chicago: Loyola University Press, 1965. 397p. LC 65-3359.

Important to local theatre history researchers, Stratman's work attempts to record books, periodical articles, theses, and dissertations on all types of theatrical activity outside New York City. Arrangement is alphabetical by state, then city, then chronological. A single index allows one to find entries by name or by subject. Most entries have a one-sentence annotation. This book must be compared to Larson (entry 64) and Gohdes (entry 39). Stratman's work covers a broader time period than Larson (late eighteenth century through 1964) and a broader range of activities than Gohdes. He lists 3,856 items to Larson's 1,481, but he has omitted newspaper articles and manuscripts that Larson includes. Larson, who worked from Stratman and Gohdes, updates and corrects errors in each of those works but stops his coverage at 1900. Gohdes' work, which concerns itself with both literary and theatrical works, also has a more limited scope than Stratman, but it does include works about New York City. Stratman should be used when looking for materials on theatrical activities after 1900 or for information on ballet, children's theatre, and puppet shows.

90. Stratman, Carl J. **Britain's Theatrical Periodicals, 1720-1967**. 2d ed. New York: New York Public Library, 1972. 160p. LC 72-134260. ISBN 0-87104-034-4.

Stratman's second edition widens the scope to include periodicals about dance, ballet, magic, music halls, opera, drama, puppets, and acting as well as all areas of theatre.

Working in many British and American libraries, the compiler has located 1,235 titles, many of them short-lived. In fact, the earliest theatre journal, published in 1720, lasted only three months! Since it is arranged chronologically by initial publication date, one can use this list to survey the history of British theatrical periodicals. An alphabetical index helps one locate titles, editors, and cities of publication. Each entry lists complete bibliographic information including the dates of the first and last issues (first issue only if the periodical is still alive). A new edition of this book is needed, but it is still useful for historical purposes.

91. Stratman, Carl J. **Dramatic Play Lists 1591-1963**. New York: New York Public Library, 1966. 44p. LC 66-22385. Reprinted from the *Bulletin of the New York Public Library*, February/March, 1966.

Stratman provides a chronological list of 99 bibliographies, indexes, and lists of English plays written between 1591 and 1963. The first item is not actually a bibliography but rather Philip Henslowe's *Diary*, the "chief source for theatrical history between 1590 and 1604." Each entry consists of a bibliographic citation and an annotation that describes and evaluates the work. In the preface Stratman describes the type of books he has omitted including manuscripts and catalogs from booksellers, auctions, and libraries. Stratman's work is important to those doing in-depth research on English drama or theatre.

92. Stratman, Carl J., David G. Spencer, and Mary Elizabeth Devine. **Restoration and Eighteenth Century Theatre Research: A Bibliographical Guide, 1900-1968**. Carbondale: Southern Illinois University Press, 1971. 811p. LC 71-112394. ISBN 0-8093-0469-4.

Growing out of the annual bibliographies published in the journal *Restoration and 18th Century Theatre Research*, this bibliography aims to be a comprehensive list of works on English theatre from 1660 to 1800 published between 1900 and 1968. As such, it includes books, journal articles, dissertations, and theses, mainly in English. The 6,560 entries are arranged within 780 subject headings in one alphabetical list. More than half of the subject headings refer to people—actors, playwrights, stage managers, and others connected with the stage at this time—while other subject headings refer to acting, theaters, farce, and many other topics. Within entries the arrangement is chronological with some topical subheadings. About 80 percent of the entries have descriptive annotations. The index is an alphabetical list of both authors and subjects with references to entry numbers. The main problem with this work is its arrangement and lack of cross-references. If one looks under "marionettes," for example, there is no pointer to "puppet theater." One cannot find all the information on theatre buildings in one place since it is scattered under "theatres," "theatre buildings," "provincial theatre," and names of individual theaters. It is best used with Frederick Link's *English Drama, 1660-1800: A Guide to Information Sources*. Because it is stronger than Link on early works and lesser-known works, this bibliography should be consulted by those wanting an exhaustive search of materials from this period.

93. Straumanis, Alfreds, ed. **Baltic Drama: A Handbook and Bibliography**. Prospect Heights, Ill.: Waveland Press, 1981. 705p. ISBN 0-917974-63-8.

This work attempts to list all plays originally written in the Estonian, Latvian, or Lithuanian languages that have been published and/or produced. Emigrants from these three Baltic countries have held on to their culture with remarkable tenacity, and many of the 4,649 plays listed are written by "exiles" living in places like Chicago and Detroit. For each country (Estonia, Latvia, Lithuania) the compiler has provided an overview of national drama and theatre activity, short biographies of important playwrights, and a list of all known playwrights and their plays written up to 1980. Each play is annotated, and its title is translated into English. Because some of these plays are available only in little-known repositories of Baltic literature, the compiler often gives locations for copies of works. Playwright, title, and subject indexes are included as well as general bibliographies on the three Baltic countries and their theatre.

93a. Taylor, Thomas J. **American Theatre History: An Annotated Bibliography**. Pasadena: Salem Press, 1992. 162p. LC 91-43961. ISBN 0-8935-6672-1.

Although not a comprehensive bibliography on American theatrical history, Taylor's book provides useful annotations to a selected list of biographies, histories, chronologies, essays, and other works. He divides American theatre into three periods: pre-1914, 1914 to 1945, and post-World War II. Additional chapters introduce works that deal with regional theatre, materials about specialized theatrical forms such as children's theatre, and periodicals related to theatre. Within each section, works are arranged by author, necessitating use of the index. Taylor's annotations describe and evaluate each work. This will be most helpful to college students writing term papers on American theatre history.

94. Toole-Stott, Raymond. **A Bibliography of Books on the Circus in English from 1773 to 1964**. Derby, England: Harpur, 1964.

Toole-Stott lists 1,100 English-language books on the circus. Each entry consists of a citation and physical description of the book. With no annotations and no indexes, this work is not nearly as useful as Toole-Stott's *Circus and Allied Arts: A World Bibliography* (entry 96).

95. Toole-Stott, Raymond. **A Bibliography of English Conjuring, 1581-1876**. Derby, England: Harpur, 1976. 288p. LC 77-362191.

Well-known for his definitive circus bibliography (entry 96), Toole-Stott here turns his bibliographic skills to the subject of conjuring and magic. His book divides into a main section devoted to conjuring books per se (752 items) and a secondary part devoted to legerdemain or sleight-of-hand (160 items). Each section is further arranged alphabetically by author. The compiler examined all but two of the books as he visited most of the important magic collections, both public and private, and he adds many explanatory notes to his citations. Library locations are given for most titles. For later works see Gill (entry 38).

96. Toole-Stott, Raymond. **Circus and Allied Arts: A World Bibliography**. Derby, England: Harpur, 1958-1971. 4v. LC 58-2986.

Written by a passionate bibliographer and circus fan, this wonderful bibliography was Toole-Stott's labor of love for more than forty years. Published over a thirteen-year period and based on four great collections—those of the Library of Congress, the British Museum, the Bibliothèque Nationale, and of Toole-Stott himself—this work includes books, pamphlets, and periodical articles on all aspects of the circus. The author explains in the first volume that he has arbitrarily widened his scope to gather in books that he considers related to the circus, at least tangentially. For this reason the researcher will find references to books about juggling, equitation, "hocus-pocus," wild west shows, and many other fascinating topics. References to fiction concerning the circus and children's circus books are here also. Toole-Stott includes many biographies of those who influenced circus greatly such as Philip Astly and P. T. Barnum. He locates materials on so-called "phenomenes" or "freaks" like General Tom Thumb and the Siamese Twins. One can trace the career of the Hottentot Venus. (The subject of a London court case in 1809, she told the court she did not mind being put on exhibition.) The four volumes contain in all 13,086 items. Volume 4 is a supplement. Because this is a world bibliography, Toole-Stott includes work in many languages. His coverage of periodical articles is weaker than his treatment of books. Many American and British magazines and journals and some from other countries are covered. Judging from the references to the *New York Times*, however, coverage is not complete. Each entry for a book gives a complete citation and a physical description; often a location code is listed for the Library of Congress, the British Museum, or the Bibliothèque Nationale. Toole-Stott annotates books that he considers important, often with quite a long explanation. Volume 3 contains an index of authors and subjects and some titles. Appended are Toole-Stott's "Best 100 Circus Books" and a limited "Circus Who's Who" of nineteenth-century European circus performers. Toole-Stott also describes major circus collections worldwide. Because it was published as a limited edition, this work may be difficult to find. Nevertheless, it is essential to any serious circus researcher. Readers who are looking for more recent materials about American and British circuses should consult Wilmeth's *American and English Popular Entertainment* (entry 97) and his *Variety Entertainment* (entry 12). Two useful catalogs are Sokan's description of the Illinois State University's collection (entry 185) and the Amsterdam University catalog (entry 150).

97. Wilmeth, Don B. **American and English Popular Entertainment: A Guide to Information Sources**. (Performing Arts Information Guide series, vol. 7; Gale Information Guide Library). Detroit: Gale Research, 1980. 465p. LC 79-22869. ISBN 0-8103-1454-1.

One of two works that Wilmeth has written on the "fringe elements" of the performing arts world, this bibliography annotates 2,478 items concerning American and English "live amusements created by professional showmen for profit and aimed at broad, relatively unsophisticated audiences" (preface). Most of these entertainments flourished during the nineteenth century before motion pictures, radio, and television made them obsolete. Wilmeth focuses primarily on American amusements with a secondary emphasis on English forms. This book cites works on the circus, wild west shows, carnivals, fairs, amusement parks, magic shows, minstrel shows, burlesque, puppets, toy theatres, pantomimes, music halls, showboats, early musical theatre, and the Chautauqua movement. With such a broad scope, coverage is not comprehensive. Senelick's work on the music hall (entry 82) is much more complete, for example. Wilmeth has chosen to annotate sources that are histories or analyses of the form of entertainment. He omits texts of materials used in performance such as burlesque sketches or music hall songs. This work is arranged by subject areas with author, title, and subject indexes. An appendix lists significant serials, special collections, museums, and organizations pertaining to popular entertainment. This book lacks the bibliographic essays that are found in Wilmeth's *Variety Entertainment and Outdoor Amusements* (entry 12). It lists materials published through May 1978 while *Variety Entertainment* contains materials published through 1981.

98. Wilmeth, Don B. **The American Stage to World War I: A Guide to Information Sources**. (Performing Arts Information Guide series, vol. 4; Gale Information Guide Library). Detroit: Gale Research, 1978. 269p. LC 78-53488. ISBN 0-8103-1392-8.

Emphasizing biographies and local theatre histories, Wilmeth provides citations and brief annotations for 1,480 published books or journal articles. Because he has omitted dissertations, newspaper and popular magazine articles, series of articles in periodicals, and unpublished material, this work suffers in comparison to Larson (entry 64). Wilmeth arranges his bibliography by broad subject categories including a chapter on "paratheatrical forms" such as vaudeville and the circus, and one on foreign-language theatre in the United States. Readers can use the indexes to find authors, titles, and specific subjects.

Dance Bibliographies

99. Adamczyk, Alice J. **Black Dance: An Annotated Bibliography.** (Garland Reference Library of the Humanities, vol. 558). New York: Garland, 1989. 213p. LC 88-29217. ISBN 0-8240-8808-5.

The author claims this is a "first attempt to compile published material documenting black dance in all its forms" (introduction). It is mainly an annotated listing of materials held by the New York Public Library collections. With 1,392 items it is not a comprehensive work, and its method of compilation presents the reader with at least one serious problem. The majority of items are articles from New York newspapers along with some books. Because Adamczyk includes articles from clipping files, she lists many citations that do not have page numbers. Readers are certain to experience difficulties in obtaining material that is not cited fully. Adamczyk's coverage of regional dance companies is spotty. Only one reference to the Dayton Contemporary Dance Company appears, for instance. The arrangement of works by author presents another problem. Most readers will want to find material on a topic, a dancer, a company, or a choreographer. The index allows that access, but its lack of detail impedes its use. Fourteen entry numbers are listed under the subject Alvin Ailey and twenty-nine additional entries are found under "Alvin Ailey: Reviews." Despite these caveats, this bibliography should be used along with the New York Public Library's *Dance Catalog* (entry 195) and its annual bibliography (entry 193) to find information on African-American dance.

100. American Association for Health, Physical Education, and Recreation. Dance Division. **Compilation of Dance Research, 1901-1964.** Washington, D.C.: AAHPER, 1964. 52p. LC 64-56415. 52.

This bibliography lists all available dance theses and dissertations written at the graduate level between 1901 and 1963, 704 items in all. The main body of the work is an alphabetical list of authors with the titles of their work, the degree granted, the university awarding the degree, and the date. The subject classification is of limited use because its categories are broad: rhythm, ethnic, and so on. This work is continued by *Research in Dance*, also published by AAHPER (entry 109).

101. Beaumont, Cyril W. **A Bibliography of Dancing**. New York: B. Blom, 1963. 228p. LC 63-23181.

A pioneer bibliography in the field of dance, Beaumont's work is a list of important books in the British Museum that are concerned with all forms of dance. Entries contain bibliographical and physical descriptions of each book along with an explanatory note that ranges from a brief phrase to more than a page of description and evaluation. When a book deals with more than one subject, Beaumont carefully lists all the contents. The annotation for *The Country Dance Book* by Cecil J. Sharp, for example, lists more than 300 titles of dances that are described in the six-volume work. Because Beaumont arranges the work by author, readers will find the subject index invaluable. It lists all dances that are mentioned either in the title or the description of each book. It also lists subjects such as "funeral dances," "ballroom dancing," and "tracts against dancing." Beaumont's work, while it obviously displays a British bias, is one of the classic dance bibliographies along with Paul Magriel's *Bibliography of Dancing* (entry 107). Readers who need more recent material should consult Forbes (entry 104) and the *Bibliographic Guide to Dance* (entry 193).

102. **Completed Research in Health, Physical Education, Recreation, and Dance.** Reston, Va.: American Alliance for Health, Physical Education, Recreation, and Dance. Annual. 1981- . ISSN 0898-2775.

An annual bibliography, this title compiles abstracts of theses and dissertations written in the field of physical education and dance. Some, but not all, volumes also present an unannotated list of periodical articles published on the same topics. Although the thesis section is arranged by university where the research was performed, readers can find information on topics through the subject index. When it appears, the article section is arranged by author without any subject access. Thus, it is more useful to faculty who wish to keep abreast of their colleagues' work rather than to students seeking information on a topic. Note that the year listed in the title of each volume is actually one year later than the research listed within. This work's predecessor, *Completed Research in Health, Physical Education, and Recreation* (1959-1980), also lists theses and articles written about dance even though dance does not appear in its title. Dance researchers will find it easier to consult *Compilation of Dance Research, 1901-1964* (entry 100) and *Research in Dance* (entry 109), which covers the years 1964 to 1981.

103. Dunin, Elsie Ivancich, and Nancy Lee Chalfa Ruyter. **Yugoslav Dance: An Introduction and List of Sources Available in United States Libraries.** Palo Alto, Calif.: Ragusan Press, 1981. 108p. LC 80-51688. ISBN 0-918660-11-4.

This is a specialized work of 505 books and periodical articles about all aspects of folk dance in what is now the former Yugoslavia. The compilers believe that they have located most of the materials published in Yugoslavia and the United States between 1840 and 1980 on this subject. As an aid to American readers the work is divided into a section of 110 works written in English and a second part listing 396 items written in other languages. Each section is arranged by author. Titles in the foreign language section are translated into English. The index lists entry numbers for dances from each geographical subdivision of Yugoslavia: Bosnia-Hercegovina, Croatia, Macedonia, Montenegro, Serbia, Slovenia, Kosovo-Mehohija, and Vojvodina; and for topics such as dance notation. However, names of particular dances are not indexed. The compilers also list important library collections and periodicals and organizations that publish information on Yugoslavian dance.

34 / 2—Bibliographies

104. Forbes, Fred R. **Dance: An Annotated Bibliography, 1965-1982**. (Garland Reference Library of the Humanities, vol. 606). New York: Garland, 1986. 261p. LC 85-45150. ISBN 0-8240-8676-7.

Modeled after Paul Magriel's *Bibliography of Dancing* (entry 107), Forbes' work is "an annotated list of current references on dance in the areas of aesthetics, anthropology, education, history, literature, physiology, psychology, and sociology" (preface). All materials listed are written in English and were published between 1965 and 1982. Most are periodical articles, but Forbes has included books, book chapters, dissertations, and theses as well. He arranges the work by broad subject classifications and provides author and subject indexes. The 1,166 entries consist of bibliographic citations and short annotations. Readers will find references to articles on many choreographers and dancers and to works about dance's place in many of the world's cultures. This book is a good beginning point for research, especially for college students. Those who need greater amounts of information should consult the New York Public Library's *Bibliographic Guide to Dance* (entry 193).

105. Forrester, F. S. **Ballet in England: A Bibliography and Survey**. (Library Association Bibliographies, no. 9). London: The Library Association, 1968. 224p. LC 68-116063. ISBN 0-85365-230-9.

Growing out of a library school project, Forrester's bibliography lists and annotates books and periodicals that deal with dance in England. The compiler arranges her material into chapters on reference works, general works, histories, technical works, biographies, and periodicals. She also lists British libraries and archives where one can find additional materials. Her work partially bridges the gap between the older bibliographies such as Beaumont (entry 101) and Magriel (entry 107) and the later Forbes (entry 104).

106. Kaprelian, Mary H., comp. **Aesthetics for Dancers: A Selected Annotated Bibliography**. Washington, D.C.: American Alliance for Health, Physical Education, and Recreation, 1976. 87p. LC 76-360816.

Kaprelian begins this bibliography by noting a lack of research on the aesthetics of dance and suggesting the need for work to be done in applying general aesthetic theory to dance. Accordingly, her bibliography includes many books and journal articles on the aesthetics of art, music, and so on. Only a few pertain directly to the aesthetics of dance. At the same time Kaprelian admits that this bibliography is not complete in terms of the field of aesthetics as a whole. The reader should approach it as a starting place from which to explore. Each entry includes a bibliographic citation and a short descriptive annotation. The bibliography is arranged by subject areas. Within each chapter are separate sections for books and for periodical articles, and separate indexes provide access by book authors and article authors.

107. Magriel, Paul David. **A Bibliography of Dancing: A List of Books and Articles on the Dance and Related Subjects**. New York: H. W. Wilson, 1936. 229p. Fourth Cumulated Supplement, 1936-1940. New York: H. W. Wilson, 1941. 104p. LC 37-842.

Aiming to provide a comprehensive list of "reference works" on dance and related arts, Magriel has arranged his book according to broad subject areas with an index to authors and subjects. Because the compiler worked out of American libraries such as the Library of Congress and the New York Public Library, his work complements Beaumont's list of dance books in the British Museum (entry 101). Unlike Beaumont, Magriel lists not only books but also periodical articles and parts of books. His scope extends to mime, masques, dance halls, and church dancing as well as the more traditional topics of ballet and folk dance. Most of the materials cited are written in English or French with a few in other European languages. The supplement follows the same format and updates the work to 1940. This bibliography is still useful for older works. Use it with Beaumont, Forbes (entry 104), Oswald's chapter in *Arts in America* (entry 54) and the *Bibliographic Guide to Dance* (entry 193).

108. Parker, David L., and Esther Seigel. **Guide to Dance in Film: A Catalog of U.S. Productions Including Dance Sequences, with Names of Dancers, Choreographers, Directors, and Other Details**. Detroit: Gale Research, 1978. 220p. LC 76-20339. ISBN 0-8103-1377-4.

Parker and Seigel collected and listed 1,700 American and foreign films in which dancing appears. Arranged by film title, the entries include the production company, running time, choreographer, dancers, and genre. The last categorizes films that are not primarily musicals or dance films by type such as drama, melodrama, opera, and so forth. The work is well indexed by personal name, production company, and foreign country name. (All foreign films included have been distributed in the United States.) Unfortunately, the authors list neither locations of copies nor distributors of films; instead, they advise readers to check recent film catalogs.

109. **Research in Dance**. Washington, D.C.: American Association for Health, Physical Education, and Recreation, 1968-1982. 3v.

Continuing the work of *Compilation of Dance Research, 1901-1964* (entry 100), this series lists theses and dissertations completed in partial fulfillment of advanced degrees in the field of dance between 1964 and 1981. Volume 1 covers the years 1964-1967, volume 2 lists works written between 1967 and 1970, and volume 3 includes titles from 1971 to 1981. The main body of each volume is divided into sections for master's degree research and doctoral research and then arranged by author. Additionally, each volume lists previously unreported earlier works in a separate section. Because it is not very detailed, the subject index offers only limited help. Main entries list author, title, degree granted, university, and date. For research past 1981, consult *Completed Research in Health, Physical Education, Recreation, and Dance* (entry 102).

110. Robinson, Doris. **Music and Dance Periodicals: An International Directory & Guidebook**. Voorheesville, N.Y.: Peri Press, 1989. 382p. LC 89-151380. ISBN 0-9617844-4-X.

Intended as a comprehensive list of all current publications about music and dance that appear at least once a year, this bibliography lists 139 dance periodicals from around the world. They are arranged within the dance chapter alphabetically by title. The amount of information about each title varies, but generally includes subscription information, advertising data, and a short description of the periodical's purpose and scope. Much of this information is available in updated form in *Ulrich's International Periodicals Directory*. Some of the periodicals are also included in Katz's *Magazines for Libraries* (7th ed., New York: R. R. Bowker, 1992). This title provides annotations for those titles that are not in Katz.

36 / 2—Bibliographies

111. Schwartz, Judith L., and Christena L. Schlundt. **French Court Dance and Dance Music: A Guide to Primary Source Writings 1643-1789**. (Dance and Music, no. 1). Stuyvesant, N.Y.: Pendragon Press, 1987. 386p. LC 87-14888. ISBN 0-918728-72-X.

To "facilitate reconstruction of French court dancing of the 17th and 18th centuries in its contemporary setting" (introduction), the authors have compiled a bibliography of 340 sources printed between 1643, the year of Louis XIV's ascension to the throne, and 1789, the beginning of the French Revolution. Schwartz and Schlundt have divided their work into three parts: writings on dance and dance notation; writings pertaining to dance music; and writings on the performing arts, including the theatre. A short-title list combines titles from all three sections into one chronological list, and the index allows access by subject and name. Besides author, date, and title of the first edition, and an annotation, the entries provide a list of subsequent editions published before 1800 and of modern editions and translations. This will interest those working on French court history, social history, and dance history.

112. **Ten Years of Films on Ballet and Classical Dance 1956-1965**. Paris: UNESCO, 1968. 105p. LC 68-102723.

Not as recent as Parker and Seigel's work (entry 108), but more international, this bibliography resulted from a UNESCO survey of films on dance. Organized by country, the entries list title, production company, choreographer, composer, subject of the film, and distributor. Surprisingly few entries overlap with Parker and Seigel, even in the United States section. Indexes to choreographer and composer provide additional access. Altogether, twenty-three countries are represented. This bibliography deserves an update.

113. Thompson, Donald, and Annie F. Thompson. **Music and Dance in Puerto Rico from the Age of Columbus to Modern Times: An Annotated Bibliography**. (Studies in Latin American Music, no. 1). Metuchen, N.J.: Scarecrow, 1991. 339p. LC 91-40519. ISBN 0-8108-2515-5.

Donald Thompson, a music historian and columnist for the *San Juan Star*, and Annie Thompson, the director of the University of Puerto Rico's School of Library and Information Science, list and annotate 995 references to books, articles, and theses on Puerto Rican music and dance. Each chapter deals with a different subject, and dance topics are included in sections on folk music and dance, urban music and dance, "lyric theatre and ballet" (that is, stage performances), and the "Danza Puertorriqueña," the national dance of Puerto Rico. Although most of the cited works are written in Spanish, a fair number are written in English. The informative and comparative annotations demonstrate the Thompsons' excellent grasp of their subject. Author and subject indexes complete this well written bibliography, which should take its place as a standard source on Puerto Rican dance.

114. Towers, Deirdre. **Dance Film and Video Guide**. Pennington, N.J.: Princeton Book, 1991. 233p. LC 91-25015. ISBN 0-87127-171-0.

Towers lists more than 2,000 films and videos produced over the last 100 years and available for rent or sale from U.S. distributors for noncommercial use. She does not rate the quality of the films, but provides a brief description of their contents. Additional information found in each title entry includes the distributor's name, the production date, the work's length and format (film or video), and credits and cast. Well indexed by choreographer, composer, dance company, dancer, director, and subject, the filmography concludes with a directory of distributors. Commercial films such as *White Nights*, starring

Mikhail Baryshnikov and Gregory Hines, may be found here, but also instructional works and films concentrating on the careers of famous dancers or choreographers. Towers' book is the fourth such work to issue from the Dance Films Association, a nonprofit organization that promotes the awareness and use of dance films and videos. Currently, it is the best source for finding these materials.

115. Troxell, Kay, ed. **Resources in Sacred Dance: Annotated Bibliography from Christian and Jewish Traditions**. Compiled by the Sacred Dance Guild. rev. ed. Peterborough, N.H.: Sacred Dance Guild, 1991. 56p. LC 91-187899. ISBN 0-9623137-1-8.

Written for dancers, researchers, and clergy and laity who want to know more about "dance/movement as it is used in relation to worship and religion" (introduction), this compilation lists 300 books, articles, and other materials related to sacred dance. Theoretical essays, organizational works, and practical manuals all have a place here, and the works represent Roman Catholic, reformed, and fundamentalist Christian views as well as Jewish traditions. Arranged by type of medium, the citations list bibliographical information, price, and a description taken from either a publisher's catalog or the editor's research. References to films and audio and video tapes constitute a separate chapter, and "Reference Sources" lists helpful libraries and associations. Because of its arrangement, the book could use a subject index which, unfortunately, it lacks.

116. Van Zile, Judy. **Dance in India: An Annotated Guide to Source Materials**. Providence, R.I.: Asian Music Publications, Music Department, Brown University, 1973. 129p. LC 73-90410. ISBN 0-913360-06-6.

Van Zile lists and annotates briefly 839 books, papers, and periodical articles in English on the subject of Indian dance. After listing reference works and materials related to the history and theory of Indian dance, she discusses works in classical dance forms; works on folk and tribal dance; and materials on dance that fit neither the classical nor the folk model. In each case, books and papers are followed by periodical articles. Separate chapters describe films, recordings of dance music, Labanotation scores available at the Dance Notation Bureau (entry 753), and resource organizations. Indexes locate materials by periodical title and by author. In need of an update, this bibliography will be useful for older materials on the subject.

Play Bibliographies

117. Bergquist, G. William. **Three Centuries of English and American Plays: A Checklist. England: 1500-1800; United States: 1714-1830**. New York: Hafner, 1963. 281p. LC 63-18015.

Compiled as an index to the Readex Microprint edition of *Three Centuries of English and American Plays*, this checklist can stand on its own as a bibliography of 5,500 plays written between 1500 and 1830. Bergquist includes most of the plays listed by Greg (entry 123), Woodword and McManaway (entry 142), and Hill (entry 128), and he gives entry numbers from the first two books when applicable. The entries are arranged by playwright and list the earliest edition known and significant later editions for each play. Readers can find the many anonymous works under their titles. Entries include brief bibliographical information and chronological period to which the play belongs. As there is no title index, readers must know the playwright's name when looking for a specific play.

118. Binger, Norman. **A Bibliography of German Plays on Microcards**. Hamden, Conn.: Shoe String Press, 1970. 224p. LC 78-117199. ISBN 0-2080-0891-8.

Binger provides bibliographic citations to 4,000 German plays published between the sixteenth century and the early twentieth century. Arranged alphabetically by author, the entries follow a catalog card format. An index allows one to locate plays by title. Binger includes both plays written in German and foreign works translated into German, most taken from collected editions or from collections such as the Loewenberg Collection at Johns Hopkins University (see entry 171). Although not rivaling the coverage in the New York Public Library's catalog (entry 179), this collection may help readers verify bibliographic information about German plays.

119. Brenner, Clarence D. **A Bibliographical List of Plays in the French Language 1700-1789**. New York: AMS Press, 1979 (c.1947). 1v. LC 76-43909. ISBN 0-404-60152-9.

With the aim of listing all "dramatic pieces composed in French between 1700 and 1789 inclusive" (preface), Brenner catalogs 11,662 stage works including plays, operas, and ballets, both professional and amateur. Arranged by playwright's name with a title index, entries provide title, type of work (drama, ballet), number of acts, place and date of its first performance, composer's name if a musical piece, and whether it is composed in prose or verse. The 1979 reprint contains a composer index to the plays with music, operas, and ballets prepared by Michael A. Keller and Neal Zaslaw. They created the index while researching eighteenth-century French music for the *New Grove Dictionary of Music and Musicians*. Researchers who need similar information for nineteenth-century French plays should consult Wicks (entry 586), which covers the years 1801-1900.

120. Bzowski, Frances Diodato. **American Women Playwrights, 1900-1930: A Checklist**. (Bibliographies and Indexes in Women's Studies, 15). Westport, Conn.: Greenwood, 1992. 420p. LC 92-12301. ISBN 0-313-24238-0.

Prompted by an interest in the writings of America's "new woman" during the first decades of the twentieth century, Bzowski has compiled a list of thousands of plays written by hundreds of women during that time. Without attempting any evaluation of the works, she has included all American women playwrights including those who wrote children's and holiday plays, those who wrote for little theatre groups, and those who composed church plays. Most of these women are obscure, although one finds an occasional famous name, such as Edna Ferber or Dorothy Fields. Entries, arranged alphabetically by name, list birth and death dates, codes for biographical dictionaries containing information about the woman, titles of plays with publication or performance date, type of play, and a reference to a play anthology or a library collection where a copy of the play may be found. Bzowski includes a short bibliography of other play indexes and of works on American theatre. Her preface contains information important to interpreting the entries and should be read before using the book. Her work will be most useful to students in women's studies courses.

121. Cohen, Edward M., ed. **Plays of Jewish Interest**. rev. ed. New York: Jewish Theatre Association; Distr., National Foundation for Jewish Culture, 1982. 126p. LC 82-223030.

Cohen, a director at the Jewish Repertory Theatre in New York City, tries to be as inclusive as possible in his definition of a Jewish play. Readers will find references to plays by Jewish authors as well as plays with Jewish themes and/or characters. In an unusual arrangement Cohen lists plays from the *Samuel French Catalog* (entry 188), those from the *Dramatists Play Service Catalogue* (entry 187), and catalogs of other publishers. Next he cites winners of various Jewish playwriting competitions and other unpublished plays and then Yiddish and Hebrew plays in English translations. Indexes allow access by title and playwright. Entries describe the plot and tell the number of sets and actors required. Unfortunately, neither date of first performance nor publication date appears. For plays that are not listed in the major catalogs Cohen tells where to write for scripts and permission to produce. Useful to school and community groups who want to stage a play with Jewish associations, this bibliography needs updating to include such recent plays as *Crossing Delancey* and *The Cemetery Club*.

122. Ellis, James, comp. and ed. **English Drama of the Nineteenth Century: An Index and Finding Guide**. New Canaan, Conn.: Readex Books, 1985. 345p. LC 85-062391. ISBN 0-918414-15-6.

Based on the enormous collection of nineteenth-century English and American plays filmed onto microcard by the Readex Corporation, Ellis' bibliography lists 9,000 English plays, opera librettos, and translations of foreign plays. Arranged alphabetically by author with title cross-references, the bibliography generally gives author, title, place of publication, publisher or printer, date of publication, and number of pages for each play. If the filmed copy of a play was used as a promptbook, that fact is noted. Appendices provide a variety of information including lists of women dramatists, of pseudonyms, of privately printed plays, of series of acting editions, and of promptbooks, manuscripts, and typescripts. If the microcard collection is available, this bibliography, along with Hixon and Hennessee's *Nineteenth-Century American Drama: A Finding Guide* (entry 129) will help unlock its riches.

122a. Furtado, Ken, and Nancy Hellner. **Gay and Lesbian American Plays: An Annotated Bibliography**. Metuchen, N.J.: Scarecrow, 1993. 217p. LC 93-17078. ISBN 0-8108-2689-5.

Published thirteen years after Terry Helbing's ground-breaking bibliography (entry 127), Furtado and Hellner's work is a welcome addition to the literature of gay and lesbian theatre. Basing their work on Helbing's manuscript and his notes, the authors list 700 plays whose primary themes are gay or lesbian or whose characters' "gay or lesbian sexuality is integral to the plays' message" (introduction). Furtado and Hellner concentrate on American plays with just a few foreign works. Helbing, on the other hand, included more foreign plays. Entries, arranged alphabetically by author and then title, present a plot summary, number of acts, sets, and actors required, and the location and year of the first production. The entries also cite availability through published editions and/or theatrical agents. Furtado and Hellner provide directories of agents, playwrights, and gay theatres. A short bibliography, a list of plays for which only titles are known, and a play title index complete the book. Readers may find plays with certain characteristics (AIDS related, one-acts, musicals, performance pieces, and so on) by using the codes found in the title index.

123. Greg, Walter W. **A Bibliography of the English Printed Drama to the Restoration**. Oxford, England: Oxford University Press for the Bibliographical Society, 1939-1959. 4v. LC 40-30318.

A monumental achievement, Greg's four volumes describe all known editions to 1700 of all English plays written before 1643 or first printed before 1660. Translations

40 / 2—Bibliographies

from other languages are included unless they were intended primarily for educational purposes. Working from records of the Stationer's Company and other sources, the author lists plays by "supposed date of publication of the earliest surviving edition" (Provisional Memoranda). Greg numbers each play and letters each different edition. Citations include both bibliographic and physical descriptions and locations of copies in twenty-six libraries, nine in Britain and seventeen in the United States. Greg establishes separate lists of Latin plays, of works that are thought to have been printed but for which no early edition exists, and for works known only through the record of the Stationer's Company. Readers will find an explanation of the author's method and the symbols he employs in the "Provisional Memoranda" at the beginning of the first volume. Harbage (entry 555) and Kawachi (entry 558) cover much of the same time period but are more concerned with performance than with publication. Although the three sources do not always agree on publication details, scholars of early English theatre are presumably aware of the problems posed by historical research.

124. Greg, Walter W. **List of Masques, Pageants, etc.: Supplementary to a List of English Plays**. London: Bibliographic Society, 1902. 1v. LC 03-0302.

A supplement to Greg's *List of English Plays Written Before 1643 and Printed Before 1700* (London: Bibliographical Society, 1900), this bibliography provides bibliographic citations, physical descriptions, and one or more British library locations for masques, pageants, entertainments, and shows presented at Court prior to the English Civil War. The work, arranged by author, also contains extensive addenda and corrigenda to the earlier volume on plays. An early work, this should be used with Steele (entry 579).

125. **Guide to Play Selection: A Selective Bibliography for Production and Study of Modern Plays**. Compiled by the NCTE Liaison Committee with the Speech Communication Association and the American Theatre Association. 3d ed. Urbana, Ill.: National Council of Teachers of English; Distr., R. R. Bowker, 1975. 292p. LC 74-33724. ISBN 0-8352-0862-1; 0-8141-1946-8 pa.

To help English teachers, play producers, and theatre lovers choose plays for performance or study, this bibliography discusses 850 plays written between 1870 and 1970 by world authors. Although British and American playwrights wrote most of the selections, other European writers such as Günter Grass and Jean Giraudoux are represented here. Works are divided by category: short plays, plays by African Americans, full-length plays, musicals, and television plays. Within sections entries are listed by author. An appendix lists anthologies and collections in which the selected plays appear, and the title index keys plays to the anthologies, a particularly useful feature. Other indexes provide access by author, topic, and actor requirements (number of men and women needed). Entries discuss set and costume requirements, number and gender of actors required, licensing and royalty information, a plot summary, and the play's suitability for various audiences. Until the National Council of Teachers of English issues a fourth edition, this work will continue as a convenient location to find basic information about a large number of modern plays.

126. Hatch, James V. **Black Image on the American Stage: A Bibliography of Plays and Musicals 1770-1970**. New York: DBS Publications, 1970. 162p. LC 72-115695.

Differing from Hatch and Omanii's *Black Playwrights, 1823-1977* (entry 5), this bibliography lists plays that contain at least one Black character or present a Black theme as well as those that were written by an African-American. Hatch's scope includes musicals, operas, and dance drama as well as all forms of stage plays. He omits radio, television, and film scripts. More than 2,000 works appear including thirteen produced before 1800 in America. Only brief information about each play is listed—author, title, year first produced, publishing information if the play was published, and location of a library copy if known. Arrangement is chronological by decade, with author and title indexes providing good access. This work is still useful for earlier plays.

127. Helbing, Terry. **Gay Theatre Alliance Directory of Gay Plays**. New York: JH Press, 1980. 122p. LC 79-91529. ISBN 0-935672-00-1.

Helbing lists and describes 400 English-language plays "with major gay characters and/or predominant gay themes" written any time before 1980. The entries, which appear alphabetically by play title, list author, genre, number of acts and sets required, the location and year of the first performance if known, and publishing and licensing information. If an agent represents the author, the agent's name and address are given. A plot synopsis completes each entry. Helbing includes an appendix of "lost plays" for which he has found no information other than author and title. He also lists gay theatre companies as of 1980. An author index locates plays by playwright. Helbing's work supplements Furtado and Hellner's more recent bibliography (entry 122a).

128. Hill, Frank Pierce, comp. **American Plays Printed: 1714-1830; A Bibliographical Record**. Stanford, Calif.: Stanford University Press, 1934. 152p. LC 34-6532.

Hill lists published plays written by Americans or American residents and supersedes the list of printed plays found in Wegelin (entry 141). Because Hill does not cite plays in manuscript form, however, Wegelin is still necessary. This work is arranged by playwright with a title index and a chronological list of plays. Entries give bibliographical citations, physical descriptions, library locations, and, sometimes, short annotations. Roden's *Later American Plays, 1831-1900* (entry 133) continues Hill's bibliography.

129. Hixon, Don L., and Don A. Hennessee. **Nineteenth-Century American Drama: A Finding Guide**. Metuchen, N.J.: Scarecrow, 1977. 579p. LC 77-12057. ISBN 0-8108-1083-2.

The Readex Corporation's *English and American Drama of the 19th Century* microprint collection is a monumental work, containing thousands of plays. Unfortunately, access to the particular play one wants has not been easily achieved. Hixon and Hennessee attempt to remedy this situation by creating an index to that part of the collection entitled "American Plays, 1831-1900." That section includes 4,500 plays. Authors and titles are alphabetically arranged with all titles cross-referenced to authors. Because Readex classified some plays under their adapters' names instead of their authors (for instance Shakespeare's works are listed under various adapters' names), Hixon and Hennessee provide cross-references. Appendices include one for series of plays (mostly publishers' series); an ethnic/racial index ("Irish in cast," "Blacks in cast," and so on); and a subject/form index. This last section locates children's plays, minstrel plays, temperance plays, and so forth. If the Readex collection is available, this book should enhance its usefulness greatly. The English portion of the collection is indexed in Ellis' *English Drama of the Nineteenth Century: An Index and Finding Guide* (entry 122).

42 / 2—Bibliographies

130.   Johnson, Albert. **Best Church Plays: A Bibliography of Religious Drama**. Philadelphia: Pilgrim Press, 1968. 180p. LC 68-22572.

Intending to make a wide range of plays available for performance by church groups, Johnson lists by title hundreds of works he considers suitable for religious organizations. Both specifically religious and other plays find a place here. Works such as Wilder's *Our Town*, Albee's *The American Dream*, and Shakespeare's *Othello*, which examine moral and ethical questions, are included. Entries feature a short abstract and royalty information. Although a subject index provides access by topics such as Biblical plays, Easter plays, and so on, regrettably there is no author index. The bibliography needs an update to include plays written in the past twenty-five years. Nevertheless, church performing groups should find something to interest them here.

131.   Nicoll, Allardyce. **A History of English Drama, 1660-1900**. rev. ed. Cambridge, England: Cambridge University Press, 1952-1959. 6v. LC 52-14525.

Each of the first five volumes in Nicoll's history stands alone, and the five together comprise a history of 240 years of British theatrical and dramatic history. Although Nicoll's work follows chronologically the works of Chambers and Bentley (entries 548, 545), he devotes nearly half of each volume to lists of plays produced or printed during the time period in question. The sixth volume, a short-title catalog of English plays 1660-1900, serves as both an index to the preceding works and as a stand-alone bibliography. In this way, Nicoll is also the successor to Greg (entry 123). Each play, in order by title, is listed with its author and year of original production or publication, and a volume and page reference to one of the first five books. Those volumes discuss the condition of the theatre and the drama for the period in question: 1660-1700 in volume 1; 1700-1750 in volume 2; 1750-1800 in volume 3; 1800-1850 in volume 4; and 1850-1900 in volume 5. An appendix in each work gives the history of the playhouses and theatres of the time. A bibliography of plays follows as well as an index of persons and subjects.

132.   O'Brien, Robert. **Spanish Plays in English Translation: An Annotated Bibliography**. New York: Published for the American Educational Theatre Association by Las Americas Publishing Company, 1963. 1v. LC 63-22756.

The result of a project by the American Educational Theatre Association to provide translations of foreign plays to students and producers, O'Brien's bibliography locates translations of Spanish plays from medieval drama to mid-twentieth-century works. For each chronological period—early drama, the Golden Age, eighteenth and nineteenth centuries, and the modern period—he lists authors by birth date with a list of selected plays. A brief description contains a plot summary, the number of acts, and the number of men and women players needed. One or more published or unpublished translations are listed. O'Brien concentrates on plays of interest to students. Spanish language teachers and drama instructors will find this useful for suggesting older titles to study or produce.

133.   Roden, Robert F. **Later American Plays, 1831-1900: Being A Compilation of the Titles of Plays by American Authors Published and Performed in America Since 1831**. (Burt Franklin Bibliography series, no. 76). New York: Dunlap Society, 1900. Reprint. New York, Burt Franklin, 1964. 132p. LC 71-6518.

A continuation of Wegelin (entry 141) and Hill (entry 128), this bibliography cites plays written by Americans and published between 1831 and 1900. Although the work is not comprehensive, the author claims he has included all important plays of the period.

Arranged by playwright with a title index, the entries contain a bibliographic citation, a physical description, and, sometimes, an annotation. Following Wegelin's example, Roden provides a paragraph of biographical information for most of the playwrights.

134. Sibley, Gertrude Marian. **The Lost Plays and Masques 1500-1642**. Ithaca, N.Y.: Cornell University Press, 1933. 205p. LC 33-4381.

Reading this book is somewhat like looking at photographs of art work destroyed in World War II. One can experience only the record of the artistic creation, not the work itself. Sibley combed public and private records of the sixteenth and early seventeenth centuries to find references to plays and court masques whose texts are now lost. Arranged by title, entries tell when the play was performed and report scholarship on the probable nature of the plot. Sibley lists many references to histories, bibliographies, and other works that are listed in a separate bibliography at the front of her volume. She provides separate sections for lost masques with known titles and for English plays acted in Germany. An index by playwright name completes the book, which complements Greg's works (entries 123 and 124).

135. Stratman, Carl J., comp. and ed. **Bibliography of English Printed Tragedy, 1565-1900**. Carbondale: Southern Illinois University Press, 1966. 843p. LC 66-19720.

Father Stratman lists 1,483 tragedies printed in Great Britain between 1565 and 1900. Shakespeare's tragedies and translations of foreign plays are omitted. Stratman arranges this work by playwright with a title index. Each entry lists bibliographic information, a library location, and an explanatory note when necessary. The appendix gives locations of manuscripts of plays listed in the bibliography. Stratman covers a larger time period than Bergquist (entry 117) but includes only English plays and only tragedies. For comedies and for American plays, see Bergquist.

136. Stratman, Carl J. **Bibliography of Medieval Drama**. 2d ed., rev. and enl. New York: Frederick Ungar, 1972. 2v. LC 78-163141. ISBN 0-8044-3272-3.

Intended to help the student of English drama who is looking for parallel developments in Continental and English literature, Stratman's bibliography includes both citations to manuscripts and texts of medieval plays and references to critical material. The author devotes the first volume to liturgical Latin plays and English plays. Volume 2 is divided into chapters on the drama of various European countries, especially Germany and France. The author lists holding libraries in the United States and Britain for most of the 9,000 works cited. The unannotated entries follow standard bibliographic form and Stratman has marked important works with an asterisk. By locating manuscripts and texts of medieval plays in several languages, this bibliography allows readers to compare, for example, the German, French, and English texts of an Easter play such as *Visitatio Sepulchri*. Clearly a specialized work, this bibliography will interest medievalists. It has been supplemented by Maria Spaeth Murphy in the Spring 1986 issue of the *Emporia State Research Studies* (vol. 34, no. 4).

137. Thompson, Lawrence S. **A Bibliography of French Plays on Microcards**. Hamden, Conn.: Shoe String Press, 1967. 689p. LC 67-13750.

As a bibliography separate from the microcard collection it accompanies, this work presents problems. Although it does record some 7,000 French plays up to the early twentieth century, its compiler has chosen only works from the Library of Congress and the University of Kentucky collections. Further, he includes only titles that are in the public domain, and not necessarily first editions. Entries vary in completeness. Those describing plays from the Library of Congress collections are more complete than entries for University of Kentucky materials. Without a title index, access is limited to the author entries, which generally include play title, publication information, pagination, and size. This will be more useful as a guide to the microcard collection than to a serious scholar of French bibliography.

138. Thompson, Lawrence S. **A Bibliography of Spanish Plays on Microcards**. Hamden, Conn.: Shoe String Press, 1968. 490p. LC 68-20280. SBN 208-00703-2.

Thompson based his selection of titles for this bibliography and the accompanying microcard collection on his personal library and that of the University of Kentucky. He has chosen about 6,000 Spanish, Spanish-American, and Catalonian plays written from the sixteenth to the twentieth centuries. Although the compiler cites mostly first editions, he has included some revised editions and school texts. Entries list author's name, play title, place, publisher, date of publication, pagination, and size. Although a few plays are entered by title, the majority are by playwright. Because Thompson has not provided a title index, readers must know the author's name to find a play, a drawback to the bibliography's use. Those looking for *comedias sueltas* should prefer the catalogs compiled by Boyer (entry 158), Bainton (entry 154), or Bergman and Szmuk (entry 155), which are more recent and more informative.

139. Thompson, Lawrence S. **Nineteenth and Twentieth Century Drama: A Selective Bibliography of English Language Works, Numbers 1-3029**. Boston: G. K. Hall, 1975. 456p. LC 75-29255. ISBN 0-8161-7842-9.

As part of a microfilming project launched by the General Microfilm Company, Thompson compiled this bibliography of plays. Despite its title the work includes not only English and American plays but also English translations of foreign playwrights such as Racine. Equally misleading is the inclusion of eighteenth- and nineteenth-century editions of earlier works, including many of Shakespeare's plays. The main entries list author, title, genre (comedy, melodrama, and so on), publisher, date, and number of pages. Numerous indexes allow access by title, editor, joint author, translator, pseudonym, illustrator, composer, and subject of the play. Without any annotations and with an unfocused selection policy, this work is not as helpful as Hixon and Hennessee (entry 129) or Ellis (entry 122).

140. Wagner, Anton, ed. **The Brock Bibliography of Published Canadian Plays in English, 1766-1978**. Toronto: Playwrights Press, 1980. 375p. ISBN 0-88754-157-7; 0-88754-155-0 pa.

Incorporating the work of the earlier bibliography and the supplements prepared by students at Brock University, this edition cites Canadian plays written during the eighteenth, nineteenth, and twentieth centuries. Arranged by century, then by author, and then by play title, entries include a bibliographic reference for each play, the number of acts, the number of characters, and a plot summary. Both radio plays and children's plays are cited, as well as more traditional stage plays for adults. The great majority date from the twentieth century. Together with Ball and Plant (entry 23) and McCallum (entry 497), this bibliography is essential to anyone researching Canadian theatre history.

141. Wegelin, Oscar. **Early American Plays, 1714-1830: Being a Compilation of the Titles of Plays by American Authors Published and Performed in America Previous to 1830**. (New York: Dunlap Society, 1900. Reprint: New York: Haskell House, 1968.) LC 68-25316.

Now largely superseded by Hill (entry 128), this list is still useful for its citations to plays in manuscript (Hill includes only printed plays.) Wegelin also includes a paragraph of biographical information about each playwright.

142. Woodward, Gertrude L., and James G. McManaway, comps. **A Check List of English Plays 1641-1700**. Chicago: The Newberry Library, 1945. 155p. Supplement: Bowers, Fredson. **A Supplement to the Woodward & McManaway Check List of English Plays 1641-1700**. Charlottesville: Bibliographical Society of the University of Virginia, 1949. 22 leaves. LC 46-3987.

Woodward, of the Newberry Library, and McManaway, of the Folger Library, drew on the extensive resources of their institutions as well as the collections of other American libraries to "record the plays and masques, with the variant editions and issues, printed in the English language in the British Isles or in other countries during the years 1641 to 1700 inclusive, and to give the location of copies in a number of American libraries" (preface). Arranged by author's name with anonymous plays filed under title, the citations include translations, adaptations of classical plays, and royal and civic pageants as well as English plays. Entries list author, title, publication date, size, and, occasionally, a reference to an earlier standard bibliography. An addendum lists editions discovered when rare books were returned from protective storage to the Folger library and the Library of Congress at the end of World War II. Woodward and McManaway provided holdings for sixteen American libraries. In his supplement Bowers added holdings for ten additional institutions and listed new acquisitions of the original libraries. He also corrected and added to the original bibliography. Most of the titles in Woodward and McManaway are in Donald Wing's *Short-title Catalogue of Books Printed in England, Scotland, Ireland, Wales, and British America, and of English Books Printed in Other Countries, 1641-1700* (2d ed. New York: Index Committee of the Modern Language Association of America, 1992), but some readers may prefer the convenience of this shorter work which concentrates on plays. Greg's bibliography (entry 123) provides information on plays written before 1642 or printed before 1660.

Discographies

143. Debenham, Warren. **Laughter on Record: A Comedy Discography**. Metuchen, N.J.: Scarecrow, 1988. 369p. LC 87-35938. ISBN 0-8108-2094-3.

With a scope considerably wider than Ronald L. Smith's discography (entry 149), Debenham lists 4,367 comedy long-playing records garnered from private collections, record stores, libraries and archives, and the Schwann record catalogs issued between 1949 and 1988. He includes records that have even one comedy cut, for example, *The Four Freshmen in Person*. With an alphabetical arrangement by name of performer, the discography is limited to records issued in the United States, but not to American comedians alone. English groups such as Monty Python and Beyond the Fringe are included, for instance. Entries consist of the record title, the label and number, and a short descriptive phrase. In contrast, Smith critiques each record in his discography. The indexes locate entries by broad subject areas such as advertising, medicine, and women (but not men!). A directory lists addresses for record companies and for sources of out-of-print records. If one is simply trying to identify a record title, one should use Debenham, which covers more titles, but those who are seeking guidance on selecting comedy records should use Smith.

144. Harris, Steve. **Film, Television and Stage Music on Phonograph Records: A Discography.** Jefferson, N.C.: McFarland, 1988. 445p. LC 87-42509. ISBN 0-89950-251-2.

Harris has cataloged all important phonograph recordings of film, television, and stage music from United States and British productions and foreign productions presented or recorded in the United States or Britain. The stage music section lists recordings of "original or adapted music composed specifically for stage musicals" (introduction). Entries give title, date of recording, composer, and record label and number. Harris includes both records of completed scores and those that contain highlights from a show. He notes if the original cast performs. Harris is not as complete or informative as Raymond (entry 146), but his book is a good supplementary source.

145. Hummel, David. **The Collector's Guide to the American Musical Theatre.** Metuchen, N.J.: Scarecrow, 1984. 2v. LC 83-7520. ISBN 0-8108-1637-7 set.

Concentrating on recordings of the American musical comedy, Hummel lists shows by title with credits for the music, lyrics, and book, song titles, members of the original cast, and conductor. He then provides information on the original cast recording and, sometimes, other recordings as well. For *My Fair Lady*, for example, he lists the original Mexican, Italian, German, and Austrian cast recordings. Hummel also includes recordings of revival productions and privately produced tapes. He marks records as monaural, stereo, or four-channel, evaluates private tapes for quality, and lists record label and number for each commercial recording. When he has located songs for a musical on albums of excerpts, he notes those, and the appendix lists these albums. Volume 2 serves as an index to personal names, which are referenced to show titles.

145a. Miletich, Leo N. **Broadway's Prize-Winning Musicals: An Annotated Guide for Libraries and Audio Collectors.** New York: Haworth, 1993. 255p. LC 92-4125. ISBN 1-56024-288-4.

Aimed at the record collector who wishes to purchase recordings of the best American musicals, Miletich's discography guides readers to the plays which won the Tony Award, the New York Drama Critics Circle Award, the Pulitzer Prize, or the Grammy Award. Chapters are arranged by award and then by year. Entries discuss the plot, songs, critical reception, and other awards received. Miletich provides original cast recording record labels and numbers for both the Broadway and the motion picture versions of a show. Musicals which won more than one award are described only once with appropriate cross-references from subsequent chapters. In a separate chapter Miletich discusses a number of musicals which did not win prizes but which he considers important or entertaining nevertheless. A general index locates people and play titles, and a separate index finds song titles. Because it concentrates on prize-winning musicals, this work is not as comprehensive as Raymond's *Show Music on Record: The First 100 Years* (entry 146).

146. Raymond, Jack. **Show Music on Record: The First 100 Years**. Washington, D.C.: Smithsonian Institution Press, 1992. 429p. LC 91-23483. ISBN 1-56098-151-2.

Raymond lists, in chronological order, "all commercially issued recordings of show music for the American stage, screen, and television as performed by members of the original cast and subsequent casts, including studio productions" (introduction). The earliest show noted, *The Bohemian Girl*, opened in 1843, but its songs were recorded in 1909. The latest shows listed opened on Broadway in 1990. A title index together with a coded numbering system allows readers to find recordings by play title. Raymond includes recordings of individual songs only if performed by a cast member or composer or lyricist of the song. Thus, cast member Michael Crawford's rendition of "The Music of the Night" from *The Phantom of the Opera* is here, but Judy Collins' "Send in the Clowns" from *A Little Night Music* is not. A separate list of anthology albums on which many of these individual songs appear is linked to the main body of the discography by a special numbering system. Users must read the introduction to understand the book's organization and to discover both the author's rules for inclusion of records and his admitted tampering with those rules. Entries group all recordings of the same show together. Thus the original cast version and all subsequent recordings of *Camelot* are listed together under 1960, the year of the opening production. Raymond lists composer, lyricist, singers, year of recording, and record label and number. This work represents a tremendous amount of effort and should remain a standard discography of the American musical for many years. Those interested in manuscript material on songs from American musicals should consult Krasker and Kimball (entry 61).

147. Rust, Brian A. L. **British Music Hall on Record.** Harrow, England: General Gramophone Publications, 1979. 301p. LC 79-322094. ISBN 0-902470-07-9.

A companion to Rust's *The Complete Entertainment Discography* (entry 148), this volume lists 78 rpm recordings made by British music hall performers. The earliest performers are not represented here because the phonograph had not yet been invented. As recordings became affordable to the mass population in the second decade of the twentieth century, more and more artists entered studios to record their performances. Arranged alphabetically by artist's name, entries list date of recording, songs recorded, and record label and number. See also the discography in *British Music Hall, 1840-1923* (entry 82).

148. Rust, Brian A. L. **The Complete Entertainment Discography from the Mid-1890s to 1942**. New Rochelle, N.Y.: Arlington House, 1973. 677p. LC 73-13239. ISBN 0-87000-150-7.

Rust lists phonograph recordings made between 1890 and 1942 by American minstrel singers, vaudeville stars, film and radio personalities, and actors. Europeans who toured and recorded in the United States, such as Maurice Chevalier and Beatrice Lillie, have been included. Rust's companion volume, *British Music Hall on Record* (entry 147), concentrates on English performers. This work excludes recordings of jazz bands, dance bands, and blues singers. Arranged by performers' names, entries list the recording date, the record label and number, and the names of the songs recorded. Representing an enormous amount of research, this specialized work should help collectors and popular culture researchers.

2—Bibliographies

149. Smith, Ronald L. **Comedy on Record: The Complete Critical Discography**. New York: Garland, 1988. 728p. LC 87-35969. ISBN 0- 8240-8461-6.

Smith has tried to list every comedy album released in the United States between 1957 and 1987, including those by British performers who were successful in the American market. He also includes a few ten-inch discs manufactured in the early 1950s. His compilation is based on record catalogs, library collections, and his own extensive record library. Each performer's listing gives biographical and career information. Each album is described, critiqued, and rated on a one to four star system. Although a performer's albums appear to be listed in chronological order, they are not dated. Only title and record label and number are provided. Smith can be quite critical when he thinks a record is not funny, and few albums receive four stars. Acknowledging that appreciation of the humorous is an individual matter, he quotes many jokes to give the flavor of various albums. A supplement lists Grammy comedy awards 1958-1986 and gold and platinum comedy records 1962-1986. This is the first place to look for evaluations of comedy on recordings. Debenham (entry 143) lists more records but does not provide critical commentaries.

Chapter 3

Catalogs

Works listed in this chapter enumerate and describe the collections found in libraries and archives in the United States, Canada, and England. A few works describe European collections.

Theatre and Related Arts Catalogs

150. Amsterdam University Library. **Catalogus van de Circus-Bibliotheek Nagelaten door K. D. Hartmans**. Amsterdam: Universiteit-Bibliotheek, 1968. 279p. LC 71-488068.

Along with Toole-Stott (entry 96) and Sokan (entry 185), the catalog of the Amsterdam University Library's circus collection forms a triumvirate of circus bibliography. Arranged in alphabetical order by author, entries cite 2,410 books. If an item also appears in Toole-Stott's list, his entry number is given in the book's description. A table at the end of this volume lists Toole-Stott's numbers with corresponding Amsterdam numbers. This collection contains many items not found in the other bibliographies. English-language readers should use Toole-Stott and Sokan before turning to this excellent supplement.

151. Angotti, Vincent L. **Source Materials in the Field of Theatre: An Annotated Bibliography and Subject Index to the Microfilm Collection**. Ann Arbor, Mich.: University Microfilms, 1967. 73p.

Angotti has cited and annotated every work in University Microfilms' collection *Source Materials in the Field of Theatre*. This collection of eighty books, periodicals, manuscripts, personal journals, and diaries contains materials written in English and European languages. Without any explanation of the rationale behind the choice of sources, it is difficult to understand the purpose of the collection, a major weakness. If one is looking for an obscure or rare theatrical document, however, one should check Angotti on the chance it will be in this collection. The subject index is so brief that it is less helpful than the main citations, arranged by author.

152. Arizpe, Victor. **The Spanish Drama Collection at the Ohio State University Library: A Descriptive Catalogue**. Kessel, Germany: Edition Reichenberger, 1990. 224p. LC 91-101990. ISBN 3-923593-92-9.

In this catalog of Ohio State's Spanish plays, Arizpe first lists all plays, both bound and unbound, by title. In this title listing, a traditional arrangement for catalogs of *comedias sueltas*, he describes only the unbound works. The second section describes the bound plays, each of which contains plays written by only one author. In this section, Arizpe uses an author arrangement that allows the reader to scan the contents of each volume. Altogether, 426 items receive bibliographic and physical description and Ohio State call number.

3—Catalogs

153. Ashcom, B. B. **A Descriptive Catalogue of the Spanish Comedias Sueltas in the Wayne State University Library and the Private Library of Professor B. B. Ashcom**. Detroit: Wayne State University Libraries, 1965. 103p.

Ashcom was a collector of *comedias sueltas*, Spanish plays that were published in pamphlet form during the seventeenth and eighteenth centuries. He donated his collection to Wayne State University and undertook a catalog of the university's collection. It describes, by title, 566 different plays by 108 dramatists. The bibliographic descriptions lack annotations. An index provides access by author.

154. Bainton, A. J. C., comp. **Comedias Sueltas in Cambridge University Library: A Descriptive Catalogue**. (Cambridge University Library Historical Bibliography series, no. 2). Cambridge, England: The University Library, 1977. 281p. LC 78-379523. ISBN 0-902205-23-4.

Bainton broke with catalog traditions previously applied to *comedias sueltas* and deliberately included much more information about each book in the Cambridge University Library's collection. Hoping to improve on the previous efforts of Ashcom (entry 153) and Rogers (entry 182), Bainton carefully describes each of 900 works in minute detail. Arranged by title, each book's title page is transcribed along with any printing from the end of the title to the end of the second line of dialogue. The compiler includes the collation, the number of pages, the verso and recto running heads, the colophon (all material printed after the end of the play), the type size, and the library's classification number. With continuing care to detail, Bainton indexes his catalog by author and by printer and bookseller. Readers should consult the introduction to understand the compiler's use of symbols within entries. Bainton influenced Boyer (entry 158) and other catalogers by redefining the proper form of a *comedias sueltas* catalog.

155. Bergman, Hannah E., and Szilvia E. Szmuk. **A Catalogue of Comedias Sueltas in the New York Public Library**. (Research Bibliographies and Checklists). London: Grant & Cutler, 1980. 2v. ISBN v. 1: 0-7293-0090-0; v. 2: 0-7293-0113-3.

Restricted to *comedias sueltas* (Spanish plays issued in pamphlet form) printed before 1834, Bergman and Szmuk's catalog describes 1,210 plays in the New York Public Library's collections. Their title arrangement is augmented by indexes for authors, printers, booksellers, theatres, and actors. The compilers provide both bibliographic and physical descriptions of the titles.

156. Birmingham Public Libraries. **A Shakespeare Bibliography: The Catalogue of the Birmingham Shakespeare Library**. London: Mansell, 1971. 7v. LC 71-873519. ISBN v. 1: 0-7201-0135-2; v. 2: 0-7201-0136-0; v. 3: 0-7201-0137-9; v. 4: 0-7201-0138-7; v. 5: 0-7201-0139-5; v. 6: 0-7201-0140-9; v. 7: 0-7201-0141-7.

Founded in 1864 to commemorate the 300th anniversary of Shakespeare's birth, the Birmingham (England) Shakespeare Library holds more than 40,000 volumes relating to the playwright and his works. Volumes 1 through 3 of this work reproduce catalog cards for the materials collected before 1932 while the last four volumes provide records for the books collected after 1931. The division results from a major change in cataloging practice that took place in 1932 and the impossibility of integrating the two files for purposes of photographing the records. In each section of the catalog works are arranged by type: editions of Shakespeare's works, first in English, then in foreign languages; and then Shakespeareana, again in English, then in foreign languages, with authors and subjects interfiled. Editions are indexed by editor, translator, illustrator, and series. For Americans, the Birmingham catalog supplements the catalog of the Folger Shakespeare Library (entry 167) which describes a more accessible collection.

157. Boston Public Library. **Catalogue of the Allen A. Brown Collection of Books Relating to the Stage in the Public Library of the City of Boston**. Boston: Trustees of the Boston Public Library, 1919. 952p. LC 19-8165.

Bostonian Allen A. Brown collected books and other materials related to the theatre during the nineteenth century, leaving his collection to the Boston Public Library when he died in 1916. Brown's wide-ranging interests led him to collect books on the circus, minstrel shows, vaudeville, and magic, as well as the legitimate stage and drama. Although many of the books were published during the nineteenth or early twentieth centuries, some have earlier imprints. Altogether, the catalog lists 3,500 volumes written in English, French, and German. Books on the history of the stage are listed in dictionary catalog style, followed by books on the drama, arranged alphabetically by author. The citation accompanies the Boston Public Library's call number. The Brown Collection is currently housed in the Boston Public Library's rare books department.

158. Boyer, Mildred Vinson. **The Texas Collection of Comedias Sueltas: A Descriptive Bibliography**. (Reference Publications in Latin American Studies). Boston: G. K. Hall, 1978. 620p. LC 78-2714. ISBN 0-8161-8117-9.

One of many catalogs of *comedias sueltas* collections, Boyer's work lists and describes 1,119 plays in the University of Texas collection. All of these plays were published between 1670 and 1834. Readers should note that the University collections also hold another 10,000 uncataloged plays published after 1834. Arranged alphabetically by author, the entries provide bibliographical and physical descriptions of each title. The catalog is amply indexed by author, title, printer, publisher, both place and date of printing, numbered series, and persons and places named in play titles. Boyer has taken great care to make this catalog as useful to researchers as possible. Her list of references leads one to other bibliographies and catalogs of *comedias sueltas*, including those of Oberlin College (entry 182), Cambridge University (entry 154), and the University of Toronto (entry 176).

159. British Drama League. Library. **The Player's Library: The Catalogue of the Library of the British Drama League**. London: Faber and Faber, 1950. 1,115p. First Supplement, 1951. Second Supplement, 1954. Third Supplement, 1956. LC 50-4789.

In 1919 the founders of the British Drama League declared as one of their purposes the formation of a theatrical library. By the time this catalog was published thirty years later, the League had amassed a collection of 70,000 volumes. The bulk of the library consists of English-language plays, citations to which are entered in the catalog by author. Each play's entry discusses its requirements in terms of sets, costumes, and cast. The second part of the work describes books about the theatre. Using a subject arrangement, the catalog cites works on acting, dance, puppets, theatre history, and other topics of interest to actors. A title index to the plays and an author index to the books about the theatre complete the catalog. Supplements follow the same format as the original volume. The third supplement also contains a list of all French-language plays in the collection. The Library, which subsequently grew to some 300,000 volumes, became part of the Theatre Museum in Covent Garden, London, in December, 1991.

160. Clubb, Louise George. **Italian Plays (1500-1700) in the Folger Library: A Bibliography with Introduction**. (Biblioteca di Bibliografia Italiana, 52). Firenze, Italy: Leo S. Olschki Editore, 1968. 268p. LC 77-352612.

Clubb cites and describes 890 Italian plays in the Folger Library. After listing collections of plays, anonymous works, and plays written by members of academies, she lists works by individual authors. Befitting rare book scholarship, she provides detailed bibliographic and physical descriptions. Clubb indicates if a title can be found in the University of Toronto or University of Illinois libraries, both of which hold large collections of sixteenth- and seventeenth-century Italian plays (see entries 161 and 169). Clubb also keys the works to Allacci's *Drammaturgia*, the seventeenth-century Italian bibliography that serves as a basic source for this period. Indexes list plays by title and printers by city. This work, Herrick's catalog of the Illinois collection, and Corrigan's catalog of the Toronto collection complement each other.

161. Corrigan, Beatrice, comp. **Catalogue of Italian Plays, 1500-1700, in the Library of the University of Toronto**. Toronto: University of Toronto Press, 1961. 132p. LC 62-2703.

A catalog of one of the larger North American collections of sixteenth- and seventeenth-century Italian plays, Corrigan's work describes about 500 plays. She concentrates on bibliographic citations and does not provide as much physical description as Clubb (entry 160). Corrigan arranges her catalog into chapters on collections of plays, anonymous plays, plays by members of academies, and plays by individual authors. A title index and a list of printers by city provide additional access points. Titles are keyed to references in Allacci's *Drammaturgia* of 1666, a standard Italian source. Because Clubb's catalog of the Folger Library's holdings follows the same format as this work, readers will be able to compare the two collections easily. Supplements to this catalog appeared in *Renaissance News* 18(4): 298-307 (1963) and 19(3): 219-228 (1966).

162. Detroit Public Library. **Catalog of the E. Azalia Hackley Memorial Collection of Negro Music, Dance, and Drama**. Boston: G. K. Hall, 1979. 510p. ISBN 0-8161-0299-6.

The first public library collection to document Black achievements in the performing arts, the E. Azalia Hackley Collection of the Detroit Public Library was founded in 1943 and named in honor of a noted Detroit musician, choral director, and teacher. The catalog reproduces 12,000 cards from the collection's catalog and shelflist. The first part of the book contains cards for books and musical scores, arranged by author, title, and subject in one alphabet. A shelflist of the collection follows. The book's second part reproduces cards for historical sheet music, arranged by composer and song title. Bibliographic information is supplied with the composer entries. Part 3 catalogs posters and broadsides that advertise performing arts events featuring Black artists. Finally, the collection's photographs are cataloged by personal name and show title. When the catalog appeared in 1979 the Hackley Collection held more than 2,000 books, 1,600 scores, 2,050 pieces of sheet music, and 2,000 photographs. The collection continues to grow and remains an important resource for research on African-Americans and the performing arts. For more information about the collection, see entry 687.

Theatre and Related Arts Catalogs / 53

163. Dubois, William R., comp. **English and American Stage Productions: An Annotated Checklist of Prompt Books 1800-1900 from the Nisbet-Snyder Drama Collection, Northern Illinois University Libraries.** Boston: G. K. Hall, 1973. 524p. LC 73-11472. ISBN 0-8161-1035-2.

Promptbooks and production editions of plays are valuable resources to theatre historians because they often contain notes that illuminate historical practices in staging and production. This work catalogs more than 2,000 promptbooks and prompter's editions of plays that form a collection held by the Northern Illinois University Library. The plays were produced on the American and English stage between 1775 and 1900, and these books were used and annotated by directors and actors of those productions. Seven hundred of the books contain handwritten notes. The entries are arranged alphabetically by playwright. Each entry includes a physical description of the promptbook, a description of its covers and of any handwritten marks in the text, the date of the earliest recorded New York or London production, and references to secondary sources. Indexes provide additional access by play titles and names of persons mentioned in the text.

164. Folger Shakespeare Library. **Catalog of Manuscripts of the Folger Shakespeare Library, Washington, D.C.** Boston: G. K. Hall, 1971. 3v. Supplement. Boston: G. K. Hall, 1988- .

Intended to supplement the Folger Library's printed books catalog, the list of manuscripts follows the same dictionary arrangement of main entries, added entries, and subjects. The catalog includes complete cataloging for manuscripts acquired until the end of 1968 plus temporary cards for 1969 and 1970 acquisitions. The chief strength of the collection is its group of theatrical and dramatic manuscripts. The Loseley collection, for example, includes the papers of Sir Thomas Cawarden, Master of the Revels at the English court between 1545 and 1559; many documents connected with the Blackfriars theatres; and the earliest known manuscript of a Shakespeare play (a 1620 version of *Henry IV, Part I and II*). The Folger also holds records of the Drury Lane and Covent Garden theatres from the mid-eighteenth century to the end of the nineteenth century; promptbooks in manuscript form; autographed letters of many actors; and the theatrical drawings and promptbooks of English actor Charles Kean. As these examples demonstrate, the Library's scope reaches from the Renaissance to present day. An appendix arranges holdings in chronological order while a second lists manuscripts by former owner.

165. Folger Shakespeare Library. **Catalog of Printed Books of the Folger Shakespeare Library, Washington, D.C.** Boston: G. K. Hall, 1970. 28v. First Supplement. Boston: G. K. Hall, 1976. 3v. Second Supplement. Boston: G. K. Hall, 1981. 2v.

Besides owning the largest collection of Shakespeare folios and quartos in the world, the Folger Shakespeare Library (entry 688) holds extensive collections on British and American theatre history with emphasis on Shakespeare production. It also collects on all aspects of British civilization during the Tudor and Stuart reigns. Shakespeare and other dramatists through the mid-eighteenth century are well represented by their works, as are Continental European playwrights. The collection on theatre extends to the present, and includes works on acting, opera, mime, theatre history, theatre portraits, and many other topics. The catalog arranges its entries in one alphabet with full bibliographic information at the main entry, usually the author entry. An appendix lists the periodicals in the collection. The two supplements present cataloging for acquisitions from 1970 to 1975 and from 1976 to 1980, respectively. They also follow a dictionary catalog format. The

54 / 3—Catalogs

Folger's catalogs unlock the treasures of one of the most important theatre history libraries in the United States.

166. Folger Shakespeare Library. **Catalog of Prints, Engravings, Photographs, and Original Art Materials / Folger Shakespeare Library**. Boston: G. K. Hall, 1984. 4v. ISBN 0-8161-0438-7.

The Folger's collections are rich in visual materials related to Shakespeare "either as illustrations to his works or scenes of actual productions, theatrical portraits, interpretations of Shakespearean characters, and representations of Shakespeare's homes and haunts" (introduction). The first three volumes of this title function as a dictionary catalog of artists, engravers, titles, and subjects of art works. Generally, complete information is found under the artist's name, and works by unknown artists are put under the "Anonymous" heading. Each entry lists the medium and size of the work and its location code. Subject access allows one to find, for example, portraits of actors David Garrick, Henry Irving, and Fanny Kemble; pictures of the Globe Theatre; or material illustrating the play *Macbeth*. The last volume contains part of a new catalog in progress called "Original Works on Paper" that aims "to locate original material in extra-illustrated volumes or in the uncataloged material of the visual arts collections, as well as recataloging the loose drawings and sketches previously cataloged" (introduction). These works receive fuller cataloging, including an indication of provenance and a fuller description of the piece if possible. The Folger recommends searching both the original catalog and the new catalog for complete coverage of the art collection. Volume four also includes a catalog of photographs and a chronological file of pre-1800 engravings. By describing the large number of art works at the Folger Shakespeare Library, this catalog supplements well the library's catalogs of printed books and manuscripts (entries 164, 165).

167. Folger Shakespeare Library. **Catalog of the Shakespeare Collection**. Boston: G. K. Hall, 1972. 2v. LC 72-6446. ISBN 0-8161-1009-3.

A subset of the Folger's larger catalog of printed books (entry 165), this catalog records the library's rich holdings of Shakespeare editions and works about Shakespeare. The Folger owns copies of 90 percent of all known sixteenth- and seventeenth-century editions of Shakespeare's plays. It holds the plays in translations into fifty languages. Subject cards appear for "most of the significant Shakespeareana that has been published over the years." The collection also includes critical works, source materials, adaptations, and parodies. The catalog, which consists of photographs of catalog cards, is divided into complete works of Shakespeare; works in translation; selections from Shakespeare's works; separate plays; works that have Shakespeare as the subject; and works in which Shakespeare is the first word of the title. Since each section is further subdivided, readers should use the table of contents in each volume as a guide.

168. Hall, Lillian A. **Catalogue of Dramatic Portraits in the Theatre Collection of Harvard College Library**. Cambridge, Mass.: Harvard University Press, 1930-1934. 4v. LC 30-13380.

Among the riches of Harvard University's libraries is a collection of 40,000 engraved dramatic prints housed in the College library. In the early 1930s Hall undertook the massive task of describing them in this catalog. The engravings portray actors, dramatists, composers, dancers, critics—anyone even remotely connected with the stage. In order by name, the entries give a description of the pose, the type of print (lithograph, woodcut, stipple), and the artist's and engraver's names. Actors' personal portraits precede pictures of them in character. Indexes of artists and engravers locate their works in the collection. Listing the names of some of the portraits' subjects demonstrates the breadth of this collection: the great English actor Henry Irving; Swedish singer Jenny Lind; the Italian ballerina Carlotta Grisi; and the great clown Joseph Grimaldi.

169. Herrick Marvin T. **Italian Plays, 1500-1700, in the University of Illinois Library**. Urbana: University of Illinois Press, 1966. 92p. LC 66-17248.

Herrick describes 500 Italian plays in the University of Illinois Library's collection. Most were published in the sixteenth century with a few dating from the seventeenth century. The entries, which are arranged by author, list title and publication data and number of acts, and indicate whether the play is written in verse. The work is indexed by play title. Herrick includes a list of intermedia or brief entertainments bound with regular plays in the collection. Herrick's work complements Clubb's more detailed catalog of the Folger Library's Italian plays (entry 160).

170. Hunter, Frederick J., comp. **A Guide to the Theatre and Drama Collections at the University of Texas**. Austin: The Humanities Research Center, The University of Texas at Austin, 1967. 85p. LC 67-65517.

Published soon after the University of Texas made a number of important theatre acquisitions, this guide describes briefly the many theatre collections the university owns and gives a partial listing of contents. Examples include the papers of John Gassner, the well-known theatre critic and of Norman Bel Geddes, the famous designer, director, and producer; the Messmore Kendall collection of engraved portraits of actors and actresses; the Albert Davis-Messmore Kendall collection of 150,000 playbills; and the Stanley Marcus collection of Sicilian marionettes. The amount of detailed description varies with each collection. While Hunter's guide whets the researcher's appetite, only a detailed catalog will fully unlock the riches in the Texas collection. It is to be hoped that the university eventually issues such a work.

171. The Johns Hopkins University Library. **Fifty Years of German Drama: A Bibliography of Modern German Drama, 1880-1930. Based on the Loewenberg Collection in the Johns Hopkins University Library**. Baltimore, Md.: The Johns Hopkins University Press, 1941. 111p. LC 41-11617.

Collected by Dr. Alfred Loewenberg, noted theatre and opera bibliographer (see entry 68) and acquired by Johns Hopkins, the German drama collection comprises some 3,000 volumes, mostly first editions. This straightforward catalog records bibliographic and physical descriptions of each title along with the date and place of each play's first performance. Arthur Schnitzler and Maurice Maeterlink are two of the many writers included. The playwrights cited are mostly German or Austrian; foreign playwrights translated into German such as Galsworthy and Claudel are also included.

172. Kaminsky, Laura J., ed. and comp. **Nonprofit Repertory Theatre in North America, 1958-1975: A Bibliography and Index to the Playbill Collection of the Theatre Communications Group**. Westport, Conn.: Greenwood, 1977. 268p. LC 77-71869. ISBN 0-8371-9536-5.

This work is most useful in conjunction with the collection of playbills owned by the Theatre Communications Group of New York and available in microfiche from the

Congressional Information Service. Kaminsky claims that this collection is the largest of its type, and she records more than 2,500 programs from American resident theatre companies. The catalog is organized by city, then by theatre or company name such as The Acting Company, then by year. In all, 75 companies are represented. Each year's productions are listed with information taken from the playbills: play title, author, director, and, if appropriate, translator, adaptor, or musical director. The book is well indexed, and one can locate information by any of the elements found in the entry. The limited amount of information given, however, suggests that the reader will need access to the collection itself in most cases. As an example, one can learn that the New York Shakespeare Festival presented Vaclav Havel's *The Memorandum*, directed by Joseph Papp, during its 1967-1968 season. But if one wants to know names of actors, a synopsis of the play, or even the exact dates of performance, one must consult either the collection or another source such as the *New York Times*.

173. Kerslake, J. F. **Catalogue of Theatrical Portraits in London Public Collections**. London: The Society for Theatre Research, 1961. 63p. LC 62-4419.

Kerslake lists portraits that are owned by the British Museum, the Dulwich Art Gallery, the National Portrait Gallery, the Victoria and Albert Museum, and other public art collections in London. He lists individual portraits and group portraits with indexes by artist and portrait title. Entries provide the subject's name, the role if portrayed in character, the length and pose of the figure, the artist's name, the date of the work, the medium, the work's dimensions, and the name of the collection that owns the work. Group portraits are named by play title. Kerslake omits engravings, works in collections outside London, and reproductions of works in books or journals. Readers who wish to see reproductions must check elsewhere to see if the appropriate collection has published an illustrated catalog of its holdings. Hall (entry 168) has catalogued the engraved portraits in Harvard's collection, and Highfill (entry 331) lists locations of portraits of his biographees.

174. McKnight, William A., and Mabel Barrett Jones. **Catalogue of Comedias Sueltas in the Library of the University of North Carolina**. (University of North Carolina Library Studies, no. 4). Chapel Hill: University of North Carolina Library, 1965. 240p. LC 65-64331.

Basing its organization on the University of Toronto's catalog (entry 176), this work describes 1,911 *comedias sueltas* published before the 1820s and housed in the University of North Carolina library. Entries are alphabetized by title with an author index. McKnight and Jones describe each book and provide the play's first and last lines and a library location code. As the catalog of one of the larger collections in North America, this work will be useful to students of the *comedia suelta*.

175. Miller, George B., Jr., Janet S. Harris, and William E. Hannaford, Jr., comps. and eds. University of New Mexico. Fine Arts Library. **Puppetry Library: An Annotated Bibliography Based on the Batchelder-McPharlin Collection at the University of New Mexico**. Westport, Conn.: Greenwood, 1981. 172p. LC 80-23474. ISBN 0-313-21359-3.

The late Paul McPharlin and Marjorie Batchelder McPharlin owned two of the world's largest private puppetry libraries. After McPharlin's death most of his collection went to the Detroit Institute of Arts (entry 708) while his widow kept some items. She later sold her collection to the University of New Mexico. This catalog records and describes monographs of fifty pages or more in the collection, over 500 titles in all. Books written in Western languages are followed by books written in Cyrillic alphabet languages. Each entry consists of a bibliographic and a physical description and a short annotation. Appendices list journals in the collection and indicate the number of uncataloged nonbook items. The compilers have provided indexes of names, subjects, and puppet play titles.

176. Molinaro, J. A., J. H. Parker, and Evelyn Rugg, comps. **A Bibliography of Comedias Sueltas in the University of Toronto Library**. Toronto: University of Toronto Press, 1959. 149p. LC 61-892.

One of the first catalogs of the Spanish *comedias sueltas* published, this book describes the works contained in the University of Toronto's collection in 1959. Most of the 723 plays date from the eighteenth century with publication dates ranging from 1703 to 1825. Entries are arranged alphabetically by title with indexes by author and by publisher and bookseller. The compilers describe each book bibliographically and physically and supply the first and last lines of the play.

177. Mullin, Michael, and Karen Morris Muriello. **Theatre at Stratford-upon-Avon: A Catalogue-Index to Productions of the Shakespeare Memorial/Royal Shakespeare Theatre, 1879-1978**. Westport, Conn.: Greenwood, 1980. 2v. LC 79-8578. ISBN 0-313-22126-X.

The Shakespeare Centre Library in Stratford-upon-Avon collects and preserves materials dealing with productions of plays by the Royal Shakespeare Theatre. This catalog/index of the microfilmed archives of the library acts as a basic reference to both Shakespeare and non-Shakespeare productions mounted by the company and its predecessor, the Shakespeare Memorial Theatre. Organized by play title and then chronologically by production, entries list credits, cite the promptbook, which is housed in the archives, list the cast, and cite reviews when available. Promptbook descriptions are keyed to Shattuck's *The Shakespeare Promptbooks* (entry 83) allowing the reader to look up more complete descriptions if desired. Mullin and Muriello include a calendar of productions and indexes to playwrights, theatre personnel, and reviewers. Even if readers cannot use the Stratford archives or the microform copy at the University of Illinois, they can discover quite a lot about an individual production. Because the authors cite reviews by newspaper and date, one should be able to locate many of them as well. For information on set and costume design for many of these productions see *Shakespeare at Stratford upon Avon* (entry 184).

178. New York Public Library. The Research Libraries. **Bibliographic Guide to Theatre Arts**. Boston: G. K. Hall, 1975- . Annual. LC 76-647338. ISSN 0360-2788.

An annual subject bibliography of theatre publications cataloged by the New York Public Library, this supplements the *Catalog of the Theatre and Drama Collections* (entry 179). The compilers define theatre broadly to include puppets, magic, vaudeville, circus, and many other entertainment forms. Nonbook materials account for the majority of items cataloged. The richness of this collection is demonstrated by the materials listed: scripts, promptbooks, drawings, materials on "stage history, production techniques, acting, theatre criticism, biography, and material on individual theatres" (introduction). Authors, titles, and subjects are found in one alphabet with full catalog information given in the main entry only. Consulting this title and the *Catalog of the Theatre and Drama Collections* is absolutely necessary to a thorough search for material about the theatre. Use the corresponding catalog and bibliographies for dance (entries 193 and 195) when looking for works on that subject.

179. New York Public Library. The Research Libraries. **Catalog of the Theatre and Drama Collections**. Boston: G. K. Hall, 1967-1976. 51v. LC 68-5330. ISBN part 1A: 0-8161-0660-2; part 1B: 0-8161-0106-X; part 2: 0-8161-1476-5; part 3: 0-8161-0058-6.

The New York Public Library owns the best theatre collection in the United States, perhaps the world. Its enormous holdings encompass printed and manuscript plays, books on theatre topics, and a huge variety of nonbook material including clippings, photographs, manuscript collections, theatre programs, and scrapbooks. The *Catalog* lists materials acquired up to the early 1970s and is supplemented by the annual *Bibliographic Guide to Theatre Arts* (entry 178), which lists materials acquired during the previous year. Of the catalog's fifty-one volumes, the first twelve, known as Part 1, catalog records for printed plays. Volumes 1 to 6 are arranged by author's name while volumes 7 to 12 follow a country arrangement. For example, one looks under "Drama, French–Translated into English" to find translations of Molière's plays. Altogether, Part 1 records 120,000 plays in Western languages, omitting children's plays, Christmas plays, and those written in Cyrillic, Hebrew, and Oriental alphabets. The nine volumes of Part 2 form a dictionary catalog of 23,500 books about the theatre, broadly defined to include the stage, cinema, radio and television, carnivals, nightclubs, vaudeville, marionettes, magic, and other forms of entertainment. Catalog records for typescripts of plays, for promptbooks, and for selected periodical articles are found here as well. Finally, the thirty volumes of Part 3 record the nonbook material, most of it unique to the New York Public Library Theatre Collection. Materials cover entertainment throughout the world from the eighteenth to the twentieth centuries. Many famous and important theatre personalities have donated their papers to the library, including playwright and producer David Belasco, whose archives formed the nucleus of the collection in 1931, critic Brooks Atkinson, actress Helen Hayes, and producer Leland Hayward. If one looks up the musical *Anything Goes*, one finds references to newspaper clippings, programs from various productions of the show, photographs, copies of reviews, and scrapbooks. The catalog uses a classification system unique to the library, and readers should consult the introduction for advice on using it. The catalog helps to make the vast resources of this collection known to researchers throughout the world. Its value cannot be overestimated.

180. Regueiro, José M. **Spanish Drama of the Golden Age: A Catalogue of the Comedia Collection in the University of Pennsylvania Libraries**. New Haven, Conn.: Research Publications, 1971. 106p. LC 75-172289.

When the microform publisher Research Publications filmed the University of Pennsylvania's collection of Spanish *comedias*, it also published Regueiro's catalog. The plays, which have publication dates through 1846, are both *comedias sueltas* that have been bound into collections and individual works. The catalog's arrangement follows that of the microfilm reels with author and title indexes. Regueiro provides full catalog descriptions including a contents note.

181. Regueiro, José M., and A. G. Reichenberger. **Spanish Drama of the Golden Age: A Catalogue of the Manuscript Collection at the Hispanic Society of America**. New York: The Society, 1984. 2v. LC 84-231923.

Complementing the many catalogs of published Spanish plays, this volume describes manuscripts held by the Hispanic Society of America containing dramatic works of Spain's Golden Age of the sixteenth and seventeenth centuries as well as later periods. The compilers have divided the work into plays with a definite author, anonymous plays, and collections of plays by various authors. Each description quotes the beginning and ending lines of each act and provides the total number of lines. The entry also gives a physical description of the manuscript. The compilers conclude the work with a general index.

182. Rogers, Paul P. **The Spanish Drama Collection in the Oberlin College Library: A Descriptive Catalog**. Oberlin, Ohio: The Oberlin Printing Company, 1940-1946. 2v. LC 40-36008.

One of the earliest catalogs of Spanish play collections, Rogers' work lists and describes 7,500 plays in Oberlin's library. The collection includes all types of plays, most dating from the eighteenth, nineteenth, and twentieth centuries. Rogers' bibliographic and physical descriptions are occasionally augmented by a note on the date and place of the play's first performance. The second volume, which appeared six years after the first, indexes the work by title, printer, and theatre.

183. **The Rosalynde Stearn Puppet Collection**. Montreal: McGill University Library, 1961. 1v. LC 84-230214.

Listing the books and other materials that comprise one of the largest puppetry collections in North America, this catalog describes the collection of Rosalynde Osborne Stearn, Canadian puppet theatre director. Mrs. Stearn donated her collection to McGill University Library in 1952 (see entry 704). The library later added some additional titles. The catalog lists more than 600 books by author and provides bibliographic information. Many of the books are written in French, German, Italian, or other European languages. The collection includes both puppet plays and critical and descriptive works on puppetry. A separate section lists puppets, toy theatres, theatrical portraits, and puppet-related art works that complete the Stearn collection. Besides serving as a guide to McGill's holdings, this catalog will help puppet historians identify European puppet-related materials. Unfortunately, there is no subject index.

184. **Shakespeare at Stratford upon Avon: The Libraries of the Royal Shakespeare Theatre and the Shakespeare Birthplace Trust**. Haslemere, England: Emmett; Boston: G. K. Hall, 1989. 1 v. ISBN 1-869934-20-2 (set).

The Shakespeare Centre Library, formed by the merger of the libraries of the Royal Shakespeare Theatre and the Shakespeare Birthplace Trust in Stratford-upon-Avon, England, holds a great deal of archival material relating to performances of Shakespeare's plays and other productions. These materials have been microfilmed, and this guide provides access to the 3,319 microfiches in the set. Part 1 indexes set and costume designs, 1879-1974, while part 2 accesses press clippings about the Royal Shakespeare Theatre and its predecessors, 1872-1975. Part 3 is a guide to posters, programs, playbills, photographs, and pictures in the libraries, and part 4 indexes the pamphlet collection. Part 5 guides the reader to production records (property lists, rehearsal notes, fight plans, and so on) for plays produced between 1947 and 1975. The sixth part of the guide locates books printed before 1701 which are in the libraries. The seventh part includes a guide to the subject classification schedule of the libraries. Part 7 also indexes the productions of the Royal

Shakespeare Company and its predecessors by play title and personal name. Because the microfiches are available from a limited number of depositories, most users will have to obtain access through interlibrary loan. The guide will help them determine which section of microfiche to request.

185. Sokan, Robert, comp. **A Descriptive and Bibliographic Catalog of the Circus & Related Arts Collection at Illinois State University, Normal, Illinois**. Bloomington, Ill.: Scarlet IBIS Press; Distr., Rare Book Room & Special Collections, Milner Library, Illinois State University, 1976. 173p. LC 76-382583.

During the first half of the twentieth century, Bloomington, Illinois, was the winter home of many flying and trapeze circus acts. Their presence inspired some residents to begin collecting circus materials, and these collections eventually became the Circus and Related Arts Collection at Illinois State University in nearby Normal, Illinois. This work is a catalog of 1,373 books in the collection, arranged alphabetically by author. For each title Sokan gives standard bibliographical information and, sometimes, a short annotation. Books that are listed in R. Toole-Stott's bibliography (entry 96) or the Amsterdam University work (entry 150) are not included in the main body of this work. Instead, Sokan lists by number those titles that the Illinois State collection holds (about 2,000 books from Toole-Stott and 1,000 from Amsterdam). Thus, the reader seeking a particular book will have to have Toole-Stott and the Amsterdam work available to use with this work. The researcher should note that this collection holds over 100,000 items of ephemera for which no descriptive catalog exists. Much of this ephemera is broadly arranged, but its existence could be verified only by an inquiry to the library. (See entry 695 for additional information about this collection.)

Commercial Catalogs of Plays

186. **Baker's Plays**. Boston: Walter H. Baker. Annual. LC 88-12703.
Along with Samuel French (entry 188) and the Dramatists Play Service (entry 187), Baker rents and licenses plays to performing groups. The company's annual catalog lists its offerings. Plays are presented in no particular order within categories such as full-length, one-act, and children's plays, monologues, orations, and plays for women. Readers should use the title index to find individual plays. Entries list number of acts, author, cast requirements, settings, and a plot summary. If one does not find a given play in the French or Dramatists catalogs, one should check Baker.

187. Dramatists Play Service. **Complete Catalogue of Plays**. New York: Dramatists Play Service. Annual. ISSN 0419-7178.
Published annually by one of the two major American suppliers of theatre scripts, the catalog lists and describes plays for which Dramatists Play Service holds performance rights in the United States. See also the catalogs of the Samuel French Company (entry 188), the other major supplier of scripts and of Baker's (entry 186), a smaller supplier. This work divides its plays by audience (community, high school) and by length of play (full-length or one-act). For each play the catalog indicates the type of play (comedy, drama), author, number of characters and sets needed, plot, and licensing fee. Sometimes the catalog quotes excerpts from reviews of the play. Since the company wants to sell its product, the annotations and excerpts are uniformly positive. A separate section lists plays

available in manuscript form only. Indexes provide access by title, author, and number of characters.

188. **Samuel French's Basic Catalog of Plays and Musicals.** New York: Samuel French. Triennial with annual supplements. ISSN 0361-6495.

Founded in 1830, Samuel French is the best-known supplier of plays and performance licensing in the United States. Its catalog lists titles of all plays published or controlled by French. Author and title indexes lead to entries that list cast and set requirements, summarize the plot, excerpt (favorable) reviews, and present royalty fees. Plays are listed in no particular order within categories such as "full-length low-royalty plays" and "murder mystery weekend plays." Libraries should keep on hand the Samuel French and the Dramatists Play Service catalogs (entry 187) as an inexpensive way to verify playwright's names, play titles, and licensing information.

Dance Catalogs

189. Bellingham, Susan, comp. **A Catalogue of the Dance Collection in The Doris Lewis Rare Book Room, University of Waterloo Library.** 2d ed. (University of Waterloo Library Bibliography, v. 10). Waterloo, Ont.: University of Waterloo Library, 1983. 201p. LC 84-182057. ISBN 0-920834-30-2.

The University of Waterloo owns the largest collection in Canada of rare books on dance and ballet. More than 1,000 works published between the fifteenth and twentieth centuries make up the collection which is especially strong in choreography and dance notation. Most of the books are written in English or French. This catalog provides bibliographic references to each title along with the library's call number and the book's provenance. Titles that are also found in the holdings of the New York Public Library (entry 195), Derra de Moroda's catalog (entry 190), or Niles and Leslie's holdings (entry 192) are referenced to those catalogs. Arranged by author, the book needs the subject index it lacks. It will be most useful to Canadian readers who are looking for a particular work.

190. Derra de Moroda, Friderica. **The Dance Library, A Catalogue.** Munich: Robert Wölfle, 1982. 576p. LC 82-227561. ISBN 3-87913-197-X.

Friderica Derra de Moroda, a dancer, teacher, and dance researcher, left her collection of 2,700 dance books to the Institüt für Musikwissenschaft, Salzburg University in Austria. This important collection contains books published between 1480 and 1980. Derra de Moroda herself prepared most of the notes for this catalog but died before it was published. Descriptions of the books are arranged by author, and the book is well indexed by title, subject, place, and personal name. For a catalog of another personal collection now in institutional hands, see Leslie (entry 192).

191. Fletcher, Ifan Kyrle, comp. **Bibliographical Descriptions of Forty Rare Books Relating to the Art of Dancing in the Collection of P. J. S. Richardson, O.B.E.** London: Dancing Times, 1954. Reprint. London: Dance Books, 1977. 1v. ISBN 0-903102-28-5; 0-903102-29-3 pa.

Now in the library of the Royal Academy of Dancing in London, the books described here were collected by P. J. S. Richardson, longtime editor of *Dancing Times* (entry 673). The bibliography fully describes each book and relates it to other books in the collection.

62 / 3—Catalogs

The book's chronological organization helps one trace the development of dance as an art form. An index provides author access. Fletcher notes if the books, published between 1549 and 1807, are included in either Beaumont's or Magriel's bibliographies (see entries 101 and 107). This small bibliography will interest those researching the beginnings of classical ballet as it contains some titles not found in the two bibliographies named above.

192. Leslie, Serge. **A Bibliography of the Dance Collection of Doris Niles and Serge Leslie**. London: C. W. Beaumont, 1966-1981. 4v. LC 66-77781.

Dancers and bibliophiles, Serge Leslie and his wife Doris Niles collected more than 2,000 books on dance. When Leslie asked Cyril Beaumont, the noted London bookseller and balletomane to edit and publish his bibliographical notes, the collection was still in his and his wife's hands. Currently housed in the Wurttenbergische Landesbibliotek in Stuttgart, Germany, the collection contains technical manuals, works by famous choreographers such as Bournonville and Petipa, memoirs of dancers, and reference books. Each volume presents descriptions of books in alphabetical order by author, and each volume contains a subject index. The first three volumes cite many older works while the fourth volume contains mostly references to twentieth-century materials. In the catalog of her own collection Friderica Derra de Moroda asserts Leslie's catalog contains many errors. One should verify its information when possible by using Derra de Moroda's work (entry 190) or other bibliographies.

193. New York Public Library. Dance Collection. **Bibliographic Guide to Dance**. Boston: G. K. Hall, 1975-. Annual. LC 76-641841. ISSN 0360-2737.

As an annual supplement to the *Dictionary Catalog of the Dance Collection* (entry 195) this title lists works cataloged by the New York Public Library Dance Collection each year. Since 97 percent of the Dance Collection is composed of nonbook materials, this bibliography lists many materials that will not be found anywhere else: oral history tapes, papers of famous dancers and choreographers, drawings and designs for costumes, and much more. Since all forms of dance are within the scope of this collection, one can locate materials about social dancing, burlesque, and folk dance besides ballet, modern dance, and theatrical dance. Access is by author, title, series, and subject in one alphabetical sequence with full catalog information given at the main (usually author) entry. Because the Dance Collection's cataloging practices vary somewhat from those of the *Anglo-American Cataloging Rules* (AACR2), readers should consult the preface before using this work. And, of course, the Dictionary Catalog itself should be consulted along with this work. Any dance researcher will find both titles essential.

194. New York Public Library. Performing Arts Research Center. **Dance on Disc: The Complete Catalog of the Dance Collection of The New York Public Library on CD-ROM**. Boston: G. K. Hall, 1992. ISBN 0-8161-1651-2.

195. New York Public Library. The Research Libraries. **Dictionary Catalog of the Dance Collection: A List of Authors, Titles, and Subjects of Multi-Media Materials in the Dance Collection of the Performing Arts Research Center of the New York Public Library**. Boston: New York Public Library; Astor, Lenox, and Tilden foundations; & G. K. Hall, 1974. 10v.

The largest collection of dance materials in the United States, the New York Public Library's collection includes all types of media—books, pamphlets, journals, films, videotapes, photographs, manuscripts, pictorial materials, scrapbooks, and clippings—describing all types of dance. Nonbook materials comprise 97 percent of the collection. A few statistics give some idea of the breadth of the collection: it holds more than 26,000 books, 6,000 librettos, 150,000 photographs, and 500,0000 manuscripts and letters. The catalog describes materials cataloged prior to October 1973 in a dictionary arrangement of authors, titles, and subjects. The library has developed its own subject headings to augment the Library of Congress headings, and readers should consult the introduction for directions on their use and on other rules for using the catalog. *Dance on Disc*, also published by G. K. Hall, offers this catalog plus its supplements, the *Bibliographic Guides to Dance*, on a compact disc, updated annually. In addition, those with access to the Internet (see the chapter on Electronic Discussion Groups for a list of books about the Internet) may telnet to the catalog using the following commands: Telnet 192.94.250.2. Login: NYPL. Password: NYPL. A subset of the catalog and its supplements, the *Index to Dance Periodicals* (entry 221) indexes periodical articles about dance.

196. Vaughan Williams Memorial Library. **The Vaughan Williams Memorial Library Catalogue of the English Folk Dance and Song Society: Acquisitions to the Library of Books, Pamphlets, Periodicals, Sheet Music and Manuscripts, from Its Inception to 1971**. London: Mansell, 1973. 769p. LC 74-165155. ISBN 0-7201-368-1.

Named for the great English composer who often integrated folk melodies into his compositions, the Vaughan Williams Memorial Library is actually based on the collection of rare book collector Cecil Sharp. The collection focuses on "the traditional arts of song and dance particularly as they have developed in the British Isles" (foreword). The catalog describes the more than 7,000 books, pamphlets, and periodicals of the collection. Both the author catalog and the classified subject catalog present complete bibliographic information for each item, eliminating the need to move back and forth between the two. The catalog lists journals under their names or the names of sponsoring societies with holdings. In the subject catalog some journals have been analyzed, and individual articles are cited, such as "The Lancashire Clog Dance" by Julian Pilling in *Folk Music Journal*, 1967. This will be useful to researchers of folk dancing and its performance.

197. Wentink, Andrew Mark. **The Doris Humphrey Collection: An Introduction and Guide**. New York: Readex Books, 1974. 142p. (Originally published as the *Bulletin of the New York Public Library* 77(1): 80-142, Fall, 1973.)

Recognized as a pioneer of American modern dance, Doris Humphrey performed until arthritis tragically ended her dancing career. She continued to choreograph, teach, and write until her death in 1958. Her papers, donated to the New York Public Library Dance Collection, comprise about 7,000 items, mostly correspondence. Wentick chronicles Humphrey's life, relates events in her career to her writings, and describes the organization of the collection. A complete folder list follows. Besides correspondence, the holdings include essays, articles, and unpublished manuscripts written by Humphrey. Wentick indexes the catalog by correspondent's name, dance title, and subject. Because Humphrey worked with Ruth St. Denis, Ted Shawn, Charles Weidman, José Limón, and others important to the modern dance movement, this collection will interest anyone researching twentieth-century American dance history.

Chapter 4

Indexes

The following titles index newspapers, magazines, journals, and other periodicals covering dance, theater, and related arts. Many of them are available in a number of formats: paper copies, online databases, and compact discs. Choosing the format to use is an individual decision based on the information sought, the formats readily available, and cost. As more libraries purchase commercially produced databases and add them to local library systems, some of these titles, especially those produced by H. W. Wilson and Information Access Company, may be available through the reader's local library catalog.

A second group of indexes locates plays, monologues, and directions for dances in books and periodicals. Finally, the *Costume Index* helps readers find illustrations of historical dress useful to the stage costumer.

Theatre and General Indexes Covering the Performing Arts

198. **ABI/INFORM**. Database. (UMI/Data Courier).
 Online Services: American Library Association; BRS; Data-Star; DIALOG; Mead Data Central; ORBIT.
 Online Coverage: Varies (1971- on BRS and Mead Data Central). Update Frequency: Varies (weekly on most services).
 CD ROM Version: ABI/Inform Ondisc (UMI/Data Courier).
 CD Rom Coverage: Latest five years. Update Frequency: Monthly.
 Anyone who has worked with a theater or dance company knows that as much effort is spent on fundraising and finance as on artistic performance. ABI/Inform indexes *Fund Raising Management*, the periodical devoted to the nonprofit sector's constant battle for funds. Recent articles indexed include "Choosing the Right Options in Prospect Cultivation" and "Working with Volunteers: No Pain, No Gain." Other journals indexed here cover the arts from a business viewpoint. This database fills a specialized but vital information need.

199. **Alternative Press Index**. Baltimore, Md.: Alternative Press Center, 1969- . Quarterly. LC 76-24027. ISSN 0002-662X.
 This is the source to consult for articles about the performing arts and what is loosely termed the "counter culture." Indexing many gay, feminist, Black, Marxist, social justice, and activist periodicals, this title provides access to articles on theatres and plays that are not covered by the regular press. One example is "Fighting Apartheid/Soweto Youth Drama Society." *Spare Rib* 214:28 (July 1990). Quarterly issues without cumulation and a computer generated typeface are drawbacks to use, but this is essential for alternative views.

200. **American Humanities Index.** Troy, N.Y.: Whitston Press, 1975- . Quarterly. LC 76-645931. ISSN 0361-0144.

A useful adjunct to H. W. Wilson's *Humanities Index*, this work indexes articles in over 450 "little magazines" and specialized periodicals. "All of the journals indexed in the AHI since 1975 are held in the little magazine collection of the College of William and Mary" (preface). Because the index lists creative works (poems, plays, stories) as well as critical works, one can find texts of plays under the subject heading "Plays." Note that these works are not commercial, Broadway-bound plays but rather more experimental, noncommercial works. There is more material here on the theater than on dance. A sampling of articles includes "William Inge, Great Voice of the Heart of America" by Patricia McIlrath in the *Kansas Quarterly* 18(4):45-53 (1986); "Unmasking the Spirits, Theatre in Malawi" by David Kerr in the *Drama Review* 31(12):115-125 (1987); and "Balanchine Woman: Of Hummingbirds and Channel Swimmers" by Ann Daly in the *Drama Review* 31(1):8-21 (1987). The computerized typeface and layout is not pleasing to use, but readers who can ignore it will find this a good access point to the little magazines. For coverage of these periodicals before 1970, Marion Sader's *The Comprehensive Index to English-Language Little Magazines, 1890-1970* (Millwood, N.Y.: Kraus-Thomson, 1976) may be of limited use.

201. **Art Index.** New York: H. W.Wilson, 1929- . Quarterly with annual cumulations. LC 31-7513. ISSN 0004-3222.
   Art Index. Database. (Wilson).
   Online Services: WILSONLINE; BRS.
   Online Coverage: September, 1984- . Update Frequency: Twice weekly.
   CD ROM Version: WILSONDISC.
   CD ROM Coverage: September, 1984- . Update Frequency: Quarterly.

Art Index's interest in the performing arts is concentrated on the visual aspects of performance or on the intersection of art and theatre known as performance art. It is strong on information about the architecture of theatre buildings (for example, "Space and Performance," a ten-article special section in *Architectural Review*, June 1989), on stage lighting and scenery, and on costume. Because it indexes *High Performance*, it is also a good source for performance art.

202. **Arts & Humanities Citation Index.** Philadelphia, Pa: Institute for Scientific Information, 1977- . Semiannual. LC 79-642953. ISSN 0162-8445.
   Arts & Humanities Search. Database. (Institute for Scientific Information).
   Online Services: BRS; DIALOG.
   Online Coverage: 1980- . Update Frequency: Varies (weekly on DIALOG).
   CD ROM Version: Institute for Scientific Information.
   CD ROM Coverage: 1980- . Update Frequency: 3/year.

The citation indexes published by the Institute for Scientific Information work on the principle that by locating the works that cite an older item on the subject, one can move forward in time through the bibliography of a subject. This index selects articles from about 6,100 journals—1,000 of which are fully covered, including dance and theater reviews. In the other 5,000 titles all arts and humanities articles are selected for coverage. The cited references include creative works (plays, dance, and theater performances) as well as the more usual scholarly articles. An example is a group of dances by American choreographer Ted Shawn that are cited in "The American Indian Imagery of Ted Shawn,"

Dance Chronicle 12(3): 366-382. Using this work requires some training, and it is faster and easier to search online.

203. Belknap, S. Yancey. **Guide to the Performing Arts**. New York: Scarecrow, 1960-1969. 11v. LC 60-7266. ISSN 0072-873X.

As a continuation and expansion of Belknap's *Guide to Dance Periodicals* (entry 219), this series indexes dance, theatre, and media articles in professional and general periodicals. Author and subject entries combine to form an alphabetical index in each volume from 1957 to 1967. Because Belknap's subject headings are not always consistent, one may need to search in several places to find a desired citation. The indexer puts reviews of ballets and operas under their titles (e.g., *Swan Lake*), but reviews of Shakespeare's plays fall under his name. On the other hand, articles about and some reviews of plays fall under title. The 1957 volume indexed seventy periodicals, the 1967 volume, fifty-nine. Many of these are general titles such as *Colliers, Forbes, Holiday*, and *Reader's Digest*, most of which are indexed in the *Readers' Guide to Periodical Literature* (entry 215). However, Belknap's coverage of dance and theatre titles renders the index still useful.

204. **Black Newspapers Index**. Ann Arbor, Mich.: University Microfilms International, 1987- . Quarterly with annual cumulation. LC 88-659594. ISSN 0149-7502. Also, **Index to Black Newspapers** (1977-1986); **Bell & Howell's Index to the Black Newspapers** (1984-1985).

Indexing eight African-American newspapers published in various United States cities, this index does more than provide access to many articles about Black performers, dance and theater companies, and playwrights. It also locates articles in the Black press about all types of productions. For example, the *Chicago Defender*'s regular dance and theatre critic reviews many productions that play in Chicago, not just specifically African-American works. Reviews are found under the subject headings "Theater" and "Dance." Indexing can be inconsistent with some articles listed under the name of the work and some under the subject headings noted above; check both places.

205. **British Humanities Index**. London: Library Association, 1962- . Quarterly. LC 63-024940. ISSN 0007-0815. Also **Subject Index to Periodicals**. London: Library Association, 1916-1961. LC 85-20167.

This "guide to articles appearing in newspapers and journals published in Britain" ("Guide for Users") indexes more than 300 periodicals. It does not index any reviews, but it does index a large number of articles on the theatre and fewer on dance. Two important sources that are indexed are *Theatre Research International* and the *Times Literary Supplement*. This is a good place to look for articles on British productions, British actors, and the British viewpoint.

206. **Business Periodicals Index**. New York: H. W. Wilson, 1958- .
Monthly. LC 58-12645. ISSN 0007-6961.
Business Periodicals Index. Database. (Wilson).
Online Services: WILSONLINE; BRS.
Online Coverage: July, 1982- . Update Frequency: Twice weekly.
CD ROM Version: WILSONDISC, SilverPlatter.
CD ROM Coverage: July, 1982- . Update Frequency: Monthly.

This work's interest in the arts is limited, but it is a useful place to look for articles on the financing of, insuring of, and accounting for theatrical enterprises. Theatrical agencies are also covered. For a complete look at the business of the performing arts, use this with the *ABI/Inform* database (entry 198).

207. Cornyn, Stan. **A Selective Index to Theatre Magazine**. New York: Scarecrow Press, 1964. 289p. LC 64-11778.

Calling *Theatre Magazine*, which appeared between 1900 and 1930, a "unique record of a vital span of theatre history" in America, Cornyn has indexed its 360 issues. In one alphabet the 45,000 entries refer to authors, subjects, and dramatic works selected for possible scholarly interest. Entries give issue and page numbers, and an issue numbering code translates the numbered code to a year and volume number. The introduction lists a number of abbreviations used for such features as play reviews, fiction, book reviews, and play synopses. With articles by famous theatre people such as John Barrymore and Al Jolson, critical reviews of Broadway openings, and records of foreign productions, *Theatre Magazine* contains much of interest to the theatre scholar. This index will unlock those interesting items.

208. **Cumulated Dramatic Index, 1909-1949**. Boston: G. K. Hall, 1965. 2v. LC 68-4712. ISBN 0-8161-0402-6.

This title, "a cumulation of the forty-one annual volumes of the *Dramatic Index* published by the F.W. Faxon Company," indexes more than 150 American and British periodicals and provides 300,000 entries for articles about "the stage and its players" (introduction). The index includes both subject-oriented periodicals such as *Drama* and *Players Magazine* and general interest periodicals such as *Collier's* and *Harper's Weekly*. The main section of the work is an alphabetical subject index. Many personal names are included, and this is an especially good place to look for references to portraits of actors and dancers who were working during the first half of the twentieth century. The scope of this work includes not only theatre but also dance (ballet and modern dance), puppetry, the circus, clowns, vaudeville, and burlesque ("The Strip Tease Olympics in Paris." A. Baer. il. *Cosmopolitan* 118: Je. '45, 14). Reviews are listed under the name of the work, and there are good cross-references from playwrights and choreographers to their works. Although most of the material indexed is American or British, many articles on theatre in other countries can be found under the subject headings beginning, "Theatre in." Following the subject index, three appendices provide a record of 6,500 books on drama; a title list of 24,000 plays published between 1909 and 1949; and a list of 20,000 authors of plays with bibliographic information on each play. This work is essential for anyone researching theatre, dance, or allied arts during the early twentieth century. It is also a useful companion to *Biography Index* (entry 321) for anyone in show business during that time.

209. **Essay and General Literature Index**. New York: H. W. Wilson, 1900- . Semiannual, with annual cumulation and multi-year cumulations. LC 34-14581. ISSN 0014-083X.
Essay and General Literature Index. Database. (Wilson).
Online Services: WILSONLINE; BRS.
Online Coverage: January, 1985- . Update Frequency: Every two weeks.
CD ROM Version: WILSONDISC, SilverPlatter.
CD ROM Coverage: January, 1985- . Update Frequency: Annually.

4—Indexes

The *Essay and General Literature Index* provides subject and author access to books of collected essays, primarily in the humanities and social sciences. Both theatre and dance can be found in essays indexed here, with theatre coverage fuller than that of dance. Locate play reviews under the name of the play. Recent topics include "Masques," "Melodrama," "Theater and Society," "Women in the Theater," "Choreography," and "Modern Dance." Because its indexing is not likely to be duplicated elsewhere, this is an important index.

210. **Humanities Index**. New York: H. W. Wilson, 1974- . Quarterly with annual cumulations. LC 75-648836. ISSN 0095-5981.
   Humanities Index. Database. (Wilson).
   Online Services: WILSONLINE; BRS.
   Online Coverage: February 1984- . Update Frequency: Twice weekly.
   CD ROM Version: WILSONDISC, SilverPlatter.
   CD ROM Coverage: February, 1984- . Update Frequency: Quarterly.

   Separated from its twin, the *Social Sciences Index*, in 1974, this work covers both dance and theatre as well as auxiliary topics. It is an excellent source of reviews, provided the reader follows instructions for finding them. Briefly, dance reviews are found under "Ballet Reviews" but citations to play reviews are listed under the playwright's name. Theatre is covered by dozens of subject headings including "Make-up, Theatrical," "Dance Festivals," "Homosexuality and the Theater," "Acting," and "Costume, Theatrical." The last heading yields an intriguing article title, "The Spectacle of Absent Costume: Nudity on the Victorian Stage," published in *New Theatre Quarterly* in 1989. School and amateur theatre are included, and the index is especially helpful for finding articles on the history of theatre in various countries. Important dance journals are indexed, and the emphasis is on reviews of dance productions and the artistic aspects of dance. Of the H. W. Wilson indexes, this is the most important one for the performing arts.

211. **MLA International Bibliography of Books and Articles on the Modern Languages and Literatures**. New York: Modern Language Association, 1921- . Annual. LC 64-20773. ISSN 0024-8215.
   MLA International Bibliography. Database. (Modern Language Association of America).
   Online Services: WILSONLINE.
   Online Coverage: 1981- . Update Frequency: 9/year.
   CD ROM Version: WILSONDISC, SilverPlatter.
   CD ROM Coverage: 1981- . Update Frequency: Quarterly.

   "The *MLA Bibliography* provides a classified listing and subject indexing for books and articles published on modern languages, literature, folklore, and linguistics" ("Guide for Users"). The *MLA* has a remarkably wide scope that goes well beyond the purpose quoted. Its compilers cast their net over thousands of books and journals every year. Where else can one find, all in the same volume, references to an article on Japanese-American music and dance in Los Angeles from 1930 to 1942; a study of Elizabethan theatre companies at Gloucester, England; and an item on break dancing? Since each citation is listed only once in the classified list, it is essential to use the subject index, available since 1981 as the second volume of the printed index, or to search the online or CD-ROM database. The CD-ROM covers articles back to 1981 while the online database extends back to 1963. References to theatre listings include works about avant-garde theater, Black theater, theatrical production, acting, and many others. Indexed dance articles tend to deal with folk dance (for example morris dancing) or to treat dance as an adjunct to theatre ("The Madmen's Song and Dance in *The Duchess of Malfi*.") Those who are doing a comprehensive search in theatre or dance should not skip the *MLA*.

212. **National Newspaper Index**. Foster City, Calif.: Information Access, 1979- . Monthly with annual cumulations. LC 83-9488. ISSN 0273-3676.
    National Newspaper Index. Database. (Information Access).
    Online Services: BRS; DIALOG.
    Online Coverage: Varies (most newspapers, 1970-). Update Frequency: Monthly.
    CD ROM Version: INFOTRAC.
    CD ROM Coverage: Latest five years. Update Frequency: Monthly.
    Available in microform, CD-ROM, and online formats, this index provides subject access to five important newspapers: the *New York Times*, the *Wall Street Journal*, the *Washington Post*, the *Christian Science Monitor*, and the *Los Angeles Times*. The importance of this index is demonstrated by its inclusion of more than 1,000 theatre reviews, complete with a rating, the reviewer's name, and length of review. The reviews are listed by play title in alphabetical order, and many of them deal with the New York stage. London and other cities are not as well represented. Coverage of the *Washington Post* provides information on the National Endowment for the Arts, government officials, and other institutions that have an interest in both financing and censoring the arts. Articles on dance, vaudeville, and the circus are also indexed. Although Information Access has improved the authority control of its indexes in recent years, it is still not as good as it could be. To find all of Sir Laurence Olivier's indexed obituaries, for example, one must look in three subheadings under his name.

213. **New York Times Index**. New York: The *New York Times*, First Series, 15 volumes, 1851-1912; Second Series, 68 volumes, 1913-1929; Third Series, 1930- . Semimonthly with annual cumulations. LC 13-13458. ISSN 0147-538X.

Because New York is still the most important city for the performing arts in the United States, the *New York Times* remains an important source of information about theatre, dance, and related subjects. Almost since its beginning the *Index* has covered the arts. Play reviews are found under "Theater" while all dance articles are listed under "Dancing." (Nineteenth-century indexes use "Amusements" and "Dramatic" for theatre entries, as well.) Other subjects such as "Juggling and Jugglers" are used when relevant. The newspaper's obituaries are an excellent source of information about the famous and less-famous in the performing arts. This is an important source for both theatre and dance information.

214. **Newsbank Review of the Arts: Performing Arts**. Stamford, Conn.: Newsbank, 1975- .
    CD ROM Version: Newsbank
    CD ROM Coverage: 1980- . Update Frequency: Monthly.
    Newsbank's Review of the Arts: Performing Arts makes available on microfiche articles on music, theatre, dance, and other performing arts from 450 U.S. newspapers. This index provides access to the collection, which includes news stories, interviews, and reviews of performances. Arranged alphabetically by subject or name of performer, the entries refer to microfiche number and grid location on the fiche itself. Readers should consult the directions for use before using this index. Newsbank supplements the better-known

newspapers by providing glimpses into American cultural life outside New York and California. Because it includes only selections from many newspapers, however, it cannot be viewed as providing exhaustive or even comprehensive coverage.

215. **Readers' Guide to Periodical Literature.** New York: H. W. Wilson, 1900- . LC 05-14769. ISSN 0034-0464.
  Reader's Guide to Periodical Literature. Database. (Wilson).
  Online Services: WILSONLINE; BRS.
  Online Coverage: January, 1983- . Update Frequency: Twice weekly.
  CD ROM Version: WILSONDISC, SilverPlatter.
  CD ROM Coverage: January, 1983- . Update Frequency: Monthly.

Small libraries that own the *Readers' Guide* as their only index need not despair. Even they can offer access to a considerable amount of periodical literature on the performing arts. The index is strong on both theatre and dance reviews. It indexes *The New Yorker, Nation, America, Newsweek, Time, New Republic, Commonweal,* and other magazines that feature regular reviews of the arts. Its coverage of *TCI* (formerly *Theatre Crafts*) adds many articles on technical aspects of theater. With the exception of articles from *Dance Magazine,* coverage of dance companies is limited to those based in New York City. This source should not be overlooked, especially because so many of the magazines included are readily available.

216. **The Times Index.** Reading, England: Research Publications, 1973- . Monthly with annual cumulation. ISSN 0260-0668. Also **Index to the Times** (1906-1972, Times); **Palmer's Index to the Times Newspaper** (1790-June 1941, Palmer); **The Times Index** (1785-1790, Newspaper Archive Developments).

Every year the British send plays to the United States. American audiences enjoy the works of Tom Stoppard, Andrew Lloyd Webber and many of their compatriots. *The Times* is an important source of information for the London stage and for British performing arts in general. The *Index* allows access to articles about and reviews of plays (use "Theatrical Productions"), dance performances (use "Ballet and Dancing"), puppet theatre productions, and other subjects of interest to British and American readers.

217. **Wall Street Journal Index.** New York: Dow Jones, 1957- . Monthly with annual cumulations. LC 59-35162. ISSN 0083-7075.

Generally thought of as a business newspaper, the *Wall Street Journal* covers a number of nonbusiness topics including the arts. The "Leisure and Arts" page presents articles and reviews of plays (eighty-eight productions in 1989) and dance performances. Befitting the *Journal*'s status as a national newspaper, it covers performances not just in New York City but in other major cities in the United States and abroad. Recent features include a review of Mark Morris' ballet production of Henry Purcell's opera *Dido and Aeneas* and an article on the American Ballet Theatre's artistic disarray following Mikhail Baryshnikov's departure from the company. The *Index* offers good access to the 3 Star Eastern Edition, which is available on microfilm from UMI Corporation. Use the "General News" volume and the subject headings "Actors and Actresses," "Dance," and "Theater Reviews."

218. **Washington Post Index**. Ann Arbor, Mich.: University Microfilms International, 1989- . Monthly with quarterly and annual cumulations. LC 88-8011. ISSN 1041-1534. Also **Official Washington Post Index**. 1979-1988. ISSN 0193-9580.

This index is a good source of articles dealing with the relationship between the federal government and arts organizations. For example, the paper covered the Robert Mapplethorpe-National Endowment for the Arts controversy extensively. It also indexes reviews of and articles about productions in Washington and elsewhere.

Dance Indexes

219. Belknap, S. Yancey. **Guide to Dance Periodicals.** Gainesville: University of Florida Press; New York: Scarecrow, 1950-1962. 10v. LC 60-7273.

Belknap retrospectively indexed dance periodicals, covering the years 1931 to 1950 in the first four volumes of the series and continuing with biennial volumes through 1962. The indexes combine author and subject entries into one alphabet. Readers should use the index carefully, as subject headings may vary from standard practice. For example, articles about the Bolshoi Ballet are found under the subject "Russia." Belknap continued her work with her *Guide to the Performing Arts* (entry 203).

220. **Dance Current Awareness Bulletin**. Guild, England: National Resource Centre for Dance, 1983- . 3/year. ISSN 0265-6523.

For those interested in British dance, this index provides access to up to twenty-four journals, both British and foreign. Arranged by subject headings, a list of which appears at the back of each issue, entries include a bibliographic citation and a short annotation. References to reviews of dance books and reviews of film and television dance performances add value to the index.

221. **Index to Dance Periodicals**. Boston: G. K. Hall, 1992- . Annual. LC 92-662050. ISSN 1058-6350.

A subset of the New York Public Library's *Bibliographic Guide to Dance* (entry 193), this new annual index "gathers and organizes in a single resource references to current periodical literature on dance and dance-related topics" (preface). Volume 1 covers 1990 and was published at the beginning of 1992. It indexes fifty-one periodicals, fourteen selectively. About half the titles are American, 18 percent are British, and the rest originate in various countries around the world. Journals that are not devoted solely to dance such as *Medical Problems of Performing Artists* or *The New Yorker*, are selectively indexed. Readers will locate scholarly and popular articles in this index, which puts authors, subjects, and dance titles together in one alphabet. The subject headings correspond to the New York Public Library's adaptation of Library of Congress headings used in its *Dance Catalog* (entry 195). A generous use of cross-references helps one locate topics. Under "Balanchine," for instance, are listed cross-references for each of his ballets. Citations sometimes include brief annotations. Readers should note that some cross-references refer to the *Dance Catalog* or the *Bibliographic Guide to Dance* rather than to this index. Subjects run a wide gamut from "Injuries and Accidents" to "Religious Dancing" to reviews of performances on stage and screen. More affordable than the *Bibliographic Guide to Dance*, the *Index* should prove to be a popular and useful work to everyone interested in any form of dance.

222. **Music Index**. Detroit: Information Coordinators, 1949- . Monthly with annual cumulations. LC 50-13627. ISSN 0027-4348.

The preface to volume 39-40 (1987-1988) of the *Music Index* states, "Beginning with Volume 39-40, dance periodicals and publications not specifically devoted to music are no longer indexed." Nevertheless, one finds articles and many book reviews concerning dance indexed. Because of the index's worldwide scope, it covers quite a few articles on dance in various countries. An important inclusion is coverage of relevant dissertations from *Dissertation Abstracts International*. One finds, for example, J. A. Lazarus's thesis, "Contemporary Dance and Feminist Aesthetic." This is also a good source for those topics that theatre and dance share with music, for example stage fright, theatre buildings, stage design, and lighting.

223. **Physical Education Index**. Cape Girardeau, Mo.: BenOak, 1978- . Quarterly with annual cumulations. LC 82-644892. ISSN 0191-9202.

This subject index covers dance from a number of perspectives: dance as art; dance as a physical activity; dance as a business; and, especially, dance education. It indexes a number of important periodicals including *Dance Magazine*, *Dance Research Journal*, and *Dance Chronicle*. Important articles will be found in other journals, such as *The American Journal of Sports Medicine*, as well. Coverage of the physiology of dance, dance injuries, and dance education is especially strong. *Physical Education Index* is the first source to use for articles on the physical activity of dancing while the *Humanities Index* (entry 210) is the best source for artistic aspects of dance.

Indexes to Plays, Monologues, and Dances

224. **Actors Guide to Monologues: An Index of 700 Monologues from Classical and Modern Plays for Auditions and Classwork**. New York: Drama Book, 1972. 35p. LC 72-182373.

Helpful to both the aspiring actor and the speech student, this work indexes 700 monologues taken from published plays. It is arranged by gender and age of the speaker and by type of monologue: serious, comic, or serio-comic. The plays indexed come from both the classical and the modern repertoire. Entries give enough information to identify the location of the monologue in each play and to describe briefly the character speaking. Although not as recent as Emerson and Grumbach's volumes (entries 229, 230), this guide supplements their more complete works.

225. Bell, Richard O., and Joan Kuder Bell. **Auditions and Scenes from Shakespeare**. Boulder, Colo.: Armado & Moth, 1979. 161p. LC 79-54914. ISBN 0-9603626-0-6.

Teachers and directors who flinch at the thought of enduring one more rendition of the balcony scene from *Romeo and Juliet* can recommend this handbook to students and auditioning actors. It lists 700 scenes from Shakespeare's plays which can be used for monologues and scene work by up to five actors in various combinations. Using a code system, the Bells have arranged the scenes according to the number and gender of actors needed. Their introduction explains how to read the codes. The authors have also marked scenes that suffer from overuse, and in their introduction they strongly suggest avoiding these passages if possible. Acknowledging the shortage of roles for women, they have coded some roles, such as Puck and Ariel, for women as well as men. Entries list play title,

Indexes to Plays, Monologues, and Dances / 73

act, scene, and beginning and ending lines and a short description of the action. The index lists play titles with characters and codes, and an appendix refers to scenes in which fencers and singers can display their skills.

226. Chicorel, Marietta, ed. **Chicorel Index Series**. New York: Chicorel Library Publishing, 1970- .

Chicorel's index series includes several volumes devoted to plays. The first three list plays in anthologies and periodicals and on records and tapes, almost 30,000 citations in all. Volume 7 includes additional citations to the "spoken arts" on recordings, while volume 8 reports on additional plays in periodicals—another 10,000 entries. Volume 9 covers plays for children, the twenty-first volume functions as an unannotated drama bibliography, and volume 25 supplements volumes 1 to 3 plus 9. Now quite old, these works should be consulted only after checking other sources such as *Play Index* (entry 248), *Ottemiller's* (entry 227), Keller (entries 235, 236), and Trefny and Palmer (entry 239).

227. Connor, Billie M., and Helene G. Mochedlover. **Ottemiller's Index to Plays in Collections: An Author and Title Index to Plays Appearing in Collections Published Between 1900 and 1985**. 7th ed., rev. and enl. Metuchen, N.J.: Scarecrow, 1988. 564p. LC 87-34160. ISBN 0-8108-2081-1.

Indispensable for even the smallest library, *Ottemiller's* is useful not only for its primary purpose of locating full-length plays in anthologies and collections, but also for verifying information such as the author's name, birth and death dates, the year the play was first produced, and variant titles. This last is especially helpful for foreign plays translated into English. The seventh edition indexes 1,350 collections and 6,548 plays. *Ottemiller's* worldwide scope covers plays of any period in English or translated into English. Coverage has been extended from the United States and England to all English-speaking countries. The great majority of collections, however, were published in New York or London with a handful of Canadian, Australian, South African, and other imprints. Plays in foreign languages are included if they appear in a collection published in an English-speaking country. It is important to remember what is not included: one-act plays and children's, radio, television, holiday, and anniversary plays. In addition, anthologies are included only if they contain works of three or more playwrights. Access to plays is by author, by title, and by collection. The author index contains the information noted above about the author and each play and notes the collection(s) in which the play appears. The list of collections provides bibliographic information and a list of contents for each collection. The title index refers the user to the author index. This work is the first choice for anyone looking for a play in a collection.

228. Drone, Jeanette Marie. **Index to Opera, Operetta, and Musical Comedy Synopses in Collections and Periodicals**. Metuchen, N.J.: Scarecrow, 1978. 171p. LC 77-25822. ISBN 0-8108-1100-6.

Although most of the synopses Drone cites summarize opera plots, she does include references to summaries of the Gilbert and Sullivan operettas and of a number of musical comedies. Representative composers include Richard Adler, Irving Berlin, Richard Rodgers, Frederick Loewe, and Jerome Kern. She has checked 74 collections and four periodicals—*The Journal of the American Musicological Society, Musical Times, The New Yorker*, and *Opera News*—to find synopses of 1,605 titles by 627 composers. The books is divided into four parts: a list of the indexed collections with codes, a title index with location codes, a composer index, and a bibliography of musical dictionaries and additional sources that contain summaries of operas.

229. Emerson, Robert, and Jane Grumbach, eds. **Guide to Monologues: Men; An Index of Over 800 Monologues from Classical and Modern Plays.** New York: Drama Book, 1988. 56p. LC 88-33483. ISBN 0-89676-103-7.

230. Emerson, Robert, and Jane Grumbach, eds. **Guide to Monologues: Women; An Index of Over 800 Monologues from Classical and Modern Plays.** New York: Drama Book, 1988. 44p. LC 88-33482. ISBN 0-89676-104-5.

Each of these volumes indexes monologues from published plays, using acting editions for modern plays and standard editions for classical works. Each book is arranged by type of play: classical or modern; and then by type of role: serious, comic, serio-comic, or one-character plays; and, finally, by age of character. This arrangement allows users to find the appropriate role quickly. Entries list play title, author, character's name and age, approximate time of performance, the first line of the speech, and the scene and act numbers. Modern monologues are cited by edition and page number. For example, "DPS 35" means page 35 in the Dramatists Play Service edition. Classics are cited using line numbers. These volumes are preferred to the older *Actors Guide to Monologues* (entry 224).

231. Firkins, Ina. **Index to Plays, 1800-1926.** New York: H. W. Wilson, 1927. 307p. LC 27-27608. Supplement, 1927-34. New York: H. W. Wilson, 1935. 140p.

An older work, this is nevertheless valuable because it helps one find often obscure nineteenth- and early twentieth-century plays. The original volume indexes 7,872 plays written by over 2,000 playwrights and includes plays published in collections, in periodicals, and separately. All plays are written in English or translated into English. (Ibsen, Strindberg, and Checkhov are represented in translation.) The entries are arranged alphabetically by author with a single title and subject index following. The supplement extends coverage to 1934. Because *Ottemiller's* coverage of plays in collections (entry 227) begins with 1900 and *Play Index* (entry 248) begins in 1949, Firkins remains a necessary source.

232. Grumbach, Jane, and Robert Emerson. **Actors Guide to Scenes.** New York: Drama Book, 1973. 28p. LC 73-75246. ISBN 0-910482-42-X.

A book for would-be actors needing to prepare a scene for an audition, this book locates more than 600 scenes suitable for two actors to perform. Most of the scenes are taken from twentieth-century plays, but separate chapters list scenes from Shakespearean plays and from musical comedies. The index is arranged by gender and type of scene (for instance, male-male serious scenes or male-female comic scenes). Each entry lists the play title, the playwright, the characters' names and ages, the approximate time needed to play the scene, the act and scene from which the excerpt is taken, and its first line. The entry also lists the excerpt's location in the acting edition and the publisher of that edition. Grumbach and Emerson also compiled *Guide to Monologues: Men* and *Guide to Monologues: Women* (entries 229, 230), which contain more recent materials.

233. Hoffman, Herbert H. **Latin American Play Index**. Metuchen, N.J.: Scarecrow, 1983-1984. 2v. LC 83-8736. ISBN v. 1: 0-8108-1671-7; v. 2: 0-8108-1633-4.

Indexing 3,300 plays written by 1,000 Latin American authors, this work locates plays published separately, in collections or anthologies, and in periodicals between 1920 and 1980. Citations to most of these plays can also be found in the *Handbook of Latin American Studies* (Gainesville: University of Florida Press, 1935-). Librarians who have the *Handbook* on their shelves may prefer to consult it directly as the *Handbook* entry provides more information about each play. The author index is the main body of the book. For each play, either a bibliographic citation or a reference to the list of collections and anthologies is given. The title index refers the reader to the author index. Both the list of collections and anthologies and the list of periodicals indexed employ abbreviations and entry numbers taken from the *Handbook of Latin American Studies*. These conventions may prove confusing to readers not familiar with that work. Hoffman does not provide information about number of acts, sets, characters, or subject matter of the play. Nevertheless, readers who lack access to the *Handbook* will find basic author and title access in this work.

234. Karp, Rashelle S., and June H. Schlessinger. **Plays for Children and Young Adults: An Evaluative Index and Guide**. (Garland Reference Library of Social Science, vol. 543). New York: Garland, 1991. 580p. LC 90-44195. ISBN 0-8240-6112-8.

Karp and Schlessinger report on 3,560 plays published between 1975 and 1989 for young people. With the goal of helping teachers and others choose suitable titles for production, the authors selected from publishers' catalogs, *Play Index* (entry 248), Trefny and Palmer's 1975-1984 volume (entry 239), and *Plays: The Drama Magazine for Young People* (entry 631). They include both individual plays and those published in anthologies or periodicals. Although the entries are arranged by play title, the indexes provide multiple and helpful access points by author, cast requirements, grade level, subject or play type, and playing time. The co-authors recruited a group of contributors to review each play and either recommend or not recommend it. Reviewers do not hesitate to criticize weak plays with phrases such as "trite, condescending, historically inaccurate, and inappropriate" or "thin, uninteresting plot." Many other works, on the other hand, warrant the phrase "highly recommended." Besides a review, each entry describes the plot and specific cast and set requirements and playing time. Sources and royalty information (as of 1988) are also given. This title's strength is its evaluations, not duplicated in any other index of children's plays, and its recency. Teachers and others will find it invaluable for play selection.

235. Keller, Dean H. **Index to Plays in Periodicals**. rev. and exp. ed. Metuchen, N.J.: Scarecrow, 1979. 824p. LC 92-962. ISBN 0-8108-1208-8.

236. Keller, Dean H. **Index to Plays in Periodicals, 1977-1987**. Metuchen, N.J.: Scarecrow, 1990. 391p. LC 90-8075. ISBN 0-8108-2288-1.

These two volumes together help the reader locate over 14,000 plays published in periodicals. They supersede Charlotte Patterson's *Plays in Periodicals*, which locates only 4,000 plays. Keller also indexes more periodicals than does Marietta Chicorel in her *Chicorel Theater Index to Plays in Anthologies, Periodicals, Discs and Tapes* (entry 226). Although Keller does not state any language limitations, the plays are all written in English, French, German, or Italian, with English predominating. The supplement not only continues the indexing of periodicals covered in the first volume, but it also indexes older volumes of additional periodical titles such as *The Instructor*. It should be consulted along with the first volume for older works. The main body of the work is the alphabetical author index that lists the title of each play, number of acts, and the periodical citation. Works in or translated into foreign languages are so noted. The title index refers the reader to information in the author index. Keller's work supplements *Ottemiller's* (entry 227), which locates plays in collections only. Since a great many plays are published in periodicals, Keller should be consulted with *Ottemiller's* for thoroughness.

237. Kreider, Barbara A. **Index to Children's Plays in Collections**. Metuchen, N.J.: Scarecrow, 1972. 138p. LC 72-3008. ISBN 0-8108-0494-6.

238. Kreider, Barbara A. **Index to Children's Plays in Collections**. 2d ed. Metuchen, N.J.: Scarecrow, 1977. 227p. LC 76-49666. ISBN 0-8108-0992-3.

239. Trefny, Beverly Robin, and Eileen C. Palmer. **Index to Children's Plays in Collections, 1975-1984**. Metuchen, N.J.: Scarecrow, 1986. 108p. LC 86-6418. ISBN 0-8108-1893-0.

Although *Play Index* (entry 248) accesses children's plays, it is easier to use this source, which confines itself to plays written for children in kindergarten through grade 12. The three volumes together index almost 2,000 plays, all published in the United States. Authors, titles, and subjects are arranged in one alphabetical list with bibliographic information given under author. Standardized subject headings are presented in the front of each book and vary slightly from volume to volume. They may represent a genre (mystery plays) or an occasion (Christmas plays) rather than an actual subject. A cast analysis list, a bibliography of all collections cited, and a publisher's directory round out each volume. The compilers refrain from commenting on the merits of these plays, perhaps a wise decision given titles such as *The Rhyme's the Crime or the Verse Is Yet to Come*. This work is useful to teachers, church educators, camp counselors, and others who work with children and teenagers.

240. Logasa, Hannah, and Winifred Ver Nooy. **Index to One-Act Plays**. (Useful Reference series, no. 30). Boston: Faxon, 1924. 327p. LC 24-21477.

241. Logasa, Hannah, and Winifred Ver Nooy. **Index to One-Act Plays. Supplement 1924-1931**. (Useful Reference series, no. 46). Boston: Faxon, 1932. 432p. ISBN 0-87305-046-0.

242. Logasa, Hannah, and Winifred Ver Nooy. **Index to One-Act Plays. Second Supplement 1932-1940**. (Useful Reference series, no.68). Boston: Faxon, 1941. 556p.

243. Logasa, Hannah. **Index to One-Act Plays for Stage and Radio. Third Supplement 1941-1948**. (Useful Reference series, no. 78). Boston: Faxon, 1950. 318p.

244. Logasa, Hannah. **Index to One-Act Plays for Stage, Radio, and Television. Fourth Supplement 1948-1957**. (Useful Reference series, no. 87). Boston: Faxon, 1958. 245p. ISBN 0-87305-087-8.

245. Logasa, Hannah. **Index to One-Act Plays for Stage, Radio, and Television. Fifth Supplement 1956-1964**. (Useful Reference series, no. 94). Boston: Faxon, 1966. 260p. ISBN 0-87305-094-0.

Because one-act plays are rarely published by themselves, they must be located in periodicals or collections of plays. This index locates one-act plays written in English or translated into English that have been published in books or magazines. It also includes one-act adaptations of longer works such as Strindberg's *Miss Julie*. The supplements extend coverage to 1964. Readers looking for one-act plays published after that date should consult *Play Index* (entry 248) or Keller's *Index to Plays in Periodicals* (entries 235, 236). Many one-act plays for children can be found using *Index to Children's Plays in Collections* (entries 237-239). Logasa's work is arranged alphabetically by play title with author and subject indexes following the main section. The bibliographical reference listed under each title is augmented by an indication of the number of men and women necessary, the stage setting required, and, if appropriate, suitability for children or adolescents.

246. Minneapolis Public Library. Music Department. **An Index to Folk Dances and Singing Games**. Chicago: American Library Association, 1936. 202p. LC 36-11219. Supplement. Chicago, American Library Association, 1949. 98p.

This book and its supplement direct the reader to books where instructions for various folk dances and singing games can be found. It is now very old, and its usefulness depends on the availability of the works indexed. Readers with access to large public or academic libraries will probably find this more useful than those confined to smaller collections and interlibrary loan service. The book lists entries under title of dance (Sword Dance), type of dance (morris dance, for example), and nationality of dance in one alphabet. The main volume analyzes 110 collections and the supplement adds sixty-eight additional books. A list of collections indexed at the back of each volume gives bibliographical information for each collection. Given the reviving interest in clogging and other forms of folk dance, this work may find a new audience in those who wish to know how to perform the "Russian Haymaking Dance," the "Cumberland Road," and other dances.

247. Pence, James Harry, comp. **The Magazine and the Drama: An Index**. (Theatre and Drama Series, 12). New York: Burt Franklin, 1970 (c. 1896). 190p. LC 75-130093. ISBN 8337-2707-9.

An early attempt to index theatre articles in the periodical literature, Pence's work locates articles about "acted drama" in 166 nineteenth-century magazines. These include *Blackwood's*, *Godey's*, *Lippincott's*, *McClure's*, and the *Spectator* as well as other lesser-known titles. Most were published in London, New York, Boston, or Philadelphia, but all regions of the United States are represented by at least a few titles. Although Pence does not state the years he has indexed, they seem to be from around 1872 to 1896. Subjects and authors appear in one alphabet, and citations list periodical, volume, beginning page, and (sometimes) date. The most reliable indexing is by personal name, but one can find information on topics such as "Voice, culture of" and "German stage." The usefulness of this index depends, in part, on the availability of nineteenth-century periodicals. At any rate, it will be of most interest to historians. The *Cumulated Dramatic Index, 1909-1949* (entry 208) takes up indexing of theatre periodicals after a thirteen-year gap.

248. **Play Index**. New York: H. W. Wilson, 1949- . LC 64-1054. ISSN 0554-3037.

A standard work with a new volume now published every five years, *Play Index* provides information on thousands of plays, both in collections and published as separate works. Its scope is broader than *Ottemiller's* (entry 227) as it includes children's plays, puppet plays, pageants, and one-act plays, for example. All plays indexed are written in English or translated into English. The work includes authors, titles, and subjects in one alphabetical sequence with information about the play listed under the author entry. Besides the standard bibliographical information, the number of acts, number of sets required, number of cast members, and a short description are listed for each play. To help those choosing plays for production, a cast analysis section lists plays according to the number of men, women, boys, and girls required for the cast. *Play Index* is especially useful because it allows access by subject, not possible with *Ottemiller's*.

249. Samples, Gordon. **The Drama Scholars' Index to Plays and Filmscripts: A Guide to Plays and Filmscripts in Selected Anthologies, Series, and Periodicals**. Metuchen, N.J.: Scarecrow, 1974-1986. 3v. LC 73-22165. ISBN v. 1: 0-8108-0699-1; v. 2: 0-8108-1249-5; v. 3: 0-8108-1869-8.

Samples has made an effort to differentiate his index from the other major play indexes by choosing selectively what plays to index. He attempts a balanced coverage but with an emphasis on foreign-language plays, lesser-known works, foreign translations of English plays, and eighteenth- and nineteenth-century collections. His purpose is "to provide for the serious student of drama and film an advantage in finding plays and filmscripts in anthologies, series, and periodicals in the original language, or in translation" (introduction, volume 3). The three volumes are not cumulative but rather complimentary, although both volumes 2 and 3 contain cumulative lists of anthologies, of publishers' series of plays, and of periodicals indexed. The main body of the index contains one alphabetical list of authors and titles, with bibliographic information listed under author. Samples has designed his index for the reader/scholar/critic rather than the play producer. He omits all production information such as number of sets and characters required. This index itself is a fine production and a useful work to consult for unusual or obscure plays.

250. Studwell, William E. **Opera Plot Index: A Guide to Locating Plots and Descriptions of Operas, Operettas, and Other Works of the Musical Theater, and Associated Material**. (Garland Reference Library of the Humanities, vol. 1099). New York: Garland, 1990. 466p. LC 89-37920. ISBN 0-8240-4621-8.

Studwell locates plot summaries not only of operas but also of operettas and musical comedies in 169 books. Most of the works are written in English, although ten languages are represented, and some of them are books suitable for children and adolescents. Readers needing a summary of a musical comedy by Richard Rodgers, Jerome Kern, or Stephen Sondheim will find it here. The alphabetical title section lists the composer, date of first production, alternate or translated titles, and the collections in which a plot summary appears. If the summary has any special features, such as illustrations, musical examples, or historical background information, Studwell notes them. The composer index (which incorrectly indexes Andrew Lloyd Webber under Webber instead of Lloyd Webber) and cross-references in the title section (for example, from *The Bat* to *Die Fledermaus*) help the reader find the needed entry.

251. Studwell, William E., and David A. Hamilton. **Ballet Plot Index: A Guide to Locating Plots and Descriptions of Ballets and Associated Material**. (Garland Reference Library of the Humanities, vol. 756). New York: Garland, 1987. 249p. LC 87-19758. ISBN 0-8240-8385-7.

This companion to Studwell's *Opera Plot Index* (entry 250) indexes plots and descriptions of 1,600 ballets in fifty-four books. It also indicates the presence of illustrations, criticism, musical themes, historical background, and summaries. The indexed books are written in several languages. The authors arrange their work by title of the ballet in its original language. Exceptions are Russian and other non-Roman language titles, which have been entered under their English or other Western European language names. Each entry lists variants of titles, date of first performance, and the name of the composer of the music as well as the codes for the books in which the plot may be found. An index allows the reader to find ballets by composer's name. Unfortunately, Studwell and Hamilton have not furnished any information on choreographers. Despite this flaw, the book will be useful to those seeking basic information about a ballet.

252. Thomson, Ruth Gibbons. **Index to Full Length Plays, 1895 to 1925**. (Useful Reference series, no. 85). Boston: Faxon, 1956. 172p. LC 57-13522.

253. Thomson, Ruth Gibbons. **Index to Full Length Plays, 1926 to 1944**. (Useful Reference series, no. 71). Boston: Faxon, 1946. 306p. LC 46-3756.

254. Ireland, Norma Olin. **Index to Full Length Plays 1944 to 1964**. (Useful Reference series, no. 92). Boston: Faxon, 1965. 296p. LC 66-18982.

Thomson compiled the first two volumes of this work, and Ireland wrote the third volume after Thomson's death. Together, the three volumes index over 3,000 titles of English-language plays published separately and in collections. Criteria for a play's inclusion in this work include the importance of the playwright, suitability of the play for production, and the personal tastes of the compilers. The third volume differs in arrangement from the first two. Volumes 1 and 2 contain separate title, author, and subject indexes as well as a bibliography of collections and individual plays. In volume 3 Ireland places authors, titles, and subjects in one alphabetical index and separates the collections and individual plays into two separate lists. In both cases, the main entry is the title entry. Ireland introduced other changes, and readers should consult her "Foreword" before using the book. They may also wish to read her highly opinionated introduction in which she blames the downfall of modern theatre on Freud, Communism, and our "antiheroic age!" *Ottemiller's* (entry 227) contains entries for most of the collections indexed here, but does not index individually published plays. Firkins' coverage (entry 231) overlaps the first years of this work, and *Play Index* overlaps most of volume 3. This title, therefore, is the preferred source for individual plays published between 1935 and 1948 and a secondary source for the other years covered.

A Costume Index

255. Monro, Isabel, and Dorothy E. Cook, eds. **Costume Index: A Subject Index to Plates and Illustrated Text.** New York: H. W. Wilson, 1937. 338p. LC 37-7142. Supplement. Edited by Isabel Stevenson Monro and Kate M. Monro. New York: H. W. Wilson, 1957. 210p.

A reference classic, this venerable work and its supplement index illustrations of costumes in 962 books and one magazine, *National Geographic*. Both volumes are arranged by subject. Some headings can be quite specific: for example, chasuble; noble-women-England-15th century; and petticoats and slips. The entries refer to the specific book and page where the illustration can be found. This title is still useful to the stage costumer for finding pictures of historical costume.

Chapter 5

Dictionaries, Encyclopedias, and Companions

Distinguished by alphabetical arrangement and brief, factual entries, the books in this chapter define and explain theatrical, dance, and entertainment terms and phrases. They identify persons, institutions, movements, and other names associated with the performing arts.

Theatre and the Related Arts

256. Ayre, Leslie. **The Gilbert and Sullivan Companion**. New York: Dodd, Mead, 1972. 485p. LC 72-2430. ISBN 0-396-06634-8.

The best feature of Ayre's work is the extensive entry for each of the operettas on which Gilbert and Sullivan collaborated. Each contains a complete plot summary and the words to every song. Other entries in this dictionary are quite brief and deal with actors, characters, allusions, and song titles associated with the Savoy operas. The introduction presents a summary of the two men's accomplishments before their meeting and a history of their partnership thereafter.

257. Band-Kuzmany, Karin R. M. **Glossary of the Theatre. In English, French, Italian and German**. (Glossaria Interpretum). New York: Elsevier, 1969. 130p. LC 68-57152. SBN 444-40716-2.

This little book translates 1,115 theatrical terms into English, French, German, and Italian. The words are arranged alphabetically by the English terms with their equivalents in the other three languages spread across the page. Each entry is numbered, and both the indexes (in French, German, and Italian) and the cross-references in the text refer to these numbers. Although some of the English phrases sound stilted, they do convey the meaning intended. The compiler has selected terms used by performers (to give the cue; stage fright) and by critics (thesis play; cycle of plays). Her book is a convenient short-cut for someone translating stage directions or a play review.

258. Banham, Martin, ed. **The Cambridge Guide to World Theatre**. New York: Cambridge University Press, 1988. 1,104p. LC 88-25804. ISBN 0-521-26595-9.

This excellent one-volume survey of theatre around the globe, published in 1988, is more up-to-date than the *Oxford Companion* (entry 279). Its articles, written by 115 contributors, include entries for actors, directors, playwrights, theatres, dramatic forms such as melodrama and masque, and many other topics related to theatre and popular stage entertainments. Long articles on the theatre of various countries take an historical approach. Even small countries such as Honduras and the Netherlands are represented. Some articles contain bibliographies, but there is no separate bibliography. This is currently the best one-volume encyclopedia of theatre in English.

5—Dictionaries, Encyclopedias, and Companions

259. Barba, Eugenio, and Nicola Savarese. **The Dictionary of Theatre Anthropology: The Secret Art of the Performer**. Translated by Richard Fowler. London, New York: Routledge Kegan Paul in association with the Centre for Performance Research, 1991. 272p. LC 90-26604. ISBN 0-415-05308-0.

This profusely illustrated book is unlike any other theatre dictionary. It seeks to find and present a repertory of "bits of good advice" or common principles of performing styles. The author defines theatre anthropology as "the study of human beings' socio-cultural and physiological behaviour in a performing situation" (introduction), and argues that while the theatre traditions of Asia include codified stage behaviors, those of the West do not. Much of this work is devoted to "translating" those Oriental traditions into behaviors that Westerners can understand and adapt. The book is arranged by general topic, some of which are "anatomy," "balance," "opposition," and "energy." Actors, dancers, and others interested in stage movement and movement techniques will benefit most from this work.

260. Barnes, Philip. **A Companion to Post-War British Theatre**. Totowa, N.J.: Barnes & Noble, 1986. 277p. LC 86-17367. ISBN 0-389-20669-5.

Barnes defines and explains or describes the important concepts, persons, events, and institutions of British theatre from 1945 to 1985. This has been a period of change and growth, beginning even before John Osborne's 1956 bombshell play *Look Back in Anger*, which changed the face of British theatre considerably. Here, Barnes lists the major work of important actors, playwrights, and others and reviews the history and accomplishments of institutions such as the National Theatre. Most of the terms he defines, such as "agit-prop" or "theatre of the absurd," can be found in other dictionaries. The American reader will appreciate its information about British performers and groups, however. Many of the longer entries have bibliographic references attached. Arranged alphabetically, the work also has an index of play titles.

261. Benford, Harry. **The Gilbert and Sullivan Lexicon in Which Is Gilded the Philosophic Pill**. 2d ed., rev. and enl. Ann Arbor, Mich.: Sarah Jennings Press, 1991. 270p. LC 90-24994. ISBN 0-931781-08-6.

Written by a longtime fan of the Savoy operas, this dictionary defines about 2,500 words and phrases used by William S. Gilbert in the librettos of those operas. Each chapter presents words and phrases from one of the operas in the same order as their appearance in the libretto, facilitating the use of Benford's lexicon with a libretto. The necessary index allows one to look up a word alphabetically. Writing in an informal style, Benford defines and discusses each phrase, often presenting alternative explanations if these exist. From the term "washing bill" (laundry list) to "mad as any hatter," Gilbert used many allusions unfamiliar to modern audiences. Given the continuing popularity of Gilbert and Sullivan works, this book will help solve those mysterious lyrics. ("Mad as any hatter," by the way, comes from *Alice in Wonderland*. Originally, however, it referred to the unfortunate tendency of hatters to contract St. Vitus' Dance from breathing fumes of mercurous oxide used in making felt hats.)

262. Benson, Eugene, and L. W. Conolly, eds. **The Oxford Companion to Canadian Theatre**. Toronto and New York: Oxford University Press, 1989. 662p. LC 90-126294. ISBN 0-19-540672-9.

The first Oxford companion devoted solely to Canadian theatre contains 703 entries written by 160 contributors. The editors have taken care that both English and French

Canadian theatre are well represented, as well as the theatrical traditions of native Canadian tribes. Entries deal with theatrical history, genres, theatres, theatre companies, biographies, dramatic criticism, and plays. Opera and dance are omitted, perhaps to make room for separate entries for fifty major Canadian plays. A good place to find brief information on playwrights, actors, and institutions, this companion testifies to Canadian theatre's emergence from the shadows cast by British, French, and American theatre.

263. Bloom, Ken. **Broadway: An Encyclopedic Guide to the History, People, and Places of Times Square**. New York: Facts on File, 1991. 442p. LC 90-32632. ISBN 0-8160-1249-0.

Focusing on the people, institutions, buildings, and other cultural icons of the Times Square/Broadway area, Bloom writes informally of theatres, composers, lyricists, conductors, actors, theatre owners, the Automat, the Astor Hotel, and Lindy's Delicatessen. Articles, longer than those in the *Oxford Companion to the American Theatre* (entry 264), are improved by the selection of portraits and photographs. Nevertheless, the book suffers from bad cross-referencing, and readers must use the index, partially defeating the purpose of the alphabetical arrangement. For example, Moss Hart is cross-referenced to Kaufman and Hart, but Lorenz Hart is not cross-referenced to Rodgers and Hart, even though Bloom describes Hart's career in that article. Similarly, the entry for Rodgers and Hammerstein refers one to the article on Hammerstein alone, but not to the Rodgers and Hart entry. Finally, critics are listed together under "Critics," but there is no cross-reference to the article about the famous critic Alexander Woolcott. Readers will find this work handy for answering trivia questions about the heyday of Broadway, but serious questions should be directed to the *Oxford Companion*.

264. Bordman, Gerald. **The Oxford Companion to the American Theatre**. New York: Oxford University Press, 1984. 734p. LC 83-26812. ISBN 0-19-503443-0.

Similar in format to Phyllis Hartnoll's *Oxford Companion to the Theatre* (entry 279), this A-to-Z dictionary concentrates on the personalities, institutions, and plays of the American theatre. Popular entertainment is covered briefly, and, in contrast to Hartnoll's selective coverage of plays, this companion attempts to list all important American plays. Each play entry summarizes the plot, lists production information, and provides a sampling of its critical reception. Entries for persons and for institutions detail their importance. While there is no bibliography, some entries do contain references to biographies and autobiographies. This is a good general source for American theatre. *The Concise Oxford Companion to American Theatre* (New York, Oxford University Press, 1987) contains about 60 percent of the present volume's material with a few added entries and some updating of articles.

265. Bowman, Walter Parker, and Robert Hamilton Bull. **Theatre Language: A Dictionary of Terms in English of the Drama and Stage from Medieval to Modern Times**. New York: Theatre Arts Books, 1961. 428p. LC 60-10495.

A scholarly work and a classic, Bowman's glossary covers theatre language of the past 500 years in English-speaking countries. Bowman's main concern is the language of the legitimate stage and drama, but he admits terms for musical comedy and vaudeville, as well as a few from ballet, the circus, and other performing arts. Over 3,000 terms fall into one of three categories: technical terms; standard nontechnical terms; and slang, jargon, and cant. Arranged in alphabetical order, the entries are short and clearly written.

If a term is British rather than American, it is so marked. Now largely superseded by Trapido's *International Dictionary of Theatre Language* (entry 300), this dictionary remains a useful supplementary source.

266. Boyce, Charles. **Shakespeare A to Z: The Essential Reference to His Plays, His Poems, His Life and Times, and More**. New York: Facts on File, 1990. 742p. LC 90-31239. ISBN 0-8160-1805-7.

Designed "for the information and entertainment of the student and general reader," the dictionary's 3,000 entries define and explain names, terms, and phrases associated with Shakespeare. Included are actors, characters, contemporaries of the playwright, historical references, places, and theatrical terms. Appendices list entries within categories such as those named above and thus function as a thematic index. Boyer writes clearly but does not provide footnotes or references. His work will answer the needs of those looking for a quick answer or explanation. A bibliography of suggested readings will aid those who want to read further.

267. Campbell, Oscar James. **The Reader's Encyclopedia of Shakespeare**. New York: Thomas Y. Crowell, 1966. 1,014p. LC 66-11946.

Campbell's encyclopedia offers "in a single volume all the essential information available about every feature of Shakespeare's life and works" (preface). The author describes persons, places, literary works, acting companies, scholars, musicians, and other subjects associated with the playwright. Each play is described and followed by its stage history in Great Britain and the United States, selected criticism, and a bibliography. Appendices offer a chronology of events related to Shakespeare and a selected bibliography of primary and secondary sources. Although older, Campbell's work is more complete than Wells (entry 305).

268. Courtney, Richard. **Dictionary of Developmental Drama: The Use of Terminology in Educational Drama, Theatre Education, Creative Dramatics, Children's Theatre, Drama Therapy, and Related Areas**. Springfield, Ill.: Charles C. Thomas, 1987. 153 p. LC 86-30193. ISBN 0-398-05313-8.

The author, who has written extensively in education and theatre, defines developmental drama as the study of practical uses of dramatic activity. In this work he attempts to codify and clarify terms used by educators, psychologists, and others who use drama for didactic or therapeutic reasons. Many of the words and phrases can be found in standard theatrical dictionaries or psychological dictionaries. Nevertheless, practitioners may find this book a convenience. A three-page bibliography provides sources for further reading.

269. Dunn, George E. **A Gilbert & Sullivan Dictionary**. New York: Oxford University Press, 1936. 175p. LC 918765.

Although it is old, this dictionary still offers descriptions and explanations of characters, allusions, obscure words, and topical names used in Gilbert and Sullivan's operettas. As Gilbert liked to insert contemporary jokes and allusions into his song lyrics, today's audiences need to have certain terms explained. For example, these lyrics from *Iolanthe*, "Oh, Captain Shaw...Could thy brigade, With cold cascade, Quench my great love, I wonder?" refer to Sir Eyre Massey Shaw, chief of London's Fire Brigade and a regular theatre-goer in the 1880s. Dunn also includes brief entries for each play and for actors who created roles in the operettas. See also Moore (entry 434).

270. **Enciclopedia dello spettacolo**. Rome: Casa Editrice La Maschere, 1954-1964. 9v. LC 55-2513. **Supplement**, 1955-1965. Rome, Unione Editoriale, 1966. **Index**. Rome, Unione Editoriale, 1968.

The most ambitious encyclopedia of performing arts has not been translated into English. Published over an eight-year period, the *Enciclopedia* aims to cover all aspects of all performing arts from earliest times to the present. As such, it includes drama, theatre, opera, operetta, dance, variety shows, puppetry, motion pictures, television, and the circus. Many contributors helped write the 30,000 articles on persons, institutions, cities, nations, artistic forms, and much more. Long articles are divided into parts. The entry for Chicago, Illinois, for example, contains sections for theatre, musical theatre, and ballet. This work is not without error; for example, it calls Chicago the state capital of Illinois. Also, coverage of Asian performance is weak. Nevertheless, the sheer amount of information is amazing. Arrangement is alphabetical with an index of titles. Readers must remember that Italian names and titles are used. For instance, *Hamlet* is found under the Italian "Amleto." A supplement brings coverage up to 1965. Both the encyclopedia and the supplement are lavishly illustrated with black-and-white drawings and photographs and color plates. This work is a basic source for the performing arts.

271. **The Encyclopedia of World Theater: With 420 Illustrations and an Index of Play Titles**. Introduction by Martin Esslin. New York: Charles Scribner's Sons, 1977. 320p. LC 76-19741. ISBN 0-684-14834-X.

Based on *Friedrichs Theaterlexicon* but with changes made for British and American audiences, this encyclopedia devotes more space to theatrical people and institutions of both Western and Eastern Europe than most other theatre dictionaries and encyclopedias. The short entries, often illustrated, present many biographies as well as explanations of terms such as "afterpiece" and "theatre of the absurd." Readers can locate plays by title through the index. Although the English edition is dated 1977, it is based on the original German work of 1969 and thus is considerably outdated. It is probably of most use when looking for historically obscure Europeans.

272. Gassner, John, and Edward Quinn, eds. **The Reader's Encyclopedia of World Drama**. (A Crowell Reference Book). New York: Thomas Y. Crowell, 1969. 1,030p. LC 69-11830.

Published after John Gassner's death, this book is one of the last of the many he edited or wrote about drama and theatre. With contributions by many people, this well-written encyclopedia presents articles about plays, authors, theatrical forms, and other terms. Like the *Cambridge Guide to World Theatre* (entry 258), the *Reader's Encyclopedia* contains long articles describing the historical development of theatre in many countries of the world. Gassner's work concentrates on the dramatic elements, however, while the Cambridge work emphasizes performance. Although now more than twenty years old, this is still valuable for its historical material and its bibliographic references. The appendix reprints twenty-four documents in dramatic theory, starting with Aristotle's *Poetics* and ending with essays by Northrop Frye and Friedrich Durrenmatt.

273. Geisinger, Marion. **Plays, Players, & Playwrights: An Illustrated History of the Theatre**. New York: Hart, 1975. 800p.

While almost half of this book is devoted to the American theatre, its strength is the chapter on the Russian theatre. It focuses on the Moscow Art Theatre, founded in 1897 by

86 / 5—Dictionaries, Encyclopedias, and Companions

Stanislavsky and Nemirovitch-Danchenko. Other chapters give the history of Greek and Roman, medieval, Renaissance, and English theatre. The book is weak in the history of other countries and contains nothing on the Asian stage. Within chapters, smaller sections explain, define, and describe movements, playwrights, events, and so on, much the same way an encyclopedia does, but in chronological rather than alphabetical order. A general index provides alphabetical access. This work supplements more important titles such as the *Oxford Companion to the Theatre* (entry 279) and the *McGraw-Hill Encyclopedia of World Drama* (entry 282).

274. Giteau, Cécile. **Dictionnaire des arts du spectacle: Français-anglais-allemand**. Paris: Dunod, 1970. 429p. LC 79-499699.

This tri-lingual dictionary translates terms used in the theatre, ballet, circus, puppetry, and media worlds into French, German, and English. Chapters are arranged by type of performance with separate alphabetical indexes for each language. A separate section, all in French, defines many of the terms. Translating 3,200 terms (about one-third of which refer to the theatre), Giteau's work is more comprehensive than Band-Kuzmany's dictionary (entry 257).

275. Granville, Wilfred. **The Theater Dictionary: British and American Terms in the Drama, Opera, and Ballet**. New York: Philosophical Library, 1952. 227p. LC 52-9717.

Granville's background was the theatre rather than academe, and he wanted to record the many phrases and terms of early twentieth-century British theatre before they died with those who used them. Thus, the book is especially strong on British slang and technical terms. Granville's frequent use of anecdotes or humorous explanations makes this book fun to browse in as well as consult. Granville is particularly good at distinguishing British and American terms for the same idea. The British equivalent to the American "Don't call us. We'll call you," for example, is "The part is already cast!" Although now quite old, this work can still be useful as a supplement to Trapido (entry 300).

276. Green, Stanley. **Encyclopedia of the Musical Theatre**. New York: Dodd, Mead, 1976. 488p. LC 76-21069. ISBN 0-396-07221-6.

This book contains information about "the most prominent people, productions, and songs of the musical theatre, both in New York ... and London" (preface). Green includes standard musical comedies, musical plays, revues, and operettas, but omits foreign musicals, one-person shows, and productions of Gilbert and Sullivan operettas. Entries for plays, songs, actors, lyricists, composers, and others are arranged in one alphabet. Individuals' theatrical careers are summarized. For plays Green provides details of the New York and London openings, plot, songs, film versions, and additional important productions. Each song is listed with the names of the composer, the lyricist, the source play, and the first person to sing it. This book is useful for musical plays produced up to the mid-1970s.

277. Griffiths, Trevor R., and Carole Woddis. **The Back Stage Theater Guide**. New York: Back Stage Books, 1991. 466p. LC 91-29166. ISBN 0-8230-7573-7.

Emphasizing writers one is apt to encounter in today's theatre, Griffiths and Woddis have compiled about 300 short entries for playwrights and their work. They also discuss a few theatre companies and some theatrical subjects such as African-American theatre and Asian theatre in Britain. Entries include, for writers, birth and death dates, nationality, a list of significant plays with date of first appearance or publication, a short biography, and a description of one of the writer's major plays. Very important playwrights, such as Tennessee Williams, rate more than one play description. The "Try These" box, which accompanies most entries, refers readers to "other plays or authors who have tackled similar topics, share similar interests, or offer marked contrasts to the one you started with" (introduction). After discussing Lillian Hellman's *The Children's Hour*, a play that demonstrates the destructiveness of a schoolgirl's rumor on her teachers, for example, the authors recommend Arthur Miller's *The Crucible* for another work on the "consequences of spiteful rumor" and the plays of Ben Jonson for "characters as embodiments of moral evil." This feature may be of use in reader's advisory work. The authors have chosen not just American and British writers, but also those of French, Swedish, German, and other nationalities. A comparison with *The Oxford Companion to the Theatre* (entry 279) and *The Cambridge Guide to World Theatre* (entry 258) shows that Griffiths and Woddis have included many writers not found in either of the two better-known guides. This work is especially useful for women and gay playwrights. It deserves a place on the shelves next to the Oxford and Cambridge works.

278. Halliday, F. E. **A Shakespeare Companion, 1564-1954**. rev. ed. New York: Schocken Books, 1964. 569p. LC 64-14747.

A standard companion to all aspects of Shakespeare's life, work, and influences, Halliday's alphabetically arranged guide discusses characters, scholars, actors, acting companies, and others associated with the writer. It also features short essays on topics such as abridgement of the plays and maps of London in Shakespeare's time. Halliday offers genealogies of the English royal houses for use with the history plays. The bibliography includes both primary and secondary works. Plates, which follow the text, illustrate stage productions. Easy to read and use, Halliday's companion supplements Campbell (entry 267) and Wells (entry 305).

279. Hartnoll, Phyllis, ed. **The Oxford Companion to the Theatre**. 4th ed. Oxford, England and New York: Oxford University Press, 1983. 934p. LC 83-235664. ISBN 0-19-211546-4.

The fourth edition of this classic work concentrates on identifying and defining terms of the legitimate theatre, especially persons, theatres, companies, theatrical forms, and production terms. Hartnoll has eliminated references to opera and dance and has treated vaudeville, musical comedy, and other popular entertainments superficially. Although she includes a few of the many experimental and alternative theatre companies that have come into existence since the third edition was published in 1967, Hartnoll believes more time is needed to discover which groups will have a lasting influence on the theatre. The alphabetically arranged entries emphasize the historical aspects of the subject. Articles for countries of the world review the history of their theatrical forms and describe today's theatre. Plays are discussed under their authors, as there are no entries for play titles. This book is an essential source for any theatre collection, although it now has strong competition from the newer *Cambridge Guide to World Theatre* (entry 258). *The Concise Oxford Companion to World Theatre*, based on the third edition of the companion, is now outdated.

88 / 5—Dictionaries, Encyclopedias, and Companions

280. Hawkins-Dady, Mark, ed. **International Dictionary of Theatre**. Chicago: St. James Press, 1992- . v. 1- . LC 91-64335. ISBN 1-55862-095-8.

St. James Press plans to issue three volumes in this dictionary: Plays, which has been published; Playwrights; and Actors, Directors, and Designers. The first volume discusses 620 plays from ancient to modern times, originally written in more than twenty different languages, representing many cultures. They were chosen on the recommendation of an advisory board assembled by the publisher. Entries for plays, arranged alphabetically by title, list date of the work's first production, if known; date of its first publication; and a list of recent critical books and articles about the play. Contributors, most of whom are professors of literature or theatre in the United States, Canada, or the United Kingdom, provide a critical essay analyzing the play. An alphabetical list of authors serves as an author index. Nicely illustrated with photographs of stage productions, this complements the *McGraw-Hill Encyclopedia of World Drama* (entry 282) well. Although not as many plays are described here, each receives a fuller critical and descriptive treatment. The advisory board has taken care to include plays representative of many countries, including Australia, Japan, and China.

281. Hay, Henry, ed. **Cyclopedia of Magic**. New York: Dover, 1975. (c. 1949). 498p. LC 74-27511. ISBN 0-486-21808-2.

Although this encyclopedia was first published in 1949, it is still a valuable source of information about the performance of magic. Hay bases his work on the writings of many others including Harry Houdini and Professor Louis Hoffmann whom Hay calls the greatest writer on magic ever. Arranged alphabetically, the articles, longer than those in Lamb (entry 285), are more oriented to the performance and showmanship aspects of magic than Lamb's. Thus Hay includes entries for "patter," "presentation," "publicity," and "stage settings." A fascinating chapter on "costume" illustrates the specially made hiding places sewn into a magician's clothing. Hay also includes short biographies of famous magicians. This book will be of interest to aspiring magicians and to those who wonder "how did he do that?"

281a. Hischak, Thomas S. **Stage It with Music: An Encyclopedia Guide to the American Musical Theatre**. Westport, Conn.: Greenwood, 1993. 341p. LC 92-35321. ISBN 0-313-28708-2.

Narrower in scope than either the *Oxford Companion to American Theatre* (entry 264) or the *Cambridge Guide to American Theatre* (entry 306a), Hischak's work provides information on more than 300 American musical plays and the people who created them. In an encyclopedia format, the entries also include information on genres such as rock musicals, musical series like the Ziegfield Follies, and general subjects such as dance in musicals. Entries vary in length according to the importance of the person or show in the history of American musical theatre. Play entries include Broadway opening dates and number of first run performances. Although the encyclopedia itself does not contain bibliographical references, Hischak provides a general bibliography at the end of the volume. A chronology lists plays produced from 1866 through 1992. The extensive index locates persons, song titles, play titles, and other subjects. A welcome addition to the literature of the musical theatre, Hischak's book will quickly answer many readers' questions.

282. Hochman, Stanley, ed. **McGraw-Hill Encyclopedia of World Drama**. 2d ed. New York: McGraw-Hill, 1984. 5v. LC 83-9919. ISBN 0-07-079169-4.

Although this second edition is 25 percent larger than the 1972 first edition, it still emphasizes the literature of the stage rather than its performance. The editor and contributors have expanded coverage of theatre in the articles on non-Western drama as well as adding coverage of musical comedy, important directors, and some theatrical companies such as the Comédie Française and the Moscow Art Theatre. Nevertheless, most articles deal with playwrights and their works. There are no entries for actors or for the technical aspects of theatre. Articles for major dramatists contain a biography, an analysis of the author's work, synopses of major plays, a play list of works other than those mentioned in the text, and a bibliography. Less-famous playwrights are represented with more perfunctory entries accompanied by bibliographic references. The encyclopedia is arranged alphabetically and illustrated with many photographs. Volume 5 contains a glossary of dramatic terms, an index, and play title list. The latter is a list of plays mentioned in the play lists, not an index to plays mentioned in the text. For this reason, it is safer to use the index when looking for a play.

283. Hodgson, Terry. **The Drama Dictionary**. New York: New Amsterdam, 1988. 432p. ISBN 0-941533-40-9.

This book is a dictionary of "terms used in the theatre and by theatre critics" (preface). It differs from many of the titles in this chapter in that it emphasizes concepts, not persons, plays, and theatrical companies. Some of the terms that are defined are circle of attention, masque, over the top, and thesis play. Entries define the phrase, sometimes give its origins, and often provide a lengthy explanation of its use. Some entries include bibliographic references. Clearly, Hodgson has in mind the dramatist, the actor, the audience, and the critic when choosing his terms. He gives them the language by which they can express themselves and communicate with each other. Both the choice of material and the well-written definitions make this work a top choice in dictionaries.

284. Kellner, Bruce, ed. **The Harlem Renaissance: A Historical Dictionary for the Era**. Westport, Conn.: Greenwood, 1984. 476p. LC 83-22687. ISBN 0-313-23232-6.

Browsing through this book will convince anyone that the Harlem Renaissance certainly encompassed a great deal more than the Cotton Club and Langston Hughes. The flowering of African-American cultural life that took place roughly between 1917 and 1935 is ably described in this work. Although most entries refer to people, others describe plays, books, organizations, and events. Many refer to theatres, actors, playwrights, and little theatre groups. Several bibliographies, a chronology, and a glossary of Harlem slang make this book even more valuable.

285. Lamb, Geoffrey. **Illustrated Magic Dictionary**. New York: Elsevier/Nelson Books, 1979. 157p. LC 80-17050. ISBN 0-525-66689-3.

Lamb, an amateur magician, addresses this dictionary to those who want to know more about magic but who are not experts. Lamb's emphasis is on the many tricks and stunts used by magicians in their routines, and his explanations of how they are accomplished are accompanied by explanatory line drawings. He identifies prominent magicians of all time periods, but readers will find better biographies in Hay's *Cyclopedia of Magic* (entry 281). Lamb includes a bibliography for those who want to read about (and perhaps attempt) the tricks behind the performance of magic.

286. Leiter, Samuel L. **Kabuki Encyclopedia: An English-Language Adaptation of "Kabuki Jiten."** Westport, Conn.: Greenwood, 1979. 572p. LC 78-73801. ISBN 0-313-20654-6.

The English version of a Japanese reference book, this encyclopedia has been altered considerably to make it more useful to Western readers. Leiter has arranged entries in English alphabetical order, expanded some articles, especially those that deal with individual plays, and has removed some material. The author's aim is to make kabuki accessible to non-Japanese theatre lovers. Most entries define and explain technical terms, give plots of more than 200 plays, summarize the careers of famous actors and playwrights, or otherwise clarify the nature of this special type of performance. Appendices include a chronology, a list of major plays with variant play titles (kabuki plays often have both formal and popular names), a bibliography, and kabuki actor family genealogies. A helpful subject guide to main entries links all articles on broad topics such as actors or scenic techniques. Leiter also includes a general index. Because most standard dictionaries and encyclopedias treat Japanese theatre superficially, this book should be consulted first when looking for information on kabuki. The Halfords' handbook (entry 405) concentrates on explaining the plots of kabuki plays.

287. Lounsbury, Warren C., and Norman Boulanger. **Theatre Backstage from A to Z.** 3d ed., rev. Seattle: University of Washington Press, 1989. 213p. LC 89-14715. ISBN 0-295-96829-X; 0-295-96828-1 pa.

Changes in the techniques and equipment of sound and electronic control prompted this new edition. After an introductory history of scenery and lighting practices in the United States, the authors present a dictionary of terms with definitions, explanations, and/or directions for use. For example, the entry for birdcall tells the reader to use an Audubon birdcall available from the Audubon Society. Entries range from the mundane—"chair glide; small metal disks used on the bottom of furniture to make sliding easy"—to the exotic—"flash powder; used for smoke and flash effects where legal. Available in slow, medium, and fast speed. Check with local fire department." The authors add a list of manufacturers and distributors and a bibliography. See also Reid's *ABC of Stage Lighting* (entry 294a) and Wehlburg's *Theatre Lighting* (entry 304).

288. Matlaw, Myron. **Modern World Drama: An Encyclopedia**. New York: E. P. Dutton, 1972. 960p. LC 71-185032. ISBN 0-525-15902-9.

Matlaw defines modern playwrights as all major nineteenth-century writers whose lives extended into the twentieth century and all major twentieth-century writers. Most of the writers are American, European, or Japanese. Survey articles, integrated into the alphabetical arrangement, review major authors and plays of many countries and regions. These articles are accompanied by bibliographies as are many other articles in the encyclopedia. Entries for plays discuss the plot in great detail and list dates of the first production and publication. Playwrights' careers are discussed along with some criticism of their work. Matlaw is most useful for the plot summaries and for critical information about authors. The index to characters broadens its range of uses. The *Cambridge Guide to World Theatre* (entry 258) presents more information about each nation's theatre heritage.

289. Mobley, Jonnie Patricia. **NTC's Dictionary of Theatre and Drama Terms.** Lincolnwood, Ill: National Textbook, 1992. 166p. ISBN 0-8442-5345-6.

Briefly defining 750 theatre and drama terms, Mobley writes clearly and often uses examples from plays to illustrate her explanations. Lacking both a bibliography and a list of sources, this dictionary is not scholarly. It will be useful in a school library, however, to answer young people's questions about theatre words.

290. Mordden, Ethan. **The Fireside Companion to the Theatre.** New York: Simon & Schuster, 1988. 312p. LC 88-18444. ISBN 0-671-67188-X; 0-671-62553-5 pa.

Short on facts but excellent on interpretation, Mordden deliberately narrows his focus to major persons, developments, and backstage terms in the theatre worldwide. Arranged alphabetically, the book is written in an entertaining style and is full of Mordden's opinions. Referring to American actress Maude Adams and her ability to play Shakespearean roles, he writes, "contrary to what we read in most theatre encyclopedias she was scarcely acceptable as Juliet." Of Molière he says, "Today, Corneille and Racine are generally performed only in France, and at least partly as a matter of national honor. Molière remains internationally vital." The work is illustrated with photographs from the New York Public Library's Performing Arts Collection. Although it does not seriously challenge the authority of the *Oxford Companion* (entry 279) or the *Cambridge Guide* (entry 258), this secondary work is interesting and fun to read.

291. Onions, C. T. **A Shakespeare Glossary.** 3d ed., rev. and enl. throughout by Robert D. Eagleson. Oxford, England: Oxford University Press, 1986. 326p. LC 84-7912. ISBN 0-19-811199-1; 0-19-812521-6 pa.

Onions, and now Eagleson, supply "definitions and illustrations of words or senses of words which are now obsolete or which survive only in archaic or provincial use" (preface) and which are used by Shakespeare. New scholarship has led to new definitions, amendments, and corrections in this third edition. Entries define each word and give up to three references from Shakespeare to illustrate the definition. In the third edition Eagleson incorporates foreign words and phrases alphabetically with English words rather than separating them as in the first two editions. As the world gets further and further away from the Elizabethan age, this dictionary makes clear Shakespeare's intent. It should be preferred to the older *A Shakespeare Word-Book* by John Foster (New York: Russell & Russell, 1969, [c. 1908]).

292. Packard, William, David Pickering, and Charlotte Savidge, eds. **Facts on File Dictionary of the Theatre.** New York: Facts on File, 1988. 556p. LC 88-28379. ISBN 0-8160-1841-3, 0-8160-1945-2 pa.

Not as scholarly or as complete as either Trapido or Bowman and Bull (entries 300 and 265), this dictionary defines words, phrases, and names associated with the British and American stage. Some entries also refer to European and non-Western forms of theatre. Entries, for the most part 50 to 150 words, define and explain terms. Entries for persons summarize their important work in the theatre. Those for plays present plot summaries. The arrangement is alphabetical with many cross-references. However, there are no bibliographies or bibliographical references included.

5—Dictionaries, Encyclopedias, and Companions

293. Philpott, Alexis Robert. **Dictionary of Puppetry**. Boston: Plays, 1969. 286p. LC 69-18110.

Compiled by an experienced puppeteer and puppet magazine editor, this book provides information on people, groups, books, and terms associated with puppets and marionettes. Philpott concentrates on the history of puppetry internationally, but with some emphasis on Great Britain. The entry for Samuel Pepys, for example, notes that he recorded in his diary seeing puppet shows several times. Philpott also includes technical terms, some of which are quite specialized. One example is "kilim arasi," literally, "between carpets," a puppet stage used in Azerbaijan, composed of a folded carpet held by two men. Entries for books are annotated. This work is the first choice for a puppetry dictionary.

294. Rae, Kenneth, and Richard Southern. **An International Vocabulary of Technical Theatre Terms, in Eight Languages: American, Dutch, English, French, German, Italian, Spanish, Swedish**. New York: Theatre Arts, 1960. 139p. LC 60-4780.

Small enough to be carried in a stage manager's pocket, this little book provides equivalents in eight languages to 637 technical theatre terms. It places the words in order alphabetically by the English/American term with the other six languages spread across the page. Separate indexes allow the foreign speaker to find the correct numbered entry for the term needed. The American index lists only terms that differ from the British. Americans sit in orchestra seats, for example, while Britons sit in stalls. Use as a supplement to Band-Kuzmany (entry 257) which contains almost twice as many terms.

294a. Reid, Francis. **The ABC of Stage Lighting**. London: A & C Black, New York: Drama Book Publishers, 1992. 129p. ISBN 0-89676-119-3.

Presented in dictionary format, Reid's illustrated glossary defines and explains stage lighting terms for pieces of equipment, techniques, and abbreviations. Reid also identifies persons and lighting companies who have played important roles in the development of the field. Although written with a British slant, the book identifies and cross-references American terms. Reid, who has spent thirty years as a lighting designer including ten years with the Glyndebourne Festival Opera, accounts for the latest advances of computerized lighting technology in the glossary. He also defines older terms seldom used today. His book should be consulted before Wehlburg's older dictionary (entry 304).

295. Sergel, Sherman Louis. **The Language of Show Biz: A Dictionary**. Chicago: Dramatic, 1973. 251p. LC 73-173320.

Despite its irritating coffee table book format and coy style, this dictionary defines many slang terms of American show business. Arranged alphabetically, the definitions range from one line—"scale; a list of box office prices"—to one and one-half pages on "the producer." Many of these words will be found in other dictionaries, but Sergel's use of "consultants" from the world of "show biz" lends a certain breeziness and authenticity to the definitions. Compared with Wilmeth's *The Language of American Popular Entertainment* (entry 306), Sergel concentrates more on the legitimate stage while Wilmeth's emphasis is on the circus, the carnival, and other popular entertainments. This is a supplemental choice to be used after consulting Trapido (entry 300), Bowman and Bull (entry 265), and Wilmeth.

296. Simon, Alfred. **Dictionnaire du théâtre français contemporain**. Paris: Larousse, 1970. 255p. LC 73-577348.

Simon asserts the contemporary French theatre began with Jacques Copeau, the actor and director whose work influenced European and American theatre enormously during the first part of the twentieth century. Accordingly, Simon's dictionary covers persons, plays, and terms important to French theatre between 1913 (when Copeau became director of La Nouvelle Revue Française) and 1969. The alphabetically arranged dictionary is profusely illustrated and is accompanied by a history of French theatre in the twentieth century and by a bibliography. To an American reader this work is probably most useful for information about French actors, directors, playwrights, and plays. The technical terms are defined equally well in English dictionaries.

297. Sobel, Bernard. **The New Theatre Handbook and Digest of Plays**. 8th ed., completely revised. New York: Crown, 1959. 749p. LC 58-12876.

Now aging, Sobel's work uses a dictionary arrangement to provide information on plays, persons, groups, and terms of the theatre. Plot summaries are given for the many plays included. Entries for persons cover their careers. When terms are defined, the entries are generally longer than those found in Trapido (entry 300) or Bowman and Bull (entry 265). Some entries are quite long, especially those that cover the dramatic literature of various countries. Sobel is weak on theatre slang. This is a supplementary source only.

298. Taylor, John Russell. **The Penguin Dictionary of the Theatre**. Harmondsworth, England: Penguin Books, 1966. 293p. LC 68-2861.

Essentially a dictionary of names of dramatists, actors, directors, and plays, this work also includes some theatrical terms such as makeup, curtain, and so on. The short definitions are arranged alphabetically. Except for the play titles, most of the entries can be found in the *Oxford Companion to the Theatre* (entry 279). This is a supplemental source.

299. **Teaterord [Theatre Words]**. Stockholm: Nordiska Teaterunionen, 1977. 207p. ISBN 91-85366-01-3.

Concentrating on Scandinavian languages, this multilingual glossary of theatrical terms fills a niche left vacant by the other works of this type. Arranged by Danish words, it includes equivalent terms in Finnish, Icelandic, Norwegian, Swedish, German, English, and French. Indexes are provided for each language. A pictorial section keys entries with technical illustrations, allowing the reader to find the proper term in any of the languages. *Teaterord* is a specialized item, to be sure, but useful if one is producing, acting, or researching a play in a Scandinavian language.

300. Trapido, Joel, ed. **An International Dictionary of Theatre Language**. Edward A. Langhans, ed. for Western Theatre; James R. Brandon, ed. for Asian Theatre. Westport, Conn.: Greenwood, 1985. 1,032p. LC 83-22756. ISBN 0-313-22980-5.

The most important dictionary of theatre, this work benefits from a list of contributors that reads like a "Who's Who" of current theatrical scholarship. By recruiting the expertise of their colleagues, Trapido and his fellow editors have been able to collect and define 10,000 English terms and 5,000 foreign terms "from theatre throughout the world, both historical and extant, as used in the English-speaking world" (preface). All areas of drama, theatre production, acting, technology, management, and much more are covered.

Proper names are generally excluded as are terms from the fields of mass media and popular entertainment. Foreign terms are included if they have appeared in English-language theatre publications. The user should read the preface for further information on the inclusion or exclusion of various subjects. After a short history of theatrical glossaries and dictionaries, the main body of the dictionary is arranged alphabetically. The seventy-seven-page bibliography follows and includes dictionaries, histories, handbooks, and many other works cited in the body of the dictionary. Entries include the term; language (if other than English); a definition and sometimes a further discussion that enriches the meaning; and, often, one or more citations to a book in the bibliography. If a term is historical, its entry indicates the time period of its usage. Comprehensive, scholarly, and up-to-date, this dictionary should be consulted first when looking for a theatrical term.

301. Trilse, Christoph, Kalsu Hammer, and Rolf Kabel. **Theater Lexikon**. Berlin: Henschelverlag Kunst und Gesellschaft, 1978. 624p.

Readers will find short biographies of playwrights, directors, and actors as well as definitions of theatrical terms in this dictionary. Since it was published in the former East Germany, it contains more entries for Eastern Europeans than other dictionaries and handbooks. Until a new work provides information about both Western and Eastern Europe, this dictionary should be useful.

302. Vince, Ronald W., ed. **Companion to the Medieval Theatre**. New York: Greenwood, 1989. 420p. LC 88-21337. ISBN 0-313-24647-5.

Stressing that medieval theatre encompassed more than just the literary texts that exist today, Vince emphasizes performance in this work. His aim is to introduce European theatre of the middle ages, defined here as A.D. 900-1550, to the nonspecialist. Articles by many contributors cover "place-names, personal names, technical terms, theatrical forms and genres" (preface). Examples include "folk drama," "dance of death," and "traveling players." The alphabetical arrangement is supplemented by numerous cross-references and four indexes. In addition to bibliographical references at the end of most articles, a bibliography and chronology appear at the end of the book.

303. Waters, T. A. **The Encyclopedia of Magic and Magicians**. New York: Facts on File, 1988. 372p. LC 87-13464. ISBN 0-8160-1349-7.

Waters' encyclopedia has two aims: "to provide a basic description of most known effects and routines and, when feasible, briefly describe the techniques involved" (introduction), and to present a "Who's Who" of performers and creators of magic, both past and present. Articles appear in alphabetical order with cross references but no index. Compared to works by Hay (entry 281) and Lamb (entry 285), Waters' strength is his inclusion of modern magicians whom the others do not discuss. Biographical entries are noticeably uneven, however. Waters has not included birth and death dates, for example, and many biographies lack dates at crucial points in the narrative. Waters does emphasize giving credit for the invention of tricks and illusions if he can prove provenance. Technical entries also display unevenness. Some descriptions go into considerable detail on how an illusion is created while others simply describe the trick's effect. Although Waters lists some bibliographical references in the text, he could have strengthened his book by providing a bibliography.

304. Wehlburg, Albert F. C. **Theatre Lighting: An Illustrated Glossary**. New York: Drama Book, 1975. 62p. LC 75-19332. ISBN 0-910482-69-1.

Aimed at lighting technicians and designers, this book defines about 750 terms concerned with theatrical lighting. Only words and phrases used in the United States are covered. In contrast, Francis Reid's *The ABC of Stage Lighting* (entry 294a) includes British and American terms. Entries are usually one or two sentences. Line drawings in the margins illustrate many terms. This work will be most helpful to someone who is already somewhat familiar with theatre technology. Consult Reid first because his dictionary is more recent. Use Wehlburg as a supplement.

305. Wells, Stanley. **Shakespeare: An Illustrated Dictionary**. New York: Oxford University Press, 1978. 216p. LC 77-18370. ISBN 0-19-520054-3.

Written to be a "companion and guide to reading Shakespeare's plays and to experiencing them where they belong, in the theatre," this dictionary defines and discusses Shakespeare's life, contemporaries, and works. It also includes entries for actors associated with Shakespearean productions such as Sir Ben Greet, a pioneer in presenting the plays outdoors, and contemporary English actress Judi Dench. Even composers, such as Tchaikovsky, who wrote music inspired by the plays, warrant an entry. Each play merits a long entry, which gives its background and the history of its theatrical productions. Other entries, illustrated with photographs and drawings, tend to be shorter. Wells includes a selective finding list of characters in the plays, but readers should use May (entry 431) or Rowse (entry 443) for information about characters. Wells will answer many inquiries about the Bard, but it is not as complete as Campbell's encyclopedia (entry 267) which is preferred if available.

306. Wilmeth, Don B. **The Language of American Popular Entertainment: A Glossary of Argot, Slang, and Terminology**. Westport, Conn.: Greenwood, 1981. 305p. LC 80-14795. ISBN 0-313-22497-8.

Wilmeth, the author of several bibliographies of popular entertainment, terms this work a glossary of "a reasonable cross section of the slang, argot, and terminology of major American popular entertainment forms" (preface). While most of the terms come from the circus and the carnival, both of which possess highly developed insider languages, Wilmeth also covers vaudeville, tent shows, medicine shows, and other entertainments. The 3,200 words and phrases, arranged alphabetically, include terms that have crossed over into the common language such as "rube: a rustic or a hayseed," and others that have not, such as "lumber-buster: minstrel show term for a wooden shoe dancer." Inasmuch as most of these entertainment forms have died out or are terminally ill, Wilmeth has provided an important service in collecting the colorful and sometimes obscure language employed by their practitioners. This work is more comprehensive than Sergel (entry 295) in the areas of vaudeville and burlesque, but it does not deal with slang of the legitimate theatre as Sergel does.

306a. Wilmeth, Don B., and Tice L. Miller, eds. **Cambridge Guide to American Theatre**. New York: Cambridge University Press, 1993. 547p. LC 92-35030. ISBN 0-521-40134-8.

Under the able editorship of Wilmeth and Miller, Cambridge has produced a work that rivals the *Oxford Companion to the American Theatre* (entry 264) in its ability to provide short, factual answers to questions about the world of American theatre. Eighty

96 / 5—Dictionaries, Encyclopedias, and Companions

writers, including many of the best-known theatre historians, inform readers about all subjects related to the theatre and to vaudeville, burlesque, the circus, magic, and folk festivals. Cambridge is more inclusive than Oxford whose scope includes only legitimate theatre. Cambridge also does a better job with the histories of major American cities such as Baltimore and Philadelphia. Oxford, however, provides many more entries for individual plays and persons. Cambridge includes a bibliography written by Wilmeth and an introductory historical survey. At the moment, Cambridge is more up-to-date than Oxford, but that advantage will alternate as additional editions are issued. Most readers and libraries will find uses for both volumes.

Dance

307. Beaumont, Cyril William, comp. **A French-English Dictionary of Technical Terms Used in Classical Ballet**. rev. and enl. ed. London: C. W. Beaumont, 1970. 43p.

Addressed to dance students, this little volume defines the French terms used in ballet. As it has no illustrations and does not contain as many terms as either Grant or Kersley (entries 311, 312), it should be used only as a supplement to these two sources. It is arranged alphabetically with an appendix containing a highly simplified explanation of French grammar.

308. Chujoy, Anatole, and Phyllis Winifred Manchester, comps. and eds. **Dance Encyclopedia**. rev. and enl. ed. New York: Simon & Schuster, 1967. 992p. LC 67-28038.

Chujoy, founder of the now defunct *Dance News*, and Manchester, managing editor of that periodical, enlisted the help of a number of distinguished contributors to compile this encyclopedia. Now aging, it remains a useful place to find information on ballets, companies, dancers, composers, types of dance, and other dance-related subjects. Topics that are not found in the other dance reference works include "dance criticism" and "accidents while dancing." The book is arranged alphabetically and does not contain a bibliography. Articles tend to be longer than those in Clarke and Vaughan (entry 309). Koegler's work (entry 313) is more recent but concentrates on ballet only.

309. Clarke, Mary, and David Vaughan, eds. **The Encyclopedia of Dance and Ballet**. New York: G. P. Putnam's Sons, 1977. 376p. LC 76-52325. ISBN 0-399-11955-8.

Clarke's encyclopedia concerns itself not only with ballet of all time periods, but also with contemporary dance as it has been performed in the twentieth century. Short entries identify choreographers, dancers, ballets, and dance companies. Although the main alphabetical section of the work does not define any technical terms, Clarke provides a glossary of technical terms and a bibliography at the end of the book. This work is similar to Wilson (entry 317), although it does include entries for non-ballet dancers such as Josephine Baker and Twyla Tharp. It is not as recent as Koegler (entry 313). Readers looking for more extensive information about modern dance should consult *The Complete Guide to Modern Dance* (entry 373).

310. Gadan-Pamard, Francis, and Robert Maillard, eds. **Dictionary of Modern Ballet**. Translated from the French by John Montague and Peggie Cochrane. New York: Tudor, 1959. 360p.

A translation of *Dictionnaire du ballet moderne*, this book covers persons, ballets, and dance companies in one alphabetical order. Techniques of dance are not included. Although most of the information found in this work can be found in other dance dictionaries and handbooks, the real reason to look at it is the profuse and beautiful illustrations, many in color. Drawings, which reproduce sets and costumes from various ballets, are particularly useful to the reader who wishes to know what a ballet looks like.

311. Grant, Gail. **Technical Manual and Dictionary of Classical Ballet**. 3d ed., rev. New York: Dover, 1982. 139p. LC 67-26481. ISBN 0-486-21843-0.

The third edition of a work originally published in 1950, this book concentrates on defining and explaining 1,100 terms used to describe the movements that compose a dance. Because the great majority of terms are French, Grant includes a phonetic pronunciation guide. Definitions are clearly written, and illustrations show the differences in positions according to the French, the Italian, and the Russian schools. Grant's manual presents much more detail about the technical aspects of ballet than any other dance dictionary except that of Kersley and Sinclair (entry 312). A small bibliography provides additional material. Readers who are interested in the positions and steps of Broadway show dancing should consult Jacqueline Lowe and Charles Selber's *The Language of Show Dancing* (entry 475), a pictorial dictionary of those movements.

312. Kersley, Leo, and Janet Sinclair. **A Dictionary of Ballet Terms**. 3rd rev. ed. London: A & C Black, 1977. Reprint. New York: DaCapo, 1981. 112p. LC 78-27421. ISBN 0-306-80094-2 pa.

Similar to Gail Grant's dictionary (entry 311), but directed to the audience rather than to the dancer, this book defines words and phrases associated with the classical ballet, including positions and steps that are used to form dances. It also includes terms such as "abstract ballet," "rake of the stage," and "arque" (bow-legged) that may be helpful to know when reading about or discussing ballet. The authors do not include any pronunciation aids, however. The dictionary is well illustrated with black-and-white drawings that recreate moments from ballets mentioned in the text. The drawing that accompanies the term "fouette," for instance, is of Odile performing one of her 32 fouettes in the Black Swan pas de deux in *Swan Lake*. This well-written book will be useful to those who wish to know more about what they are seeing on stage.

313. Koegler, Horst. **The Concise Oxford Dictionary of Ballet**. 2d ed. New York: Oxford University Press, 1982. 459p. LC 82-237993. ISBN 0-19-311330-9.

Koegler presents a reworking of his *Friedrichs Ballettlexicon von A-Z* for English and American audiences. This book attempts "to cover the whole ballet scene, past and present, its personalities, works, companies, places of performance, and technical terms, with some considerations of modern dance, ethnic dance, and ballroom dance" (foreword). For the second edition, the author has deleted and replaced many older entries with newer material. Entries are short except for those describing individual ballets; here Koegler presents more detail than Wilson (entry 317). He does not emphasize technical terms, and the reader should use Grant (entry 311) or Kersley and Sinclair (entry 312) for descriptions of dance steps and movements. The coverage of ethnic and ballroom dance is not as complete as that of Raffe (entry 316).

5—Dictionaries, Encyclopedias, and Companions

314. Love, Paul. **Modern Dance Terminology**. New York: Kamin Dance, 1953. 96p. LC 53-11674.

Love scanned dance publications and conducted interviews to compile this glossary of terms representing "the aims, theories, and objectives of the modern dance" during the first half of the twentieth century (preface). Most of the definitions and descriptions are quite long, at least one paragraph, and Love quotes many well-known dancers such as Doris Humphrey and Mary Wigman. Some entries contain a reference to a bibliography listed on the final page. Since many of the terms defined in the book are not found in standard dance dictionaries, this source is important to the modern dance researcher. Because modern dance is so much more open to change than classical ballet, one wishes an update existed to record the changes that have taken place in the last forty years.

315. Mara, Thalia. **The Language of Ballet: An Informal Dictionary**. Brooklyn, N.Y.: Dance Horizons, 1972 (c.1966). 120p. LC 78-181477. ISBN 0-87127-037-4.

This work defines and describes French terms used for positions and movements in classical ballet. Phonetic spelling for each word helps readers pronounce terms correctly. The work is arranged alphabetically, and variations of steps are listed as subheadings under a main entry. For instance, "croise" is followed by "croise derriere," "croise devant," and other variations. Although some words are illustrated, the drawings are not as fine as those in Kersley and Sinclair (entry 312). Mara's book is a good supplement to Grant's dictionary (entry 311) and to Kersley and Sinclair.

316. Raffe, W. G., comp. **Dictionary of the Dance**. New York: A. S. Barnes, 1975. 583p. ISBN 0-498-01643-9.

Definitely the book to use for information on folk dance and social dancing, this dictionary's purpose is to define terms relating to all types of dance from over 100 countries and in all time periods. Terms defined include names of individual dances such as polonaise and waltz, but not the names of individual ballets. Raffe writes in a knowledgeable, opinionated, and humorous style. He compares the Japanese Cherry Blossom Dance to a Westerner's invitation to "come up and see my etchings." His criticism of "ice dancing" is crushing and funny. Readers may enjoy browsing in this work just to sample Raffe's prose. This is indispensable to any dance collection.

317. Wilson, G. B. L. **A Dictionary of Ballet**. 3d ed. New York: Theatre Arts, 1974. 539p. LC 73-88212. ISBN 0-87830-039-2.

Wilson concentrates on defining the terms of classical ballet, with some entries for modern dance. This wide-ranging work includes definitions for technical terms, descriptions of ballets, and short biographies of dancers, choreographers, and teachers. Entries for ballets include names of the choreographer and composer and information about opening performances. This work is similar to Koegler (entry 313) and less technical than Grant (entry 311).

Chapter 6

Biographical Sources

These books locate information about people. They include both biographical dictionaries and indexes to biographical information in periodicals.

318. Backscheider, Paula R., ed. **Restoration and Eighteenth-Century Dramatists. First Series**. (Dictionary of Literary Biography, vol. 80). Detroit: Gale Research, 1989. 397p. LC 89-1070. ISBN 0-8103-4558-7.

319. Backscheider, Paula R., ed. **Restoration and Eighteenth-Century Dramatists. Second Series**. (Dictionary of Literary Biography, vol. 84). Detroit: Gale Research, 1989. 456p. LC 89-11870. ISBN 0-8103-4562-5.

320. Backscheider, Paula R. **Restoration and Eighteenth-Century Dramatists. Third Series**. (Dictionary of Literary Biography, vol. 89). Detroit: Gale Research, 1989. 396p. LC 89-36563. ISBN 0-8103-4567-6.

In the fashion of the Gale Research Dictionary of Literary Biography series, these describe the lives and works of fifty-four playwrights who worked between 1642 and 1800. Articles are arranged roughly chronologically by the playwright's birthdate (volume 1 contains those born between 1621 and 1666; volume 2, 1670 and 1729; and volume 3, 1699 and 1762) and then alphabetically within the volume. The playwrights include major figures such as Dryden, Goldsmith, Sheridan, Wycherly, Farquhar, and Congreve. Among the women dramatists represented are Aphra Behn, Frances Sheridan, and Elizabeth Inchbald. The illustrated articles include a bibliography of plays and other work, an essay on the dramatist's life and plays, and a bibliography of criticism.

321. **Biography Index**. New York: H. W. Wilson, 1946- .
Biography Index. Database. (Wilson).
Online Services: WILSONLINE; BRS.
Online Coverage: July, 1984- . Update Frequency: Twice weekly.
CD ROM Version: WILSONDISC, SilverPlatter.
CD ROM Coverage: July, 1984- . Update Frequency: Quarterly.

Indexing biographical material from the other Wilson indexes as well as other periodicals and books, this is an excellent source in which to find information about performing artists. Because the obituaries from the *New York Times* are indexed, a library that lacks the *New York Times Index* (entry 213) should remember to look in this source. Arrangement is alphabetical by name, but an index of professions leads the reader to articles about dancers, drama critics, make-up artists, puppeteers, and even chorus girls ("Rice, Mary Alice, d. 1989, chorus girl and fashion show producer"). It is easier to use this source than to check each Wilson index separately, and multi-year cumulations add to this title's utility.

322. Bowers, Fredson, ed. **Elizabethan Dramatists**. (Dictionary of Literary Biography, vol. 62). Detroit: Gale Research, 1987. 492p. LC 87-19779. ISBN 0-8103-1740-0.

Relating the careers of twenty playwrights who wrote for the Tudor and Stuart stage, this book is part of Gale Research's Dictionary of Literary Biography series. Shakespeare dominates this volume as he does the period (87 of 387 pages are devoted to the man from Stratford-upon-Avon), but one also finds criticism of Christopher Marlowe, Thomas Kyd, Ben Jonson, and others. As usual with this series, the alphabetically arranged entries include a list of plays and other works, a critical essay, and a bibliography. Illustrations reproduce title pages, manuscript pages, and costume designs of the period. The clearly written essays can serve as beginning points for further study.

323. Bryan, George B., comp. **Stage Deaths: A Biographical Guide to International Theatrical Obituaries, 1850 to 1990**. Westport, Conn.: Greenwood, 1991. 2v. LC 91-10304. ISBN 0-313-27593-9 (set).

Bryan offers a useful guide to obituaries and biographies of both famous and obscure "theatrical artists" (introduction). He includes thousands of actors, dancers, circus performers, film stars, and theatre historians in two volumes of alphabetically arranged entries. Besides brief biographical information to identify the person, entries cite obituaries in nine newspapers including the *New York Times* and *The Times* (London) as well as book-length biographies and autobiographies. Because date and place of death are given, readers can check local newspapers for additional death notices. This set complements the *Variety* obituaries (entry 362) well because it extends further back in time and because it cites additional sources.

324. Bryan, George B., comp. **Stage Lives: A Bibliography and Index to Theatrical Biographies in English**. Westport, Conn.: Greenwood, 1985. 368p. LC 84-19833. ISBN 0-313-24577-0.

With a broader scope than the works of Moyer (entry 76), Wearing (entry 364), and the Johnsons (entry 53), Bryan's bibliography lists collections and individual biographies written in English that deal with anyone connected with theatre (including vaudeville, opera, and other performing arts) from earliest times to the present. As might be expected, most of the biographees lived in the seventeenth century or later. The geographical scope includes the Americas, Europe, Asia, and Australia. A good many of the collective biographies are eighteenth- and nineteenth-century publications. However, the 2,597 individual biographies include many more recent books. Entries are standard citations without annotations and are arranged by author. An index of names provides subject access. This well-organized work will be helpful to anyone doing biographical research in theatre.

325. Busby, Roy. **British Music Hall: An Illustrated Who's Who from 1850 to the Present Day**. Salem, N.H.: Paul Elek, 1976. 191p. LC 77-351040. ISBN 0-236-40053-3.

Described by Senelick (entry 82) as the best biographical dictionary of music hall performers to date, Busby's work profiles British, American, and Continental performers who appeared on the British stage. Thus, it includes Americans such as Harry Houdini and Sophie Tucker, who was a great favorite with English audiences. The narrative entries, arranged alphabetically, focus on the performers' careers. Most entries are short except for the most famous stars. The introduction contains a history of music halls and variety theatres. For American vaudeville see Slide (entry 358).

326. **Canada's Playwrights: A Biographical Guide**. Downsview, Ont.: CTR Publications, 1980. 191p. LC 81-134066. ISBN 0-920-644-49-X; 0-920-644-47-3 pa.

Both French-Canadian and English-Canadian playwrights find a place in this biographical dictionary put together by the publishers of *Canadian Theatre Review*. Brief biographies are accompanied by portraits and bibliographies of plays and other writings. Both well-known writers like Robertson Davies and lesser-known authors are included. Because of the book's age, readers should prefer the *Oxford Companion to Canadian Theatre* (entry 262).

327. **Contemporary Authors**. Detroit: Gale Research, 1962- . V. 1- . New Revision Series. 1981- . V. 1- . LC 62-52046. ISSN 0010-7468; New Revision Series, 0275-7176.

Since 1962, *Contemporary Authors* has provided brief biographical information on writers of all types, both established authors and newcomers, including playwrights. With more than 130 volumes in the original set and over thirty volumes in the New Revision series, this set has profiled thousands of writers. Volume 133, for example, includes an entry for Alfred Uhry, winner of the 1988 Pulitzer Prize for drama for his play *Driving Miss Daisy*. Entries include personal information, address, career highlights, awards, and a list of writings. A section called "sidelights" presents an essay on the writer, sometimes supplemented by an interview, and is followed by a list of secondary sources. The New Revision series, started in 1981, contains entries from the original set that have been substantially revised. The cumulative index covers both series.

328. **Current Biography**. New York: H. W. Wilson, 1940- . V. 1- . Monthly with annual cumulations. LC 40-27432. ISSN 0011-3344 (monthly); 0084-9499 (annual).

Beginning with its first volume in 1940, *Current Biography* has consistently profiled actors, playwrights, dancers, and other famous practitioners of the performing arts. The work fulfills very well its goal of providing "brief, objective, accurate, and well-documented biographical articles" that are easily located and accompanied by a photograph. Especially helpful are the short bibliographies that conclude each biography and a list of references at the end of each volume. Obituaries are now located at the end of the volume rather than interspersed with the alphabetically arranged entries as they originally were. The fifty year cumulative index (1940-1990) speeds the search process for older biographies.

329. Davis, Thadious M., and Trudier Harris, eds. **Afro-American Writers After 1955: Dramatists and Prose Writers**. (Dictionary of Literary Biography, vol. 38). Detroit: Gale Research, 1985. 390p. LC 85-1673. ISBN 0-8103-1716-8.

A volume of the Dictionary of Literary Biography, this book profiles thirty-five Black playwrights and novelists. Both living and dead writers are included, and there is some overlap with another work in this series, *Twentieth-Century American Dramatists* (entry 338). The alphabetically arranged entries highlight the writers' careers and lives and include bibliographies. Lorraine Hansberry and Ed Bullins are included but August Wilson, unfortunately, achieved fame too late for this volume. An appendix provides a "research list" of Black theatres and theatre organizations, giving name, founder or director's name, and address.

102 / 6—Biographical Sources

330. **Earl Blackwell's Entertainment Celebrity Register.** New York: Visible Ink Press (Gale), 1991. 610p. LC 90-48123. ISBN 0-8103-9400-6 pa.

Arranged alphabetically, short, gossipy biographies focus on the lives and careers of 500 famous people. The book includes actors who have appeared on stage as well as in films. Most of this information can be found in *Variety's Who's Who in Show Business* (entry 332) or *Current Biography* (entry 328).

331. Highfill, Philip H., Kalman A. Burnim, and Edward A. Langhans. **A Biographical Dictionary of Actors, Actresses, Musicians, Dancers, Managers & Other Stage Personnel in London, 1660-1800.** Carbondale: Southern Illinois University Press, 1973- . Vols. 1-16. LC 71-157068. ISBN v. 1: 0-8093-0517-8; v. 2: 0-8093-0518-6; v. 3: 0-8093-0692-1; v. 4: 0-8093-0693-X; v. 5: 0-8093-0832-0; v. 6: 0-8093-0833-9; v. 7: 0-8093-0918-1; v. 8: 0-8093-0919-X; v. 9: 0-8093-1129-1; v. 10: 0-8093-1130-5; v. 11: 0-8093-1280-8; v. 12: 0-8093-1281-6; v. 13: 0-8093-1525-4; v. 14: 0-8093-1526-2; v. 15: 0-8093-1802-4; v. 16: 0-8093-1803-2.

The purpose of this monumental undertaking is to offer brief biographies of all performers in theatres and other places of entertainment in London between 1660 and 1800. Relying on original sources as much as possible the authors will have produced biographies of more than 8,500 performers when the set is completed. Information about each person varies, of course, with the fame of the subject and the amount of material that can be verified. Frances Abington, the actress who provided the model for Lady Teazle in Sheridan's *The School for Scandal*, merits eight pages while "Mr. Powell" is represented by one sentence: "A Mr. Powell acted the Footman in *The Country Girl* at the Haymarket Theatre on 18 September 1797." The most complete entries present both personal and career information as well as interesting anecdotes if they can be verified. An especially pleasing aspect is the large number of portraits, and the authors also list locations of all known portraits of each subject. This scholarly and readable work is vital to anyone researching Restoration or eighteenth-century English theatre.

332. Kaplan, Mike, ed. **Variety's Who's Who in Show Business.** rev. ed. New York: R. R. Bowker, 1989. 412p. LC 89-178637. ISBN 0-8352-2665-4.

The third edition of *Variety's* biographical dictionary covers 6,500 entertainers, either alive or very recently dead (persons who died before June 30, 1985 are not included). Arranged alphabetically by name, the short entries list standard "Who's Who" type information. One can always quibble about selection in this type of book (why include Daniel Barenboim but not Claudio Abbado? Why Denholm Elliott but not Leo Kern?), but generally this is a useful source for basic information on people connected with show business. For those who have died, see *Variety Obituaries 1905-1986* (entry 362).

333. Kaye, Phyllis Johnson. **American/Soviet Playwrights Directory.** Waterford, Conn.: O'Neill Theater Center, 1988. 144p. LC 88-17819. ISBN 0-96051601-8.

The result of a collaboration between the Eugene O'Neill Theater Center and the former USSR copyright agency, this little book provides basic information in English about the Soviet Union's leading playwrights and in Russian about major American dramatists. Close to 100 writers from each country are profiled, each with a photograph. Lacking a statement of scope, the reader can infer that most of these people worked in the twentieth century. Although most were living when the book was published, some, such as Eugene O'Neill, were dead. The alphabetical entries in each of the book's two parts briefly describe the writer's career and list plays, often with the year and theatre of first performance. Some plays have short synopses given. With the break up of the Soviet Union, it is interesting to note that many of the "Russian" playwrights were born in one of the other republics. The book's section on American playwrights, besides requiring a knowledge of Russian, contains material easily found in other works such as the *Oxford Companion to American Theatre* (entry 264).

334. Kirkpatrick, D. L., ed. **Contemporary Dramatists**. 4th ed. Chicago: St. James Press, 1988. 785p. LC 88-182947. ISBN 0-912289-62-7.

The bulk of this book is devoted to critical analyses of more than 300 living dramatists and their work. Each entry includes a biography, a signed critical essay, and primary and secondary bibliographies. Some entries are amplified with comments from the playwright. If a library or archive holds a playwright's papers, it is noted. The contributors are a combination of professional writers and academics, and their essays exhibit a personal style that makes this book an interesting read. Supplements contain brief biographical listings for writers who work exclusively in films or television; for musical librettists; and for theatre companies that sometimes compose their own works (such as the San Francisco Mime Troupe or New York's Mabou Mines). A special supplement treats seven playwrights who are dead "but whose reputations are essentially contemporary" (Editor's Note) including Lorraine Hansberry, William Inge, and Joe Orton. A play title index allows one to find information about its author. The high quality of the critical essays makes this source an important one.

335. Kolin, Philip C., ed. **American Playwrights Since 1945: A Guide to Scholarship, Criticism, and Performance**. Westport, Conn.: Greenwood, 1989. 595p. LC 88-10245. ISBN 0-313-25543-1.

The forty American dramatists profiled in this bio-bibliography achieved fame after World War II. The contributors, mostly academics working in English or theatre departments, have written assessments of the playwright's work and bibliographic essays stressing the important sources for analyzing that work. Bibliographies of the dramatist's plays and of secondary sources accompany the essays. The alphabetically arranged chapters include essays on relative newcomers Beth Henley, August Wilson, and Wendy Wasserstein as well as older playwrights such as Robert Lowell, Arthur Miller, and Tennessee Williams. A personal name index and a play and screenplay title index complete the volume. This is a good source to consult when looking for both biographical and bibliographic information about a recent American playwright.

336. Lacy, Robin Thurlow. **A Biographical Dictionary of Scenographers: 500 B.C. to 1900 A.D.** Westport, Conn.: Greenwood, 1990. 762p. LC 90-14004. ISBN 0-313-27429-0.

Lacy, formerly professor of theatre and head of the theatre production design program at Ohio University, has based his book on forty years of work in American and European archives, checking playbills and theatre programs as well as other materials. He attempts to list all known scenographers who flourished from antiquity to 1900. Arranged alphabetically by name, the entries list name, dates the scenographer flourished, theatre(s) and location(s) where he worked, career information, and codes that represent sources in the bibliography at the end of the book. These 435 sources are composed of books, journal articles, and library collections that contain material on one or more of the subjects. The appendix contains a list of names arranged by country and time period. Readers should

104 / 6—Biographical Sources

note that this work deals only with European and American scenographers. Bobbi Owen profiles modern American scenographers in her *Scenic Design on Broadway; Designers and Their Credits, 1915-1990* (entry 351), but she does not list bibliographic references for many of the designers and her general bibliography is only two pages long.

337. Lyman, Darryl. **Great Jews on Stage and Screen**. Middle Village, N.Y.: Jonathan David, 1987. 279p. LC 87-4214. ISBN 0-8246-0328-1.

Lyman provides biographical sketches of 100 famous Jews both living and dead who have acted in theatre or films. The book also contains brief biographical information about 200 lesser-known Jewish actors, musicians, and entertainers. Both sections are arranged alphabetically. Lyman follows Jewish law in determining who is Jewish, that is, anyone born of a Jewish mother or converted to the faith. For that reason, biographies of converts Elizabeth Taylor and Sammy Davis, Jr. are found here as well as those of Barbra Streisand and Zero Mostel. Although not all biographees are Americans, most have worked in American theatre or films. The informally written sketches are noncritical and are accompanied by a photograph and a list of selected performances. This work is a convenient supplement to *Current Biography* (entry 328) and *Contemporary Theatre, Film, and Television* (entry 348) if one is interested specifically in Jewish actors. Lyman has written another book, The J*ewish Comedy Catalog* (Middle Village, N.Y.: Jonathan David, 1989), which contains much of the same material as this title. Because it does not include any serious actors, however, it is not as useful as *Great Jews on Stage and Screen*.

338. MacNicholas, John, ed. **Twentieth-Century American Dramatists**. (Dictionary of Literary Biography, vol. 7). Detroit: Gale Research, 1981. 2v. LC 81-564. ISBN 0-8103-0928-9 (set).

Starting with David Belasco, whose plays *Madame Butterfly* and *The Girl of the Golden West* inspired two of Puccini's operas, and ending with David Mamet, Sam Shepard, and others working today, this title describes the lives and work of seventy-nine American playwrights. All biographees have created major works during the twentieth century. The alphabetically arranged entries center around long essays on the writers' lives and careers. Bibliographies of the authors' works and of criticism are included along with many illustrations. A useful appendix profiles major regional theatres. Part of Gale's Dictionary of Literary Biography, this work includes seven playwrights who are also treated in another volume in the series, *Afro-American Writers After 1955: Dramatists and Prose Writers* (entry 329). Because each volume employs different critics, however, readers may want to check both titles. See also Kolin's *American Playwrights Since 1945* (entry 335).

339. Mapp, Edward. **Directory of Blacks in the Performing Arts**. 2d ed. Metuchen, N.J.: Scarecrow, 1990. 594p. LC 89-30477. ISBN 0-8108-2222-9.

Superseding the first edition, this new volume now contains information on 1,100 African-American performers, both living and dead. The alphabetically arranged entries include basic factual information such as education, theatre credits, honors received, and family relationships to other Black performers. A bibliography and an index by occupation complete the book. Mapp has included both famous and obscure actors, choreographers, producers, and critics. This work is essential for locating basic facts about Blacks in the theatre.

Biographical Sources / 105

340. Martin, Linda, and Kerry Segrave. **Women in Comedy**. Secaucus, N.J.: Citadel Press, 1986. 449p. LC 86-23206. ISBN 0-8065-1000-5.

Like Unterbrink (entry 361) Martin and Segrave have written short biographies of comediennes and comic actresses who performed in the United State from around 1860 to 1985. The authors cover the lives and careers of sixty-nine "comic superstars" using the information to demonstrate the discrimination faced by women in the theatre. For instance, Gracie Allen, Judy Holliday, and others suffered from being identified with their "dumb blond" stage personalities. Each fairly long article is written in an informal style and discusses both the woman's career and her personal life. This book is arranged chronologically with a bibliography. Unfortunately, it lacks an index.

341. McGill, Raymond D., ed. **Notable Names in the American Theatre**. Clifton, N.J.: James T. White; Distr., Gale, 1976. 1,250p. LC 76-27356. ISBN 0-88371-018-8.

Although this book and its predecessor, Rigdon's *Biographical Encyclopaedia and Who's Who of the American Theatre*, were once important sources for biographical information about theatre personalities, they have been largely superseded by newer works including *Contemporary Theatre, Film, and Television* (entry 348). This title can be used to find information on people working in theatrical professions in the mid-1970s. The alphabetically arranged entries provide credits for work on stage and in all media as well as personal information. The volume also contains lists of New York play productions, premieres of American plays, histories of theatre companies, and other miscellaneous information. Alas, most of it is too old to be useful to anyone other than the theatre historian.

342. McNeil, Barbara, and Miranda C. Herbert, eds. **Performing Arts Biography Master Index**. 2d ed. (Gale Biographical Index series, no. 5). Detroit: Gale Research, 1981. 701p. LC 81-20145. ISBN 0-8103-1097-X.

A subset of Gale's *Biographical and Genealogical Master Index*, this work provides 270,000 citations to biographical articles in 110 books. Arranged alphabetically by name, the citations list name, dates (if available), and abbreviations for sources that contain biographical information. Persons included are of all nationalities and time periods. Because names are not standardized, the reader should check all variations to find every source. If one's library owns most of the books indexed, this is a useful source. See also Wearing's *American and British Theatrical Biography: A Dictionary* (entry 364).

343. Mikotowicz, Thomas J., ed. **Theatrical Designers: An International Biographical Dictionary**. Westport, Conn.: Greenwood, 1992. 365p. LC 91-28086. ISBN 0-313-26270-5.

In an ambitious undertaking, Mikotowicz and his fellow contributors provide information on 270 "set, costume, and lighting designers of drama, opera, dance, and film productions, as well as theatre architects and theoreticians" (preface). Covering the years 84 B.C. to 1957, the work overlaps Lacy (entry 336) who gives basic information on scenographers dating from 500 B.C. to 1900 and Owen (entries 349, 350, and 351) who covers the period after 1915. Chosen for their significance and for the availability of research materials, most of the designers described in this book are Americans or Western Europeans. In order by designer's name, entries provide basic biographical information and an essay on the designer's career. Lists of important productions and of awards are often accompanied by a short bibliography. Appendices present designers in chronological order and by country of birth. Mikotowicz lists important periodicals and theatre collections where readers could expect to find more information, and provides an annotated bibliography on theatre design. The index contains names of plays and designers. Mikotowicz complements Owen, who confines herself to designers working on Broadway, and Lacy, whose coverage stops at 1900.

344. Morley, Sheridan. **The Great Stage Stars: Distinguished Theatrical Careers of the Past and Present**. New York: Facts on File, 1986. 425p. LC 85-27548. ISBN 0-8160-1401-9.

Morley has chosen 200 actors whom he asserts could fill a theatre on the basis of their name alone, even if the play and playwright were unknowns. His choices mostly come from the nineteenth- and twentieth-century British and American stage, although the earliest noted is Edward Alleyn, the famous Elizabethan actor. Arranged alphabetically the entries are factual, uncritical, narrative biographies. Because most of the subjects can be found in other biographical sources, this is a supplementary work.

345. Mullin, Donald, comp. and ed. **Victorian Actors and Actresses in Review: A Dictionary of Contemporary Views of Representative British and American Actors and Actresses, 1837-1901**. Westport, Conn.: Greenwood, 1983. 571p. LC 83-1407. ISBN 0-313-23316-0.

Mullin has collected excerpts of Victorian criticism of 234 actors and actresses of the period. So that the reader can consider the leading players in relation to their supporting actors, Mullin includes reviews of both stars and unknowns. For both, he selects criticism of the actors' abilities in general and criticism of their performance of specific roles. The critics whose writings are quoted include George Bernard Shaw, Otis Skinner, and William Winter, the "doyen of New York theatre critics." The entries are arranged alphabetically and include the actor's dates and nationality. Excerpts are then arranged chronologically. Readers will find full bibliographic information for each citation in the bibliography. A subject index completes the volume. For American actors see also Young (entry 371).

346. **New York Times Biographical File**. The *New York Times* Company, June, 1980- . Biweekly database from Mead Data Central.

This file, accessible on Mead Data Central's Nexis service, provides full-text biographical stories from the final New York City edition of the *New York Times* beginning June 1980. About fifty articles per week are selected from the newspaper and added to the file. Included are profiles, interviews, and obituaries for many theatre personalities. Two other files in Nexis offer more limited coverage of theatre people. They are the *Los Angeles Times Biographical Stories* (beginning January 1990) and the *Washington Post Biographical Stories* (beginning January 1989). Because New York is still the center of American theatre life and because the *New York Times Biographical File* is much larger, it should be consulted first.

347. Nungezer, Edwin. **A Dictionary of Actors and Other Persons Associated with the Public Representation of Plays in England before 1642**. New Haven: Yale University Press, 1929. Reprinted. New York: Greenwood, 1968. 437p. LC 68-57633.

Citing from an extensive list of sources, Nungezer writes biographies of people associated with the theatre in England before the year 1642. Arranged alphabetically by name, most of the entries are for actors from the Elizabethan and Stuart periods. Nungezer includes the famous such as Richard Burbage and Edward Alleyn, the greatest actors of the Tudor stage, as well as the many obscure players mentioned in court records. Theatre owners and managers find their place here as well, including the famous diarist and theatre proprietor Philip Henslowe. See Highfill and others (entry 331) for biographies of actors working in London between 1660 and 1800. (English theatres were closed during Cromwell's rule between 1642 and 1660.)

348. O'Donnell, Monica M., ed. **Contemporary Theatre, Film, and Television**. Detroit: Gale Research, 1984- . 1- . Annual. LC 84-649371. ISSN 0749-064X.

After the publisher Gale Research bought *Who's Who in the Theatre* and published the seventeenth edition (1981), it decided to transform the series into a format similar to its *Contemporary Authors* (entry 327). Thus, this title is a series of volumes that constantly add biographies of new performers and revise older biographies as necessary. Gale also expanded the work's scope to include film and television actors, directors, and so forth. Each volume contains a cumulative index to all previous volumes in addition to *Who Was Who in the Theatre* (entry 368) and all seventeen editions of *Who's Who in the Theatre* (entry 370). The alphabetically arranged entries supply date of birth, personal and career information, a record of achievements, sources of additional information, and address. Photographs accompany some entries. While most of the biographees are alive and active in show business, Gale's new format makes it possible to create an entry for the dead. (For example, Lucille Ball and Laurence Olivier are profiled in volume 8, 1990.) This is an important source for current information about theatre people.

349. Owen, Bobbi. **Costume Design on Broadway: Designers and Their Credits, 1915-1985**. (Bibliographies and Indexes in the Performing Arts, no. 5). Westport, Conn.: Greenwood, 1987. 254p. LC 87-7515. ISBN 0-313-25524-5.

Contending that costume design has become important only in the twentieth century, Owen has profiled 1,021 costume designers who worked on Broadway between 1915 and 1985. In addition, she has chosen 100 costume renderings to include as examples of design through those seventy years. The entries, arranged by name, feature a paragraph about the designer and a list of credits. Appendices list winners of various costume awards including the Tony awards for costume design. This well-researched title spotlights a group of people whose work adds a great deal to the success of Broadway productions. Owen has also produced books on lighting and scenic designers (entries 350, 351), and a considerable amount of overlapping information exists within these titles.

350. Owen, Bobbi. **Lighting Design on Broadway: Designers and Their Credits, 1915-1990**. (Bibliographies and Indexes in the Performing Arts, no. 11). Westport, Conn.: Greenwood, 1991. 159p. LC 91-24007. ISBN 0-313-26533-X.

Lighting design is a relatively new profession and a craft that has changed rapidly because of technological innovations. Owen examined thousands of playbills and found that even as late as the 1943-1944 theatre season only 25 percent of Broadway productions listed a lighting director in their programs. Only since the 1960s have credits for lighting designers become common. Owen describes the careers of about 400 artists including Jennifer Tipton, Theron Musser, and Raoul Pene Du Bois. Biographical details are followed by lists of credits for lighting, scenery, and costumes. Readers should note that credits for designers who also work in scenery or costumes are exactly the same in this

108 / 6—Biographical Sources

book and in Owen's other titles (entries 349, 351). Lists of Tony and other award winners for lighting design and an index by play title complete this book.

351. Owen, Bobbi. **Scenic Design on Broadway: Designers and Their Credits, 1915-1990**. (Bibliographies and Indexes in the Performing Arts, no. 10). Westport, Conn.: Greenwood, 1991. 286p. LC 91-25254. ISBN 0-313-26534-9.

Owen here turns to scenic designers, those responsible for the stage scenery and the general "look" of the play. She provides short biographies of more than 1,000 designers who have worked on Broadway since 1915 and lists their credits for scenic design followed by credits for costume and lighting designs, if any. Note that the entries in this book and in Owen's *Lighting Design on Broadway* are exactly the same for individuals who have worked in both stage and lighting design. It is not necessary to check both volumes. Appendices list winners of design awards and a few books on stage design. The index of plays helps those who wish to know the name of a particular show's designer. Because Owen begins with 1915, readers should consult Lacy (entry 336) for information about scenographers who worked before 1900.

352. Pascoe, Charles Eyre, ed. **The Dramatic List: A Record of the Performances of Living Actors and Actresses of the British Stage**. 2d ed., rev. and enl. London: Bogue, 1880. Reprint. Bronx, NY: B. Blom, 1969. 432p. LC 70-91911.

This work is still a standard source of information about nineteenth-century British actors. It contains biographies of about 300 performers living in Britain and working on the British stage in 1879. Included are critical comments extracted and summarized from contemporary newspapers and periodicals. The work is arranged alphabetically with an appendix for recently deceased actors and an index of names. Readers who need biographical information on British actors prior to 1800 should consult Highfill and others (entry 331) or Nungezer (entry 347). Be aware that this book has been reprinted many times, sometimes with slightly different titles. *American Reference Books Annual 1972*, entry 1147, contains a history of the book's many reprintings.

353. Perry, Jeb H., comp. **Variety Obits: An Index to Obituaries in Variety (1905-1978)**. Metuchen, N.J.: Scarecrow, 1980. 311p. LC 80-10424. ISBN 0-8108-1289-4.

Until *Variety* published its set of obituaries (entry 362) researchers had to use Perry's index to locate death notices in the entertainment industry's weekly newspaper. More selective in its coverage, Perry does not index obituaries of people who were dancers, musicians, or performers in burlesque, cabaret, the circus, nightclubs, or carnivals. Nor does he include citations for people in the business and financial side of the industry. Perry indexes professional names only, and he indexes only the obituary columns, not related news stories. The alphabetical entries do give date of death (not given in the index of the *Variety* set), date and page of *Variety* obituary, and age at death. Readers should prefer the *Variety* set if available, not only for convenience, but also for its superior indexing.

354. Peterson, Bernard L., Jr. **Contemporary Black American Playwrights and Their Plays: A Biographical Directory and Dramatic Index**. Westport, Conn.: Greenwood, 1988. 625p. LC 87-17814. ISBN 0-313-25190-8.

Although flawed by the author's difficulties in obtaining information, Peterson's bio-bibliography remains the best source currently available on African-American playwrights and their works. Peterson covers Black playwrights, either American citizens or

U.S. residents, who were living in 1950 or have been born since then. Entries concentrate on both the playwright's life and work. Plots of major plays are summarized, and other plays are listed with their production histories. The book's strength is the large number of authors it describes (more than 700). Its weakness is its reliance on printed sources for information. Peterson points out in his preface that 60 percent of the entries were compiled from existing material. One playwright has not lived at the address given for at least fifteen years. The biographical information can be used only if it is checked. The bibliographies are more reliable but not as current as they should be. For these reasons Peterson's book should be used, but with caution.

355. Peterson, Bernard L., Jr. **Early Black American Playwrights and Dramatic Writers: A Biographical Directory and Catalog of Plays, Films, and Broadcasting Scripts**. Westport, Conn.: Greenwood, 1990. 298p. LC 90-2961. ISBN 0-313-26621-2.

To complement his work on modern Black playwrights (entry 354), Peterson examines the lives and work of 218 early writers. These playwrights wrote at least one play before 1950, were Black or partly Black, and were American citizens or longtime residents of the United States. The main directory includes 136 writers while two appendices include librettists of musicals and lesser-known writers. Within each section Peterson lists playwrights alphabetically. Entries follow a common pattern. Following a biographical essay Peterson lists dramatic works and a short bibliography of other biographical materials. A chronology of plays by writers profiled in this volume and a bibliography on early Black theatre add to the book's usefulness. Besides play title and general subject indexes the author includes an index of Black American theatre organizations. Peterson's book should be especially helpful in finding information about important but little-known writers such as Randolph Edmonds, a prolific playwright and a founder of the National Association of Dramatic and Speech Arts.

356. Poorman, Susan, comp. **The Neal-Schuman Index to Performing and Creative Artists in Collective Biographies**. New York: Neal-Schuman, 1991. 155p. LC 91-2116. ISBN 1-55570-056-X.

Poorman indexes biographies of artists found in 127 collective biographies published for children and young adults between 1970 and 1989. Entries, arranged by the artist's professional name, list date of birth (and death if appropriate), country of birth and book(s) in which biographical material appears. Poorman indicates the presence of illustrations and the relative length of each biography, perhaps in response to class assignments that insist on articles of so many pages and illustrated homework. Many, although not all, of the 1,291 people listed are performing artists. They can be located through the index of professions. Other indexes help the reader find women artists and artists by country of origin. By far the greatest number are Americans. A bibliography provides complete citations for all indexed books and could be used as a selection guide by school and public libraries.

357. Robinson, Alice M., Vera Mowry Roberts, and Milly S. Barranger, eds. **Notable Women in the American Theatre: A Biographical Dictionary**. New York: Greenwood, 1989. 993p. LC 89-17065. ISBN 0-313-27217-4.

Designed to correct the historical record and show that women have made significant contributions to the American stage throughout its history, this book contains over 300 biographies of American women involved in the theatre. The biographees were chosen for their achievements, influence, or innovative work in any aspect of theatrical activity, including regional theatre, children's theatre, and theatre education. Some examples of the book's range are Edna Ferber, playwright; Patricia McIlrath, founder of the Missouri Repertory Theatre; and Jennifer Tipton, lighting designer. Written by many contributors, the signed biographical sketches describe the subject's life and career. Each is followed by a bibliographic essay listing the most important sources for the study of the person. The articles are arranged alphabetically by name with an index by place of birth, one by profession, and a general subject index. Well researched and written, this book is an excellent source for information about women in the American theatre.

358. Slide, Anthony. **The Vaudevillians: A Dictionary of Vaudeville Performers**. Westport, Conn.: Arlington House, 1981. 172p. LC 81-3565. ISBN 0-87000-492-1.

Anthony Slide has written extensively on the early days of American cinema. Here he shifts his focus to take a lighthearted look at the personalities of American vaudeville. Slide presents short biographies of 172 performers, both "headliners" and minor acts. The latter include the singing Cherry Sisters, "an act which was so bad it was good," and Power's Dancing Elephants. The stars of vaudeville's later years are better known even today because many of them made the transition to radio, film, and even television: the Marx Brothers, Burns and Allen, and Abbott and Costello, for instance. Relatively unknown today is its biggest female star "for almost vaudeville's entire existence," the temperamental Eva Tanguay. She and all the rest are profiled by Slide in informal, anecdotal articles. He includes bibliographical references if available, and portraits acccompany most articles. See also Busby's work on English music halls (entry 325), as many entertainers worked on both sides of the Atlantic.

359. Smith, Ronald L. **The Stars of Stand-up Comedy: A Biographical Encyclopedia**. New York: Garland, 1986. 227p. LC 84-48408. ISBN 0-8240-8803-4.

What do Mark Russell, Red Skelton, and Anna Russell have in common? They are among the 101 comedians selected by Ron Smith for this book. Without trying to be comprehensive, Smith has chosen people who are representative of different types of comedy and who are, in his view, unique, funny, famous, or influential. Both living and dead comics are included. Based on interviews and secondary sources, the biographies are uncritical, informal narratives punctuated with quotations from their subjects. Entries are arranged alphabetically, and there is no index.

360. **20th Century Drama**. (St. James Reference Guide to English Literature). Chicago: St. James Press, 1985. 316p. ISBN 0-912289-25-2.

For each of about 100 playwrights, this book provides a short biography, a bibliography, and a signed critical essay focusing on the playwright's work. The bibliography cites both the author's work, including nondramatic writings, and criticism. Essays rarely exceed one and one-half pages. The playwrights covered here are American, British, Irish, and South African. A place to find a small amount of information quickly, the work does not provide in-depth coverage of dramatists.

361. Unterbrink, Mary. **Funny Women: American Comediennes, 1860-1985**. Jefferson, N.C.: McFarland, 1987. 267p. LC 85-43595. ISBN 0-89950-226-1.

This book and another, *Women in Comedy* (entry 340), provide an object lesson in how two different interpretations can be given to the same material. Both books cover

Biographical Sources / 111

almost exactly the same group of women, comediennes and comic actresses who worked on the American stage from the mid-nineteenth century through the mid-1980s. Both present a short biography of each subject, and both provide bibliographic references. Unterbrink writes in an uncritical style, providing some personal information and much career information about her subjects. She uses many quotations from published interviews to illustrate the lives of many of these women. The authors of *Women in Comedy*, writing from a feminist viewpoint, use their biographies to demonstrate the discrimination faced by many of these women during their careers. Unterbrink includes more women comics who were working in the 1980s than does *Women in Comedy*. Her book is arranged chronologically with a bibliography and an index.

362. **Variety Obituaries 1905-** . New York: Garland, 1988- . LC 87-25931.

A thorough search of 750,000 pages of *Variety* yielded 90,000 obituaries and related articles about theatrical and show business personalities. Because of its extensive system of "stringers" *Variety* published death notices for actors and performers located all over the United States, not just in New York. This set reprints the actual obituaries and articles in chronological order. Volume 11 constitutes the index, which is arranged alphabetically by name with the date of the *Variety* issue carrying the obituary. Note that the date is not the death date. A great deal of care went into the index, which makes it easy to use. Alternate names are listed in full, and publication dates are listed under each name. Subentries for relatives appear (for example "Cole Porter - mother"), and relatives are also listed under their own names if known. (In the early years the newspaper did not always print the actual name of the relative in the obituary.) The index also lists premature obituaries and retractions. Seventy prominent show business persons who did not receive *Variety* obituaries are also indexed with "No *Variety* obituary" and year of death. The index helps make this work essential for research in American theatrical history.

363. Vinson, James, ed. **Great Writers of the English Language: Dramatists**. Associate ed. D. L. Kirkpatrick. New York: St. Martin's Press, 1979. 648p. LC 78-78303. ISBN 0-312-34570-4.

Based on the recommendations of a board of advisors, the editors chose 230 English-language dramatists to profile. Entries, in alphabetical order, feature a short biography, a complete list of published works, a selected list of bibliographies and of critical works, and a signed critical essay. The essays concentrate on dramatic criticism rather than considering the theatrical aspects of a writer's work. This work supplements the drama volumes of the Dictionary of Literary Biography (see entries 318, 319, 320, 322, 329, 338, 365, 366).

364. Wearing, J. P. **American and British Theatrical Biography: A Directory**. Metuchen, N.J.: Scarecrow, 1979. 1,007p. LC 78-31162. ISBN 0-8108-1201-0.

Theatre historian Wearing has produced an index to 171 sources that contain biographical information about performers in British and American theatre. For this work theatre is used broadly to mean vaudeville, ballet, and circus as well as the legitimate stage. Further, Wearing includes costumers, directors, playwrights, and critics as well as actors in his compilation. Entries are arranged alphabetically by name with cross-references from stage names, pseudonyms, and women's maiden or married names. They contain birth (and death) dates, nationality, occupation, and codes to sources containing biographical information. Indexed sources include long runs of *The Best Plays* (entry 375) and *Who's Who in the Theatre* (entry 370). Wearing also indexes standard sources such as the *Dictionary of American Biography* and *Current Biography* (entry 328). A good time-saver, this work can be used with the *Performing Arts Biography Master Index* (entry 342).

365. Weintraub, Stanley, ed. **British Dramatists Since World War II.** (Dictionary of Literary Biography, vol. 13). Detroit: Gale Research, 1982. 2v. LC 82-15724. ISBN 0-8103-0936-X (set).

This work profiles sixty-nine British dramatists whose careers were made after World War II. Each article's critical essay emphasizes the playwright's work and its critical reception. Details of the writer's life are included as well as portraits and bibliographies. Appendices present information on postwar theatre companies and on the dismantling of the British stage censorship system. Part of the Dictionary of Literary Biography, this work provides a useful beginning for the study of post-war British theatre.

366. Weintraub, Stanley, ed. **Modern British Dramatists, 1900-1945.** (Dictionary of Literary Biography, vol. 10; A Bruccoli Clark Book). Detroit: Gale Research, 1982. 2v. LC 81-19234. ISBN 0-8103-0937-8 (set).

Part of the Dictionary of Literary Biography series (Gale Research), this set presents essays on the lives and work of seventy-two British playwrights working between 1900 and 1945. The articles also include bibliographies and portraits. Among the biographees are the famous (Barrie, Coward, Shaw, Yeats, Wilde), those whose reputations have faded with time (Arthur Pinero, Frederick Lonsdale, Clemence Dane), and those who are usually associated with other genres (A. A. Milne, Dorothy L. Sayers). This work also contains interesting essays on theatre during the two world wars and on censorship and the Lord Chamberlain's office. Together with the biographies, they present a clear picture of British drama during the first part of the twentieth century.

367. Wemyss, Francis Courtney. **Wemyss' Chronology of the American Stage from 1752 to 1852.** New York: William Taylor, 1852. 191p.

An early attempt at a biographical dictionary of actors, Wemyss's work is a group of brief sketches of thespians who acted in American productions between 1752 and 1852. Information in the entries, which are in rough alphabetical order, should be checked in other sources if possible. Wemyss did not indicate his sources of information and may not be totally reliable. The book also contains a suspect list of "all" theatres in the United States, a list of playhouses destroyed by fire, and a list of theatre managers, 1752-1852.

368. **Who Was Who in the Theatre: 1912-1976: A Biographical Dictionary of Actors, Actresses, Directors, Playwrights, and Producers of the English-Speaking Theatre.** (Gale Composite Biographical Dictionary Series, no. 3; An Omnigraphics Book). Detroit: Gale Research, 1978. 4v. LC 78-9634. ISBN 0-8103-0406-6.

This compilation of 4,100 short entries represents theatre people dropped from the first fifteen editions of *Who's Who in the Theatre* (entry 370) because of death or inactivity in their profession. Death dates have been added when available for all who died before 1977. Not only actors but also dramatists, critics, managers, and other theatrical types will be found in these pages. Entries emphasize careers, especially roles played and plays produced or directed. The subjects of most of the profiles worked in the British or American theatres with a sprinkling from Ireland, Australia, and New Zealand. For current

Biographical Sources / 113

biographies of living actors, see the seventeenth and last edition of *Who's Who in the Theatre* and its successor, *Contemporary Theatre, Film and Television* (entry 348).

369. **Who's Who in Entertainment.** Wilmette, Ill.: Marquis Who's Who, 1988- . 1- . LC 89-25121.

Issued periodically, the latest edition of this work was published in 1992. It uses a format similar to another Marquis publication, *Who's Who in America*, to provide short biographies of 17,000 North Americans who work in the entertainment business: music, theatre, motion pictures, dance, broadcast media, puppetry, clowning, and other performing arts. Inclusion is based on one's importance as determined by the editors. About one-fourth of the people listed here live in the two entertainment capitals of the United States, New York and Los Angeles. Alphabetical entries briefly list one's occupation; parents, spouse, and children; education; career and writings; civic, military, and political activities; awards; memberships in clubs, lodges, and organizations; religion; and home and office addresses. Although the most famous performing artists can be found in *Who's Who in America*, this specialized work covers the less famous.

370. **Who's Who in the Theatre.** 1-17th eds. London: Pitman; Detroit, Gale Research, 1912-1981. LC 12-22402.

All editions of this classic reference book are still useful for historical purposes. The last edition not only includes biographical information for 2,400 people connected with the English-speaking stage in the late 1970s but also reprints playbills for plays produced in London and New York, Stratford-upon-Avon, and Stratford, Ontario, between 1976 and 1979. Starting with the fourth edition, earlier editions also contain playbill information, making them valuable as well. Biographical information is the type one finds in *Who's Who*. Check *Who Was Who in the Theatre: 1912-1976* (entry 368) for persons removed from editions 1-15 because of death or inactivity in the theatre. For more recent information consult *Contemporary Theatre, Film, and Television* (entry 348), which is this work's successor.

371. Young, William C. **Famous Actors & Actresses on the American Stage: Documents of American Theater History.** New York: R. R. Bowker, 1975. 2v. LC 75-8741. ISBN 0-8352-0821-4.

Young's purpose is to present information about 225 American actors, mostly from the eighteenth and nineteenth centuries. He uses excerpts from articles, interviews, and reviews published at the time the actor was working to present both the actor's views on the profession and the critical reception of his or her work. Young chose the 225 biographees based on their importance in American theatre history or for their colorful life stories. Chapters are arranged alphabetically by name, and excerpts are presented with citations at the end of each chapter. Unfortunately, the excerpts leave the reader dissatisfied, and the number of excerpts is necessarily small. Thus, the book is useful only as a beginning point. Young includes a general index and a chronological index as well as a bibliography at the end of the volume. For nineteenth-century actors see also Mullin's *Victorian Actors and Actresses in Review* (entry 345).

Dance Biographies

372. Cohen-Stratyner, Barbara Naomi. **Biographical Dictionary of Dance**. (A Dance Horizons Book). New York: Schirmer Books/Macmillan, 1982. 970p. LC 81-86153. ISBN 0-02-870260-3.

A comprehensive biographical work, this book supplies information for 2,900 people important to dance history during the past 400 years in Europe and the Americas. All types of dance and all occupations associated with dance fall within Cohen-Stratyner's scope. The reader will find a biography of impresario Sol Hurok here as well as those of dancers, choreographers, and set designers. The biographies emphasize professional achievements, and some have bibliographic references. Articles for choreographers list all known works. The author has tried to verify all facts in three independent sources and has omitted questionable or unverified information. She often adds her own evaluation of an individual's influence or importance. The book's only disappointment is its lack of portraits.

373. McDonagh, Don. **The Complete Guide to Modern Dance**. Garden City, N.Y.: Doubleday, 1976. 534p. LC 75-21235. ISBN 0-385-05055-0.

McDonagh's book is a welcome source on modern dance. He profiles 116 modern dance choreographers, primarily Americans. He ranges from the earliest modernists, Maud Allan and Isadora Duncan to those like Twyla Tharp who made their reputations in the 1970s. The biographies are arranged in rough chronological order with an index, a chronology of modern dance, and a bibliography appended. The end papers illustrate modern dance "choreographic families" helping the reader understand influences of older choreographers on younger ones. Each short biography is followed by descriptions and analyses of major works and a chronology of the person's works. This is an important source for modern dance through the early 1970s. Readers looking for information about more recent choreographers should check *The Dance Handbook* (entry 478).

Chapter 7

Handbooks and Yearbooks

Compilations of information on a subject, handbooks and their cousins, yearbooks, contribute the broadest range of materials in this book. Included are annuals that discuss theatre and dance seasons, such as the *British Theatre Yearbook* (entry 419); practical handbooks including those on set construction, costume making, and stage makeup; and works demonstrating basic steps and movements in ballet.

374. American Theatre Planning Board. **Theatre Check List: A Guide to the Planning and Construction of Proscenium and Open Stage Theatres**. Middleton, Conn.: Wesleyan University Press, 1969. 72p. LC 69-19619.

The American Theatre Planning Board, "a committee of theatre specialists," designed this work to guide new theatre builders through the essential steps of the planning process. The book raises questions that must be answered satisfactorily if the new theatre is to succeed both as a performance space and as a workplace for actors and crew. A preliminary chapter presents illustrations and plans of several successful buildings and lists general points to consider in the early planning period. The chapters that follow consist of checklists, one for theatres with proscenium stages and the other for those with open stages. A final section deals with topics applicable to both types of buildings. Line drawings and photographs illustrate the prose, and an index helps locate specific subjects. Theatre builders will find this guide necessary but not sufficient for today's requirements. Although most of its advice remains sound, it says nothing about handicapped access, for example. Nevertheless, it does raise important questions that should not be overlooked in the planning process.

375. **The Applause/Best Plays Theater Yearbook** (formerly *The Burns Mantle Theater Yearbook*). New York: Applause Theatre Book Publishers, 1920- . Annual. LC 92-2902. ISSN 1063-620X.

The best-known American theatre reference book has chronicled the New York season since 1921, with retrospective volumes that extend coverage back to 1894. Each volume combines an overview of the theatre season with a statistical section, a listing of awards, and condensations of the year's ten best plays as determined by the book's editors. Since the 1970s *The Best Plays* has placed more emphasis on theatre outside New York City, mirroring the growing importance of regional theatre in the United States. A special section lists details of new plays produced by companies around the country. The editors also cover Broadway, off-Broadway, revivals, and off-stage events. The many lists published in each volume include plays produced on Broadway, off-Broadway, and off-off-Broadway, cast replacements and touring companies, and plays that closed prior to Broadway openings. Long-running plays warrant a separate listing. A bibliography of plays published during the year and a necrology are annual features, as is a list of all "Best Plays" since 1894. An index facilitates use of each volume. Put together with care, this series is the first place to look for information about past American plays. An index to the first seventy-seven years can be found in *The Directory of the American Theater 1894-1971* (entry 404).

376. Arnold, Janet. **A Handbook of Costume**. New York: S. G. Phillips, 1980 (c. 1973). 336p. LC 79-29663. ISBN 0-87599-231-5.

Although not specifically addressed to theatrical costumers, Arnold's handbook directs them to primary sources such as paintings, sculptures, coins, drawings, dolls, and tapestries where they can research details of costume. Each chapter describes the use and limitations of a particular type of source and suggests books with useful illustrations. A separate chapter describes costuming for the stage. Arnold's bibliography updates Hiler and Hiler (entry 47) but is not as complete as Kesler (entry 56). The final third of the book is a guide to the many costume collections in the United Kingdom. This well-written and illustrated guide should be useful to costume researchers and designers for many years.

377. Barsis, Max. **The Common Man Through the Centuries: A Book of Costume Drawings**. New York: Frederick Ungar, 1973. 354p. LC 68-31447. ISBN 0-8044-1075-5.

While designing costumes for Hollywood studios, Barsis had trouble finding details of dress worn by common people through the centuries. Subsequently he researched, wrote, and illustrated this guide to the apparel worn by those of small or no means who had to struggle just to make a modest living. Almost 700 figure drawings illustrate common apparel in Europe from the time of the ancient Greeks to the late eighteenth century. Because the costumes are presented chronologically, the author provides an index by occupation, country, and other characteristics. For those who wish to research further, Barsis discusses his sources at the beginning of the book. Under each drawing he includes information gleaned from his studies, often quoting contemporary sources. His wonderfully expressive drawings depict not just clothes but also the people who wore them. This is a useful source for anyone designing period costumes.

378. Barton, Lucy. **Historic Costume for the Stage**. Boston: Walter H. Baker, 1963 (c. 1935). 609p. LC 77371827.

Despite its age, Barton's handbook remains the definitive work on period stage costume. It describes and illustrates hundreds of costumes and accessories worn by ancient Egyptians, Greeks, Romans, and Byzantines, and by Europeans from the Gothic period to the early twentieth century. Arranged chronologically, each chapter begins with some notes about the period and its costumes. Barton then methodically describes every aspect of men's, women's, and children's dress from head to toe. She notes popular colors and materials, surface decorations, jewelry, and accessories that fit the period. A section on practical reproduction of the period's clothing for theatrical purposes is followed by illustrations and suggested readings. Because Barton follows the same format in each chapter, the reader can compare, for example, the cut of women's sleeves from one century to the next. Barton's organization is equaled by her attention to detail. She describes underwear and stockings as well as outer garments, illustrates specialized costumes for military and ecclesiastical wear, and distinguishes between middle class and upper class manners of dress. Because Barton's survey stops at the beginning of the twentieth century, those interested in modern costume should consult O'Donnol's handbook (entry 437), which continues Barton's work up to the 1970s.

379. Baygan, Lee. **Makeup for Theatre, Film & Television**. New York: Drama Book, 1982. 183p. LC 81-1911. ISBN 0-89676-023-5.

Written by the director of makeup for NBC, Baygan's manual falls into two parts. First, he offers step-by-step directions for applying makeup, illustrated with small photographs. Second, he shows how to properly attach and wear beards, sideburns, and other hairpieces. Commercial sources are given for both makeup and hairpieces. Because this book provides specific instructions, it complements Corson's more theoretical work (entry 388) well.

380. Bergan, Ronald. **The Great Theatres of London: An Illustrated Companion**. San Francisco: Chronicle Books, 1988. 200p. LC 88-15337. ISBN 0-87701-571-6.

Acknowledging his debt to Raymond Mander and Joe Mitchenson's works (entries 429 and 430) in his introduction, Bergan has produced a popular handbook of information about sixty-four theatres in London. This work's illustrations, including exterior and interior views of the forty-four most important sites and scenes from plays produced in them, provide the most compelling reason to consult Bergan along with Mander and Mitchenson. Bergan describes each theatre's architecture and its relationship to its surroundings and gives a short history of productions, actors, and managers associated with it. Twenty theatres of less importance are described briefly. Bergan will be more useful to travelers while Mander and Mitchenson's works are more suitable for researchers.

381. Berger, Thomas L., and William C. Bradford, Jr. **An Index of Characters in English Printed Drama to the Restoration**. Englewood, Colo.: Microcard Editions Books, 1975. 222p. LC 75-8052. ISBN 0-910972-44-3.

Basing their work on W. W. Greg's *Bibliography of English Printed Drama to the Restoration* (entry 123), Berger and Bradford index all characters appearing in 836 plays cited by Greg. The compilers examined first editions of all these plays and subsequent editions if they contained changes in characters' names. They have indexed not only proper names but also nationalities, occupations, and other identifying characteristics named in the play's text. Users must read the introduction in which the compilers discuss their problems with indexing variant texts and the decisions they made. For example, a few common character names such as "servant" and "maid" are not indexed, but more specific variations such as "butler" or "kitchenmaid" are included. Each alphabetical entry refers to a number for each play in which the character appears. The "Finding List" is arranged by these numbers, which also correspond to Greg's numbers. The compilers list the play's author, the dates of its first printing and first performance, and either Pollard and Redgrave's (*Short-title Catalogue of Books Printed in England, Scotland, & Ireland ... 1475-1640*. 2d ed. London: Bibliographical Society, 1976-1991) or Wing's (*Short-title Catalogue of Books Printed ... 1641-1700*. 2d ed. New York: Index Committee of the Modern Language Association of America, 1972-) short-title catalog number. Berger and Bradford suggest that scholars may use their index in various ways such as tracing the English view of Norway through the portrayal of "Norwegians" in the period's plays. The possibilities for this kind of scholarship are expanded greatly thanks to this work.

382. Billington, Michael. **The Guinness Book of Theatre Facts and Feats**. Enfield, England: Guinness Superlatives; Distr., Sterling, 1982. 240p. LC 82-220438. ISBN 0-85112-239-6.

118 / 7—Handbooks and Yearbooks

Unlike *The Guinness Book of Records*, which is a genuinely useful reference book, this work is frustrating to use to find information. Lavishly illustrated and arranged by broad subjects such as theatre, actors and actresses, and plays and playwrights, chapters present trivia in no logical order. Although an index provides access by subject and name, the information provided is hardly worth looking up. Readers should beware: not all Guinness books are equally worthwhile.

383. **Black Arts Annual.** New York: Garland, 1989- . Annual. ISSN 1042-7104.

An especially pleasing feature of this new yearbook is its willingness to cover African-American artists and artistic groups based outside New York City. Covering all arts, each volume thus far has included chapters on theatre and dance. The theatre chapter contains description of major productions, and the dance chapter lists personnel of major companies. Both list obituaries of famous Black performers and artistic personnel. The 1990 annual devotes considerable attention to the Alvin Ailey Company's thirtieth anniversary but also spotlights the debut of Judith Jamison's new company, the Jamison Project. The theatre chapter excerpts reviews of major productions and profiles regional companies. It covers the National Black Theatre Festival and includes an article about Black women playwrights. As this new publication grows, its coverage may change slightly from year to year. If it maintains its focus, however, it should provide a valuable record of Black arts activity in the United States.

384. Bloom, Ken. **American Song: The Complete Musical Theatre Companion.** New York: Facts on File, 1985. 2v. LC 84-24728. ISBN 0-8719-6961-0 set.

With a wider scope than Lewine and Simon (entry 423), Bloom lists 42,000 songs that were written for American musical productions between 1900 and 1984, including Broadway, off-Broadway, and off-off-Broadway shows. He also includes vaudeville, burlesque, and selected nightclub productions; regional productions by major artists; shows that closed before reaching Broadway; straight plays with original music; and English and French productions of shows by major American composers. Volume 1 lists shows alphabetically with opening date and number of performances, a list of artistic personnel (composer, librettist, and so forth), the song titles, the cast, and notes on the score. Volume 2 indexes song titles and names as well as providing a chronological list of shows. Listing 42,000 songs to Lewine and Simon's 17,000, Bloom provides more information but requires more work to use. Bloom is preferred, however, because it covers more productions.

385. Bonin, Jane F. **Prize-Winning American Drama: A Bibliographical and Descriptive Guide.** Metuchen, N.J.: Scarecrow, 1973. 222p. LC 73-3111. ISBN 0-8108-0607-X.

Bonin has selected seventy-eight American plays which won one or more of the following prizes between 1917, the year the first Pulitzer Prize in drama was awarded, and 1971: the Pulitzer Prize, the New York Drama Critics Circle Award, the Tony Award, the Obie Award, and the Players' Workshop Award. Arranged chronologically, the entries feature a description of the play, a history of its production, a plot summary, and a bibliography of reviews and criticism. Regrettably, not all plays that have won these prizes are included. For example *Luther* won both the Tony and the Drama Critics Circle awards in 1964 but is not described here. Because one cannot say all prize winners are present, the only way to know if information about a particular play will be found here is to look.

Toohey's *A History of the Pulitzer Prize Plays* (entry 458) lists all Pulitzer-winning plays, and Stevenson's *The Tony Award* (entry 453) lists all Tony winners through 1987. *World of Winners* (Detroit: Gale Research, 1989) lists winners of all five of the awards.

386. Bronner, Edwin. **The Encyclopedia of the American Theatre 1900-1975**. San Diego: A. S. Barnes, 1980. 659p. LC 75-2439. ISBN 0-498-01219-0.

Bronner's handbook provides information about American plays produced between 1900 and 1975. The alphabetical entries list the name of the play, date and place of its first performance, the length of its initial run, cast and production credits, and a plot summary. Several appendices report on actors' and playwrights' debuts, long-running Broadway and off-Broadway plays, awards, and number of plays produced in each season. The index leads readers to information in both the alphabetical section and the appendices. Bronner has written a useful handbook for the first three-quarters of twentieth-century American theatre. For more complete information about a particular season see *The Best Plays* (entry 375).

387. Buerki, F. A. **Stagecraft for Nonprofessionals**. 3d ed., rev. by Susan J. Christensen. Madison: University of Wisconsin Press, 1983. 171p. LC 83-1244. ISBN 0-299-09350-6; 0-299-09354-9 pa.

Emphasizing relatively simple designs and techniques suitable to amateur theatre, Buerki discusses scene design and stage setting as well as more specific subjects like stage lighting, scene painting, and construction of doors and windows. Arranged by topic with a subject index and short bibliography, the book also includes a glossary of stage terms. Because he covers so many topics, Buerki cannot treat each one in depth, and readers may wish to use other works if they are actually constructing scenery or properties. Thurston James' book on props (entry 412) offers better instructions on their construction, for example. Buerki is more valuable for his background information, such as his explanation of color theory in the stage painting chapter.

388. Corson, Richard. **Stage Makeup**. 8th ed. Englewood Cliffs, N.J.: Prentice-Hall, 1989. 411p. LC 89-3447. ISBN 0-13-840539-5.

Every actor must know how to apply makeup to present a proper stage appearance. Corson has provided a textbook and reference work for actors, makeup designers, and teachers. Through numerous photographs he illustrates various features of facial anatomy, principles of light and shade, and the effects of lighting on makeup. Chapters treat topics such as analyzing one's character, designing the makeup; applying makeup; using corrective makeup; and applying hair and wigs. Especially interesting chapters show nonrealistic makeup applications for characters such as ghosts, angels, clowns, and elves, quick-change makeups executed during a play, and sex reversal makeups. Corson discusses creating racial and ethnic looks through makeup and illustrates makeup and hair for period plays. Appendices define and explain makeup terminology and list commercial sources of stage makeup. This is a good basic introduction to the art of stage makeup. Its directions are not as detailed as those in Lee Baygan's work (entry 379).

389. Currell, David. **The Complete Book of Puppet Theatre**. Totowa, N.J.: Barnes & Noble, 1987. 342p. LC 86-22246. ISBN 0-389-20685-7.

Providing basic information on many aspects of puppetry, Currell relates the history of puppets in various parts of the world including the Middle East and Asia. Puppeteers will appreciate his chapters on the design and construction of puppets and on technical aspects of puppet theatre such as lighting and sound. Appendices list puppet organizations, museum collections worldwide, and a list of suppliers in Britain and America. Currell includes a bibliography that, although shorter than Crothers' two-volume work (entries 31 and 32), includes more recent materials. A subject index facilitates access to the various parts of this handbook, which should be a useful starting place for information about puppets.

390. Dixon, Geoffrey. **The Gilbert and Sullivan Concordance: A Word Index to W. S. Gilbert's Libretti for the Fourteen Savoy Operas**. (Garland Reference Library of the Humanities, vol. 702). New York: Garland, 1987. 2v. LC 86-33484. ISBN 0-8240-8505-1 (set).

Dixon bases his concordance on Macmillan's 1926 edition of *The Savoy Operas* plus the text of *Thespis*, which is reprinted in Dixon's appendix. (Gilbert and Sullivan's first collaboration, *Thespis*, was not a Savoy production.) Following standard concordance procedure, each word is surrounded by enough quoted context to retain "integrity as a semantic entity." Each phrase is followed by a letter denoting the operetta in which it appears and a page reference to the Macmillan edition. *Thespis* entries refer to line numbers of the reprinted text. A concordance can be one of the dryest of reference books, but Gilbert's facility with words shines throughout this one with phrases like "the people who eat peppermint and puff it in your face" (*The Mikado*) and "each Christmas day he gave each stoker a silver shovel and a golden poker" (*Thespis*). The book will serve both those who are studying Gilbert's prose and those who simply want to know where to find "I always voted at my party's call, and I never thought of thinking for myself at all."

391. Durham, Weldon B., ed. **American Theatre Companies, 1749-1887**. Westport, Conn.: Greenwood, 1986. 598p. LC 84-27947. ISBN 0-313-20886-7.

392. Durham, Weldon B., ed. **American Theatre Companies, 1888-1930**. Westport, Conn.: Greenwood, 1987. 541p. LC 85-30213. ISBN 0-313-25359-5.

393. Durham, Weldon B., ed. **American Theatre Companies, 1931-1986**. Westport, Conn.: Greenwood, 1989. 596p. LC 88-32039. ISBN 0-313-25360-9.

Demonstrating the long history and vitality of the American theatre, these three volumes contain short histories of resident acting companies in the American colonies and the United States from 1749 to the present. Entries, written by professors of theatre, are presented alphabetically by company name within each of the chronological volumes. Although the heart of each entry is the history, which focuses on both the artistic and the financial characteristics of the groups, each chapter also lists all known personnel, a list of the repertory, and a bibliography. One finds information about the first known company in colonial America, the Murray and Kean Company, which performed Joseph Addison's *Cato* in Philadelphia in August 1749. Volume 3 recounts the history of many companies still operating today, such as the Negro Ensemble Company, the Guthrie Theatre Company, and Chicago's innovative Steppenwolf Theatre Company. The "Chronology of Companies" and "Theatre Companies by State" help the reader approach the material by date or place. An index of personal names and play titles provides additional access points. Although not exhaustive, this set includes 264 of the most important companies and should help students of American theatrical history.

394. Eaker, Sherry, comp. and ed. **The Back Stage Handbook for Performing Artists**. New York: Back Stage Books/Watson-Guptill, 1991. 309p. LC 91-29379. ISBN 0-8230-7569-9.

Sherry Eaker, editor of *Back Stage* (entry 600) since 1977, has based her handbook on articles written for that periodical. The book's thirty-five chapters discuss various aspects of show business from training and breaking into the business to working in various types of theatres to producing one's own shows. Separate chapters detail the theatre scene in New York, Chicago, and Los Angeles. Because it contains many lists of theatres, theme parks, comedy clubs, and other potential employers, the book can be used as a directory as well. It will be most useful to beginning actors.

395. Ewen, David. **New Complete Book of the American Musical Theater**. New York: Holt, Rinehart & Winston, 1970. 800p. LC 70-117257. ISBN 03-085060-6.

Ewen's handbook provides information about musical shows and revues produced in the United States between 1866 and 1970. The main body of the work describes about 500 productions. Besides credits, Ewen lists the major cast members, the opening theatre, the opening date, and the number of performances. Each narrative describes the genesis of the show, its plot, and a summary of its critical and popular reception. Occasionally he notes revivals and motion picture versions. Drawing on his extensive background as a writer on musical theatre, Ewen intersperses his narratives with his own critical comments. The second part of the book presents brief biographies of leading composers, lyricists, and librettists, both living and dead, of the American musical theatre with lists of their major works. Appendices provide a chronology of musicals from 1866 to 1970 and a list of outstanding songs from the shows. Because both main sections are arranged alphabetically, the index lists only persons and show titles mentioned within the entries, not the entries themselves. Consult this work for information on musicals produced before 1971. For British musicals see Gänzl(entry 552)

395a. Field, Shelly. **Career Opportunities in Theater and the Performing Arts**. New York: Facts on File, 1992. 235p. LC 91-39650. ISBN 0-8160-2579-7; 0-8160-2580-0 pa.

Profiling 71 careers associated with the performing arts, Field describes each job's working conditions, salary range, education and skill requirements, and advancement prospects. She also suggests ways to gain entrance to the field. Careers are grouped by type: performance, artistic composition, production, arts management, theatre technology and design, education, and so on. Appendices list colleges and training programs; internships; and theatres, ballet companies, orchestras, and employers. A bibliography suggests books and periodicals to those who want further information on a career, and a glossary defines "abbreviations, acronyms, and industry jargon." By providing current, factual information about many careers in the performing arts, this book will help high school and college students to become aware of careers other than performance that exist in the field.

396. Fletcher, Steve, and Norman Jopling. **The Book of 1000 Plays**. New York: Facts on File, 1989. 352p. LC 88-38121. ISBN 0-8160-2122-8.

Fletcher and Jopling offer plot synopses and other information such as genre, number of acts, and a list of characters, for 1,000 plays chosen for their popularity with theatre audiences. Summaries are written in an interesting, informal style but with little evaluation. While the plays of Shakespeare, Shaw, Noel Coward, and Tennessee Williams appear frequently, so do musicals by Rodgers and Hammerstein and translations of foreign plays. With a title arrangement and author index, the book presents a handy guide to popular works.

397. Franks, Don. **Tony, Grammy, Emmy, Country: A Broadway, Television and Records Awards Reference**. Jefferson, N.C.: McFarland, 1986. 202p. ISBN 0-89950-204-0.

Readers who do not have access to Stevenson's *The Tony Award* (entry 453) can locate winners of the American Theatre Wing's Tony Awards from 1947 to 1984 in this useful handbook. Other chapters cover winners of television's Emmy Awards, the Country Music Association Awards, and the recording industry's Grammys. Each chapter is arranged chronologically. The volume's index helps readers locate persons, plays, songs, and television programs by name.

398. Gänzl, Kurt, and Andrew Lamb. **Gänzl's Book of the Musical Theatre**. New York: Schirmer Books/Macmillan, 1989. 1,353p. LC 88-18588. ISBN 0-02-871941-7.

Intended as a companion to Gustav Kobbe's well-known *Complete Opera Book* (10th ed. London: Bodley Head, 1987), Gänzl's handbook acts as a source of information on the theatrical, broadcast, and recorded performances of 300 musical shows. The author has selected the most popular, the best, and his favorite shows from the United States and Europe. Each country has its own section, and within it shows are arranged chronologically. Most musical plays date from the twentieth century, although the earliest described is *The Beggar's Opera*, first performed in 1728. Gänzl lists details of the first and subsequent major productions, film versions, and characters. Extensive plot summaries include a paragraph detailing changes made to the original work in later productions. An index of titles, authors, composers, and lyricists is accompanied by a separate list of song titles. The strength of this book is its coverage of foreign-language musicals. France is represented by fifty-two works, Spain by seven, and the German-speaking countries by seventy-two. Gänzl sticks to facts, offering no commentary. Readers should turn here first for information on European musical plays and operettas.

399. Glazer, Irvin R. **Philadelphia Theatres, A-Z: A Comprehensive, Descriptive Record of 813 Theatres Constructed Since 1724**. Westport, Conn.: Greenwood, 1986. 277p. LC 85-27131. ISBN 0-313-24054-X.

Glazer, who has served as president of the Theatre Historical Society, documents 813 theatres that graced the City of Brotherly Love at one time. Most, alas, have been demolished. Arranged by theatre name, entries vary according to the amount of information Glazer has found. He lists the theatre's address, capacity, and architect. A paragraph or two discusses the building's opening date, its current fate, and special architectural features. If possible Glazer describes the types of entertainment that generally played the house. A map pinpoints theatre locations within Philadelphia, and a list of architects notes buildings they have built or renovated. Finally, a glossary defines both architectural and theatrical terms. This work should be of interest to historians of American theatre.

400. Gordon, Gilbert. **Stage Fights: A Simple Handbook of Techniques**. (A Theatre Arts Book). New York: Theatre Arts, 1973. 118p. LC 73-75918. ISBN 0-87830-580-7.

Gordon, a British fencer, has written a set of illustrated lessons on using various weapons on stage, including the sword, the dagger, the point rapier, and others. Aimed at amateur actors, the work also shows how to make weapons for theatrical purposes. A bibliography suggests additional sources on the art of fencing, both on and off stage. Those seeking additional information may wish to contact the Society of American Fight Directors (entry 744).

401. Green, Stanley, ed. **Rodgers and Hammerstein Fact Book: A Record of Their Works Together and with Other Collaborators**. New York: The Lynn Farnol Group; Distr., Drama Book, 1980. 762p. LC 81-113497. ISBN 0-9604002-0-6.

If any collaborators dominated American musical comedy during the 1940s and 1950s, it was the team of Richard Rodgers and Oscar Hammerstein II. Green's handbook emphasizes information about their productions together and with other partners. (Both men had enjoyed successful careers before beginning their partnership.) The first two chapters present biographical information about Rodgers and Hammerstein respectively as well as data on their early shows. The third chapter provides details of the shows they wrote together. For each, Green discusses the show's tryout prior to its Broadway opening, its New York run, its plot and musical numbers, and its cast. Green quotes generously from reviews so that readers can judge the reviewer's intent. Information about national touring companies, revivals, and film versions is included with each original production. Separate chapters deal with works created by Rodgers after Hammerstein's death and with miscellaneous songs created by one or both of them. A bibliography and discography are supplemented by a subject listing of their songs. The index locates songs and productions in the text. Green covers his subject well, and readers should look here first for information about Rodgers or Hammerstein.

402. Gruver, Elbert A. **The Stage Manager's Handbook**. rev. and expanded. New York: Drama Book, 1972. 220p. LC 72-190641.

Gruver wrote his book to help the stage manager "augment or consolidate his knowledge in terms of the Broadway production" (foreword). The book's arrangement roughly follows the stages of developing a play production: the prerehearsal period; rehearsals; the performance period; and touring the show. In each section Gruver explains the stage manager's duties and gives checklists of procedures to follow and actions to take. He explains how to mark a script for prompting and how to draft property, lighting, sound, and costume plots from the script. Although somewhat dated with its references to typescripts and carbon paper, Gruver's advice on working with actors and directors remains sound. And while he addresses Broadway productions, his checklists adapt well to other types of productions. Stern (entry 452) provides more recent advice to stage managers.

403. Guernsey, Otis L., Jr. **Curtain Times: The New York Theatre, 1965-1987**. New York: Applause, 1987. 613p. LC 86-26536. ISBN 0-936839-24-4; 0-936839-23-6 pa.

Essentially a compilation of the annual reviews Guernsey has written for *The Best Plays* (entry 375) between 1965 and 1985, this handbook provides a convenient history of New York theatre during a twenty-year period. Despite the book's title, the 1986 and 1987 seasons are merely summarized. The yearly chapters discuss Broadway, off-Broadway, revivals of older plays, and off-stage events, in that order. Combining facts and opinion, Guernsey looks at plays, writers, performers, and box office attendance figures. Each chapter contains lists of Broadway and off-Broadway plays. An index locates plays, performers, theatre companies, and other subjects. This is useful if one lacks *The Best Plays*, but not essential if one has that at hand.

404. Guernsey, Otis L., Jr. **Directory of the American Theater 1894-1971**. New York: Dodd, Mead, 1971. 343p. LC 71-180734. ISBN 0-396-06428-0.

A cumulative index to the first seventy-seven years of *The Best Plays* (entry 375), Guernsey's work accesses authors, composers, and titles of Broadway, off-Broadway, and off-off-Broadway plays. Altogether, 22,000 names of plays, playwrights, and others are listed in the two parts of this index. The first covers all the people who created these plays (authors, composers, librettists, and so on) with the volume and page numbers of their entries. The second index covers plays titles and again lists volume and page number. This index makes using *The Best Plays* much faster and easier.

405. Halford, Aubrey S., and Giovanna M. Halford. **The Kabuki Handbook: A Guide to Understanding and Appreciation, with Summaries of Favourite Plays, Explanatory Notes, and Illustrations**. Rutland, Vt.: Charles E. Tuttle, 1956. 487p. LC 55-10618.

The foreigner who attends a kabuki performance faces difficulties stemming from the language, the unfamiliar acting style, the complicated plots, and the Japanese practice of presenting bits and pieces of several plays in one performance. The Halfords help one understand kabuki by providing plot summaries for dozens of the most popular plays. They indicate acts and scenes that are commonly played separately and list alternative play titles. (Many kabuki plays are known by more than one title.) A notes section presents information on costumes, acting families, audience etiquette, the kabuki stage, and other aspects of the art. The index includes titles and alternate titles of plays and parts of plays. For more information on kabuki see Leiter's *Kabuki Encyclopedia* (entry 286) and Shaver's *Kabuki Costume* (entry 447).

406. Hay, Henry. **The Amateur Magician's Handbook**. 4th ed. New York: Harper & Row, 1982. 414p. LC 80-7878. ISBN 0-06-014865-9.

Because Hay's purpose is to help readers become good magicians, he emphasizes performance while also providing background information on the history and personalities of magic. He arranges his book by types of magic such as card tricks, coin tricks, and "hand magic." Separate chapters deal with children's shows and magic involving more elaborate apparatus. The illustrated section on performance stresses movement and pantomime as important aspects of one's presentations. Hay includes a glossary of terms, a biographical section, and a bibliography. The biographies are not as complete as those in Hay's *Cyclopedia of Magic* (entry 281), however. Because of the topical arrangement, use of the index is essential.

407. Heys, Sandra. **Contemporary Stage Roles for Women: A Descriptive Catalogue**. Westport, Conn.: Greenwood, 1985. 195p. LC 84-19218. ISBN 0-313-24473-1.

Heys identifies plays with strong female roles, defined as those that are interesting in their own right rather than those that are merely reflections of or reactions to male roles. For each play she lists title, number of male and female roles, playwright's name, date of first production, and the name of the agency that controls the play's rights. She includes a brief plot summary and a synopsis of the female characters. Additional chapters classify roles by age, by character type, and by race. Indexes by playwright and by character name follow a bibliography about women and the theatre. Heys' selection is not exhaustive. She omits *Vanities* and *Monday After the Miracle*, for instance, plays with strong women characters. Her selection is broad enough, however, to help directors and producers who are looking for plays with good parts for women.

408. Hoggett, Chris. **Stage Crafts**. New York: St. Martin's Press, 1976. 282p. LC 76-10554. ISBN 0-312-75495-7.

Although now aging, Hoggett's handbook still provide good drawings and illustrations and broad coverage of many aspects of technical theatre. Divided into chapters by subject, the work begins with an explanation and illustration of various types of stages and how to construct them. It moves on to positioning cloths, borders, and wings and constructing stairs. It then covers design, painting, properties, lighting, arms and armor, costume accessories, and makeup and masks. A short glossary and index complete the book. Readers should ignore the outdated list of suppliers and use a recent directory such as *Stearns* (entry 526) or *Theatre Crafts* (entry 514). Useful for beginners who want to know something about stage design, Hoggett supplements more complete works such as James' *Theatre Props Handbook* (entry 412) or Buerki's *Stagecraft for Nonprofessionals* (entry 387).

409. Holden, Michael, comp. **The Stage Guide: Technical Information on British Theatres**. London: Carson and Comerford, 1971. 404p. ISBN 0-901048-02-X.

Dated but still useful, Holden's 1971 guide, the first published since 1946, provides "basic information on the dimensions, equipment and accommodation in theatres in the British Isles" (introduction). London's important theatres are listed first, followed by other British cities in alphabetical order. Each theatre's entry lists its address, date of construction, and information on the stage, the house, sound and electrical equipment, and backstage facilities. Appendices list theatres arranged by seating capacity and proscenium stage theatres by proscenium width. A third section lists all towns in Great Britain that have fully licensed theatres or multipurpose halls or movie theatres used for drama. Although some information is now outdated, this work will serve as a quick reference guide to British performing spaces.

410. Howard, Diana. **London Theatres and Music Halls 1850-1950**. London: Library Association, 1970. 291p. LC 79-476497. ISBN 0-85365-471-9.

Originally a Library Association Fellowship thesis, Howard's guide lists every known theatre and music hall that existed in London between 1850 and 1950. This century was the time of greatest activity in theatre building in that city. Altogether, 910 theatres are listed in alphabetical order with address, year licensed, names of the management, and details about the building's architecture if known. Howard includes a bibliography of materials about London theatres, a list of library collections, and a name index that cites alternate names for theatres and music halls. Howard's entry for each theatre is briefer than those of Mander and Mitchenson's books (entries 429 and 430), but she includes many more buildings than they do. Her book answers basic questions but will provide only a starting point for those needing in-depth information.

411. Jackson, Sheila. **Costumes for the Stage: A Complete Handbook for Every Kind of Play**. New York: New Amsterdam, 1988. 144p. LC 88-5289. ISBN 0-941533-36-0.

Jackson, the former Head of Costume for London Weekend Television, who designed costumes for the *Upstairs, Downstairs* television series, has written a handbook for the amateur costumer with limited funds. More than 700 illustrations clarify the author's prose as she discusses how to capture the essential details of a period costume in a simple and inexpensive way. Chapters are arranged by time period from ancient Greece to modern times with special sections for stylized productions, musicals, pageants, carnivals, and school plays. The heavily illustrated guide emphasizes practical advice. A bibliography directs readers to other helpful sources, and an index provides good subject access to Jackson's work. See also Prisk (entry 441).

412. James, Thurston. **The Theater Props Handbook: A Comprehensive Guide to Theater Properties, Materials, and Construction**. White Hall, Va.: Betterway Publications, 1987. 272p. LC 87-15924. ISBN 0-932620-88-4; 0-932620-86-8 pa.

Thurston James has been involved with educational theatre for more than twenty-five years, and in this book he shares his knowledge of constructing properties, those items that are handled by actors as part of their stage business. Arranging his work by type of prop, James provides profusely and clearly illustrated directions for making books, coins, confetti, various foods, and many other props. He also advises on the purchase of items and lists suppliers. Although the book's alphabetical arrangement makes it easy to find a topic, James includes a subject index as well. This informally written work should be helpful to those involved in stage productions.

413. Jewell, James C., and Thomas E. Howard. **Broadway and the Tony Awards: The First Three Decades 1947-1977**. Washington, D.C.: University Press of America, 1977. 281p. LC 78-100461. ISBN 0-8191-0339-X.

Written in the form of a narrative with a chapter for each year, Jewell's handbook emphasizes biographies of Tony winners, production information for winning plays, and trivia. A necrology lists Tony winners who have died, and several appendices list Tony winners who have also been nominated for Oscars, Emmys, or other drama awards. Because the work lacks an index and has a narrative format, it cannot be used as easily as Stevenson (entry 453). It does provide more biographical information than Stevenson, however.

414. Kaplan, Mike, ed. **Variety International Show Business Reference, 1983**. (Garland Reference Library of the Humanities, vol. 455). New York: Garland, 1983. 877p. LC 83-11653. ISBN 0-8240-9089-6.

If Garland had published this work annually, it would be more useful than it is. The 1983 edition and its predecessor, published in 1981, included about 6,000 biographies of living or recently deceased show business people, credits for plays, films, and television shows, and lists of award-winning and long-running plays. Most of the theatre information will be found *The Best Plays* (entry 375) and *Contemporary Theatre, Film, and Television* (entry 348).

415. Kienzle, Siegfried. **Modern World Theater: A Guide to Productions in Europe and the United States Since 1945**. Translated by Alexander Henderson and Elizabeth Henderson. New York: Frederick Ungar, 1970. 509p. LC 73-98342. ISBN 0-8044-3129-9.

Translated from German, Kienzle's work describes plots for 578 plays produced between 1945 and 1970. Arranged alphabetically by author, then by play title, entries list the first published edition of the play, its first performance date and place, and one or two sentences of commentary as well as the plot outline. Kienzle provides good coverage of French, German, English, and American playwrights and adequate coverage of other European writers. Because he does not include African, Asian, or Latin American writers, however, his title is somewhat misleading. An index of play titles completes the book. Readers should prefer Kienzle to Shipley (entry 448) for the post-war period.

Handbooks and Yearbooks / 127

416. Kullman, Colby H., and William C. Young. **Theatre Companies of the World**. Westport, Conn.: Greenwood, 1986. 2v. LC 84-539. ISBN 0-313-21456-5 (set).

Like Durham (entries 391-393), Kullman and Young present histories and descriptions of permanent theatre companies. All of the groups described were operating at publication time. Kullman and Young have recruited nine editors to oversee the essays in each of the nine geographic areas into which the book is divided. A general introduction to each country precedes the entries for the theatre companies. Each essay presents the company's history, its significance to theatrical history in its country, achievements of playwrights associated with it, and future plans. A bibliography arranged by geographical area and an index close the set. Note that because of the companion volumes edited by Durham, only the most important American companies are listed.

417. Langley, Stephen. **Theatre Management and Production in America: Commercial, Stock, Resident, College, Community, and Presenting Organizations**. New York: Drama Book, 1990. 680p. LC 90-42890. ISBN 0-89676-115-0.

Intended as a textbook for aspiring theatre managers and producers, Langley's work contains valuable reference material. For instance, he defines the roles and responsibilities of various producing, directing, and theatre operations personnel. The appendix prints samples of many forms such as rental contracts and grant applications. Langley provides a guide to national and regional arts service organizations, lists of theatrical unions and guilds, and a directory of management associations. His bibliography directs readers to additional sources dealing with theatrical management. The book is arranged by broad subject categories like financial management, public relations, and sales. Langley helped create Brooklyn College's program in performing arts management. His book is a useful source not only to his students, but to anyone seeking information about the business of the performing arts.

418. Lawliss, Chuck. **The New York Theatre Sourcebook**. New York: Simon & Schuster, 1990. 367p. LC 90-38394. ISBN 0-671-68870-7.

Theatre-goers will appreciate having a guide to the theatres, restaurants, theatre collections in museums and libraries, and theatre shops in New York. Arranged by location (Broadway, Lincoln Center area, New Jersey suburbs, and so on) with an area street map for each section, each theatre's entry includes a house seating plan, details of handicapped access, address, and box office telephone. Aside from these important facts, entries relate the history of each theatre including famous plays performed. Lawliss recommends nearby restaurants and night spots in each district. This guide is a convenient starting place for those planning a theatre trip to New York City, but telephone numbers and addresses, especially of shops and restaurants, should be verified in current telephone directories.

419. Lemmon, David, ed. **British Theatre Yearbook**. New York: St. Martin's Press, 1989- . Annual. LC 90-648598. ISSN 1047-7101.

As an overview of the British theatre season, this yearbook devotes chapters to activities in the West End, the National Theatre, the Royal Shakespeare Company, and outer London, regional, and touring companies. Each chapter lists theatres and companies alphabetically. It also provides credits, descriptions, and critiques of each play produced during the season. Illustrated with black-and-white photographs and indexed by play title, the annual provides a record of British theatrical activity for the year.

420. Leonard, William Torbert. **Broadway Bound: A Guide to Shows That Died Aborning**. Metuchen, N.J.: Scarecrow, 1983. 618p. LC 83-15042. ISBN 0-8108-1652-0.

Leonard records the detail of plays that became victims of out-of-town tryouts. For one reason or another, these shows, including dramatizations of *Gone with the Wind* and *Lady Chatterley's Lover*, closed in Connecticut or New Jersey or Peoria before making it to "The Great White Way." Each play's production is described along with information on the principal actors, producers, and directors; a plot synopsis; and a summary of reviews. A chronological index lists the shows in order by opening date, 1931-1981. See also Simas (entry 450).

421. Leonard, William Torbert. **Once Was Enough**. Metuchen, N.J.: Scarecrow, 1986. 282p. LC 86-11855. ISBN 0-8108-1909-0.

Advice that went unheeded, dreams that went sour, reviews that ripped apart performances—all these contributed to this list of Broadway plays that were so bad they ran for one night only. The alphabetical entries consist of play title, date, credits, and plot summary. Leonard provides background information on the production, sidelights on various people connected with the play, and a summary of the (mostly bad) reviews. (Of *Onward Victoria*, a musical based on the life of suffragette Victoria Claflin Woodhull, *New York Times* critic Frank Rich wrote "The book and lyrics battle to a standoff as they attempt to top each other in witlessness.") A chronological index titled "Bombs in Season" lists the failures by date. Additional indexes allow one to locate actors, choreographers, directors, and other creative artists involved with any of the shows.

422. Leonard, William Torbert. **Theatre: Stage to Screen to Television**. Metuchen, N.J.: Scarecrow, 1981. 2v. LC 80-22987. ISBN 0-8108-1374-2.

Providing information about plays that became motion pictures, television plays, ballets, operas, or musicals, Leonard demonstrates the ease with which some works can cross genres while other fail to make the transition. He includes American and English plays but excludes Shakespeare's works, Gilbert and Sullivan operettas, most foreign plays, and all ancient Greek dramas. Arranged by title of the original play, entries include information about all subsequent versions. To find *My Fair Lady*, therefore, one looks under *Pygmalion*. Leonard presents credits for stage, screen, and television productions and discusses each production's history. He also reports on the critical reception of each version. For Arthur Miller's *The Crucible*, for example, he discusses nine versions including the original New York production; French, British, and Canadian productions; an opera version; a French film: and three separate television broadcasts. Indexes allow one to locate composers, lyricists, librettists, authors, and playwrights.

423. Lewine, Richard, and Alfred Simon. **Songs of the Theater**. New York: H. W. Wilson, 1984. 897p. LC 84-13068.

Lewine and Simon present information about songs written for the American stage between 1891, the year *Robin Hood*, "America's first successful and enduring theater piece," debuted, and 1983. For the years up to World War I the authors include all important legitimate shows but not vaudeville productions. From 1915 they deal with "virtually every theater piece seen on Broadway" plus off-Broadway productions that ran for fifteen or more performances. Even film and television songs by established theatre composers and lyricists are noted, for example, Rodgers and Hammerstein's "It Might As Well Be Spring" from the film *State Fair*. The book's first section lists 17,000 songs with composer and lyricist, the name of the show, the year it opened, and type of production: on or off Broadway, film, or television show. The second part of the book provides information on the shows themselves: opening date, composer and lyricist, number of performances, and a list of songs. If recordings, piano vocal scores, or sheet music for vocal selections are available, they are noted. Lewine and Simon also provide a chronology of stage productions, an index of film and television productions in which listed songs appeared, and an index of composers, lyricists, authors, and others mentioned in the book. Lewine and Simon's work is quite similar to Ken Bloom's *American Song* (entry 384), which covers songs performed between 1900 and 1984. Because Bloom's scope is wider, he covers more songs. Lewine and Simon's work is slightly easier to use, however, because all information is in the song entry in section 1. Bloom requires the use of a song index in volume 2 which refers one to the play's entry in volume 1. Either book will answer a great many song questions, but only Bloom will answer those about songs from obscure shows.

424. Leyson, Peter. **London Theatres: A Short History and Guide**. London: Apollo Publications, 1970. 73p. LC 76-129929. SBN 9501265-0-0.

Everything about this book from its small size to its inclusion of a London Underground map bespeaks its purpose as a guidebook for tourists interested in the London theatre. Written in an informal style, it describes about seventy theatres located in London or nearby. It also lists the location of several monuments such as Shakespeare's statue. Several paragraphs describe each theatre's history and list its address, telephone number, and closest Underground stop. Not as informative or scholarly as Mander and Mitchenson's work (entry 430), nor as well illustrated as Bergan (entry 380), Leyson's guide may answer tourist questions if the other titles are not available.

425. Lovell, John, Jr. **Digests of Great American Plays: Complete Summaries of More than 100 Plays from the Beginnings to the Present**. New York: Thomas Y. Crowell, 1961. 452p. LC 61-10482.

Of the 102 plays annotated in this work, thirty-three were first performed before 1900 and another twenty-eight before 1930. The synopses of the relatively unknown older plays (the first was *Ponteach; Or, The Savages of America*, performed in 1766) are probably most valuable to readers. Arranged chronologically, the summaries are indexed by play title. Appendices analyze plays from several angles such as act and scene structure, type of drama, themes, and so on. For each play, Lovell provides a list of characters and a plot summary.

426. Lucha-Burns, Carol. **Musical Notes: A Practical Guide to Staffing and Staging Standards of the American Musical Theatre**. Westport, Conn.: Greenwood, 1986. 581p. LC 85-10017. ISBN 0-313-24648-3.

Written to help amateur groups locate suitable musical plays for production, this handbook describes, in alphabetical order, 144 musicals. Entries provide cast and production credits for the first performance, information about the orchestra's size, suggested minimum size for the chorus, and a full synopsis of the play. Notes on production describe special problems and considerations and offer suggestions for amateur groups. Lucha-Burns pays particular attention to simplifications which can be made to sets and costumes without sacrificing the show's quality. She lists sources for scripts, scores, and recordings, and notes the proper licensing agency for each play. Appendices list representative songs suitable for classroom study and auditions, provide a chronological list of musicals, and

130 / 7—Handbooks and Yearbooks

list the longest running musicals. A bibliography and a directory of sources of scripts, music and recordings is followed by indexes of show titles, song titles, and personal names. Lucha-Burns provides more advice about each show than does Lynch in his *Musicals!* (entry 427), but he covers 400 plays compared to her 144. Both works will be useful to amateur groups.

427. Lynch, Richard Chigley. **Musicals! A Directory of Musical Properties Available for Production**. Chicago: American Library Association, 1984. 197p. LC 84-468. ISBN 0-8389-0404-1.

Lynch, the assistant curator of the Billy Rose Theatre Collection at the New York Public Library, has compiled a list of "almost 400 musical properties available for production" (introduction). Aimed at amateur groups looking for musicals to present, this guide offers access to everything from standards like *Show Boat* and *My Fair Lady* to the obscure *Minnie's Boys*, a 1970 show based on the lives of the Marx Brothers. It also includes *Fly With Me*, written by Rodgers and Hart for the 1920 Columbia University Varsity Show. Arranged by title, entries provide a plot summary as well as the date of the first New York performance and the names of the playwright, composer, and lyricist. Lynch also includes information about sound recordings, published librettos, and licensing agents for each play. An appendix lists addresses of licensing agents and music publishers, and the index locates composers, lyricists, and librettists. See also Lucha-Burns (entry 426).

428. Mackintosh, Iain, and Michael Sell, eds. **Curtains!!! or A New Life for Old Theatres**. Eastbourne, England: John Offord, 1982. 248p. LC 82-670128. ISBN 0-903931-42-7.

Mackintosh and his colleagues, who included theatre historians and architects, surveyed all pre-1914 theatres and music halls in Great Britain. Mackintosh reports their findings in this handbook. It lists address, date built, architect, and current use of the building. The theatre's history and appearance are discussed, and each building is ranked for architectural and theatrical importance. Mackintosh arranges the entries by city. A separate list of demolished theatres gives details for those that have been destroyed, and a series of maps locates the theatres. Because it describes many provincial theatres, this supplements Mander and Mitchenson's works (entries 429, 430).

429. Mander, Raymond and Joe Mitchenson. **The Lost Theatres of London**. New York: Taplinger, 1968. 572p. LC 68-29986.

To supplement their book *The Theatres of London* (entry 430), Mander and Mitchenson have written fairly lengthy histories of twenty-eight central London theatres that have been demolished. Taken in alphabetical order, each entry includes address, variant names, opening and closing dates, and a history of the theatre. An appendix lists architects who designed the theatres and an alphabetical list of theatres including all variant names. As a visual aid the authors include maps of London with the former locations of the theatres marked. This will be of interest to historians of British theatre.

430. Mander, Raymond, and Joe Mitchenson. **The Theatres of London**. new ed. London: New English Library, 1975. 344p. LC 76-366416. ISBN 0-45002-123-8.

Mander and Mitchenson give a chronology and short history for forty-one theatres in London's West End, eleven in the city's suburbs, plus eleven others scattered throughout the London area. If a theatre has had more than one location, the authors discuss each building and its history. For example, Drury Lane Theatre moved into successive buildings in 1663, 1674, 1794, and, finally, 1812. The appendices list theatres chronologically; theatres that appear on the Statutory List of Buildings of Special Architectural or Historical Interest; and architects of currently standing theatres. Both theatre and architectural researchers will find this volume useful. It should be preferred to Peter Leyson's *London Theatres: A Short History and Guide*, which is not as complete. See also the authors' *The Lost Theatres of London* (entry 429), which discusses demolished theatres.

431. May, Robin. **Who's Who in Shakespeare**. New York: Taplinger, 1973. 190p. LC 73-5334. ISBN 0-8008-8269-5.

May presents, in alphabetical order, all the characters in Shakespeare's plays, identifies the play in which each appears, and discusses their relationship to the plot and to the other characters. Major figures receive long descriptions while minor characters have shorter annotations. The book also lists Shakespeare's plays in alphabetical order with character names and the act and scene in which each first appears. May's book is very similar to Rowse's work (entry 443), and either will answer questions about Shakespearean characters.

432. McCaslin, Nellie. **Historical Guide to Children's Theatre in America**. Westport, Conn.: Greenwood, 1987. 348p. LC 85-12684. ISBN 0-313-24466-9.

McCaslin, a professor of educational theatre at New York University, has documented the growth of the children's theatre movement in the United States from its beginnings to 1985. Using primary sources when possible, the author first presents a general history of American children's theatre. She then lists major theatre companies and organizations that perform for young people. Arranged by company name, each narrative describes the company's history and, if the company is still active, its current activities. Several appendices provide a chronology of events, brief bibliographies of important people in the movement, and a list of associations involved with children's theatre. The bibliography includes published and unpublished materials. An index concludes this useful book. See also Swortzell's *International Guide to Children's Theatre and Educational Theatre* (entry 455).

433. McPharlin, Paul. **The Puppet Theatre in America: A History, 1524-1948. With a Supplement Puppets in America Since 1948 by Marjorie Batchelder McPharlin**. Boston: Plays, 1969. 734p. LC 79-97944.

Although written as a narrative, the McPharlins' work remains useful as a reference book. Really two books in one cover, the work includes Paul McPharlin's original study of puppetry in America and Marjorie Batchelder McPharlin's supplement, which brings the history to 1969. Most helpful is a list of American puppeteers from 1524 to 1948 with brief biographical information. Mrs. McPharlin supplements the list with biographies of puppeteers active in the late 1960s. She also includes an annotated bibliography and information about puppetry organizations. Because no other chronicle of puppet activities in the United States exists, researchers may want to consult McPharlin's narrative. It describes, in rough chronological order, the European traveling puppet companies and the American puppeteers who entertained American audiences from the sixteenth to the twentieth centuries. For additional information on puppets, consult Crothers' bibliography (entry 31), which is more extensive than the one published here.

7—Handbooks and Yearbooks

434. Moore, Frank Ledlie. **Crowell's Handbook of Gilbert and Sullivan**. New York: Thomas Y. Crowell, 1962. 264p. LC 61-12817.

Moore devotes a chapter to each of the operettas on which William S. Gilbert and Sir Arthur Sullivan collaborated, from *Thespis* in 1871 to *The Grand Duke* in 1896. Besides a plot summary and details about the first night's performance, Moore provides information about the conception of each work and the critical reaction to it. Short biographies of Sullivan, Gilbert, and Richard D'Oyly Carte, their producer, are followed by a list of the members of D'Oyly Carte's Savoy Company, a list of first lines and famous lines from the songs, and a bibliography. Although the book lacks an index, it is well organized and will answer many basic questions about Gilbert and Sullivan's collaborations. For a dictionary of allusions and topical names in the operettas see Dunn (entry 269).

435. Morrow, Lee Alan. **The Tony Award Book: Four Decades of Great American Theater**. New York: Abbeville Press, 1987. 274p. LC 87-11501. ISBN 0-89659-584-6.

Morrow's appendix lists Tony Award winners 1946-1987 and nominees 1956-1987 chronologically. The rest of the lavishly illustrated book, not designed for quick reference use, recounts the history of the award and offers a selection of biographical material and anecdotes about the winners. A general index locates persons, plays, and theatre companies. If Isabelle Stevenson's *The Tony Award* (entry 453) is not available, Morrow's book provides a satisfactory second choice.

436. Mullin, Donald, comp. **Victorian Plays: A Record of Significant Productions on the London Stage, 1837-1901**. (Bibliographies and Indexes in the Performing Arts, no. 4). Westport, Conn.: Greenwood, 1987. 444p. LC 86-25718. ISBN 0-313-24211-9.

Mullin lists plays produced in London during Queen Victoria's reign in about sixty of the most important theatres. Only professional performances of legitimate plays are included. Mullin lists the name(s) of the theatre(s) that produced the play, the dates of performances, the type of play such as drama or comedy, and the number of acts. Sometimes he gives names of cast members as well. Unfortunately, because no chronological arrangement supplements the alphabetical list of entries, Mullin's work cannot be seen as a continuation of *The London Stage 1660-1800* (entry 563). Neither is there an index of actors' names. By limiting access to play titles, Mullin has limited his book's usefulness.

437. O'Donnol, Shirley Miles. **American Costume, 1915-1970: A Source Book for the Stage Costumer**. Bloomington: Indiana University Press, 1982. 270p. LC 81-48390. ISBN 0-253-30589-6.

Useful as a supplement to Lucy Barton's *Historic Costume for the Stage* (entry 378), O'Donnol's guide records and illustrates seven periods of American dress between World War I and 1970. For each time period she follows Barton's pattern of discussing the general characteristics of costume followed by specific elements of men's, women's, and children's dress. She deals with material and colors appropriate to the period and suggests how to achieve the proper look in the theatre. Photographs and line drawings enhance the text, and a bibliography provides additional sources to consult. Regrettably, there is no index. Nevertheless, O'Donnol's book will help those faced with costuming a twentieth-century play.

438. **Performing Arts Annual**. Washington, D.C.: The Library of Congress, 1986- . Annual. ISSN 0887-8234.

Based on the large manuscript collection of the Library of Congress, this annual publishes articles on a variety of performing arts topics including theatre, dance, film, and television. Recently, an article described the creation of three Martha Graham dances, using Graham's correspondence to show their development, while another looked at the Children's Theatre of the Federal Theatre Project during the Depression. Beautifully and abundantly illustrated with portraits, still photographs from films, costume drawings, and reproductions of manuscript pages and musical scores, *Performing Arts Annual* is a feast for the eyes. Each volume also includes a list of the Library of Congress's performing arts publications, a description of its research facilities, and a list of the year's performances at the library.

439. **Performing Arts Resources**. New York: Theatre Library Association, 1974- . Annual. LC 75-646287. ISSN 0360-3814.

Published by the Theatre Library Association (entry 747), this annual originally reported on the resources available in North American repositories for the study of the performing arts, excluding music and dance. Through the years, the focus has broadened "to make available reference materials to scholars, curators, and the staffs of performing arts and general-readership libraries." Volume 13, for example, used materials drawn from several archives to write about two famous American acting families, the Drews and the Barrymores. Another volume dealt with nineteenth- and early twentieth-century periodicals, while a third presented a series of bibliographies on various theatre topics. Designed for theatre library professionals, these volumes will also be of interest to researchers.

440. Peterson, Richard. **The Character Catalog: Who's Who in One Hundred Fifty Modern Plays**. New York: Drama Book, 1984. 91p. LC 83-16362. ISBN 0-89676-069-3.

Peterson describes characters from "150 modern plays frequently produced in regional theatre, summer stock, and dinner theatre" (introduction). Each play's entry, presented alphabetically, lists all characters, their ages, and descriptions of their personalities, drawn from the playwrights' descriptions and from a reading of the scripts. Peterson includes an author index, but not a character index. Therefore, readers cannot use this work in the same way they can use the Sharps' indexes (entry 446). Because these plays are the most frequently performed, many of the characters will be familiar to theatre people and play-goers already. If a script is not available and a brief character description is needed, Peterson may provide the information.

441. Prisk, Berneice. **Stage Costume Handbook**. New York: Harper & Row, 1966. 198p. LC 66-10606.

Although not as detailed or scholarly as Barton (entry 378) or O'Donnol (entry 437), Prisk's guide includes chapters on building and equipping a costume workshop and on organizing and running a costume crew during a production. The first part of her book describes and illustrates various historical, national, and traditional costumes. The second section deals with construction and care of stage costumes. Both the bibliography and the directory that complete the book are outdated and should be ignored. The table of contents and the brief index together will help readers find information by subject.

134 / 7—Handbooks and Yearbooks

442. Richel, Veronica C., comp. **The German Stage, 1767-1890: A Directory of Playwrights and Plays**. (Bibliographies and Indexes in the Performing Arts, no. 7). Westport, Conn.: Greenwood, 1988. 230p. LC 87-25155. ISBN 0-313-24990-3.

Richel has used German theatre chronicles and histories to compile information about German playwrights and plays during the late eighteenth and nineteenth centuries. Beginning with 1767, the date of the first attempt to establish a German national theatre, she concludes with 1890, the year that *Neuer Theater-Almanac* (now *Deutsches Bühner-Jahrbuch*) first appeared. Entries, arranged by playwright, list place and date of birth and death and cite references to biographical material. A list of the author's plays follows with the genre and number of acts specified. Richel then provides the year of the (usually) first performance in Vienna plus nine German cities. If the first performance cannot be verified, she includes the earliest performance found. Some plays, of course, never played in all ten cities, and therefore have fewer than ten dates listed. A bibliography of sources appears in the front of the volume. Readers will need to consult the introduction for an explanation of Richel's methods and the limitations of this work. It provides very little actual information about any one play, but it may suggest avenues of exploration to German scholars.

443. Rowse, A. L. **Shakespeare's Characters: A Complete Guide**. London: Methuen, 1984. 167p. ISBN 0-413-56710-9.

Rowse's work discusses Shakespeare's characters, A-to-Z, naming the play in which they appear and relating them to other characters and to the plot. Similar to May's handbook (entry 431), this work lacks an index by play title, a feature that May provides. Readers will find much the same information in both books, and either may be used to answer questions about Shakespeare's characters.

444. Sampson, Henry T. **Blacks in Blackface: A Source Book on Early Black Musical Shows**. Metuchen, N.J.: Scarecrow, 1980. 552p. LC 80-15048. ISBN 0-8108-1318-1.

This handbook aims to present information about the Black musical theatre in the United States, that is, shows produced by African-Americans and performed in Black theatres. Despite the book's title, it does not restrict itself to shows where the actors wore blackface. Sampson divides his work into several chapters that together present the history of the Black musical, biographical sketches of both the businessmen and the performers, histories of famous Black theatres, and synopses of many shows. Sampson's information is drawn from weekly newspapers and theatre programs. He has pulled together much useful information that would be hard to find otherwise. Readers may want to check Woll's *Dictionary of the Black Theatre* (entry 462) which covers non-musical plays as well as musicals. Sampson's *The Ghost Walks* (entry 578) chronicles Black performance between the Civil War and 1910 but does not discuss theatres or present biographies.

445. Seller, Maxine Schwartz, ed. **Ethnic Theatre in the United States**. Westport, Conn.: Greenwood, 1983. 606p. LC 81-13494. ISBN 0-313-21230-9.

Finding information on the theatrical activity of immigrants to the United States, activity that hit its high point during the early twentieth century, is difficult. Many of the sources lie scattered in repositories all over the country, and much material has simply been lost. Seller and her fellow contributors summarize current research and "direct the reader to sources for further research" (introduction) for the theatre of twenty representative ethnic groups. The ethnic groups were chosen on the basis of finding an expert who could write about the topic and on locating sufficient source material to make an essay feasible. Each chapter discusses the origins, history, dramatic literature, and personnel of a particular group, from Armenian-Americans to the Yiddish theatre. Each author also covers the ethnic theatre's relation to mainstream American theatre and to its homeland theatre (e.g., Polish-American theatre vis-à-vis Polish theatre), its role in the ethnic community, and the status of current research. A short bibliography completes each chapter. A subject index helps locate information but is not as complete as it should be. Seller provides a good starting point for those who wish to research the theatrical activity of their forebears or of another ethnic group.

445a. **Shakespeare Survey**. Cambridge, England: Cambridge University Press, 1948- . Annual. LC 49-1639. ISSN 0080-9152.

Founded to document not only the study of Shakespeare's works but also "their representation on the stage" (preface, volume 1), this annual continues to record and critique performances of Shakespeare's plays. The yearbook features bibliographic essays, articles on various aspects of Shakespeare's work, and reviews of stage, film, and television versions of the plays. A noteworthy section is the annual overview of British productions. Comprising more than 45 years, this title will help readers who wish to study changes in performance practice since World War II.

446. Sharp, Harold S., and Marjorie Z. Sharp, comps. **Index to Characters in the Performing Arts**. New York: Scarecrow, 1966-1973. 4v. in 6. LC 66-13744.

The Sharps have identified thousands of characters with their respective plays, operas, operettas, ballets, and motion pictures in this monumental work. Part 1 concentrates on 30,000 characters in 3,600 non-musical plays written by 1,400 authors. The compilers include English plays and translations of foreign works written between the fifth century B.C. and 1965. Part 2 identifies 20,000 characters in 2,500 works written between the thirteenth century and 1966. It includes operas and operettas from many countries as well as musicals from Britain and America. Part 3 locates 3,000 characters in 800 ballets from the late sixteenth century to 1970. In all parts the alphabetical list of characters includes a one-line description and a list of related characters. For example, "Stanley, Major General" is followed by a list of his four daughters. In the first part the name of the play, the author, and the date of its first performance are included in each entry. Parts 2 and 3 use a symbol for each work. A second section, arranged by symbol, presents production information for each work. Although in need of a supplement, the Sharps' work is an obvious help in answering questions about characters' names in almost 7,000 plays, operas, and ballets.

447. Shaver, Ruth M. **Kabuki Costume**. Rutland, Vt.: Charles E. Tuttle, 1966. 396p. LC 66-15266.

Shaver, who studied kabuki for fourteen years while living in Japan, has written a fascinating book about the costumes, wigs, and makeup used by kabuki performers. After an historical sketch, she arranges her chapters by costume type with special chapters for wigs and makeup. She explains the costume and which character wears it, when it was first used, and plays in which it is used. Given the highly stylized nature of Japanese theatre, it is not surprising that an entire chapter is devoted to "hashori," or pulling up the kimono hem by the hand and tucking it into the obi. The way the actor pulls the hem, the hand used, and the placement of the tuck denote different attributes of the character wearing the

136 / 7—Handbooks and Yearbooks

costume. Both color and black-and-white illustrations enhance the text. Indexed by subject, play title, actors' names, and character names, the book also contains a glossary of terms and a bibliography. For information about other aspects of kabuki see *The Kabuki Handbook* (entry 405) and Leiter's *Kabuki Encyclopedia* (entry 286).

448. Shipley, Joseph T. **The Crown Guide to the World's Great Plays: From Ancient Greece to Modern Times**. rev. ed. New York: Crown, 1984. 866p. LC 83-27211. ISBN 0-517-55392-9.

In this revision of his 1956 *Guide to Great Plays*, Shipley drops some plays from the first edition and adds others, according to his judgment about their lasting value. He describes hundreds of plays written in all time periods from ancient Greece to the late twentieth century. (The most recent is David Mamet's 1983 play, *Glengarry Glen Ross*.) Arranged alphabetically by author, entries combine background information, a plot summary, and information about one or more productions with Shipley's critical comments. The book exhibits a bias toward English-language plays, although major European writers such as Ibsen, Giradoux, and Pirandello are included. Asia and Africa are ignored. For the post-World War II period, readers will find Kienzle (entry 415) more complete. Shipley remains a good basic handbook for Western European and American plays.

449. Silverman, Maxwell. **Contemporary Theatre Architecture: An Illustrated Survey; A Checklist of Publications 1946-1964 by Ned A. Bowman**. New York: The New York Public Library, 1965. 1v. LC 65-12942.

Silverman describes and illustrates fifty theatre buildings that represented trends in theatre architecture during the post-World War II period. The well known Lincoln Center and Metropolitan Opera House in New York City are accompanied by educational facilities such as the Krannert Center at the University of Illinois (in the planning stages and illustrated with architect's drawings) and the Speech Arts Building at Orange Coast College in Costa Mesa, California. Arranged by type of theatre, each building's date of construction, architect, seating capacity, and type of design is listed. In the second part of the book Bowman compiles a comprehensive bibliography on twentieth-century theatre architecture. The unannotated list of books, articles, theses, and unpublished materials is arranged by country of publication and indexed by subject. It supplements Stoddard's more recent bibliography, *Theatre and Cinema Architecture* (entry 87).

450. Simas, Rick. **The Musicals No One Came to See: A Guidebook to Four Decades of Musical-Comedy Casualties on Broadway, Off-Broadway and in Out-of-Town Tryout, 1943-1983**. New York: Garland, 1987. 639p. LC 87-25095. ISBN 0-8240-8804-2.

Convinced that many short-lived and stillborn Broadway musicals can be successfully performed by theatre groups, Simas has compiled information about 577 shows that premiered between 1943 and 1983 and that either closed in tryouts or ran for fewer than 300 performances. He divides his work into four parts: Broadway flops, off- and off-off-Broadway failures, shows that did not reach Broadway, and longer-running shows that are currently not available for production. Within these categories alphabetical entries provide credits, source of adaptation (novel, play, etc.), citations to magazine and newspaper reviews, and information on locating scripts, librettos, recordings, and sheet music. Most important, Simas lists the owner of the musical's rights, that is, the person who can give permission for a performance. Simas also advises producers about legal arrangements and working with the original authors and composers on a revival. Indexed by title, by source

Handbooks and Yearbooks / 137

of adaptations, and by librettist, composer, lyricist, and author, this handbook may help those looking for an unusual musical to produce. See also Leonard's books (entries 420 and 421), which describe all types of Broadway "casualties" including non-musical plays.

451. Somerset, J. Alan B. **The Stratford Festival Story: A Catalogue-Index to the Stratford, Ontario, Festival 1953-1990**. (Bibliographies and Indexes in the Performing Arts, no. 8). Westport, Conn.: Greenwood, 1991. 316p. LC 91-11238. ISBN 0-313-27804-0.

Inspired by Mullin and Muriello's catalog of the Royal Shakespeare Theatre's archives (entry 177), Somerset has written this work to document the Stratford, Ontario, Shakespeare Festival. In his introduction he presents a brief history of the Festival and of its archives. The chronological catalog lists credits, number of performances, and citations to reviews and notices from forty newspapers for 636 plays produced between 1953 and 1989. The author provides only cast lists and credits for 1990. Somerset's work will help those researching Canadian theatre. As he notes in his book, readers desiring more information should contact the Festival archives directly.

452. Stern, Lawrence. **Stage Management: A Guidebook of Practical Techniques**. 4th ed. Boston: Allyn & Bacon, 1991. 349p. LC 91-24955. ISBN 0-205-13466-1.

Written by an experienced stage manager, this handbook discusses the many aspects of a stage manager's job in detail. Arranged by broad subjects such as acquiring, marking, and handling scripts; scheduling; supervising stage staff; working rehearsals; running the show; and closing and moving the show, the book also includes a chronological index and a subject index. The former arranges the stage manager's duties according to the normal progression of a play production from the decision to perform to postproduction chores. Stern includes many forms and examples of letters, charts, and other communications useful in stage management. His book should help fledgling stage managers whether in school, community, or professional theatre.

453. Stevenson, Isabelle, ed. **The Tony Award: A Complete Listing, with a History of the American Theatre Wing**. New York: Crown, 1987. 197p. LC 87-5226. ISBN 0-517-56664-8.

Broadway's answer to the Oscars, the Tony Awards owe their name to Antoinette Perry, chairman of the board, and later secretary of the American Theatre Wing. Originally founded to aid the war effort during World War I, the organization continued its charitable activities during the Second World War. Its aims have changed over the ensuing years, and it now tries "to further the highest standards of the theatre," primarily by awarding prizes for the best plays and performers on Broadway every year. This book offers a chronological listing of every Tony award winner from 1947 to 1987. For years since 1956 both nominees and winners are listed. (Nominees' names were first made public in 1956.) An alphabetical list of winners (but not nominees) functions as an index. Readers can find more recent winners by using the *New York Times Index* (entry 213).

454. Suskin, Steven. **Show Tunes, 1905-1991: The Songs, Shows, and Careers of Broadway's Major Composers**. rev. and expanded ed. New York: Limelight Editions, 1992. 769p. LC 91-23643. ISBN 0-8791-0146-6.

Suskin emphasizes thirty American composers and their work in his handbook of twentieth-century musicals. By arranging the book in rough chronological order by the date of each composer's first important work, Suskin provides an historical overview of the Broadway musical from Jerome Kern to Steven Schwartz (the composer of *Pippin* and *Godspell*). Entries describe the works of each composer written through July 1991 with emphasis on the songs and their composition. Suskin lists all published and recorded scores and separately published songs. He notes songs that were cut from the production, reused from another show, revived, or added to the film version or revival. A special section provides information on important Broadway scores by composers other than Suskin's chosen thirty. These include *Hair*, *1776*, and *A Chorus Line* as well as *Big River* with music by country singer Roger Miller. A chronological list of productions, a list of collaborators (librettists, producers, etc.), and a bibliography are followed by indexes for song title, show title, and personal name. Suskin, who has acted as business manager for dozens of Broadway productions, has produced a useful handbook that emphasizes the major musicals. It is not comprehensive, however, and readers looking for information about lesser-known musicals should consult Bordman's *American Musical Theatre* (entry 547).

455. Swortzell, Lowell, ed. **International Guide to Children's Theatre and Educational Theatre: A Historical and Geographical Source Book**. Westport, Conn.: Greenwood, 1990. 381p. LC 89-12059. ISBN 0-313-24881-8.

Quoting Mark Twain's belief that "children's theatre is one of the very, very great inventions of the twentieth century," Swortzell surveys children's theatre in forty-five countries around the world. His introduction includes a short history of children's theatre from ancient Greece to the late twentieth century. Following are the alphabetically arranged national essays. Based on information provided by each country, entries give a history of children's theatre, a survey of contemporary practice, descriptions of major companies, and bibliographic references. Within this framework quite a bit of variation in terms of coverage and style exists. Events have rendered some chapters obsolete, notably the chapters for East and West Germany, Yugoslavia, and the USSR. The Czechoslovakian entry makes no mention of changes since that country's "velvet revolution." This book offers a beginning point for researchers in the growing field of children's theatre. One hopes Swortzell will expand and update the information in a second edition.

456. **Theatre World**. New York: Daniel C. Blum, 1945-1950; New York: Greenberg, 1951-1965; New York: Crown, 1973- . Annual.

Short on prose but long on photographs, *Theatre World* supplements *The Best Plays* by providing a pictorial record of each season in New York and elsewhere. The work is divided into sections on Broadway, off-Broadway, touring companies, and regional companies. Entries provide cast and credits, opening date and theatre as well as subsequent changes in casts, awards won, and closing date, as appropriate for each play opening on Broadway or off-Broadway. Each Broadway production is represented by several photographs. Off-Broadway repertory companies and regional companies are listed with personnel and repertoires, again accompanied by photographs. The book also lists productions carried over from previous years. Biographical data on cast members from many of the productions and obituaries of leading theatre personalities follow. Many of the biographies and obituaries feature portraits. An index helps readers find their way to the many facts and photographs presented in this annual look at American theatre.

Handbooks and Yearbooks / 139

457. Thomson, Peter, and Gamini Salgado. **The Everyman Companion to the Theatre**. London: J. M. Dent, 1985. 458p. LC 86-122658. ISBN 0-460-04424-9.

An opinionated, anecdotal handbook, Thomson and Salgado's book aims to put "the English-speaking theatre in its context" (preface). To that end they provide a theatrical chronology from 1500 to 1982; essays on English and American drama and theatre; a dictionary of theatres, companies, and genres; a biographical dictionary; and a section of theatrical miscellany. The authors provide an index to the essays and a play title index. The short entries often contain a bibliographic reference. Opinions abound. Of Richard Burton, whom the authors believe wasted himself making mediocre motion pictures, they write, "He is the twentieth-century theatre's leading sacrifice to the technological revolution." The last section contains amusing anecdotes, some of which may be the theatrical equivalent of urban myths, about all kinds of people and events. One A. E. Matthews forgot his lines when he answered a telephone on stage one night. "'It's for you,' he said to the only other actor on stage at the time—and left." Not a first choice among handbooks, this is nevertheless a delight to read and quote.

458. Toohey, John L. **A History of the Pulitzer Prize Plays**. New York: Citadel Press, 1967. 344p. LC 67-25654.

A chronological history, Toohey's work discusses the Pulitzer Prize-winning plays from 1916, when the award was initiated, to 1967. Besides listing credits for each plays' opening production, entries describe the plot, summarize critical reviews, and present Toohey's opinion on the year's choice. For the several seasons when no prizes were awarded (including the first year), the author gives a brief description of the season and reasons why no play won. Many black-and-white photographs and an index enhance the work. See also Bonin's *Prize-Winning American Drama* (entry 385).

459. Van Hoogstraten, Nicholas. **Lost Broadway Theatres**. New York: Princeton Architectural Press, 1991. 288p. LC 90-23520. ISBN 1-878271-06-7; 0-910413-58-4 pa.

Between 1882 and 1932 New Yorkers built ninety theatres in the Broadway area, concentrating more theatres in midtown Manhattan than anywhere else in the world. By 1990 only thirty-five playhouses continued to present live productions. Many theatres have been demolished or converted to other uses. Van Hoogstraten describes fifty-four "lost" Broadway theatres. Thirteen of these still exist, but are closed or used for other purposes. The others have fallen to the wrecker's ball. Arranged chronologically by date of construction, each chapter presents a short, readable history including a physical description of the theatre, important plays or acts that performed in the house, its eventual decline, and date of its demolition. Well chosen black-and-white photographs accompany each chapter and usually present both exterior and interior views. An appendix shows floor plans and elevations for many of the theatres. A bibliography and an index by theatre name complete the book. Sadly, many of these theatres disappeared to make room for office buildings or hotels. Van Hoogstraten has been able to preserve some of the theatres' charm in his book.

460. Walkup, Fairfax Proudfit. **Dressing the Part: A History of Costume for the Theatre**. New York: F. S. Crofts, 1938. 397p. LC 38-21125.

Like Barton (entry 378) Walkup has written an extensive handbook on historic costume and has arranged it in the same fashion. Starting with ancient Egypt, Walkup describes each era's history, provides general characteristics of costume, and then gives specific details about men's, women's, and children's clothing. The author finishes the chapter with suggestions for modern stage adaptations of the period's dress. In succeeding chapters Walkup takes the reader through history up to the early twentieth century. An appendix provides brief and now outdated notes on clothing construction, followed by a bibliography and index. Although Walkup's work is not as detailed as Barton, in most cases it is an adequate substitute if Barton is not available.

461. Watson, Lee. **Lighting Design Handbook**. New York: McGraw-Hill, 1990. 458p. LC 89-39104. ISBN 0-07-068481-2.

A complete rewriting of the author's earlier book, *Theatrical Lighting Practice*, coauthored with Joel E. Rubin, this title was published after Watson's death. He worked extensively in all fields of lighting design including Broadway and television, and his book focuses on design as opposed to technology. Although the first three chapters concentrate on basics, Watson devotes most of the work to design for particular situations such as musical theatre, outdoor theatre, puppetry, mime, dance, opera, and so forth. He also discusses the use of lighting in television and cinematography and in architectural and commercial applications. The last part of the book explains the business end of design, discussing employment prospects, unions, and professional organizations. Throughout the book, Watson uses footnotes to augment his work, and the bibliography thus created will prove useful to many. He offers more than a dozen references on lighting outdoor pageants, for example. Watson also provides photographs and lighting plots that illustrate the latest thinking on lighting design. His handbook should be consulted first when looking for information on lighting design.

462. Woll, Allen L. **Dictionary of the Black Theatre: Broadway, Off-Broadway, and Selected Harlem Theatre**. Westport, Conn.: Greenwood, 1983. 359p. LC 82-21090. ISBN 0-313-22561-3.

Woll, who is associate professor of history at Rutgers, has written extensively on film and theatre. Part 1 of this book documents more than 300 shows produced between 1898 and 1981. All were produced, acted, and/or written by African-Americans. Each of the alphabetical entries contains a cast list, a plot synopsis, a summary of critical comments from both Black and general circulation newspapers, and an evaluation of the plays' importance. Part 2 contains biographies of major Black actors, playwrights, and directors, and notes major organizations encouraging Black theatre in twentieth-century New York City. Entries, which are arranged alphabetically, often refer to materials on file in the New York Public Library's theatre collections. Appendices include a chronology of Black plays, a discography of Black shows, and a selected bibliography of Black theatre history and criticism.

463. Young, William C. **Documents of American Theater History**. Vol. 1, **Famous American Playhouses 1716-1899**. Chicago: American Library Association, 1973. 327p. LC 72-9837. ISBN 0-8389-0136-0.

464. Young, William C. **Documents of American Theater History**. Vol. 2; **Famous American Playhouses 1900-1971**. Chicago: American Library Association, 1973. 297p. LC 73-657. ISBN 0-8389-0137-9.

Young uses a mix of primary and secondary sources to document the history of theatres and playhouses in the United States. He has chosen 199 theatres based on a combination of their historical, architectural, or cultural importance. One or more excerpts from contemporary newspaper accounts, architectural journals, and other printed sources describe the theatre, generally at the time of its construction or grand opening. Selections from volume 1 tend to focus on the social aspects of the theatre's opening, while those in the second volume are more concerned with architectural and technical criticism. Young groups his playhouses into chapters by date of construction, location (such as New York and regional), and type. The indexes facilitate access by theatre name, location, personal name, and occupation (architects, theatre owners, and others). Both volumes contain selected bibliographies.

Dance Handbooks

465. Balanchine, George. **Balanchine's New Complete Stories of the Great Ballets**. Edited by Francis Mason. Garden City, N.Y.: Doubleday, 1968. 626p. LC 68-22606.

Describing 231 ballets, with some overlap with Balanchine's *101 Stories* (entry 466), this handbook also discusses the history of ballet; explains how to enjoy a performance; and provides a glossary, a bibliography, and a discography. The main body of the work lists ballets alphabetically with discussions of their plots and dancing and, often, notes on their critical reception. Balanchine also provides credits for each work's first performance and first American performance. Because it covers more ballets, this work is preferred to Balanchine's *101 Stories*.

466. Balanchine, George and Francis Mason. **101 Stories of the Great Ballets**. Garden City, N.Y.: Dolphin (Doubleday), 1975. 541p. LC 73-9140. ISBN 0-385-03398-2.

The reader of Balanchine's guide to fifty classic ballets and fifty-one new ballets created between 1968 and 1974 is treated to descriptions of and comments on the greatest works by one of the greatest choreographers. Balanchine tells the story of each ballet and describes its dancing from beginning to end. Entries, arranged by title, also provide credits for the first performance. Works set on the New York City Ballet, including Balanchine's own masterpieces, tend to be described more fully than other pieces. Interspersed personal comments add interest to the text; for example, Balanchine interrupts his discussion of *A Midsummer Night's Dream* to mention that as a child he played an elf in the St. Petersburg production, and that the play has always been a favorite of his. He goes on to discuss his choreography set to Mendelssohn's music in 1962. The subject index includes personal names. Because of its American bias this work should be used with Clarke and Crisp's handbook (entry 470), which takes a more British viewpoint.

467. **The Ballet Annual**. London: A & C Black, 1947-1963. LC 48-7447.

With a British emphasis, *The Ballet Annual* chronicled events in the dance world for eighteen years. Heavily illustrated with black-and-white photographs, each volume presented outstanding events of the year in Britain and discussed highlights of the season in other countries, including the United States, Denmark, and France. Not as inclusive as the new *World Ballet and Dance*, this series, nevertheless, contributes to the history of dance in the post-war period.

468. Beaumont, Cyril W. **Complete Book of Ballets: A Guide to the Principal Ballets of the Nineteenth and Twentieth Centuries**. rev. ed. London: Putnam, 1956. 1,106p.

Beaumont, who wrote many ballet books during his long career as a London bookseller and balletomane (see entries 101 and 307), describes more than 200 major ballets of the nineteenth and early twentieth centuries. Beaumont made his selections from a study of contemporary records and the ballets' scenarios and, in the case of twentieth-century ballets, from personal observation. Arranged chronologically by choreographer, each chapter begins with a short biography and is followed by a description of each of that choreographer's works chosen by Beaumont. The author includes many excerpts from contemporary newspaper accounts of first performances and occasionally offers his own critical comments. He describes many works not found in the other dance handbooks. For instance, he includes eight ballets by Paul Taglioni (brother of the famous nineteenth-century ballerina Marie Taglioni) that are rarely performed today. Beaumont presents an historical record while the other handbooks concern themselves with helping ballet-goers interpret currently performed works. For that reason, Beaumont is a necessary source, even though old.

469. Casey, Betty, ed. and comp. **International Folk Dancing U.S.A.** Garden City, N.Y.: Doubleday, 1981. 363p. LC 78-60283. ISBN 0-385-13308-1.

Part dictionary, part instruction manual, part directory, and part biographical dictionary, Casey's handbook provides information on all aspects of international folk dance. Profiles of major performing groups such as Duquesne University's Tamburitzans and the AMAN Folk Ensemble of Los Angeles are included as well as biographies of folk dance pioneers and descriptions of organizations and associations. Casey includes a dictionary of folk dance terms, steps, and movements. For many readers the most important part of the book will be the chapters containing directions for performing the folk dances of more than twenty-five countries. Each of these sections has been written by an expert in that dance tradition, often a native of the country. The bibliography will help readers continue their research but should be supplemented with references from periodical indexes. A general index helps one find one's way in this informative book.

470. Clarke, Mary, and Clement Crisp. **The Ballet Goer's Guide**. 1st American ed. New York: Alfred A. Knopf; Distr., New York: Random House, 1981. 367p. LC 81-47496. ISBN 0-394-51307-X.

Clarke and Crisp have written a guide to 138 ballets for the novice ballet-goer. Arranged alphabetically by ballet title, the entries list credits and details of the first performance, background information on the ballet's creation, and a plot and dance synopsis. Compared with George Balanchine's handbooks (entries 465 and 466), Clarke and Crisp exhibit a slight British slant in terms of the ballets chosen for discussion and the dancers who appear in the photographs. Clarke and Crisp include introductory material on the process of making a new ballet, a glossary of ballet terms, and short biographies of major choreographers and dancers. Along with Balanchine, this book will answer basic questions about the better-known works in the repertoire. Terry (entry 480) discusses more ballets, but in less detail.

471. **John Willis' Dance World**. (Formerly *Dance World*.) New York: Crown, 1966- . Annual. ISSN 0070-2692.

Notable for its lavish use of photographs, each year's *John Willis' Dance World* lists dance companies, their personnel, and their repertoires for the season. Both New York and regional companies appear in each volume, as do touring companies visiting New York. The annual also covers summer dance festivals. Short biographies of important dancers, both in New York and regionally, are followed by obituaries and an index. Because photographs comprise more than half of each page, this is the place to look for illustrations of specific dance events and to locate information about a company during a given year.

472. Drew, David, ed. **The Decca Book of Ballet**. London: Frederick Muller, c. 1958. 572p. LC 59-1334.

Drew's handbook differs from other ballet books in that it stresses music rather than choreography. Appropriately, the work is arranged by composer's name within two sections: scores composed especially for ballet and music that was later converted to use for dance. An example of the latter is Mendelssohn's "Scotch Symphony," which Balanchine later used for a ballet. Each entry provides details of the ballet's first production, a synopsis of the action, and notes about the music. Other chapters include a short history of ballet, brief biographies of major dancers and choreographers, and sketches of ballet companies. Given the book's age, however, its greatest use will be to those who want to know what they are hearing as well as seeing when they attend a ballet performance.

473. Dufort, Antony. **Ballet Steps: Practice to Performance**. London: Kingswood Press, 1990. 160p. ISBN 0-434-98136-2.

Dufort, an artist and sculptor, became fascinated with ballet when a friend took him to a performance. This handbook combines his artistic and dance interests. He has drawn lovely and clear illustrations of the basic steps and positions used by ballet dancers. Starting with warm-ups and barre work, the book then continues with floor movements and partner work. An index-glossary and a bibliography complete the work. Readers who prefer photographs to drawings may want to consult Warren's *Classical Ballet Technique* or Mackie's *Basic Ballet* (entries 481, 476) instead of Dufort.

474. Guillot, Genevieve, and Germaine Prudhommeau. **The Book of Ballet**. (A Spectrum Book). Englewood Cliffs, N.J.: Prentice-Hall, 1976. 418p. LC 75-35930. ISBN 0-13-079905-X.

A translation of Guillot's *Grammaire de la Danse Classique* (1969), this work defines and describes positions, steps, and combinations of movements used in classical ballet. Guillot starts with the basic positions and steps, progresses through leaps, turns, acrobatics, and arm movements, and ends with enchainements or sequences of movement designed for a single dancer or a pair. The last chapter presents examples of lessons or classes for pupils at various stages of expertise. The book suffers from a stilted translation, and Guillot's illustrations are not as informative as Dufort or Mackie (entries 473, 476). Nevertheless, she presents much useful information, especially on the more complicated combinations of steps and on acrobatics. The index allows the book to function as a dictionary, but readers should note that index numbers refer to pages, not to the numbered paragraphs.

144 / 7—Handbooks and Yearbooks

475. Lowe, Jacqueline, and Charles Selber. **The Language of Show Dancing.** New York: Charles Scribner's Sons, 1980. 1v. LC 80-10751. ISBN 0-684-16431-0.

Using photographs taken by dance photographer Martha Swope, Lowe, a Broadway dancer, and Selber, a theatre producer and director, demonstrate positions and steps used in show dancing. This style of dancing is used in Broadway musicals, motion pictures, and television specials. After consulting this book, one can talk authoritatively about the bump, the cakewalk, and the grapevine. Theatre-goers who want to identify the moves they see in *All That Jazz* or *A Chorus Line* will find this title helpful.

476. Mackie, Joyce. **Basic Ballet.** New York: Penguin Books, 1980. 127p. LC 79-28212. ISBN 0-14-046445-X.

Designed as a reference for ballet students and audiences, Mackie's handbook shows in clear photographic sequences all basic movements in classical ballet. Mackie follows the sequence of motions that all dancers follow in class, starting with basic leg and arm movements to warm up the muscles and continuing to more and more complex work, first at the barre and then away from it. The photographs help the reader work through each movement and position required for a certain step. Mackie includes a brief glossary of French ballet terms at the end of the work. This is not as complete as Warren (entry 481), but it answers basic questions about ballet technique. Dufort's book (entry 473) is similar but uses drawings instead of photographs.

477. Reynolds, Nancy, and Susan Reimer-Torn. **Dance Classics: A Viewer's Guide to the Best-Loved Ballets and Modern Dances.** Pennington, N.J.: a capella books/Chicago Review Press, 1991. 297p. LC 90-27665. ISBN 1-55652-109-X; 1-55652-106-5 pa.

First published in 1980, this handbook differs from Balanchine (entries 465 and 466) and Clarke and Crisp (entry 470) in its arrangement, which places each of fifty-three ballets into chapters by type of ballet. The categories include the romantic ballets (*La Sylphide, Giselle, Pas de Quatre*); the classic works (*Swan Lake, The Nutcracker*); classical pas de deux; comedy ballets; twentieth-century traditional ballets (*Romeo and Juliet, Cinderella*); and contemporary and modern dances of Martha Graham, Doris Humphrey, and others. Although somewhat artificial, these divisions allow one to read and compare several ballets that have in common their date of creation and a certain style. Especially for novices, this approach may be more helpful than an alphabetical arrangement. The authors have written good explanations of the action and plot of each ballet. They include a glossary of dance terms and an index. The book is illustrated, but not so well as Clarke and Crisp's guide.

478. Robertson, Allen, and Donald Hutera. **The Dance Handbook.** Boston: G. K. Hall, 1990. 278p. LC 89-77759. ISBN 0-8161-9095-X; 0-8161-1829-9 pa.

Broader in scope than Balanchine (entries 465 and 466), Clarke and Crisp (entry 470), Terry (entry 480), and *Dance Classics* (entry 477), *The Dance Handbook* discusses dance companies, choreographers, and dancers as well as ballets and modern dance works. Entries are arranged alphabetically within broad chronological chapters. The final chapter, titled "Alternatives," discusses choreographers such as Meredith Monk and Mark Morris who do not appear in older handbooks. Besides providing biographies, company histories, and ballet plot outlines, the editors include a feature called "lineage." This feature refers to other ballets that have elements in common with the work under discussion. As an example, Robertson and Hutera claim that modern choreographers such as Lucinda Childs and Trisha Brown have drawn from the famous repetitive pattern danced by the corps de ballet in *La Bayadere* to create their own choreographic repetitions as a way of "transforming real time into a seemingly endless stream of movement." Besides a short glossary and a brief bibliography, the book includes a country-by-country listing of information sources and an index. Many entries also contain suggestions for further reading or viewing. Because many of its features set it apart from other dance handbooks, Robertson and Hutera's work is an important source.

479. Schlundt, Christena L. **Dance in the Musical Theatre: Jerome Robbins and His Peers, 1934-1965: A Guide**. (Garland Reference Library of the Humanities, vol. 1213). New York: Garland, 1989. 247p. LC 89-1117. ISBN 0-8240-5547-0.

Centered on the theatrical career of choreographer Jerome Robbins, this work provides information on Broadway shows choreographed by Robbins and his contemporaries. Entries describe 191 plays in alphabetical order. Schlundt draws her information from programs and other source material from the New York Public Library's theatre collections. She lists opening and closing dates of the show, number of performances, and names of the choreographer, assistant choreographer, and everyone else associated with the show. Entries include all performers, even chorus members. She also cites references to newspaper articles and reference books. A chronological list of the shows precedes twelve indexes that allow access by occupation. Most of Schlundt's information can be found in *The Best Plays* (entry 375), but readers may find it useful to have these facts pulled into one book.

480. Terry, Walter. **Ballet Guide: Background, Listings, Credits, and Descriptions of More Than Five Hundred of the World's Major Ballets**. New York: Dodd, Mead, 1976. 388p. LC 75-20240. ISBN 0-396-07024-8.

Ballet critic Walter Terry briefly describes 500 ballets and dances one may see in the repertory of American and European companies. The entries, which appear in order by title, are much briefer than those in Balanchine's books (entries 465, 466) or Clarke and Crisp's work (entry 470). Cast and production credits for the first performance and, sometimes, for the first American performance, are followed by a summary of the plot and the dancing. However, Terry lists credits only for some works. He includes some works from the 1970s. An appendix lists London premieres of American ballets for the period 1945-1973. Terry's work supplements Balanchine and Clarke and Crisp, all of which should be preferred for their depth.

481. Warren, Gretchen Ward. **Classical Ballet Technique**. Tampa: University of South Florida Press; Distr., Gainesville: University Presses of Florida, 1989. LC 89-31141. ISBN 0-8130-0895-6; 0-8130-0945-6 pa.

Written for teachers, students, and professional dancers, Warren's handbook addresses classical ballet instruction more fully than either Dufort (entry 473) or Mackie (entry 476). A former Pennsylvania Ballet dancer and currently professor of dance at the University of South Florida, Warren not only describes the basic positions, steps, and movements that comprise ballet, but also takes a realistic look at the body structure and proportions needed by the successful dancer. She uses 2,600 photographs taken by dance photographer Susan Cook to illustrate both proper and improper positions as she guides the reader through twelve chapters of exercises from work at the barre to pointe work. Separate chapters discuss successful teaching methods and classroom etiquette. A glossary, bibliography, and index complete the book. Warren is preferred to Mackie and Dufort, which are both good second choices for handbooks on ballet technique.

482. **World Ballet and Dance**. London: Dance Books, 1989- . Annual. LC 90-24328.

A new venture, this annual features essays by various writers reviewing the dance season in their countries. These essays discuss new works, personnel changes in dance companies, and other important news. A separate section provides statistics on dance companies, by country. Only the largest and best-known groups are included, however. Because this is a British publication, both major and minor British companies are discussed. Finally, essays review various topics of interest, for example the health of dancers. This is most valuable for its coverage of dance in small countries such as Finland and Hong Kong. If it succeeds in maintaining an annual publication schedule, it will be a valuable record of the world's dance activity each year.

Chapter 8

Directories

Because directory information ages rapidly, only recent directories and works that are revised on a regular basis are included here. Readers should remember that many professional associations maintain directories of their members and may be contacted when necessary.

483.   **AudArena Stadium ... International Guide to Facilities, Supplies & Services**. Nashville, Tenn.: Amusement Business, 1990- . Annual.

Published by the periodical *Amusement Business*, this directory lists over 6,500 arenas, auditoriums, stadiums, exhibit halls, and other entertainment spaces in the United States, Canada, and other countries. The United States section, divided by state and city, lists each space with its location, personnel, seating and stage dimensions, backstage facilities, and booking and ticket information. Also listed are amenities such as parking, concession stands, and nearby hotels. The Canadian and international sections follow the same format. The editors also include a product and services directory for such things as box office systems and parking lot equipment. Published annually and filled with advertising, this provides up-to-date information for anyone scheduling plays, dance programs, and other events.

484.   Charles, Jill, comp. and ed. **Directory of Theatre Training Programs**. Dorset, Vt.: Theatre Directories, 1987- . Annual. LC 88-645976. ISSN 1041-5211.

Directed at aspiring acting students, Charles' directory lists schools offering theatre training programs in the United States. Most entries include admission information, a listing of theatre facilities, and a description of the purpose of the program along with any specializations taught. Both the arrangement by state and the index by school name will help high school students looking for an academic theatre program.

485.   Conolly, L. W. **A Directory of British Theatre Research Resources in North America**. London: The British Theatre Institute, 1978. 24p. LC 80-468671.

American and Canadian libraries hold a surprising amount of material related to the British theatre. Conolly describes thirty-six repositories in the United States and nine in Canada that hold particularly good collections. The entries, arranged first by country, then by state or province, include the Folger Shakespeare Library, the Historical Society of Pennsylvania, and the University of Texas Hoblitzelle Theatre Arts Library. Besides standard directory information, the compiler includes the library's acquisitions policy and information about catalogs and finding aids. A subject index completes this small but useful book.

486. **Contact Book**. New York: Celebrity Service International, 1958- . Irregular. LC 86-3002. ISSN 0069-1372.

Founded by Earl Blackwell, author of the *Celebrity Register* (entry 330), the *Contact Book* provides addresses and telephone numbers for "top personalities" and organizations in the entertainment industry in four American and four foreign cities: New York, San Francisco, Hollywood, Washington, D.C., Toronto, London, Paris, and Rome. For each location, addresses are arranged by type of service such as agents, rehearsal studios, music publishers, newspapers, and so on. American listings sometimes provide the name of a contact person in addition to the address. Although most of the American listings can be found in their respective local telephone books, the foreign entries would be more difficult to obtain. This book may be useful to the professional performer and to the tourist looking for theatres, nightclubs, and restaurants to patronize.

487. Delaplaine, A., ed. **The Dramatist's Bible 1989**. Chicago: St. James Press, 1989. 222p. LC 87-37045. ISBN 0-912289-77-5.

Although not as useful as *The Playwright's Companion* (entry 499), Delaplaine's directory lists "theatres that produce the work of new playwrights" (introduction), both in the United States and abroad (Canada, the United Kingdom, and New Zealand). The short entries, arranged by theatre name, vary in length and information provided. Generally, they indicate whether or not unsolicited manuscripts are accepted and read. They may also indicate a theatre's special interests, best submission times, and cast requirements. The second part lists grants, residencies, prizes, and other opportunities for playwrights and college students. Play publishers, literary agents, and writers' organizations are described separately. Besides a comprehensive index, Delaplaine includes an index of special interests such as Asian-American or feminist themes. This work is rapidly dating and does not provide as much information as *The Playwright's Companion*. It should be used only as a supplemental source.

488. **Dramatist's Sourcebook**. New York: Theatre Communications Group, 1981- . Annual. LC 82-644562. ISSN 0733-1606.

Published annually, this directory lists opportunities for playwrights, including theatre companies looking for scripts, prizes, publication opportunities, workshops, agents, artists' colonies, and organizations that help writers perfect and market their work. The general heading "Script Opportunities" includes directory and script submission information for theatre companies, prize-giving agencies, publishers, and play development workshops. The "Career Opportunities" section includes similar information for agents, fellowship and grant awarding organizations, state arts agencies, writers' colonies, and service organizations. Altogether, 900 listings provide a wealth of opportunities for a playwright to explore. Readers can find names of companies, prizes, workshops, and organizations in the index.

489. Epstein, Lawrence S. **A Guide to Theatre in America**. New York: Macmillan, 1985. 443p. LC 84-19418. ISBN 0-02-909670-7.

Unlike the *Lively Arts Information Directory* (entry 518), this guide concentrates on theatre alone, but it includes some categories that *Lively Arts* omits. For instance, it provides lists of ticket agencies, critics, agents, directors, and choreographers. Within each of the eighteen chapters, arrangement is by state and city with a personal name index/directory at the end of the book. Canadian listings follow those for the United States in each chapter.

Like its counterpart *Lively Arts*, this directory needs an update. Readers should use it with care.

490. Frick, John W., and Carlton Ward, eds. **Directory of Historic American Theatres**. Westport, Conn.: Greenwood, 1987. 347p. LC 87-10709. ISBN 0-313-24868-0.

Evidence of a flourishing American theatre prior to the advent of radio and television is found in this work, which provides details about 886 surviving historic theatres. All the theatres were built before 1915 and were used solely or principally for live entertainment. The authors based their book on data gathered from responses to a survey under the auspices of the League of Historic American Theatres and on research in theatre collections. They have deposited their data at Princeton University where it is available for further study. The first section of the book lists name, address, opening date, the theatre's style of architecture, stage and house dimensions, and amount of seating. Both free-standing theatres and performance spaces within public or commercial buildings are included, and the building's current use is given. The Weis Opera House in Frankfort, Kansas, for example, now functions as a firehouse. The authors describe the major types of entertainment produced during each theatre's heyday and name major stars who appeared on its stage. A second section lists historic theatres that are known to exist but for which there is no other information. Both sections are arranged by state and city. This directory will lead historians and architects to examples of nineteenth- and early twentieth-century theatres. This work supersedes Ward's earlier book, *National List of Historic Theatre Buildings* (Washington, D.C.: League of Historic American Theatres, 1983).

490a. Gould, Robert B., and Susan E. Lee. **Stage Specs: A Guide to Legit Theatres**. New York: League of American Theatres and Producers, 1990. 621p. LC 90-060537. ISBN 0-9625844-0-1.

Organized by state, city, and theatre name, this directory provides information on the backstage and house facilities of 300 American and Canadian theatres that host touring Broadway shows. (Canadian entries follow those for the United States.) Each 2-page entry presents a diagram of the stage and orchestra pit with dimensions as well as the theatre's address and telephone numbers, names of key personnel, and information about the theatre's electrical and sound equipment. Indexes allow readers to find theatres by major market areas, theatre name, and house capacity. A specialized work, this will help those who need specific information about a playhouse. Unfortunately, it does not cover the many theatres that do not import Broadway shows. The *AudArena Stadium ... International Guide* (entry 483) gives similar information for many more performance spaces.

491. **Handel's National Directory for the Performing Arts**. 5th ed. New York: R. R. Bowker, 1992. 2v. LC 73-646635. ISBN 0-8352-3250-6 (set).

Now in its fifth edition and under the editorial control of publisher R. R. Bowker, this directory has corrected some of the errors and omissions noted by reviewers of previous editions. Nevertheless, it remains unable to fulfill its promise of listing all dance, music, theatre, and presenter organizations, both professional and amateur, all facilities used for the performing arts and all theatre, dance, and music educational programs in the United States. Volume 1 lists performing arts organizations and facilities alphabetically by state and city. Unfortunately, it misses many facilities and organizations. To take just two examples, it omits the Dayton Theatre Guild and Rhythm in Shoes in Dayton, Ohio, both well known locally. Mixing facilities and performing groups is confusing and

150 / 8—Directories

inconsistent. The University of Illinois' Krannert Center for the Performing Arts is listed as a facility while its Assembly Hall is listed as a presenting organization. In fact, both organizations are both facilities and presenters. Volume 2 of the work lists information on performing arts programs in colleges and universities. Better information can be found in *Directory of Theatre Training Programs* (entry 484) and the *Dance Magazine College Guide* (entry 525). Nevertheless, the fifth edition does include more than 1,200 new organizations, facilities, and educational programs. Readers will appreciate the convenience of so many names and addresses in one work, flawed as it is.

492. Hill, Kathleen Thompson. **Festivals U.S.A.** New York: John Wiley, 1988. 242p. LC 87-3479. ISBN 0-471-62636-8.

More recent than Shemanski's and Wasserman's books (entries 507 and 517), Hill's work describes over 1,000 American festivals arranged first by region, then by state, then by date of the event. Although these festivals are organized around many themes, not just the arts, readers can use the index to find dance and theatre festivals. Each entry describes the festival and lists pertinent location, ticket, and accommodation information. A glossary of terms defines unusual words, including ethnic food terms. This directory should be especially useful to those who are looking for festivals that include ethnic dancing.

493. Howard, Diana, comp. **Directory of Theatre Resources: A Guide to Research Collections and Information Services**. 2d ed. London: Library Association Information Services Group and The Society for Theatre Research, 1986. 144p. LC 88-105581. ISBN 0-946347-08-5.

Based on a survey carried out in 1985-1986, Howard's directory describes 256 British collections of theatre materials and thirty-six theatre societies and associations that provide information services. The collections, arranged by city, are listed with address, telephone number, admission policies, hours of operation, and a brief description of the types of materials held. These libraries range in size from the British Library and the Public Records Office to smaller institutions like the Ellen Terry Memorial Museum, the repository for the actress's papers. The societies and associations are arranged by name in the second part of the work, and Howard lists the organization's purpose, services offered to the public, and any publications available. An index to the collections provides access by name and by subject. This book will be useful to anyone planning to do theatre research in Britain.

494. Itzin, Catherine, ed. **Directory of Playwrights Directors Designers**. Eastbourne, England: John Offord, 1983- . Biennial. ISSN 0265-0932.

Originally part of the now defunct *British Alternative Theatre Directory*, this title grew large enough to be published separately. The editor has arranged information based on questionnaires into three lists: one of playwrights, one of directors, and one of theatrical designers. By providing a list of each person's work, entries establish an historical record and also help theatre companies decide which writer, director, or designer to consider hiring for new productions.

495. Number not used.

Directories / 151

496. Leon, Ruth. **Applause: New York's Guide to the Performing Arts**. New York: Applause, 1991. 506p. LC 91-29244. ISBN 1-55783-096-7.

Leon lists and describes hundreds of performing companies and performance spaces in New York City. Entries are arranged alphabetically within chapters for theatre, music, opera, dance, cabaret, and children's events. Each performance space entry provides essential information such as directions, parking advice, an evaluation of the theatre's comfort (seats, sightlines, restrooms, bar facilities, and so on), and, if appropriate, information about the companies that regularly perform in the space. Besides the well-known Lincoln Center and Broadway theatres, Leon describes church basements and other small halls where performance takes place on a regular basis. Her entries for performing groups describe and evaluate their work. Invaluable to anyone who lives in New York, this will also help travelers find their way to musical, theatrical, and dance events in the city. As Leon writes in her introduction, the book should be used with a daily newspaper for current listings of events. The publishers plan a series of guides for major American cities, but this is the only one available now.

496a. Lynk, William M. **Dinner Theatre: A Survey and Directory**. Westport, Conn.: Greenwood, 1993. 128p. LC 92-36607. ISBN 9-313-28442.3.

Claiming to be the first book written solely about dinner theatre, Lynk's work presents a short history of the form (dinner theatre dates from the 1950s in the United States). Following an overview of theatre and restaurant operations, the author discusses marketing and other considerations that go into a successful business of this type. He then profiles forty-five theatres, including details on geographic location, ticket prices, seating capacities, stage type, and personnel. A directory of eighty theatres (including the forty-five that have been profiled) throughout the United States follows. A final chapter lists organizations, publications, and businesses that offer assistance to the dinner theatre operator. Lynk quotes dinner theatre owners extensively in this informal and advice-laden guide. His book will interest people who want to own, manage, or work in this specialized area of theatre.

497. McCallum, Heather. **Research Collections in Canadian Libraries. Pt. 2, Special Studies. Sect. 1, Theatre Resources in Canadian Collections**. Ottawa: National Library of Canada; Distr., Information Canada, 1973. 113p.

McCallum stresses nonbook materials in this inventory of theatre collections in 114 Canadian institutions. She arranges the entries by type of institution, such as provincial archives, theatre companies, dance companies, and so forth, and for each collection she provides a good description of its contents. All performing arts including puppets and film are included. Anyone researching Canadian theatre, music, or film will find this work a useful introduction to primary source materials. See also Young's *American Theatrical Arts: A Guide to Manuscripts and Special Collections in the United States and Canada* (entry 522).

498. Merin, Jennifer, and Elizabeth B. Burdick. **International Directory of Theatre, Dance and Folklore Festivals**. Westport, Conn.: Greenwood, 1979. 480p. LC 79-9908. ISBN 0-313-20993-6.

Although aging, the information in this directory is still useful in two ways. It documents 850 arts festivals taking place in 56 countries in the late 1970s, and, because it is organized by country, it suggests to travelers festivals that they may wish to investigate further. Given the shaky financial grounds of the arts, some of these events have undoubtedly folded, but the venerable festivals at Spoleto, Edinburgh, and Florence continue to draw large crowds year after year. Each festival's entry lists address, telephone, person in charge, date, and a short description of the event. A calendar of festivals lists each festival by country, then by month, a feature especially useful to tourists. Two caveats: the directory contains no information on American festivals, and all addresses should be verified in more recent sources.

499. Meserve, Mollie Ann, comp. **The Playwright's Companion: A Submission Guide to Theatres & Contests in the U.S.A.** New York: Feedback Theatrebooks, 1985- . Annual. LC 87-654261. ISSN 0887-1507.

Designed to help writers get their plays to the public, this guide is arranged by five categories, all of which an aspiring playwright can pursue. First, theatres and theatre companies that are interested in new plays are listed by name with submission policies and basic information about the company such as its size and its facilities. The second section describes playwriting contests with regulations, procedures, and prizes awarded. Third, the reader can find out about workshops, showcases, fellowships, and other types of support services open to playwrights. The final two sections list publishers and literary agents who are especially interested in plays. An index by special interests such as plays for puppets, plays dealing with disabilities, and so forth, is followed by a calendar listing contest deadlines and a bibliography of works of interest to aspiring playwrights. Anyone trying to get a play produced or published will find several paths to explore here. This provides more detail and more recent information than *The Dramatist's Bible* (entry 487).

500. **The New York Theatrical Sourcebook.** Shelter Island, N.Y.: Broadway Press, 1984- . Annual. LC 86-25818.

Compiled by the Association of Theatrical Artists and Craftspeople, this guide locates about 3,000 sources "for materials and services available to the New York area craftsperson." Although most of the listed suppliers are in New York City, their services and products will be useful to theatres throughout the United States. Products and services are listed by category from "Adhesives and Glues" to "Winemaking and Brewing Supplies." Each category lists suppliers with directory information and specialties. A company index allows access by name, and an appendix lists companies open after 1:00 A.M. or before 7:00 A.M.—useful for last minute emergencies! Other appendices list New York theatres, sound stages, and rehearsal studios; health and safety services; and theatre organizations and unions. A must for New York backstage personnel, this work should find a home in other parts of the country as well. It supersedes Simon's *Directory of Theatrical Materials, Services & Information*, now too old to be useful.

501. Niemeyer, Suzanne. **Money for Performing Artists.** New York: ACA Books, 1991. 268p. LC 91-29393. ISBN 0-915400-96-0.

To help individual performing artists of all types find programs of financial support, Niemeyer surveyed 223 organizations that provide this type of help. These include well-known programs such as the prestigious Eugene O'Neill Theater Center, which awards one-month residencies to promising playwrights, as well as lesser-known groups such as the Arts and Humanities Council of Tulsa, Oklahoma, which awards grants to local artists. Niemeyer lists each organization by name and describes its programs in two sections. The first explains direct support funding such as grants, commissions, and residency programs. The second describes technical assistance, for example touring and performing opportunities. For each organization, Niemeyer lists the number of awards and amount of money granted. A full set of indexes allows one to locate awards by geographic area, by discipline, including dance and theatre, and by type of support (competitions, emergency assistance, legal assistance, and so forth). If Niemeyer can issue the book annually, she will provide a valuable source to performing artists.

502. **The Original British Theatre Directory**. London: Richmond House, 1986- . Annual. LC 89-18400. ISSN 0306-4107.

As the continuation of the *British Theatre Directory* (Eastbourne, England: Vance-Offord, 1972-1985), this work continues to list information about London and provincial theatres, concert halls, and arts centers in Britain. In keeping with the information needs of touring companies and other producers, the directory lists each theatre's technical attributes, the size of its house, and the type of shows it presents, as well as address and telephone number. Outside London, arrangement is by city alphabetically. Separate sections list theatre, ballet, opera, and puppet theatre companies; orchestras; circuses; agents; publishers; and others involved in the arts. A final chapter lists firms that supply the technical needs of theatres such as costumes and lights.

503. **Performing Arts Libraries and Museums of the World**. 3d ed. Paris: National Center for Scientific Research, 1984. 1,181p. LC 85-131579. ISBN 2-222-03265-2.

Identification of new collections and new materials in existing collections prompted a third edition of this title fifteen years after the second edition. It includes institutions from China, Australia, and New Zealand for the first time. Written in French and English, the directory provides the address for each institution, its access and loan policies, a description of its collections, and a list of activities and publications. The book is indexed by individual name and by name of collections that are separate units within libraries, such as the Hanya Holm Collection within the New York Public Library's Performing Arts Library. Because it locates so many collections worldwide, this work is indispensable for anyone doing serious original research.

504. **Players Guide: The Annual Pictorial Directory for Stage, Screen, Radio, and Television**. New York: Players Guide, 1944- . Annual. LC 47-34214.

Designed for use by casting directors, this pictorial directory is arranged by gender and then by type and age of actor. For example, "Girls" are separated from "Young Leading Women and Ingenues" who in turn are divided from "Leading Women." Each actor's picture, a small head shot, is accompanied by name, union membership, agent's name, and telephone number. A special section lists men and women who act in commercials. At the front of the volume is an alphabetical index of all names. Although some directors, choreographers, and stage managers are listed, this directory concentrates on actors. It can be used by anyone looking for a photograph of a particular performer.

505. **Playhouse America! A Directory of Theatres and Theatre Companies in the U.S.A.** New York: Feedback Theatrebooks, 1991. 308p. LC 92-114951. ISBN 0-937657-08-5.

The most comprehensive list of addresses and phone numbers of American theatres yet published, this directory offers breadth at the expense of detail. More than 3,500 theatres are listed alphabetically by name, including Broadway and off-Broadway houses, regional professional theatres, college and university theatres, and even small-town community theatres. A sample demonstrates the book's range; the Joliet, Illinois, Drama Guild, the University of North Texas Theatre, the American Players Theatre from Spring Green, Wisconsin, and the Helen Hayes Theater on West 44th Street in New York City are all listed. However, the listings provide address and telephone number only, nothing more. An index lists specialities: Broadway theatres, ethnic theatres, dinner theatres, gay and lesbian theatres, and so on. A good addition for future editions would be a geographical index. Right now, this is helpful only if one knows the name of a theatre and needs the address or telephone number.

506. **Regional Theatre Directory**. Dorset, Vt.: Theatre Directories, 1986- . Annual. LC 86-640753. ISSN 1041-9411.

Updated each May, this directory lists hiring and casting information for 400 regional and dinner theatres in the United States. If a theatre gives internships, the directory provides information on them as well. Arranged by state, entries provide brief information on the theatre's company, season, and facilities. The "Key to Listings" explains the many abbreviations used in the entries. Additional chapters provide bibliographies of books and periodicals and lists of unions and associations of interest to theatre professionals. The index lists theatres by name. See also *Summer Theatre Directory* from the same publisher (entry 511).

507. Shemanski, Frances. **A Guide to Fairs and Festivals in the United States**. Westport, Conn.: Greenwood, 1984. 339p. LC 82-21080. ISBN 0-313-21437-9.

Written by a former newspaper editor, this guide provides information on approximately 250 festivals in every state of the union. Arranged by state, the directory lists the date (month) of the festival and describes it in several paragraphs. An appendix that lists festivals by type allows readers to find events that feature ballet and dance, drama, opera, or music. A separate calendar arranges about 2,000 events by month within state categories. The index lists festivals by name and by subject. Although it features fewer festivals, Shemanski's work contains better descriptions of events than either Wasserman (entry 517) or Hill (entry 492).

508. Slide, Anthony, Patricia King Hanson, and Stephen L. Hanson. **Sourcebook for the Performing Arts: A Directory of Collections, Resources, Scholars, and Critics in Theatre, Film, and Television**. Westport, Conn.: Greenwood, 1988. 227p. LC 87-23630. ISBN 0-313-24872-9.

Intended as a ready-reference guide, this work functions as an overall directory for researchers of theatre, film, and television. It describes important library and archival collections, arranged by state; gives brief biographical information on 200 academics, critics, historians, and others involved in research; and lists addresses for bookshops, journals, publishers, performing arts organizations, motion picture and television studios, televisions networks, and various film commissions. The index allows access by names of biographees, institutions, and collections. Although much of the information listed here can be found in other directories such as *The Encyclopedia of Associations* (Detroit: Gale Research, annual) and Lee Ash's *Subject Collections* (New York: R. R. Bowker, 1985), librarians who answer many performing arts questions will find this compilation more convenient to use.

509. Spivack, Carol, and Richard A. Weinstock. **Best Festivals of North America: A Performing Arts Guide**. 3d ed. Ventura, Calif.: Printwheel Press, 1989. 208p. ISBN 0-916401-08-1 pa.

People who want to center their vacations around a performing arts festival will find Spivack's book helpful in choosing among the hundreds of opportunities available in the United States and Canada. Arranged by type (theatre, drama, classical music, jazz, and so on) the directory reports on 142 festivals best in terms of depth and variety of performances, quality of performers, and setting and location of the festivals. Besides a narrative description of each event, Spivack includes ticket and booking information as well as nearby sightseeing and accommodations. Indexes are designed to help travelers find festivals by name, geographic location, and month of the festival's occurrence. The author also includes an index of sightseeing attractions near festivals and an index of children's activities.

510. **The Stage Managers Directory**. New York: Broadway Press, 1983- . Annual. LC 86-646929. ISSN 1048-1923.

With a goal of providing "a central source of information to employers looking for stage managers and to stage managers themselves as a reference tool," this directory lists members of the Stage Managers Association alphabetically along with their addresses and the names of shows on which they have worked. To be more useful, the entries are indexed by type of experience (e.g., Broadway productions, off-Broadway, children's theatre), by geographic region, and by foreign language spoken.

511. **Summer Theatre Directory**. Dorset, Vt.: Theatre Directories, 1984- . Annual. LC 85-643067.ISSN 0884-5840.

A companion to *Regional Theatre Directory* (entry 506), this title will help those who are looking for a summer experience in theatre, either a paying job or a training program. Arranged by state, each entry describes a summer theatre company, its facilities, and its hiring practices. Availability of apprenticeships and internships is noted. Training programs are listed with course descriptions, program dates, and application procedures. A separate chapter lists regional auditions held jointly by groups of theatres. Also included is a bibliography of periodicals that publish audition and casting information regularly. The book concludes with an index of theatres by name.

512. **The Survey of Arts Administration Training**. New York: American Council for the Arts Books, 1982- . Biennial.

Graduate programs in arts administration are scarce. This directory describes degree-granting programs with a major concentration in arts administration. All of them operate in the United States except those at York University in Canada and at the Utrecht School of the Arts in the Netherlands. They include the well-known program at the University of Wisconsin-Madison and the Brooklyn College-CUNY course run by Stephen Langley (see entry 417). For each school the directory lists address and telephone; degree granted; course, thesis, and internship requirements; and admission procedures. It also presents the program's history and its current orientation and purpose. The book will help those who wish to enter the field of arts management choose a school. Prospective students should also consult *Career Opportunities in Theater and the Performing Arts* (entry 395a). It describes careers and lists educational and training programs.

156 / 8—Directories

513. **TCG Theatre Directory**. New York: Theatre Communications Group, 1980- . Annual. LC 83-10324.

Essentially the Theatre Communications Group membership list, this directory provides a guide to the 230 constituent theatres and the 103 associate theatres in the organization. Arranged alphabetically by theatre name with an index by state, the entries list the theatre's location and telephone number, the name of a contact person, and details of the theatre's Actor's Equity Association contract. A separate section provides information on programs offered by forty-seven arts organizations. This directory is a convenient place to find information on nonprofit professional theatres in the United States. More information about each company can be found in *Theatre Profiles* (entry 515) also published by the Theatre Communications Group.

514. **Theatre Crafts Directory: Manufacturers, Suppliers, & Consultants for the Entertainment Technology Industry**. New York: Theatre Crafts Associates, 1979- . Annual. ISSN 0040-5469.

Each June/July *Theatre Crafts*, now *TCI* (entry 639), publishes this directory instead of a regular issue. It provides information on "1,500 manufacturers, suppliers, rental houses, construction shops, and consultants serving the performing arts industry." The separate manufacturers and suppliers sections, both organized by product, provide names of companies that make and sell stage curtains, costumes, and the like. The service index lists scenic painting shops, costume rental firms, and other theatrical services. The company listings describe each company in a short profile while the consultants section offers names and addresses of experts in various theatrical crafts. Compared with *Stearn's Performing Arts Directory* (entry 526) this work concentrates on the physical products needed for theatre productions while the other concentrates on the needs of dancers and musicians. Unlike *The New York Theatrical Sourcebook* (entry 500) this includes suppliers throughout the United States, not just in the New York metropolitan area.

515. **Theatre Profiles: The Illustrated Reference Guide to America's Nonprofit Professional Theatre**. New York: Theatre Communications Group, 1973- . Biennial. LC 76-641618. ISSN 0361-7947.

Calling itself "a resource book of nonprofit professional theatres in the United States," this directory describes over 200 companies. Because each theatre's play productions are listed as well as information on its facilities, finances, and artistic philosophy, each edition provides a snapshot of America's noncommercial theatre for a given two-year period. Taken together, the biennial editions of *Theatre Profiles* preserve a record of the artistic personnel and productions of the more important regional companies in the United States. Arranged by name, the theatre companies are indexed by founding date and by state. An index of play titles shows which plays are popular during a particular year, and a name index allows one to locate persons. Each company is represented by a photograph from one of its productions.

516. Thomas, James W., ed. **The Directors Directory: A National Guide to American Stage Directors**. New York: American Directors Institute/Broadway Press, 1988. 79p. ISBN 0-911747-11-7.

Providing resume and contact information on 138 people, this includes many directors who have worked off-Broadway or in summer stock theatre, but few with Broadway credits. Listed alphabetically, the resumes list plays directed and include comments from each director. The book is indexed by experience category such as Broadway, opera, summer theatre, and so forth.

517. Wasserman, Paul, ed. **Festivals Sourcebook**. 2d ed. Detroit: Gale Research, 1984. 721p. LC 84-160130. ISBN 0-8103-0323-X.

Listing more festivals than Spivack and Weinstock, Shemanski, or Hill (entries 509, 507, and 492), Wasserman's directory provides less information about each event than the other books. It lists 4,200 festivals arranged by type. Chapters that relate to the performing arts include dance, the arts, and theatre and drama. Short entries within each chapter are arranged by state and list the festival's frequency, the time it is held, address and telephone number, the year the festival began, and a two- or three-line description. A separate section lists festivals by month, and three indexes offer access by festival name, geographic location, and subject. Because of its age this directory must be used with care and its information verified. Nevertheless, it does include more festivals than any of its rival directories.

518. Wasserman, Steven R., and Jacqueline Wasserman O'Brien, eds. **The Lively Arts Information Directory: A Guide to the Fields of Music, Dance, Theatre, Film, Radio and Television, in the United States and Canada**. 2d ed. Detroit: Gale Research, 1985. 1,040p. LC 85-6949. ISBN 0-8103-0321-3.

A comprehensive directory that tries to cover many aspects of the performing arts, this work is starting to show its age. The editors have arranged 9,000 listings into thirteen sections dealing with agencies, government programs, foundations, schools, consultants, information centers, awards, publishers, festivals, and libraries. Much of the information is pulled from other sources published by Gale Research such as *The Encyclopedia of Associations* and *Awards, Honors and Prizes*. Until a new edition is published, readers should check the original source if possible for more current information.

519. Webb, Elmon, and Virginia Lim, eds. **Register: Directory of Designers, Artists, and Craftspeople**. New York: Limelite Group, 1987. 1v. ISBN 0-9615796-2-5.

Grouped by specialization, technical theatre personnel such as costume designers, art directors, and lighting designers are listed with their addresses and telephone numbers. Some entries also include union membership and names of past productions. An index locates people alphabetically by name. A subject/geographical index that mixes subject and geographical subheadings is of limited use. The directory should help those who are trying to locate the right person for a technical position. See also *Who's Where in the American Theatre* (entry 520), which complements this volume by listing performers, playwrights, and others not found in the *Register*.

520. **Who's Where in the American Theatre: A Directory of Affiliated Theatre Artists in the U.S.A.** New York: Feedback Theatrebooks; Distr., Samuel French Trade, 1989- . Annual. LC 89-2686. ISSN 1047-1715.

With the aim of providing a directory of American theatre artists, educators, and practitioners, this work is an alphabetical listing of more than 2,000 individuals with their position titles and addresses. An index by "primary fields of endeavor" helps the reader locate critics, performers, playwrights, and others by profession. The index by state has limited utility, especially for New York and California, as it is not further subdivided. This directory works best for those who have a name and want to locate that person's address.

158 / 8—Directories

521. **The Working Actor's Guide, L.A.** Los Angeles: Paul Flattery Productions; Distr., Samuel French, 1987- . Annual. LC 91-37420.

A serious study of this guide may convince an aspiring actor to stay home and pursue a career in banking instead. By the time he pays his business manager, his agency, his public relations firm, his florist, and his union dues, he may not have much of a salary left. This directory of services and organizations of interest to actors includes those named above plus casting directors, theatres, training programs, photographers, resume writers, and many others. A section on the Actors' Equity Association includes standard pay rates for theatre, film, and television work.

522. Young, William C. **American Theatrical Arts: A Guide to Manuscripts and Special Collections in the United States and Canada.** Chicago: American Library Association, 1971. 166p. LC 78-161234. ISBN 0-8389-0104-2.

In a book that covers dance and film collections as well as theatre materials, Young describes the holdings of 138 libraries, archives, and manuscript repositories in the United States and Canada. Arranged by country, then by state or province, and then by National Union Catalog symbol, the entries describe in a list format one or more collections held by each repository. The address of the library or archives is also given. The second part of the book indexes the collections by persons and subjects. The numbers used in the index refer to the institution and to the collection within that institution's entry. Thus, 115:1 refers to the first collection listed for repository number 115. Young's failure to include hours of operation and other directory information matters less than it would in a more recent book. In fact, the book's age is its major drawback. As Young points out in his introduction, the field of theatre collecting and research has burgeoned during the past thirty years. Now twenty years old, this needs an update. Nevertheless, it remains useful for the collections it does include.

Dance Directories

523. Allen, Beverly, ed. **Dance Directory 1990.** 14th ed. Reston, Va.: National Dance Association, American Alliance for Health, Physical Education, Recreation and Dance, 1990. 104p. ISBN 0-88314-498-0.

Issued periodically by the American Alliance for Health, Physical Education, Recreation, and Dance, this directory lists dance programs in the United States and Canada and performing arts high schools in the United States and Australia. Although the entries are not as informative as those in *Dance Magazine College Guide* (entry 525), they do provide a listing of courses offered, names of faculty members, and a list of performing dance groups affiliated with the program. Information for high schools is generally limited to address and telephone number. Arranged by state, this should be useful to high school students seeking a college dance program. Dancers may wish to consult Field's book (entry 395a), which profiles dance careers and lists educational programs and internships.

524. Collier, Clifford, and Pierre Guilmette. **Dance Resources in Canadian Libraries.** (Research Collections in Canadian Libraries: Special Studies, no. 8). Ottawa: National Library of Canada, 1982. 1v. ISBN 0-660-51022-7.

Based on questionnaires and personal visits, Collier and Guilmette have compiled information about dance collections in Canadian libraries, collections that the compilers admit are all relatively recent. Each province's libraries are listed with address, access rules, and a description and evaluation of the collection. A serials holdings list locates dance periodicals in Canadian libraries. To help new collections improve their holdings, Collier and Guilmette provide a list of reference works that should be in every dance library. Note that this book is written in both English and French on inverted pages. For Canada's theatre collections see McCallum (entry 497).

525. **Dance Magazine College Guide**. New York: Dance Magazine, 1978- . Biennial. LC 79-643315. ISSN 0193-1202.

Both *Dance Magazine* and the American Alliance for Health, Physical Education, Recreation, and Dance publish directories of dance programs in colleges and universities. This guide lists more schools than the AAHPERD directory (entry 523) and presents information in a narrative form while AAHPERD uses a tabular style. The first section describes about 200 "important" dance programs, arranged by university name. Several paragraphs provide information on the number of majors enrolled, the emphasis of the program, facilities, performing companies allied with the program, and information on the university itself. Following is a directory listing of all the programs spotlighted in the first section plus a few additional programs that grant degrees in dance. Finally, a third section lists schools that offer dance minors and non-degree programs. Altogether, nearly 600 programs appear in the 1990-1991 edition. The index lists schools by state. Because it offers more information, *Dance Magazine*'s guide is preferred over the AAHPERD directory. See Field (entry 395a) for information about dance as a career.

526. **Stearn's Performing Arts Directory**. New York: DM, 1988- . LC 89-662150.

Stearn's Directory serves as a guide to resources for dancers and musicians. Arranged by broad topics, the directory includes both classified listings and advertising. The dance section lists performers, teachers, schools, notators, and health services for dancers. "Music" includes similar listings for musicians. The resources chapter lists providers of services such as advertising agencies, designers, photographers, and artists' colonies; and purveyors of merchandise—dancing shoes, lights, and much more. This chapter also contains directories of government agencies and private organizations involved in the performing arts. "Sponsors" lists arts festivals worldwide, organizations that present arts events, and presenter consortia. A final chapter contains a list of performing arts periodicals. Produced yearly, *Stearns* is the best directory for the field of dance. Those interested in theatre should use *The New York Theatrical Sourcebook* (entry 500) or the *Theatre Crafts Directory* (entry 514) instead.

Chapter 9

Review Sources

The books listed in this chapter locate reviews of performances. Readers will find additional reviews by using the periodical indexes described in chapter 4.

527. Number not used.

528. Comtois, M. E., and Lynn F. Miller. **Contemporary American Theatre Critics: A Directory and Anthology of Their Works**. Metuchen, N.J.: Scarecrow, 1977. 979p. LC 77-23063. ISBN 0-8108-1057-3.

Designed to provide biographical information about theatre critics along with samples of their critical writings, Comtois and Miller's directory focuses on critics writing for local or regional newspapers and other media. Formatted entries for 291 critics provide standard biographical details, a list of writings, an estimate of their circulation or audience, and the number of plays reviewed annually. Most entries reprint one or two cited reviews. Indexed by geography and by name of newspaper or other source, this work also includes a bibliography of books and articles about twentieth-century theatre criticism in the United States. Unfortunately, the directory suffers from several faults. Since it has not been updated, much of its information is no longer correct and should be confirmed through other sources. Some entries, especially those for well-known critics, offer simply name, newspaper name, and address, because the critics did not respond to the authors' inquiries. Finally, one or two reviews do not offer enough material on which to judge the critics' styles, preferences, and biases.

529. Eddleman, Floyd Eugene, comp. **American Drama Criticism: Interpretations, 1890-1977**. 2d ed. (Drama Explication series). Hamden, Conn.: Shoe String Press, 1979. 488p. LC 78-31346. ISBN 0-208-01713-5.

530. Eddleman, Floyd Eugene, comp. **American Drama Criticism: Supplement I to the Second Edition**. (Drama Explication series). Hamden, Conn.: Shoe String Press, 1984. 255p. LC 83-25410. ISBN 0-208-01978-2.

531. Eddleman, Floyd Eugene, comp. **American Drama Criticism: Supplement II to the Second Edition**. Hamden, Conn.: Shoe String Press, 1989. 269p. LC 88-37507. ISBN 0-208-02138-5.

531a. Eddleman, Floyd Eugene, comp. **American Drama Criticism: Supplement III to the Second Edition**. Hamden, Conn.: Shoe String Press, 1992. 436p. LC 92-3977. ISBN 0-208-02270-8.

A useful place to find reviews and other criticism of plays, Eddleman's bibliography and supplements list interpretations of American plays published between 1890 and 1990. Although Eddleman has located citations in more than 200 books, most of the entries, which are arranged alphabetically by playwright, cite magazine reviews of first productions. For instance, eight of the nine citations for Herb Gardner's *A Thousand Clowns* are reviews published between April and June, 1962. The play opened on Broadway on April 5, 1962. Several indexes help the reader find information by play title, critic, and authors and titles of works from which plays have been adapted.

532. Lloyd Evans, Gareth, and Barbara Lloyd Evans. **Plays in Reviews 1956-1980: British Drama and the Critics**. New York: Methuen, 1985. 257p. LC 85-15251. ISBN 0-416-01171-3.

Concentrating on sixty-four plays written by forty-one playwrights between 1956 and 1980, the compilers reprint reviews and excerpts of reviews of the important plays of the period. The compilers have selected the works based on their own judgment of the plays' intellectual and aesthetic worth and on their goal of showing "the characteristic modes, methods and approaches" of British theatre critics during the period. Plays of all the well-known modern writers are included, for example Pinter, Osborne, Peter Shaffer, David Hare, and Stoppard; as well as left-wing playwright Arnold Wesker, two of the older generation, Eliot and Fry, and many others. Sources of all the reviews and excerpts, which are arranged in yearly chapters with introductions, are cited to help readers find the complete review if needed. The book concludes with indexes of plays, playwrights, and critics. The compilers provide an interesting look at twenty-five years of British criticism. Readers may also be interested in Stanley's *Broadway in the West End* (entry 543), which cites British criticism of American plays during approximately the same time period.

533. Marks, Patricia. **American Literary and Drama Reviews: An Index to Late Nineteenth Century Periodicals**. Boston: G. K. Hall, 1984. 313p. LC 82-23219. ISBN 0-8161-8470-4.

Marks lists reviews of plays from thirteen American periodicals published after the Civil War. She lists plays by title with citations to reviews and reviewers' names if known. Marks has chosen the periodicals to reflect "the conservative tastes of their middle-class readership" (introduction). They range in tone from gossipy, sensationalist magazines such as the *New York Illustrated Times* to political journals like the Democratic *Puck* and the Republican *Judge*. The index lists authors and adapters of plays. Since Marks covers a time period before that covered by Salem (entries 537-539), her book provides valuable indexing to reviews that would otherwise be difficult to locate.

534. **New York Theatre Critics Reviews**. New York: Critics Theatre Reviews, 1943- , Weekly with annual index. LC 42-1744. ISSN 0028-7784.

The most important source for collected reviews of American plays, this weekly publishes verbatim reviews taken from several daily newspapers plus other media. Coverage varies from year to year. In 1991 it included seven newspapers, two weekly newsmagazines, and transcriptions from one television station. An annual index locates actors, authors, producers, directors, and others associated with the production of plays. The reviews themselves are reprinted in their entirety and without further commentary. Because this publication appears weekly, its *New York Times* reviews are more current than those in the *New York Times Theater Reviews* (entry 535), which are published every two years. For reviews of London plays see the *Theatre Record*, formerly the *London Theatre Record* (entry 544).

535. **The New York Times Theater Reviews**. New York: Arno, 1920-1970: 10v.; 1870-1919: 6v.; 1971- . Biennial. LC 72-166218.

Generally conceded to be the dominant voice in American theatre reviewing, the *New York Times* and its theatre critics have been reviewing plays since just after the Civil War. The collected reviews have been issued in three sets. The first comprises reviews published between 1920 and 1970 in ten volumes. The second set goes back to gather reviews from 1870 to 1919 in six volumes. Since then, volumes have been issued at two-year intervals. Reviews are printed as they appeared in the newspaper with the cast list, a citation to the newspaper issue, and often a photograph. The two sets and the biennial volumes are indexed by personal name and play title. Later volumes also contain corporate name indexing for entities such as the New York Shakespeare Festival. Because the reviews are collected every two years, readers should use the newspaper itself and its index (entry 213) or the *New York Theatre Critics Reviews* (entry 534) for more recent reviews.

536. Palmer, Helen H. **European Drama Criticism 1900-1975**. 2d ed. Hamden, Conn.: Shoe String Press, 1977. 653p. LC 77-171. ISBN 0-208-01589-2.

Combining references to reviews and to critiques, Palmer provides the reader with citations to twentieth-century criticism of European and British plays of all time periods. Omitting only Shakespeare's works, Palmer has selected a group of playwrights who represent the best of their country's dramatists or who have acquired an international reputation. The unannotated citations are arranged by playwright, then by play, and refer to both books and periodical articles. Completing the book are an index of authors and titles and lists of indexed books and journals. For criticism of American plays, see Eddleman (entries 529-531a).

537. Salem, James M. **A Guide to Critical Reviews**. Part I, **American Drama, 1909-1982**. 3d ed. Metuchen, N.J.: Scarecrow, 1984. 657p. LC 84-1370. ISBN 0-8108-1690-3.

538. Salem, James M. **A Guide to Critical Reviews**. Part II, **The Musical, 1909-1989**. 3d ed. Metuchen, N.J.: Scarecrow, 1991. 820p. LC 84-1370. ISBN 0-8108-2387-X.

539. Salem, James M. **A Guide to Critical Reviews**. Part III, **Foreign Drama, 1909-1977**. 2d ed. Metuchen, N.J.: Scarecrow, 1979. 420p. LC 73-3120. ISBN 0-8108-1226-6.

A great timesaver, Salem's bibliographies list reviews of American plays and musicals and foreign plays produced in New York. Reviews are taken from American and Canadian periodicals, the *New York Times* and the *New York Theatre Critics Reviews* (entry 534). Part 1 covers 2,500 plays produced between 1909 and 1982 on Broadway, off-Broadway, and off-off-Broadway. Arranged by playwright and with all productions of a given play grouped together, the entries list opening date and number of performances as well as citations to reviews. Indexes of co-authors and adapters and of play titles accompany lists of awards and long-running plays. Part 2 concentrates on 2,669 musicals produced in New York between 1909 and 1989. Arranged by title of the musical, the work is indexed by names of creative personnel such as composers, designers, directors, and so forth, and by author and title of original works upon which musicals were based. For example, *Damn Yankees* is indexed under *The Year the Yankees Lost the Pennant* and under Douglass Wallop, the book's author. Part 3 lists reviews of 1,300 foreign plays produced in New York between 1909 and 1977. Playwrights are listed with their works alphabetically with a title index and an index of co-authors, adapters, and translators. Salem has tried to record both the foreign and English title for each play, but admits that not every play is listed under both. The set remains useful for the time periods it covers. It should be especially helpful to those who do not have the *New York Theatre Critics Reviews* at hand, as it provides citations that can be used when requesting photocopies.

540. Samples, Gordon. **How to Locate Reviews of Plays and Films: A Bibliography of Criticism from the Beginnings to the Present**. Metuchen, N.J.: Scarecrow, 1976. 114p. LC 76-3509. ISBN 0-8108-0914-1.

Samples lists books, newspapers, periodical indexes, and other sources one can use to find reviews and critiques of plays and motion pictures. He arranges entries by type of material such as study guides, review indexing services, newspaper indexes, and so on. Each entry cites the source and annotates it briefly. A title index locates specific works. This may be helpful to students and novice library users.

541. Slide, Anthony, ed. **Selected Theatre Criticism**. Metuchen, N.J.: Scarecrow, 1985-1986. 3v. LC 85-2266. ISBN v. 1: 0-8108-1181-6; v. 2: 0-8108-1844-2; v. 3: 0-8108-1846-9.

Slide has chosen and reprinted reviews of New York plays produced since 1900. Volume 1 contains reviews from nine periodicals of more than 200 dramas, musicals, and revues produced between 1900 and 1919. The second volume covers 200 plays reviewed in ten periodicals between 1920 and 1930, and volume 3 reprints reviews of 140 plays produced between 1931 and 1950. The reviews are listed by play title and indexed by critic and by name. The third volume also indexes all three volumes by play title. Because only one or two reviews per play are reprinted, readers will not find complete listings of reviews here. This work can be used as a supplement to the *New York Times Theater Reviews* (entry 535). Readers should also check Salem's *Guide to Critical Reviews* (entries 537, 538, 539) for additional material.

542. Slide, Anthony, ed. **Selected Vaudeville Criticism**. Metuchen, N.J.: Scarecrow, 1988. 308p. LC 87-28553. ISBN 0-8108-2052-8.

Using a mixture of reviews, interviews, and articles, all reprinted in full, Slide tries to present a picture of vaudeville's heyday, 1900 to 1920. The material covers 147 performers and groups that performed in the United States during that time. Unfortunately, coverage is quite uneven. Some performers represented by a several-page article while others receive only a one-paragraph review. Further, since Slide does not indicate how he selected his material, readers are left wondering if he merely used what was readily available. Possibly useful as a starting point, this book is not as well executed as Slide's *The Vaudevillians* (entry 358).

543. Stanley, William T. **Broadway in the West End: An Index of Reviews of American Theatre in London, 1950-1975**. Westport, Conn.: Greenwood, 1978. 206p. LC 77-89108. ISBN 0-8371-9852-6.

If American tourists are sometimes surprised to see Broadway hits running in London's West End theatres, they should remember that play traffic runs both ways across the Atlantic. Stanley has compiled a list of over 3,000 reviews of commercial productions of American plays, musicals, and revues that played in London between 1950 and 1975. His sources include seventeen newspapers and magazines including *Punch*, *The Times*, and the *Illustrated London News*. The book's first section lists reviews by playwright and then play title. Besides the citation to each review, entries include the name of the theatre, the dates of the run, and the number of performances for each play. The second section features a chronological listing of plays, and section 3 is a title index. A specialized work, this index will save the time of those researching American theatre in London.

544. **Theatre Record** (formerly *London Theatre Record* [1981-1990]). Twickenham, England: I. Herbert, 1981- , Biweekly with annual index. LC 81-646222. ISSN 0261-5282.

Published biweekly with an annual index, the *Theatre Record* presents the full cast and production details for every important show in London's West End and "Fringe" theatres plus reviews of most of Britain's major daily and weekly drama critics. The editors include a list of productions running in London during any given week, thus establishing an important historical record. Some regional productions are covered as well. Even more than in New York, the large number of critics insures a good sampling of reviews for any given play. Most plays have at least three to six reviews and important productions may receive up to nineteen or twenty notices. All reviews for the same play are grouped together, but the plays are not arranged in any discernable order. Each issue's table of contents and the annual index will help readers locate specific plays. This is an important source for anyone interested in contemporary British theatre.

Chapter 10

Chronologies and Histories

Chronologies list performances in chronological order for a theatre, a city, a country, or another geographical entity. A few histories which also contain chronology information are included.

545. Bentley, Gerald Eades. **The Jacobean and Caroline Stage**. Oxford, England: Clarendon, 1941-1968. 7v. LC 41-3671.

Carrying on the work of Chambers' *The Elizabethan Stage* (entry 548), Bentley provides historical information about English theatre companies, playwrights, and actors who worked between 1616, the year of Shakespeare's death, and 1642, the year Parliament closed the theatres. Volume 1 recounts the history of leading companies with lists of their actors and their repertories. The second volume concerns itself with biographies of actors while volumes 3, 4, and 5 include biographies and bibliographies for 220 playwrights. The sixth volume provides brief histories and bibliographies for London theatres of the period. The index to this monumental set is found in volume 7 along with a chronology of theatrical affairs for the period. Bentley's work can be used to start research in English theatre of this period. Readers interested in chronological information should consult Harbage (entry 555) or Kawachi (entry 558), which list plays by date of performance.

546. Blum, Daniel. **A Pictorial History of the American Theatre, 1860-1985**. New 6th ed., enl. by John Willis. New York: Crown, 1986. 496p. LC 87-117298. ISBN 0-517-56258-8.

In her forward to this book the late Helen Hayes wrote, "The camera as it has been used by many masters of the photographic art has an ability which is almost uncanny in capturing mood and interpretation as well as likeness." By presenting thousands of photographs depicting the American theatre and its leading actors from 1860 to 1985, Blum has captured something of the look and feel of the New York stage during that time. He presents the first forty years decade by decade and, starting with 1901, devotes a chapter to each year. Descriptions discuss important productions on and off Broadway, but prose takes second place to the dozens of pictures depicting each season's plays. The index locates actors and plays by name and makes it possible to compare different staging and costume designs over time for the same play. Although *The Best Plays* volumes (entry 375) also contain photographs, Blum reproduces more in one convenient volume.

547. Bordman, Gerald. **American Musical Theatre: A Chronicle**. New York: Oxford University Press, 1992. 821p. LC 91-15671. ISBN 0-19-507242-1.

Bordman presents a chronology of American musical theatre from its beginnings to 1990. The first known musical plays presented before 1866 are covered in a summary chapter. Following it is a year-by-year chronicle in narrative form with names of shows highlighted in bold print. Bordman concentrates on Broadway with some remarks on musical theatre in Boston, Philadelphia, Chicago, and other large cities prior to World War

166 / 10—Chronologies and Histories

I. His narrative includes not only the facts such as opening date and theatre of each show, but also his opinion on its worth and its influence on later shows. He points out popular songs and performers of each year. An appendix describes turn-of-the century second rate or "B" musicals that "toured from city to city without ever playing first-class houses" (preface). The book is well indexed by show title, title of source materials such as novels or plays, song title, and personal name. Bordman's work stands as the premiere work on the American musical.

548.   Chambers, Edmund K. **The Elizabethan Stage**. Oxford, England: Clarendon, 1923. 4v. LC 24-4078.

Chambers describes the histories of thirty-five acting companies and eighteen theatres and gives brief biographies of Elizabethan actors in his important history of the English stage during Elizabeth I's reign. He also includes biographies and primary bibliographies of playwrights. This work is indexed by play title, person, place, and subject. A court calendar lists important events from November 17, 1558, the day of Elizabeth's accession to the throne, to April 23, 1616, the date of Shakespeare's death.

549.   Champion, Édouard. **La Comédie Française, 1er janvier 1927 à 1937**. Paris: Champion, 1934-1937. 5v. LC 34-1808.

Champion continued Joannidès' work (entry 557) in his own set of chronologies, which contain lists of artistic and managerial personnel, budget figures, and several essays on each season as well as a daily listing of plays presented and information on premieres and revivals. Altogether, the reader can trace the daily performances of the Comédie Française from 1680 to 1937.

550.   **The Federal Theatre Project: A Catalog-Calendar of Productions**. Compiled by the Staff of the Fenwick Library, George Mason University. (Bibliographies and Indexes in the Performing Arts, no. 3). Westport, Conn.: Greenwood, 1986. 349p. LC 86-9780. ISBN 0-313-22314-9.

The United States' only federally sponsored national theatre, the Federal Theatre Project grew out of the Works Progress Administration during the Great Depression. The short lived theatre existed from 1935 until 1939, when the U.S. Congress, fearful of the theatre's left-wing politics, cut off its funding. At its peak it employed over 12,000 people who brought theatre to towns across America. This book draws its information from the F.T.P. records now housed at George Mason University (see entry 690). The production catalog lists in alphabetical order every play produced with the date and place of every performance. Altogether 2,745 performances are noted. A production calendar repeats information in chronological order, and several indexes provide entry points by name, type of play, and geographic location. This work illuminates an important experiment in American theatre and should be helpful to historians. Duffy (entry 33a) lists additional sources related to the Federal Theatre Project.

551.   Fitzsimmons, Linda, and Arthur W. McDonald, eds. **The Yorkshire Stage 1766-1803: A Calendar of Plays, Together with Cast Lists for Tate Wilkinson's Circuit of Theatres (Doncaster, Hull, Leeds, Pontefract, Wakefield, and York) and the Yorkshire Company's Engagements in Beverley, Halifax, Newcastle, Sheffield, and Edinburgh**. Metuchen, N.J.: Scarecrow, 1989. 1,097p. LC 88-35569. ISBN 0-8108-2187-7.

Fitzsimmons and McDonald have compiled a chronological list of plays performed by the Tate Wilkinson Company in Yorkshire theatres during the last half of the eighteenth century. Actor-manager Wilkinson toured an annual circuit of Yorkshire towns with his company and also took his actors to Sheffield, Edinburgh, and other British cities. Based on a collection of playbills in the York Minster Library, the authors list cities and dates of performances day by day. Plays listed include cast members. The book is indexed by performer name and play title. This work supplements *The London Stage 1660-1800* (entry 563) by presenting a picture of theatrical activity in the provinces.

552. Gänzl, Kurt. **The British Musical Theatre**. New York: Oxford University Press, 1986. 2v. LC 85-29705. ISBN 0-19-520509-X.

Gänzl chronicles over 100 years of British musical shows in two large volumes. The first covers 1864-1914, the second 1915-1984. The yearly chapters begin with an overview of the season that discusses the most important shows and their critical and popular reception. Cast and credits for each of that season's musicals follow. Entries also provide information on subsequent New York, Paris, and Vienna productions and on film versions. The first appendix in each volume lists printed scores and other music for the plays found in the British Library, the Library of Congress, the New York Public Library, and the author's collection. The second appendix lists recorded music from the plays. Gänzl compiled these entries from record catalogs, published discographies, and private collections. Finally, an index lists everyone mentioned in the text and listed in production credits; all play titles; and all theatres, newspapers, magazines, and journals mentioned in the text. Gänzl's love of his subject and his in-depth research shine through his informative, opinionated, and witty narratives.

553. Green, Stanley. **Broadway Musicals: Show by Show**. 3d ed. Milwaukee, Wis.: Hal Leonard, 1990. 372p. LC 90-17372.

Green has written a history and guide to more than 300 Broadway and off-Broadway musicals chosen for their lengthy runs or for their importance in subject matter, persons involved, or quality of the musical score. Beginning with *The Black Crook*, which ran for 475 performances in 1866, and ending with *Jerome Robbins' Broadway* from 1989, Green arranges his entries chronologically. He provides credits, song titles, length of run, theatre name, plot, and brief background of the show. He notes which shows have been recorded, published in book form, and/or licensed for amateur or professional productions. Several indexes help one find information by show title, theatre name, and names of persons involved with the productions. Green's remarks are not as critical as Bordman's (entry 547) nor is he as complete.

554. Hara, Arnold, ed. **Theatre Royal, Bath: A Calendar of Performances at the Orchard Street Theatre, 1750-1805**. Bath, England: Kingsmead Press, 1977. 249p. LC 77-370959. SBN 901571-79-2.

The Theatre Royal entertained the middle and upper classes of the fashionable resort of Bath, England, during its eighteenth-century heyday. This chronology lists all plays presented during the theatre's fifty-five-year career. For each season, Hara lists the members of the company and follows with a day-by-day chronology. Entries list abbreviations for the source of information: newspapers from Bath or nearby Bristol, playbills now housed in various repositories, and other manuscripts and books. Indexes provide

168 / 10—Chronologies and Histories

access by actors' names and by play titles. A specialized title, this adds to the already considerable knowledge of British theatre history outside London.

555. Harbage, Alfred. **Annals of English Drama 975-1700: An Analytical Record of All Plays, Extant or Lost, Chronologically Arranged and Indexed by Authors, Titles, Dramatic Companies Etc.** Revised by Sylvia Stoler Wagonheim. 3d ed., rev. London, New York: Routledge Kegan Paul, 1989. 375p. LC 89-14273. ISBN 0-415-01099-3.

A scholarly work with a broad scope, Harbage's chronology has been updated and corrected by Sylvia Wagonheim. It presents a chronological list of all known English plays from the earliest known, *Quam Quaeritis*, performed in 975, to those acted in 1700. Descriptions of royal receptions and entertainments are also included. Plays written in Latin or French appear if they were written in England, as well as translations, adaptations, and even unacted or "closet" plays written during the Interregnum. Within each year entries are arranged on a double page in columns listing author, title, date of performance, type of play, the company and place of the first performance, date of the first printed edition, and date of the latest modern edition. Several lists and indexes derived from the main body of the work add to the book's utility. Examples include a list of extant play manuscripts and their locations and an index of theatre companies. This is an important reference work that has been kept up-to-date as new scholarship has discovered additional information. See *The London Stage 1660-1800* (entry 563) and the *Records of Early English Drama* series (entries 568-576a) for similar information for different time periods.

556. Ireland, Joseph N. **Records of the New York Stage from 1750 to 1860.** New York: T. H. Morrell, 1866-1867. Reprint. New York: Burt Franklin, 1968. 2v. LC 68-56716.

An ancestor of Odell's *Annals of the New York Stage* (entry 566), Ireland's chronology discusses performances in various New York theatres up to the Civil War. Written in a narrative style, each chapter contains cast lists for plays produced during a particular year. Ireland comments on various actors and actresses and provides some death notices. A general index appears at the end of the second volume. Use this work to supplement Odell.

557. Joannidès, A. **La Comédie-Française de 1680 à 1900: Dictionnaire général des pièces et des auteurs.** Paris: Plon-Nourrit, 1901. Reprint. New York: Burt Franklin, 1971. 1v. LC 75-171947. SBN 8337-4190-X. Continued by *La Comédie-Française*. Annual. 1901-1919; 1920-1925; 1926. Paris: Plon-Nourrit, 1934. 21v.

Covering a longer time period than Lancaster (entry 559) Joannidès arranges his chronology of La Comédie Française into three parts. The first lists plays performed by the company in order by title with author and date of first production. The second section lists authors and their plays alphabetically. The third part is a chronological table that presents a year-by-year list of plays presented. Joannidès continued his work with supplements until his untimely death at the age of forty-seven in 1927. Champion continued the chronology until 1937 (entry 549). Although this chronology does not present information about box office receipts and finances as does Lancaster's, the length of time it covers makes it a valuable source to those interested in French theatre.

558. Kawachi, Yoshiko. **Calendar of English Renaissance Drama 1558-1642.** (Garland Reference Library of the Humanities, vol. 661). New York: Garland, 1986. 351p. LC 86-4456. ISBN 0-8240-9338-0.

Bringing together information from Harbage (entry 555), Chambers (entry 548), Bentley (entry 545), Sibley (entry 134), and many other sources, Kawachi constructs a day-by-day listing of play performances in England between 1558 and 1642. She includes plays, masques, and royal entertainments performed by professionals and amateurs. She indicates dates of tours by English acting companies. The book follows a tabular format, and entries list date, place, acting company, play title, type of play, whether the play was acted or not (if not, acting company and place are left blank), the author, the date of the earliest text, and Kawachi's source of information. Kawachi indexes the book by play title, playwright, and acting company. Because of incomplete records many entries lack complete information. Kawachi offers a daily chronology while Harbage is arranged by year and then by author's name. Readers should note that Kawachi based her book on the second edition of Harbage. Because the third edition has now been published, it should be checked for corrections and additions to Kawachi.

559. Lancaster, H. Carrington. **The Comédie Française, 1680-1701: Plays, Actors, Spectators, Finances**. (Johns Hopkins Studies in Romance Literatures and Languages, extra volume 17). Baltimore, Md.: Johns Hopkins Press, 1941. 210p. LC 41-8706.

Derived from the business records of Paris's Comédie Française, Lancaster's chronology records the plays presented day-by-day with the number of paid spectators, the receipts, and the actors' and authors' earnings between 1680 and 1701. The introduction presents a history of the company during these twenty-one years, including a fascinating explanation of its profit-sharing system. Lancaster indexes the work by play title and personal names mentioned in the introduction. Lancaster published the same type of information for the years 1701 to 1774 in the American Philosophical Society's *Transactions*, n.s., v.41, p. 593-849. Joannidès' *La Comédie-Française de 1680 à 1900* (entry 557) carries the chronology further.

560. Leiter, Samuel L., ed. **The Encyclopedia of the New York Stage, 1920-1930**. Westport, Conn.: Greenwood, 1985. 2v. LC 84-6558. ISBN 0-313-23615-1.

561. Leiter, Samuel L., ed. **The Encyclopedia of the New York Stage, 1930-1940**. Westport, Conn.: Greenwood, 1989. 1,299p. LC 88-5668. ISBN 0-313-25509-1.

562. Leiter, Samuel L., ed. **The Encyclopedia of the New York Stage, 1940-1950**. Westport, Conn.: Greenwood, 1993. 1,000p. LC 92-7397. ISBN 0-313-27510-6.

In these volumes Leiter attempts to describe every professional legitimate theatre production in New York from June 16, 1920 to June 15, 1950. His scope includes Broadway, off-Broadway, and selected ethnic theatres. Leiter has chosen an alphabetical rather than chronological approach, but one can locate plays by date using the "Calendar of Productions." Several other appendices provide information about awards, foreign theatre companies in New York, longest running shows, critics, and more. Leiter includes a bibliography and an index of proper names. The entries list play title, author, cast and credits, theatre, opening date, length of run, and a commentary. The commentaries vary and might include background on the play's creation, a plot synopsis, excerpts from reviews, or a summary of critical comments. This is an important source for historians of American theatre. For earlier periods see George Odell's *Annals of the New York Stage* (entry 566).

170 / 10—Chronologies and Histories

563. **The London Stage 1660-1800: A Calendar of Plays, Entertainments & Afterpieces, Together with Casts, Box-receipts and Contemporary Comment.** Carbondale: Southern Illinois University Press, 1960-1968. 11v. LC 60-6539.

Thirty-five years in the making, this work lists day-by-day all performances of plays, operas, operettas, oratorios, masques, and other entertainments in London from the beginning of the Restoration to 1800. Each year's chapter begins with a summary of that season's history and lists of theatre companies and their personnel and London theatres. Each introduction also lists plays that cannot be placed on a particular date but that were performed sometime during that season. Listings present title, cast, theatre, and additional comments drawn from contemporary diaries, letters, account books, and other documents. To aid the reader the editors have noted yearly events such as Lent and Passion Week during which performances were prohibited or severely limited. They have also indicated the succession of new monarchs and other political events that might have had an effect on the theatre. Although each volume has its own index, when the calendar was completed the editors decided to produce a computer-generated index to the entire set of eleven volumes. It provides 506,014 references to names and titles in the set. Users should be sure to read the foreword and the introduction to the index as both explain editors' decisions that affect the index's use. For example, generic titles such as "Dance" or "A Young Gentleman" have been omitted from indexing. Also, an actor might have appeared in two or more performances in the same theatre on the same day, but he appears only once in the index. Readers need to scan the entire entry in the calendar for that day to find all performances. The index's introduction also contains a fascinating account of the process by which the computer index was produced, a work of seven years. The calendar and index are outstanding works that will aid theatre scholars for many years to come. For biographical information on the performers of this era see Highfill and others (entry 331).

564. Loney, Glenn. **20th Century Theatre.** New York: Facts on File, 1983. 2v. LC 81-19587. ISBN 0-87196-463-5 (set).

Not as scholarly or detailed as the works of Wearing (entries 580-585a) or Leiter (entries 560-562), this chronology covers more recent years than either of the others. For each year Loney lists American and British premieres and revivals as well as notable births, deaths, and debuts. He includes a bibliography and an index. Readers who are trying to find the date of a particular opening or the debut of an actress will find Loney's book helpful.

565. Nelson, Alfred L., and Gilbert B. Cross, eds. **The Adelphi Calendar Project 1806-1850. Sans Pareil Theatre 1806-1819/Adelphi Theatre 1819-1850.** (The London Stage 1800-1900, no. 1). Westport, Conn.: Greenwood, 1990. 233p.; 31 microfiche. LC 89-11968. ISBN 0-313-25882-1.

Both on its own merits and as a model for future chronologies of individual theatres, this work deserves a close look. Developed by the collaboration of several theatre historians, its goal is to provide "objective, quantifiable data on performances and performers" at the theatre known first as the Sans Pareil and later as the Adelphi. The loose-leaf notebook contains a summary of each season; an author and play title index; an index of all actors and actresses who played the theatre; and an index of singers, dancers, and musicians who performed there. A bibliography lists sources important to the study of nineteenth-century British theatre. The microfiche, arranged by year, provide the details suggested in the annual summaries. The daily calendar lists play title, author, genre, first-night cast, music, type of scenery, and general comments. A seasonal summary provides statistics on number of performances, ticket prices, names of the theatre's management and artistic personnel, and the number of plays performed. This work represents a great deal of scholarly research and work with computers. If the editors fulfill their commitment to create calendars for all major nineteenth-century English theatres, they will add immeasurably to the knowledge of their history.

566. Odell, George C. D. **Annals of the New York Stage**. New York: Columbia University Press, 1927-1949. Reprint. New York: AMS Press, 1970. 15v. LC 77-116018. ISBN 0-404-07830-3 (set).

George Odell's entire life was spent chronicling the New York stage. Stage struck early in life, he chose Columbia as his college because of its proximity to Broadway. After graduating he remained in New York, spending his entire teaching career at Columbia and working on this chronicle. Covering both legitimate theatre and "many humble forms of diversion," Odell's chronology, written in a narrative style, lists and describes many of New York's theatrical events from its beginnings to 1894. Odell relied on contemporary newspapers, playbills, diaries of theatre-goers, and other documents to write his history. Unfortunately, he included neither footnotes nor a bibliography, a weakness for serious scholarship. His work chronicles not just Broadway but opera, foreign-language theatre, music halls, amateur plays, and much more. One can read about Henry Irving's first visit to New York in 1883 and the opening of the Metropolitan Opera House the same year, for example. Each of the fifteen volumes has its own index. The many portraits in the work are indexed in a separate work (entry 567). For later periods see Leiter's *Encyclopedia of the New York Stage* (entries 560-562).

567. Odell, George C. D. **Index to the Portraits in Odell's Annals of the New York Stage**. New York: American Society for Theatre Research, 1963. 179p.

Odell's *Annals of the New York Stage* (entry 566) contains hundreds of portraits of actors and other performers. To aid in their location, the American Society for Theatre Research published this alphabetical index by name to the portraits. Each name is cited with volume and page number. Anyone looking for theatrical portraits of the eighteenth and nineteenth centuries should also check the Harvard catalog of portraits (entry 168).

Records of Early English Drama. Toronto and Buffalo, N.Y.: University of Toronto Press, 1979- . Irregular.

568. Anderson, J. J., ed. **Newcastle upon Tyne**. (Records of Early English Drama). Toronto and Buffalo, N.Y.: University of Toronto Press, 1982. 216p. LC 83-151419. ISBN 0-8020-5610-5.

569. Clopper, Lawrence M., ed. **Chester**. (Records of Early English Drama). Toronto and Buffalo, N.Y.: University of Toronto Press, 1979. 591p. LC 79-16420. ISBN 0-8020-5460-9.

570. Douglan, Audrey and Peter Greenfield, eds. **Cumberland, Westmorland, Gloucestershire**. (Records of Early English Drama). Toronto and Buffalo, N.Y.: University of Toronto Press, 1986. 547p. LC 87-160695. ISBN 0-8020-5669-5.

571. Galloway, David, ed. **Norwich, 1540-1642**. (Records of Early English Drama). Toronto and Buffalo, N.Y.: University of Toronto Press, 1984. 501p. LC 84-218576. ISBN 0-8020-5648-2.

172 / 10—Chronologies and Histories

572. George, David. **Lancashire**. (Records of Early English Drama). Toronto and Buffalo, N.Y.: University of Toronto Press, 1992. 471p. LC 92-93351. ISBN 0-8020-2862-4.

573. Ingram, R. W., ed. **Coventry**. (Records of Early English Drama). Toronto and Buffalo, N.Y.: University of Toronto Press, 1981. 712p. LC 82-113197.ISBN 0-8020-5542-7.

574. Johnston, Alexandra F., and Margaret Rogerson, eds. **York**. (Records of Early English Drama). Toronto and Buffalo, N.Y.: University of Toronto Press, 1979. 2v. LC 78-14756. ISBN 0-8020-2304-5.

575. Klausner, David, ed. **Herefordshire and Worcestershire**. (Records of Early English Drama). Toronto: University of Toronto Press, 1990. LC 90-94294. ISBN 0-8020-2758-X.

576. Nelson, Alan H., ed. **Cambridge**. (Records of Early English Drama). Toronto and Buffalo, N.Y.: University of Toronto Press, 1989. 2v. LC 89-175453. ISBN 0-8020-5751-9.

576a. Wasson, John M. **Devon**. (Records of Early English Drama). Toronto and Buffalo, N.Y.: University of Toronto Press, 1986. 623p. LC 88-128526. ISBN 0-8020-5706-3.

A monumental project undertaken by the University of Toronto Press, Records of Early English Drama (REED) seeks "to collect written evidence of drama, minstrelsy, and ceremonial activity in Great Britain before 1642." Still in progress, the series when finished will cover all of England. For each volume, which covers a specific geographical area such as a city or a county, scholars sift through minutes of governmental meetings, city and guild accounts, ordinances, legal contracts, wills, rent rolls, letters, court records, and other materials to find evidence of theatrical activity. These records are reprinted together with an historical introduction, maps, a glossary of obsolete Latin and English words, and an index. Volumes vary according to the type and amount of information available, but generally follow the same format. The documents reveal not only the varied entertainment offered to medieval and Renaissance Englishmen, but also the constant battle between the authorities and the unruly traveling players. The Gloucester Corporation Common Council Minute Book of November 3. 1580 forbade "Players of Enterludes" within the city because they "Drawe away greate Sommes of money from diuerse persons and allure seruantes, apprentices, and iorneymen & others of the worst desposed persons to leudenes and lightnes of life." By locating and printing thousands of local documents, REED is performing an invaluable service to researchers interested in medieval and Renaissance British theatre.

577. Ritchey, David, comp. and ed. **A Guide to the Baltimore Stage in the Eighteenth Century: A History and Day Book Calendar**. Westport, Conn.: Greenwood, 1982. 342p. LC 81-13461. ISBN 0-313-22589-3.

Beginning with a short history of theatre in Baltimore between 1772 and 1799, Ritchey lists day-by-day "every production, every cast, and every performer" for Baltimore theatres during these years. Indexes allow access by play title, actors' names, and playwrights. Each entry lists, besides the play title, the author's name, the theatre in which the performance occurred, and the cast list. Subsequent productions of the same play refer to the opening date for complete information. Ritchey cites a source for his information, either a newspaper article or materials from various manuscript repositories. At the end of each season, a summary lists new performers, reappearing performers, new plays, and repeating plays.

578. Sampson, Henry T. **The Ghost Walks: A Chronological History of Blacks in Show Business, 1865-1910**. Metuchen, N.J.: Scarecrow, 1988. 570p. LC 87-27973. ISBN 0-8108-2070-6.

Intended as a prequel to his *Blacks in Blackface* (entry 444), Sampson's book chronicles the entrance of African-Americans into American show business after the Civil War. Each chapter introduces the time period and is followed by a chronology. Entries list a date and describe an event in one or several sentences. Important events warrant several paragraphs. Sampson provides more information for later years, reflecting greater availability of sources for those years. He quotes from reviews and articles in both Black and general circulation newspapers from all over the United States and from Australia. (Black performers toured Australia during the late nineteenth century.) While most entries refer to performances, others portray the hardships African-American artists encountered. The danger faced by these performers is illustrated by an account of the 1902 lynching of a member of the Georgia Minstrels in New Madrid, Missouri. Sampson's work will suggest areas of further research to students and scholars alike. And the book's title? On payday the company's manager, attired completely in white, paid the performers. Hence, "the ghost walks" meant one was getting paid for one's work.

579. Steele, Mary Susan. **Plays & Masques at Court During the Reigns of Elizabeth, James, and Charles**. New Haven, Conn.: Yale University Press, 1926. Reprint. New York: Russell & Russell, 1968. 300p. LC 67-18296.

Steele identifies and provides information about "all dramatic representation before the sovereigns and other members of the royal family, on progress as well as in their usual residences" (preface). She arranges the book chronologically, starting with Elizabeth I's ascension to the throne in November 1558, and ending March 12, 1642, shortly before Charles I lost his head. Working from official records of the court and other early sources, Steele describes each play or masque in as much detail as possible. She cites many references to court documents, letters, diaries, and other original and secondary sources. Author and title indexes conclude the work. For criticism of the court entertainments of this period, see David Bergeron's *Twentieth-Century Criticism of English Masques, Pageants, and Entertainments: 1558-1642* (entry 25).

580. Wearing, J. P. **The London Stage, 1890-1899: A Calendar of Plays and Players**. Metuchen, N.J.: Scarecrow, 1976. 2v. LC 76-1825. ISBN 0-8108-0910-9.

581. Wearing, J. P. **The London Stage, 1900-1909: A Calendar of Plays and Players**. Metuchen, N.J.: Scarecrow, 1981. 2v. LC 80-28353. ISBN 0-8108-1403-X.

582. Wearing, J. P. **The London Stage, 1910-1919: A Calendar of Plays and Players**. Metuchen, N.J.: Scarecrow, 1982. 2v. LC 82-19190. ISBN 0-8108-1596-6.

583. Wearing, J. P. **The London Stage, 1920-1929: A Calendar of Plays and Players**. Metuchen, N.J.: Scarecrow, 1984. 3v. LC 84-10665. ISBN 0-8108-1715-2.

174 / 10—Chronologies and Histories

584. Wearing, J. P. **The London Stage, 1930-1939: A Calendar of Plays and Players.** Metuchen, N.J.: Scarecrow, 1990. 3v. LC 90-8883. ISBN 0-8108-2349-7.

585. Wearing, J. P. **The London Stage, 1940-1949: A Calendar of Plays and Players.** Metuchen, N.J.: Scarecrow, 1991. 2v. LC 91-36206. ISBN 0-8108-2500-7.

585a. Wearing, J. P. **The London Stage, 1950-1959: A Calendar of Plays and Players.** Metuchen, N.J.: Scarecrow, 1993. 2v. LC 93-17179. ISBN 0-8108-2690-9.

Basing his work on the playbills of major London theatres, Wearing is providing "a daily listing of plays and players on the London stage" beginning in 1890. Starting with the opening performance date, entries include title and author of the play, name of theatre, number of performances, a cast list, and a bibliography of reviews. American readers should note that dates are written European style: 12/11/19 is November 12, 1919. Indexes provide multiple access points. Together, the seven titles already published provide information on more than 18,000 productions. Wearing is providing theatre historians a valuable reference that should aid their work considerably.

586. Wicks, Charles Beaumont. **The Parisian Stage: Alphabetical Indexes of Plays and Authors.** University: University of Alabama Press, 1950-1979. 5v. LC 50-2939.

During his lengthy project Wicks used newspapers, periodicals, previous compilations and studies, and manuscript materials to compile a list of every new play produced in Paris during the nineteenth century. Within each volume Wicks arranges entries by play title with an author index. He provides the play's genre, number of acts, and the theatre and date of its first performance. Note that dates are written in the European style: 11-1-36 is January 11, 1836. Because each part contains corrections and additions to all previous parts, readers should check all volumes for the greatest accuracy. The last volume contains a cumulative index of authors from 1800 to 1900. The five volumes document 31,879 productions. Regrettably, Wicks has not provided a chronological listing. Nevertheless, this specialized work provides the building blocks for advanced research in nineteenth-century French theatre history. Joannidès (entry 557) covers a longer time period in more detail, but only for the Comédie Française.

Dance Chronologies

587. Tintori, Giampiero. **Cronologia: opere - balletti - concerti 1778-1977.** Gorle, Italy: Grafica Gutenberg Editrice, 1979. 475p. LC 80-48458.

Written by the curator of the La Scala museum, this chronology lists operas, ballets, and concerts performed during 200 years of La Scala's existence. Although primarily associated with opera, La Scala also presents ballets, concerts, and other entertainments. In this work ballet is given its own section. Performances are listed chronologically starting with *Pafio e Mirra*, performed on August 3, 1778, with music by Antonio Salieri. Each entry lists the names of the choreographer, the composer, and the principal dancers. Using the ballet name section of the index one can find that Marie Taglioni, the world's first ballet star, danced her signature piece, *La Sylphide*, at La Scala on May 29, 1841. Ballet titles are listed in a separate section of the index that is located at the back of the book. A specialized work, this should be useful to students of nineteenth- and twentieth-century European ballet.

Chapter 11

Electronic Discussion Groups

This chapter describes discussion groups that are available through the Internet and Bitnet computer communications networks. Part of the developing National Research and Education Network (NREN), the Internet and Bitnet allow users to communicate with other individuals (e-mail) and with groups of people who are interested in the same topic (electronic discussion groups or lists). To use the Internet one must have a computer, a modem, and communications software. One also needs access to the network, either through a university, a company, or a network service reseller. As of this writing, in early 1993, several useful guides have been published. *Crossing the Internet Threshold: An Instructional Handbook* by Roy Tennant, John Ober, and Anne G. Lipow (San Carlos, Calif.: Library Solutions Press, 1993) clearly explains how to start using the Internet and provides a list of Internet service providers. Other books that explain the use of networks include Jack Kessler's *Directory to Fulltext Online Resources 1992* (Westport, Conn.: Meckler, 1992), Brendan P. Kehoe's *Zen and the Art of the Internet: A Beginner's Guide* (2d ed. Englewood Cliffs, N.J.: PTR Prentice-Hall, 1993), and Ed Krol's *The Whole Internet: User's Guide and Catalog* (Sebastopol, Calif.: O'Reilly & Associates, 1992).

Because new discussion groups appear frequently, readers should check the list of academic discussion lists available from Diane Kovacs at Kent State University by anonymous ftp from KSUVXA.KENT.EDU. (The books listed above explain how to use ftp protocols to retrieve information from remote computer sites.) A second list of lists is available from Dartmouth University by anonymous ftp from DARTCMS1.DARTMOUTH.EDU. Finally, the Office of Scientific and Academic Publishing of the Association of Research Libraries publishes the *Directory of Electronic Journals, Newsletters, and Academic Discussion Lists* periodically.

Theatre Discussion Groups

588. **ASTR-L**. Bitnet address: ASTR-L@UIUCVMD.

Acting as an information exchange for members of the American Society for Theatre Research (entry 728), *ASTR-L* is open to anyone interested in theatre history. It facilitates inquiries of the type often posed by historians, such as general calls for information on obscure persons and institutions. Because this is a new list, it has only begun to store articles, bibliographies, and other large files that can be retrieved by subscribers.

589. **PERFORM**. Internet address: PERFORM@IUBVM.UCS.INDIANA.EDU; Bitnet address: PERFORM@IUBVM.

Not to be confused with *PERFORM-L* (entry 590), this discussion group focuses on medieval performance. It distributes announcements of seminars held at such places as the Newberry Library's Center for Renaissance Studies. Perhaps because it shares the concerns and many of the same subscribers of the *Shakespeare Electronic Conference* and *REED-L* (entries 592 and 591), this newer discussion group has not been a very active list.

590. **PERFORM-L**. Internet address: PERFORM-L@ACFcluster.NYU.EDU; Bitnet address: PERFORM-L@NYUACF.

PERFORM-L exists to allow discussion of performance studies issues. Performance studies combine the social sciences and the arts in an attempt "to widen our vision of performance, studying it not only as art but as a means of understanding historical, social, and cultural processes." Recently, participants have debated the difference between performance studies and cultural studies and have discussed the impact of live versus non-live performances. The list maintains an archive of bibliographies, syllabi, and other large files of interest to its members.

591. **REED-L: Records of Early English Drama.** Internet address: REED-@EPAS.UTORONTO.CA.

A relatively quiet conference, *REED-L* exists to disseminate information about the University of Toronto's *Records of Early English Drama* series (entries 568-576a). Announcements of new volumes and occasional queries regarding medieval words or phrases make up most of the list's traffic.

592. **SHAKESPEARE ELECTRONIC CONFERENCE**. Bitnet address: SHAKSPER @UTORONTO.

Founded by Ken Steele of the University of Toronto in July 1990, the *Shakespeare Electronic Conference* facilitates conversations and information exchange among more than 300 Shakespeare scholars, students, and aficionados worldwide. It is a moderated list currently edited by Hardy M. Cook, and subscribers must submit a request to join and a short biography to HMCOOK@BOE00.MINC.UMD.EDU. The group's fileserver maintains a large collection of files including biographies of list members, scholarly papers, public domain Shakespeare texts, a directory of calls for papers and conference announcements relevant to Shakespearean and Renaissance studies, and a list of works in progress, including doctoral dissertations. Anyone researching Shakespeare or English Renaissance studies will appreciate the chance to interact with others of like mind on this active list.

593. **STAGECRAFT**. Internet address: STAGECRAFT%JAGUAR@CS.UTAH.EDU. Send requests to STAGECRAFT-REQUEST%JAGUAR@CS.UTAH.EDU.

An unmoderated list, *STAGECRAFT* encourages "the discussion of all aspects of stage work, including...special effects, sound effects, sound reinforcement, stage management, set design and building, lighting design, company management, hall management, hall design, and show production." The list manager also maintains a file of users with their specialties and skills for professional networking purposes. *STAGECRAFT* complements *THEATRE* (entry 594) well, as the latter concentrates on acting and directing.

594. **THEATRE: The Theatre Discussion List**. Internet address: THEATRE@ PUCC.PRINCETON.=DU. Bitnet address: THEATRE@PUCC.

THEATRE boasts a more eclectic membership than some electronic conferences with a good mix of theatre professors, graduate students, undergraduates, and nonprofessional theatre lovers. Members are quite generous with their advice and help when queried. Conversations range widely, from reports on professional conferences to a discussion on the role of the director vis-à-vis the actors in a production to advising a high school student on which theatre periodicals to read. Technical theatre topics are not discussed on *THEATRE* because *STAGECRAFT* (entry 593) handles that discussion.

Dance Discussion Groups

595. **DANCE-L**. Internet address: DANCE-L%HEARN.BITNET@CUNYVM.CUNY. EDU; Bitnet address: DANCE-L@HEARN.

DANCE-L focuses on folk and traditional dance. Its members are trying to build several databases that will help folk dance participants and researchers. These include a file of folk dances, an electronic bibliography, and a "multilingual folk dance terminology database."

Chapter 12

Core Periodicals

Periodicals enable one to remain current in a field. Their book reviews focus attention on new works while their articles present new findings and interpretations. The titles in this chapter were chosen for their importance or to represent an area of the performing arts. Periodicals related to magic are limited to those available to the public. As Coleman points out in *Magic: A Reference Guide* (entry 4), many magic books and periodicals are available only to magicians through professional associations. For periodicals not described in this chapter, see *Ulrich's International Periodicals Directory* (New York: R. R. Bowker, annual).

Theatre and Related Arts

596. **American Theatre: The Monthly Forum for News, Features and Opinion**. New York: Theatre Communications Group, 1984- . Monthly. ISSN 8750-3255.

Known as a lively, informative magazine, *American Theatre* focuses on American nonprofit professional theatre. It reports on productions throughout the United States and prints one full-length play in each issue. The magazine's columnists review books and report on government actions affecting theatre. Recent articles have included a piece on lighting designer Jennifer Tipton's debut as director of *The Tempest* at the Guthrie Theater and a report on playwright Marsha Norman. The April issue is an annual survey of nonprofit professional theatres in the United States.

597. **Arts & Culture Funding Report**. Arlington, Va.: Education Funding Research Council, 1989- . Monthly. ISSN 1047-3297.

Of interest to arts managers and artists seeking funding, this twelve-page monthly newsletter reports on government and business funding of the arts. Short, factual articles advocate support for the arts and keep readers informed about government legislation and trends in corporate giving. This title concentrates on funding while *Arts Management* (entry 598) deals with a broader group of management issues.

598. **Arts Management**. New York: Radius Group, 1962- . 5/year. ISSN 0004-4067.

A four-page newsletter, this title calls itself "the national news service for those who finance, manage and communicate the arts." Practical and informative, *Arts Management* reports on advertising trends in the arts, board governance, and funding issues. A useful feature is a short bibliography of recent books and articles of interest to administrators. The *Arts & Culture Funding Report* (entry 597) provides more information on grants, but *Arts Management* keeps the professional manager up-to-date on the business of the arts.

599. **Asian Theatre Journal**. Honolulu: University of Hawaii Press, 1984- . 2/year. ISSN 0742-5457.

Formerly edited by James R. Brandon (see entry 26) and now by Samuel Leiter (see entries 286; 560-562), this journal publishes "articles on Asian theatre and on the relation and mutual influences between Asian and Western theatre." Scholarly articles written by academics dominate and have included a look at fourteenth-century Japanese actor and teacher, Zeami Motokiyo's views on feeling and acting; a history and description of the Takarazuka Revue Company of Japan; and a description of Western interpretations of Indian theatre. Book reviews and an occasional playscript complete the offerings. This is a basic title for anyone interested in Asian theatre.

600. **Back Stage: The Performing Arts Weekly**. New York: Backstage Publications, 1960- . Weekly. ISSN 0005-3635.

As a trade newspaper, *Back Stage* prints casting notices for New York and regional theatres. It also reviews new play productions, reports union news, and publishes information about government and foundation changes that affect the arts. It will interest actors looking for new jobs and students considering a career in the theatre.

601. **Bandwagon**. Columbus, Ohio: The Circus Historical Society, 1957- . Bimonthly. ISSN 0005-4968.

Bandwagon covers the history of the big top and its devotees. Easily read, well-illustrated articles describe various circus organizations and families. Others discuss topics such as the impact of domestic animal diseases on circus animals and the construction of circus wagons. The advertisements will lead collectors of circus memorabilia to appropriate sources. As the official publication of the Circus Historical Society, the magazine also covers the society's annual convention and other business. For circus buffs this is a must.

602. **Black Masks**. Bronx, N.Y.: Beth Turner, 1984- . Bimonthly. LC 86-1173. ISSN 0887-7580.

A welcome addition to theatre periodicals, *Black Masks* features "information about Black performing and visual arts throughout the United States". Each issue contains two or three feature articles including one about an African-American artist. Others discuss plays written by African-Americans such as August Wilson's *The Piano Lesson*. The "Arts Hot-Line" lists current productions, exhibits, and new books of interest. *Black Masks* provides current awareness of Black performers and performances and nicely supplements the *Black Arts Annual* (entry 383).

603. **Broadside**. New York: Theatre Library Association, 1940- . Quarterly. ISSN 0068-2748.

The Theatre Library Association's newsletter publishes news of the association, reports on winners of TLA awards for the best theatre books, and reviews books appropriate to a theatre library. It also notes exhibitions of interest and reviews new periodicals. This is of interest primarily to theatre librarians, most of whom probably belong to the Association.

604. **Canadian Theatre Review**. Downsview, Ont.: Faculty of Fine Arts, York University, 1974- . Quarterly. LC 79-644805. ISSN 0315-0836.

Although always related to Canadian theatre, each issue explores a different topic. Subjects have included Canadian women playwrights; theatre in the prairie provinces; native theatre; and new voices in Canadian theatre. Well-illustrated articles focus on plays, playwrights, and actors. A number of book reviews and a playscript complete each issue. This is a must for anyone interested in contemporary Canadian theatre.

605. **Circus Report**. El Cerrito, Calif.: Circus Report, 1972- . Weekly. LC 86-10833. ISSN 0889-5996.

Although its purpose is to publish the routes taken by various circuses, *Circus Report* also features articles written by volunteer reporters from around the United States. They review circuses and report news of circus people. A directory by subject advertises the services of acrobats, dog acts, stunt shows, and many other specialties. This title will interest circus professionals and buffs alike.

606. **Dramatics**. Cincinnati, Ohio: Educational Theatre Association, 1929- . 9/year. ISSN 0012-5989.

Published for members of the International Thespian Society, *Dramatics* aims squarely at the high school student with an annual "College Theatre Directory," many advertisements for college theatre programs, and a plethora of practical advice. Hints on developing a character, on building props, and on publicizing plays are typical subjects of articles. The magazine also prints short plays and reviews books.

607. **Dramatists Guild Quarterly**. New York: The Dramatists Guild, 1964- . Quarterly. LC 64-9425. ISSN 0012-6004.

The journal of the Dramatists Guild publishes two or three short articles written by playwrights, lists new plays and books written by members, and acknowledges honors given to members. Several directories helpful to playwrights appear regularly. These include a list of professional theatres with play submission policies; a directory of producers with information on the types of plays they favor; lists of agents, festivals, artists' colonies, service organizations, and other sources of support; and a directory of college and non-Equity theatres. Designed to be useful to the practicing dramatist, the *Quarterly* will also interest aspiring writers.

608. **Essays in Theatre/Études théâtrales**. Guelph, Ont.: Department of Drama, University of Guelph, 1982- . 2/year. ISSN 0821-4425.

Written in French and English by Canadian and American academics, the articles in this refereed journal discuss "any aspect of theatre studies." About six essays and an equal number of book reviews make up each issue. Recent articles have considered Kenneth Branagh's motion picture interpretation of *Henry V* and examined Brian Friel's *Translations*. Although material on Canadian subjects is encouraged, the journal publishes articles on a much wider range of topics. This is a good general theatre title.

609. **Estreno**. Cincinnati, Ohio: Department of Romance Languages and Literatures, University of Cincinnati, 1975- . 2/year. ISSN 0097-8663.

Written in Spanish and English, *Estreno* examines drama and theatre in twentieth-century Spain. A short play appears in each issue. Although most articles focus on drama, a few deal with theatre. Book reviews are supplemented by an annual bibliography of critical books, articles, theses, and dramatic texts.

610. **Genii: The International Conjurors' Magazine**. Los Angeles, Calif.: William W. Larsen, 1936- . Monthly. LC 78-1312. ISSN 0016-6855.

Published since its beginnings by the Larsen family, who also run the Magic Castle, a club for magicians in Los Angeles, *Genii* has been in business for more than fifty years. It publishes news about magicians, descriptions of tricks, performance tips, book reviews, and obituaries. The advertisements exhort professional and amateur magicians alike to part with cash for the latest apparatus. *Genii* does not publish as many historical articles as *MAGIC* (entry 617), but it is useful for looking at the current magic scene.

611. **High Performance**. Santa Monica, Calif.: High Performance, 1978- . Quarterly. ISSN 0160-9769.

High Performance covers the world of performance art including dance, mime, theatre, video performances, cyberart (interactive, computer-generated pictures and words), art installations, and various combinations thereof. The first half of each issue presents several articles on performers and companies who engage in this type of performance, while the second half reviews performances, books, and recordings. The editors of *High Performance* state they are "devoted to progressive thinking in the arts," which translates to an interest in every trendy liberal and radical cause including AIDS, the homeless, feminism, multiculturalism, and American repression of Third World countries. The Summer 1992 issue devoted itself to presenting artists' responses to the Los Angeles riots of the previous April. While the rhetoric gets tiresome quickly, this journal reviews performances that are seldom reviewed elsewhere. For that reason it will be especially useful to theatre students who want to know what the avant-garde is up to.

612. **Inside Arts**. Washington, D.C.: Association of Performing Arts Presenters, 1989- . Quarterly. No ISSN.

The Association of Performing Arts Presenters (entry 731) represents people who book visiting performers for artists series. Their journal focuses on topics of interest to presenters such as community outreach projects, arts criticism, and commissioned works. Short articles focus on specific performers and artists series. *Inside Arts* also reports on public policies affecting the arts. The periodical should interest any series manager, whether a member of APAP or not.

613. **The Journal of Arts Management, Law, and Society**. Washington, D.C.: Heldref Publications, 1982- . Quarterly. ISSN 1063-2921.

Concentrating on the business side of the arts, particularly funding, this periodical covers "public policy, funding approaches, sociological perspectives, and cultural issues as they relate to the arts." For the most part the writers come from academe with a sprinkling of practitioners included. Recent topics explored have been the problem of succession in an arts organization when a founder retires or dies; effective use of boards of trustees; and the use of public money by the National Endowment for the Arts. The journal reviews books of interest to arts managers, the audience to whom this periodical will appeal.

614. **Journal of Dramatic Theory and Criticism.** Lawrence: Department of Theatre and Media Arts, University of Kansas, 1986- . 2/year. ISSN 0888-3202.

The interests of this journal revolve around the performance of dramatic texts and criticism of those performances. A mix of articles, interviews, book reviews, and performance reviews address "the theoretical issues associated with performance and performance texts." Recent articles have examined the state of East German theatre just prior to unification and the legal rights of American playwrights regarding performance of their works. The magazine has interviewed Ellen Stewart, found of La Mama Theatre in New York City, and Ntozake Shange, a performance artist. The journal will appeal to readers who are interested in both text and performance.

615. **Latin American Theatre Review: A Journal Devoted to the Theatre and Drama of Spanish and Portuguese America.** Lawrence: The Center of Latin American Studies, The University of Kansas, 1967- . 2/year. LC 78-369. ISSN 0023-8813.

Written in Spanish, Portuguese, and English, each issue of this journal contains a dozen articles or so, as well as book and performance reviews. With an emphasis on research and scholarship, articles focus on a specific playwright, a theatrical form such as street theatre in Colombia, or the relation of a Latin American country's theatre to the society in which it exists. With a growing interest in Latin American culture, this title should interest scholars and students at the college level.

616. **Lighting Dimensions.** New York: Lighting Dimensions Associates, 1977- . 9/year. ISSN 0191-541X.

The trade magazine for lighting professionals of all types, this periodical is heavy with advertising. The December issue functions as a directory of manufacturers, suppliers, and consultants, while the July-August issue is a buyers' guide arranged by product. Each issue reports on new products and carries several features including stories on theatre lighting. Chris Perry's designs for the Royal Shakespeare Company's production of *Les Liaisons Dangereuses* were featured recently as was the work of Dennis Parichy, the designer of *Talley's Folly* and *As Is*. Lighting professionals will find this title illuminating.

617. **MAGIC: An Independent Magazine for Magicians.** Lakewood, Calif.: Stan Allen, 1991- . Monthly. ISSN 1062-2845.

A newcomer, this slickly produced magazine features several well-written articles each month along with news notes, a question- and-answer column, and product reviews. Besides books, the reviews cover instructional videos, tricks, and even computer software helpful to magicians. Articles mix today's news with history. A recent article described Harry Blackstone's successful evacuation of 2,000 children from the Lincoln Theatre in Decatur, Illinois on September 2, 1942, minutes before flames engulfed the building. Another recounted the discovery of Howard Thurston's illusions and equipment in a Wisconsin barn in 1988 and their disposition. A third article grew out of a two-week diary recently written by a professional magician. If publisher Stan Allen can keep up the good work, his periodical will become a standard title along with *Genii* (entry 610).

618. **Marquee: The Journal of the Theatre Historical Society of America.** Springfield, Pa.: The Society, 1969- . 5/year. ISSN 0025-3928.

Besides reporting on the activities of its parent organization, *Marquee* publishes information about old theatres, both extant and demolished in the United States. Each article describes the theatre and discusses its history. Photographs accompany most articles. Although most of the buildings are movie theatres, *Marquee* occasionally covers legitimate and vaudeville theatres. This title will interest architecture and old theatre buffs. For more information on the society, see entry 746.

619. **Maske und Kothurn: Internationale Beiträge zur Theaterwissenschaft.** Vienna: Universität Wien, Institut für Theaterwissenschaft, Bohlaus Verlag, 1955- . Quarterly. ISSN 0025-4606.

Covering all aspects of theatre research, including radio, film, and television plays, *Maske und Kothurn* features articles written in German and English by scholars. Topics range widely from the plays of the ancient Greeks to modern Black South African works. A recent special issue concentrated on European views of Japanese performing arts. With many articles in English, this journal will be accessible to American theatre students despite its German title.

620. **Medieval English Theatre**. Lancaster, England: University of Lancaster, 1979- . 2/year. ISSN 0143-3784.

Specializing in "medieval and early Tudor theatre in all its aspects together with articles and records of modern survivals or equivalents in theatre and pageantry," this refereed journal covers a fascinating range of topics. Articles have included a report on the construction of pageant "waggons" on which medieval plays were performed; a biographical sketch of sixteenth-century Scottish theatrical painter Walter Binning; and a description of the Easter processions in Cordoba, Spain. Photographs enhance the articles, which describe modern reenactments of medieval theatre such as the production of the "Mary Plays" at York, England. The journal reports on play productions, new books, and meetings of interest to its audience of medievalists.

621. **Modern Drama**. Downsview, Ont.: Graduate Centre for Study of Drama, University of Toronto Press, 1958- . Quarterly. ISSN 0026-7694.

Primarily a drama journal, *Modern Drama* is included here because it publishes a bibliography of drama and theatre history every June, which is intended to supplement Charles Carpenter's *Modern Drama Scholarship and Criticism, 1966-1980* (entry 27). Most of the articles concerning the theatre can be found in the "general" section of the bibliography. Issues generally contain about ten articles on nineteenth- and twentieth-century dramatists and their works written by professors of English or drama. Recent articles have considered Strindberg, Chekhov, Sam Shepard, and Brian Friel. Several book reviews complete each issue.

622. **Modern International Drama: Magazine for Contemporary Intentional Drama in Translation**. Binghamton: State University of New York at Binghamton, 1967- 2/year. ISSN 0026-7856.

With the aim of making "the best plays of the modern foreign theatre available to American readers and producers," this periodical publishes translations of twentieth-century foreign plays. Recent works have come from Finland, Chile, Mexico, Spain, Russia, Denmark, and Hungary. The editors look for translations that capture the meaning of the original language while reading and playing well in English. Depending on submissions from volunteer translators, the journal may not always publish the "best" plays, but it does present an interesting selection of works that otherwise would not be available to American readers.

623. **New Theatre Quarterly** (formerly *Theatre Quarterly*). Cambridge, England: Cambridge University Press, 1971- . Quarterly. ISSN 0266-464X.

A scholarly journal, *New Theatre Quarterly* publishes articles on all aspects of the theatre. Several footnoted pieces written by academics appear in each issue accompanied by book reviews and announcements. Recent articles have recounted the history of the Oberammergau passion play, described the repertoire of the Britannia Theatre in nineteenth-century London, and considered the idea of androgyny in Shakespeare's plays.

624. **Nineteenth Century Theatre**. Amherst: University of Massachusetts, 1973- . 2/year. ISSN 0893-3766.

Nineteenth Century Theatre "regularly publishes essays, documents, bibliographies, review essays, reviews, and an annotated list of books received" on the theatre of the 1800s. A wide scope allows the journal to present topics in European and American theatre, dance, opera, and other performing arts. The editors emphasize the publication and use of primary source material. Recent articles have included a demographic study of Victorian theatre employees; a description of James Steele MacKaye's lighting designs for the 1893 Columbian Exposition; and excerpts from a diary kept by the manager of a Japanese acrobat troupe that toured the United States in 1867. Book reviews complete each issue. This lively journal will interest theatre and popular culture historians.

625. **The Passing Show**. New York: The Shubert Archive, 1977- . 2/year. ISSN 1061-8112.

The Shubert Archive (entry 713) contains a wide variety of source materials on the Shubert Organization and, by extension, American theatre in the nineteenth and twentieth centuries. The Archive's newsletter highlights materials from the collection by publishing historical articles based on those sources. Photographs from the collection add interest to each piece. Researchers and historians of American theatre will find *The Passing Show* a useful indicator of the riches held by the Shubert Foundation.

626. **Performance**. London: Performance Magazine, 1979- . Bimonthly. ISSN 0144-5901.

A magazine for the avant-garde, *Performance* concentrates on reviewing events in the United Kingdom and elsewhere. Reflecting a radical viewpoint, the magazine looks at performance art, political theatre, and art installations. Every number includes book reviews and a listing of future international festivals and art gatherings. Not for the conservative, this title tries to show the reader life on the performing edge.

627. **Performing Arts & Entertainment in Canada**. Toronto: Avanti Magazines, 1961- . Quarterly. ISSN 1185-3433.

A well-illustrated general arts magazine, this title serves the lay public interested in Canadian theatre, dance, music, film, and television. Interviews and notes on coming events are mixed with discussion of topics such as Toronto's play development festival. With an emphasis on people and pictures, this is a good choice for readers who want to keep up with the current scene in Canada.

628. **Performing Arts Journal**. Baltimore, Md.: The Johns Hopkins University Press, 1976- . 3/year. ISSN 0735-8393.

Using a lively mixture of essays, criticism, interviews, and creative work, *Performing Arts Journal* covers today's theatre, opera, cinema, and other creative performances. A recent article examined the implication of German reunification on that country's theatre, for example. Playwright Arnold Wesker contributed an essay on the director's role in staging a play, and another article discussed multiculturalism and the arts. Each issue contains some half-dozen articles written by academics, performers, and writers. Both books and performances are reviewed. Although theatre receives more attention than the other performing arts, this journal can serve to introduce theatre students to related arts.

629. **Play Source**. New York: Theatre Communications Group, 1980- . Bimonthly. ISSN 0789-9841.

Although *Play Source* is a small typed pamphlet that accompanies *Plays in Process* (entry 633), its importance lies in its identification and publicizing of new plays. Each issue lists a number of new works, divided into categories such as full-length, one-act, and children's plays, with plot, act, and scene information, number of actors required, and other details. Most importantly, it publishes the name and address of a person to contact for licensing information. Producers looking for new plays to stage should consult *Play Source* regularly.

630. Number not used.

631. **Plays: The Drama Magazine for Young People**. Boston: Plays, 1941- . 7/year. ISSN 0032-1540.

Providing a continuing source of plays for children and youth for over fifty years, *Plays* publishes works that regular subscribers may produce royalty-free as part of a school or drama club activity. Both grade school and high school teachers will find suitable, if somewhat innocuous, plays to present. The magazine notes the passing of the school year by publishing works of seasonal interest for Thanksgiving, Christmas, Valentine's Day, Black History Month, and other holidays. An occasional puppet play or bowdlerized classic is included. Production notes list playing time, cast and costume requirements, and other information needed to produce the play. Although schools provide the obvious market for this magazine, church groups, scouts, and other children's organizations may find it equally useful.

632. **Plays and Players**. Croyden, England: Pickwick Papers, 1953- . Monthly. ISSN 0032-1559.

Directed at the British playgoer, *Plays and Players* features five or six articles and many performance reviews each month. The magazine reports on festivals in Britain and overseas. The "Player of the Month" profiles an actor or actress. Regular columns list London openings and review television and radio programs. Interviews of actors and playwrights appear frequently. *Plays and Players* concentrates on British theatre while another British periodical, *Plays International* (entry 634), reviews productions abroad.

633. **Plays in Process**. New York: Theatre Communications Group, 1980- . Monthly. ISSN 0736-0711.

The Theatre Communications Group publishes scripts of the best new plays produced by American theatres each year and sends them to subscribers under the title of *Plays in Process*. Subscribers receive twelve playscripts per year. Accompanying this title on a bimonthly basis is *Play Source* (entry 629), which lists many other new works. The two titles should appeal to those who work in contemporary American theatre.

634. **Plays International**. Shrewsbury, England: Plays International, 1985- . Monthly. ISSN 0268-2028.

Similar to *Plays and Players* (entry 632) but covering American, Canadian, and European theatre as well as British productions, *Plays International* reviews plays, lists London shows, and prints playscripts. BBC television plays and radio plays are reviewed, as are books of interest to theatre lovers. Articles feature actors, theatres, and play productions. This commercial publication helps readers keep current on the theatre scene in Europe and America.

635. **Puppetry Journal**. Macedonia, Ohio: The Puppeteers of America, 1949- . Quarterly. ISSN 0033-443X.

Anyone interested in puppets will want to read this periodical published by the leading puppet organization in the United States. Issues publish articles on puppet collections, festivals, and performances of touring puppet troupes. Practical advice on such topics as making puppet wigs out of felt are included, and some pieces profile puppeteers from other countries. Regular columns list new books, provide a calendar of events, and summarize articles from American newspapers about puppetry. The association's news also appears.

636. **Restoration & Eighteenth Century Theatre Research**. Chicago: Department of English, Loyola University, 1962- . 2/year. ISSN 0034-5822.

Scholarly articles and book reviews in this journal concern themselves with English stage productions between 1660 and 1800. Recently, essays have analyzed the eighteenth-century Englishman's hostility to Italian opera, especially its castrati, and discussed the use of clothing to convey character in Restoration comedy. Every two to three years the journal publishes a selective bibliography of books and articles on the period. This title is of obvious value to theatre historians and students.

637. **Southern Theatre**. Greensboro, N.C.: Southeastern Theatre Conference, 1964- . Quarterly. ISSN 0584-4738.

A good general theatre magazine that emphasizes Southern playwrights and theatres, *Southern Theatre* reviews plays and publishes articles on all aspects of theatre work. Using computers to design scenery has been discussed, as well as the character of the southern belle in Beth Henley's plays and the problems faced by married couples who both work in theatre. The magazine occasionally ventures outside its region as it did to profile Vermont's Bread and Puppet Theatre. Readers will find this periodical to be an interesting introduction to theatre in the South.

638. **Stages: The National Theatre Magazine**. New York: Curtains, 1984- . Monthly. ISSN 1041-6048.

In a tabloid format *Stages* reviews plays, dance, and other performances in New York City, London, and elsewhere. The critics range widely, covering everything from performer Ann-Margret at Radio City Music Hall to the Moscow Circus. A column briefly reviews books and recordings. This is useful mainly for current awareness purposes.

639. **TCI** (formerly *Theatre Crafts*). New York: Theatre Crafts Associates, 1967- . 10/year. ISSN 0040-5469.

Useful to all backstage personnel, professional or amateur, *TCI* covers all aspects of technical theatre. Reports on trade shows and columns on new products are interspersed with advertisements that can be equally informative. Interviews with designers and articles about specific productions offer ideas to be copied or adapted. A recent piece on the set design for the short-lived *Nick and Nora*, for example, showed sets that, while too complicated for most productions, offered inspiration and adaptable ideas. Other articles deal with sound, lighting, and costume design and execution. When the magazine changed its name in August 1992, it expanded its focus to include more international news and more news about the technical aspects of television, industrial shows, and theme parks. *TCI* is essential to anyone involved in theatre technology. Its readers will also want to read *TD&T* (entry 640).

640. **TD&T: The Journal for Design & Production Professionals in the Performing Arts** (formerly *Theatre Design & Technology*). New York: United States Institute for Theatre Technology, 1965- . 5/year. ISSN 1052-6765.

Must reading for designers and production personnel, *TD&T* covers scene design, technical production, costuming, sound, and lighting. Most articles emphasize design, especially the work of a particular designer. Issues have featured British director Jonathan Miller's design ideas, and an homage to Russian artist Erté. Practical aspects of theatre are not neglected. *TD&T* has produced a special issue on the use of computers in design and has counseled students on what to look for in a graduate school. It has also instructed readers on how to make spats for Victorian productions. Along with *TCI* (entry 639), this is indispensable for anyone interested in technical theatre.

641. **TDR: The Drama Review: A Journal of Performance Studies**. Cambridge, Mass.: MIT Press, 1955- . Quarterly. ISSN 1054-2043.

Definitely coming at its audience from left of political center, *TDR* seems to attract readers who enjoy arguing controversial points in the letters column. The Fall 1992 editorial contains the sentences, "Remember, that since the late 1960s, the United States has been led and systematically exploited and brutalized by the most reactionary groups ... Think about it." Most articles deal with contemporary works and theatres. Recent topics have been the attempts of various theatre companies to deal with issues of the homeless; "the radicality of puppet theatre;" and a description of the Castillo Cultural Center, "New York's most radical art and theatre center." Although *TDR* publishes an occasional book review, this feature is not a strong point.

642. **Text and Performance Quarterly**. Annandale, Va.: Speech Communication Association, 1988- . Quarterly. ISSN 1046-2937.

A mixture of articles and book reviews written by academics examines the "nexus of texts, performers, and audiences within the expanded understanding of how far and how deeply textuality and performance reach in our lives." Far-ranging in its interests, the journal has published articles on interpretation of texts, on cross-casting in *Miss Saigon* (e.g., casting Caucasian actors in Asian roles), and even on performances associated with the use of fake identification cards by college coeds to gain entrance to campus bars! One fascinating (and depressing) study reported on campus reactions to Ball State University students who wore yellow stars on their clothes in preparation for roles in the play *Ghetto*. *Text and Performance Quarterly* also covers lectures, television broadcasts, and other performing arts. Its lively articles often present material from a slightly different perspective.

643. **Theater**. New Haven, Conn.: Yale School of Drama/Yale Repertory Theater, 1968- . 3/year. ISSN 0161-0775.

Boasting many contributors from Yale, *Theater* often devotes an issue to one theme. A recent topic was "New Artistic Directions" featuring interviews with Douglas Wager of Washington's Arena Stage and Emily Mann from Princeton's McCarter Theater. Another issue looked at Russian and Soviet classic plays while a third theme was "Theater and Time." Each issue also carries the text of a play and short essays on one or two contemporary works. Other articles that have appeared recently have considered German criticism of Robert Wilson, looked at the changing critical view of Yeats, and presented an interview with theatre designer Ming Cho Lee. Nicely illustrated with photographs, this should be a standard source for information on contemporary theatre.

644. **Theatre History in Canada/Histoire du théâtre au Canada**. Toronto: Graduate Centre for Study of Drama, University of Toronto; Kingston, Ont.: Department of Drama, Queen's University, 1980- . 2/year. ISSN 0226-5761.

Devoted to the history of theatre in Canada, articles in this journal are written in French or English. Perhaps reflecting Canada's bilingualism, each article is summarized in both languages. Because the editors define theatre broadly, they have published articles on dancers and other performers as well as on legitimate theatre. Recent articles have related the life of Canadian actor and director Donald Davis; recounted the construction of the Sherbrooke Opera House; and discussed Canadian theatre education after World War II. This is the primary journal for the history of Canadian theatre and compliments *Performing Arts & Entertainment in Canada* (entry 627), which covers the current scene.

645. **Theatre History Studies**. Grand Forks, N.D.: The Mid-America Theatre Conference, 1981- . Annual. ISSN 0733-2033.

The official journal of the Mid-American Theatre Conference, *Theatre History Studies* covers all aspects of theatre. The well-illustrated volume contains essays, book reviews, and announcements of the Conference's business. Some emphasis is placed on describing collections and manuscripts such as the Glick Stock Company Memorabilia Collection, the records of a rural Ohio touring company of the late nineteenth century. Another article, by Don B. Wilmeth (see entries 12, 97, 98, 306, and 306a), is a bibliography on popular entertainment. *Theatre History Studies* attracts important names in theatre history and, although it appears only once a year, provides interesting, well-researched history.

646. **Theatre Information Bulletin**. New York: Proscenium Publications, 1944- . Weekly. ISSN 0040-5515.

Intended for producers, publicists, agents, and others in the theatre business, this cheaply reproduced, stapled weekly lists theatre activity in New York and around the country. It lists Broadway and off-Broadway openings, closings, and previews. For currently running plays, it provides the names of the theatre, the producer, and the press agent. A calendar lists events of interest to the theatre community. Regional productions, road tours, and workshops are included, as are plays currently under option and English productions due to play the United States in the future. This title is similar to *Theatrical Index* (entry 654), and the two can be consulted interchangeably.

647. **Theatre Ireland**. Castlerock, Ireland: Theatre Ireland, 1982- . 3/year. ISSN 0263-6344.

The country that gave the world Shaw, Yeats, and Synge continues a lively theatre tradition, and *Theatre Ireland* reports on that scene. The good-looking, illustrated magazine contains about a dozen articles per issue on subjects such as lighting designers, street theatre, Irish plays currently playing in London, and a review of Dublin's theatre season. Book reviews and a letters column complete this attractive periodical, which will appeal to students of Irish theatre.

648. **Theatre Journal**. Baltimore, Md.: The Johns Hopkins University Press, 1949- . Quarterly. ISSN 0192-2882.

Continuing the *Educational Theatre Journal*, this periodical provides "an outlet for scholarship and criticism in the theatre arts." Important features are ten to fifteen signed book reviews and an equal number of reviews of professional and university theatre productions. Scholarly articles discuss both new works and more traditional plays. The May issue lists dissertations in progress in the field of theatre arts. *Theatre Journal* covers a wide range of subjects and as such will interest many students and researchers.

649. **Theatre Notebook**. London: The Society for Theatre Research, 1945- . 3/year. ISSN 0040-5523.

Published by the Society of Theatre Research, *Theatre Notebook* contains scholarly articles on the history of British theatre. Contributors are scholars from the United Kingdom, Ireland, and North America. Each issue features half a dozen book reviews and three or four essays. A "Notes and Queries" section allows readers to ask for information related to their scholarly work. In 1992 the journal started to print an annual list of "major archive collections acquired by British repositories." This title should be required reading by historians of the British theatre.

650. **Theatre Research International**. Oxford, England: Oxford University Press and International Federation for Theatre Research, 1975- . 3/year. ISSN 0307-8833.

In 1992 the editor announced a change in focus for *Theatre Research International*, promising more emphasis on the theory of theatre practice and the review of productions. The journal will continue to publish its very readable articles on theatre history, as well. Written by academics, essays deal with theatre worldwide and through history. Book reviews play a significant role in this periodical, and the titles reviewed are equally wide in scope. *Theatre Research International* is a primary journal for any theatre scholar.

190 / 12—Core Periodicals

651. **Theatre Survey**. New York: American Society for Theatre Research, 1960- . 2/year. ISSN 0040-5574.

Although published by the American Society for Theatre Research, *Theatre Survey* publishes articles "with an historical bent on a wide range of subjects, including American, African, Asian, British, European theatre." Articles and book reviews present new information and interpretations of historical subjects. Recent topics have included the popularity of the *Merry Wives of Windsor* in eighteenth-century England, the American theatre tax controversy of 1919, and Anna Benko and the Pushkin Theatre, "Moscow's first continuously-producing, professional private theatrical enterprise." Along with *Theatre Notebook* (entry 649) and *Theatre Research International* (entry 650), this is important to theatre historians.

652. **Theatre Topics**. Baltimore, Md.: Johns Hopkins University Press, 1991- . 2/year. ISSN 1054-8378.

A joint project of the Association for Theatre in Higher Education and The Johns Hopkins University Press, *Theatre Topics* publishes "in areas of dramaturgy, performance studies, and theatre pedagogy." Aiming to encourage dialogue between theatre professionals and educators, it includes descriptions of "practical applications in the various aspects of theatre" such as integrating production and curriculum in the liberal arts college. A letters column specifically invites comments from professionals in and outside of academe. Recent articles have described vocal training for use in stage combat and discussed adapting literature for children's theatre from a feminist perspective. This new journal should be especially helpful to university professors of theatre.

653. **The Theatrical Calendar**. New York: Celebrity Service International, n.d. Bi-weekly. ISSN 0882-8830.

Similar to the *Theatre Information Bulletin* (entry 646) and *Theatrical Index* (entry 654), *The Theatrical Calendar* lists current and future shows on Broadway, off-Broadway, and off-off-Broadway with information on opening date, theatre name, producer, and press agent. The section that covers theatres outside New York City is not as extensive as similar coverage in the other two titles mentioned above. A current awareness service, this is aimed at theatre management, the press, and others in the arts business in New York.

654. **Theatrical Index**. New York: Price Berkley, 1964- . Weekly. ISSN 1046-9869.

Of interest to producers, agents, actors, and managers, *Theatrical Index* provides information on Broadway and off-Broadway openings and currently running plays. It also lists previews, tryouts, and shows in rehearsal, thus providing more information than its rival publications, *Theatre Information Bulletin* (entry 646), and *The Theatrical Calendar* (entry 653). A schedule of road tours and regional theatre productions supplements the New York City coverage. Wasting no space, the periodical's covers list producers, New York agents, and Broadway theatres with addresses.

655. **Themes in Drama**. Cambridge, England: Cambridge University Press, 1979- . Annual. ISSN 0263-676X.

Each volume of *Themes in Drama* brings together articles and reviews built around a single theme in "theatrical activity of a wide range of cultures and periods." The journal has examined violence in drama, drama and philosophy, women in theatre, and the theatrical space. Within the theme, authors cover a wide range of issues. The volume on violence, for example, examines plays by Euripides, Shakespeare, Shaw, and Athol Fugard, among others. Although much of the writing relates to drama, some issues of theatre and stagecraft are discussed.

656. **TYA Today (Theatre for Young Audiences Today)**. Evansville, Ind.: International Association of Theatre for Children and Young People, 1985- . 2/year.

A publication of ASSITEJ/USA (entry 729) *TYA Today* publishes articles about and reviews of children's plays. Written by members of the association, articles deal with experiences in play production, both in the United States and in foreign countries. The magazine reports on meetings and festivals devoted to young people's theatre and reviews the occasional book. This will interest producers, directors, and writers of children's theatre.

657. **Variety: The International Entertainment Weekly**. New York: Cahners, 1905- . Weekly. ISSN 0042-2738.

Best known for its snappy headlines and tabloid appearance, *Variety* is *the* newspaper of the entertainment industry including the legitimate theatre. *Variety* records the gross sales and season box office totals for Broadway and road shows and for resident theatres across the United States. It reviews plays, and it prints theatre news from here and abroad. Anyone who was anyone in show business merits an obituary in the newspaper, and these have been compiled into a separate set of volumes (entry 362). *Variety* also covers film, video, television, and the financial aspects of show business. Besides its day-to-day usefulness, it provides a record of the entertainment business for future researchers.

658. **The White Tops: Devoted Exclusively to the Circus**. White Stone, Va.: Circus Fans Association of America, c. 1927- . Bimonthly. ISSN 0043-499X.

Produced by circus fans for circus fans, *The White Tops* features short articles on today's circuses, museum notes, and an occasional historical article. Recent issues have reported on the visit of the Cirque de Soleil to Yokohama, Japan; described Jose Cole's Circus, a small, Minneapolis-based show; and recounted the story of the worst railroad crash in circus history, involving the Hagenbeck-Wallace Circus in June 1918. Like *Bandwagon* (entry 601), this journal uses many photographs to illustrate its prose.

659. **Women & Performance: A Journal of Feminist Theory**. New York: Women & Performance Project, Department of Performance Studies, New York University, Tisch School of the Arts, 1983- . 2/year. ISSN 0740-770X.

Each issue of *Women & Performance* features several articles, book reviews, and reviews of performances by women or emphasizing feminist concerns. It also publishes original plays. Recently it printed performance artist Ellen Zweig's *The Lady and the Camel*, a monologue about "the dark side of the Victorian lady traveler." Articles tend to be scholarly but accessible and have included a discussion of feminist dramatic criticism and a look at "gender scenarios" performed by German Pina Bausch's Dance Theatre. Covering theatre, dance, and performance art, this journal is useful for women's studies students as well as dance and theatre students who are interested in women's issues.

Dance Periodicals

660. **Ballet Review.** New York: Dance Research Foundation, 1965- . Quarterly. ISSN 0522-0653.

Each issue of *Ballet Review* begins with four to six reports on performances from major cities around the world. About ten articles follow; these include interviews, biographical sketches and descriptions of choreography. Recent offerings have included a profile of Sylvie Guillem, the controversial French guest star with the Royal Ballet; an interview with the Bolshoi Ballet's Nina Ananiashvili; a review of The White Oak Dance Project; and a report on weightlifting for dancers. The well-written articles will be readily understood by the lay person.

661. **Ballett International.** Cologne, Germany: Rolf Garske, 1982- . Monthly. ISSN 0171-7995.

Written in German and English, this periodical features reports on dance from many different countries, even those not normally associated with dance such as Switzerland, Norway, and Greece. A news section lists festivals, tours, premieres, and workshops for dancers. Illustrations are a particularly strong feature of the magazine, which includes several feature articles as well. A calendar of events is arranged by country. The January issue is a directory of services and products for the dance world, and one section lists companies, their management, and their repertoires for the past three years.

662. **Ballett-Journal/Das Tanzarchiv.** Overath, Germany: Ulrich Steiner Verlag, 1981- . Quarterly. ISSN 0720-3896.

Formed by the merger of *Ballett-Journal* and *Das Tanzarchiv*, this magazine covers the ballet scene in Europe, particularly Germany, Austria, and Switzerland. Recent articles have described the Stuttgart Ballet's production of *On Your Toes* and have paid tribute to Martha Graham. Columnists review ballet books, videos, and records. Although the emphasis is on ballet, the periodical also covers modern dance. It is especially helpful to those who have a special interest in German dance.

663. **Choreography and Dance: An International Journal.** London: Harwood Academic, 1988- . Irregular. ISSN 0891-6381.

A distinguishing feature of this title is the videotape provided with each issue. With the goal of discussing "the composition of ballet and related forms of dance performed on stage," the journal concentrates on the development of choreography, using dance notation and videotapes. Recent issues have focused on Antony Tudor's work and on a revival of Nijinsky's *L'Après-midi d'un faune*. This will interest choreographers and dance researchers.

664. **Contact Quarterly Dance Journal, A Vehicle for Moving Ideas.** New York: Contact Collaborations, 1975- . 2/year. ISSN 0198-9634.

Of interest to both dance and theatre students, *Contact Quarterly* provides a forum for the discussion of "movement and its performance." Authors of articles are movement practitioners—dancers, choreographers, improvisation artists, and teachers. Topics explored have been dancing with different populations, including disabled people; movement improvisation in Russia; and a history of the Institute for Movement Exploration. Each issue's directory lists classes, "jams," and other activities important to movement specialists.

665. **Country Dance and Song**. Northampton, Mass.: Country Dance and Song Society of America, 1968- . Annual. ISSN 0070-1262.

Devoted to the traditional English folk dance as performed in the United States and elsewhere, the annual *Country Dance and Song* features a half dozen articles written by teachers, performers, and amateur enthusiasts. Topics discussed recently have been morris dancing in pre-World War I America; dancing during the Civil War; and folk songs from Sussex, England. The magazine will appeal to country dancers, dance historians, and popular culture researchers.

666. **Dance and Dancers**. London: Orpheus Publications, 1950- . Monthly. ISSN 0011-5983.

A commercial magazine for fans of dance, this monthly features articles by well-known writers such as Clive Barnes, reviews of performances both in Britain and elsewhere, and news and events of the English dance scene. The "Danceguide" lists coming events in Britain and abroad. Black-and-white photographs enhance the periodical's appeal.

667. **Dance Chronicle: Studies in Dance and the Related Arts**. New York, Marcel Dekker, 1977- . 3/year. ISSN 0147-2526.

With an editorial board that includes dance writers Horst Koegler and Ivor Guest, and former curator of the New York Public Library's Dance Collection, Genevieve Oswald, *Dance Chronicle* is clearly a serious, scholarly publication. Each issue features four or five articles written by scholars on all aspects of dance and its history. A recent article considered Diaghilev's lighting designs for his ballets, for instance, while another dealt with sixteenth century Italian dance. Several book reviews and a list of books received help scholars keep current in their fields. *Dance Chronicle* is a must for serious students of dance history.

668. **Dance Magazine**. New York: Dance Magazine, 1927- . Monthly. ISSN 0011-6009.

Americans living on a desert island would choose *Dance Magazine* to keep them up-to-date on the dance world. (Britons might choose *Dancing Times*.) Covering all areas of dance with articles, reviews, news columns, obituaries, and a directory of dance services, the magazine reports on the dance scene both in the United States and abroad. Although the big cover stories tend to emphasize stars such as Twyla Tharp and Mikhail Baryshnikov, regional companies are not neglected. Clive Barnes provides a monthly column in which he muses about a topic or two. Illustrations and a good number of advertisements make this an easy read. *Dance Magazine* is indispensable to American dancers, choreographers, and dance fans.

669. **Dance Medicine Health Newsletter**. Los Angeles: International Center for Dance Orthopaedics and Dance Therapy, 1982- . Quarterly. No ISSN.

Not as scholarly as *Kinesiology and Medicine for Dance* (entry 676), this newsletter reports on issues of interest to dancers, sport physicians, and health professionals. Dance injuries, iron deficiencies in adolescent dancers, and suitable physiques for dance careers have all been subjects of articles. The *Newsletter* also lists conferences that might interest its readers. This is a supplementary choice to *Kinesiology and Medicine for Dance*.

670. **Dance Notation Bureau Newsletter**. New York: The Bureau, 1943- . 2/year. No ISSN.

The Dance Notation Bureau (entry 753) preserves choreographed works of dance using a notation system called Labanotation. The *Newsletter* reports on the bureau's work, including notices of meetings, appeals for funds, and news of new notation projects. Most importantly, the *Newsletter* also reports on notated works newly acquired by the Bureau's library. This periodical will be most useful to choreographers and producers looking for records of dances.

671. **Dance Research Journal**. New York: Congress on Research in Dance, 1974/75- . 2/year. ISSN 0149-7677.

Dance Research Journal reflects the wide interests of its parent organization, the Congress on Research in Dance (entry 751). Refereed articles and reports discuss theory and methods and evaluate the state of knowledge in various fields of dance research. In recent issues authors have considered the impact of dancer recruitment patterns on ballet and modern dance; discussed the "Aesthetic of Yoruba Recreational Dancers as Exemplified in the Oge Dance;" and described eighteenth-century dancing in Philadelphia. This title definitely will attract an academic audience.

672. **Dance Theatre Journal**. London: Laban Centre for Movement and Dance, 1983- . Quarterly. ISSN 0264-9160.

Reflecting ballet, modern dance, and other forms of movement in performance, this well-written periodical features articles and interviews with many of today's dance newsmakers. Recent interviewees have been contemporary choreographers Trisha Brown and Lucinda Childs. After Dame Margot Fonteyn's death *Dance Theatre Journal* published a careful, critical assessment of her technique. The magazine reviews dance festivals and provides a calendar of events for the United Kingdom. Less earnest than the *Contact Quarterly Dance Journal* (entry 664), this will appeal to a wide audience.

673. **Dancing Times**. London: Dancing Times, 1894-1910; New Series, 1910- . Monthly. ISSN 0011-605X.

The grandfather of dance magazines, *Dancing Times* currently operates under the direction of Mary Clarke (see entries 309, 470). One of the best all-around ballet periodicals, albeit with a British slant, it reviews performances, reports on sales of ballet antiques and collectibles, runs obituaries of dance luminaries, and reports ballet news. Recent articles have discussed Judith Jamison's leadership of the Alvin Ailey company and provided a delightful recollection of Cyril Beaumont's famous bookshop. A large number of advertisements tout schools and teachers, and the calendar lists upcoming events both in the United Kingdom and overseas. Of interest to any balletomane, *Dancing Times* runs a close second to *Dance Magazine* (entry 668) as the first choice for any library or personal ballet collection.

674. **Folk Dance Scene**. Los Angeles: Folk Dance Federation of California, South. 10/year. ISSN 0430-8751.

Publishing articles on folk dance, music, costume, and culture worldwide, *Folk Dance Scene* devotes one or two articles in each issue to a specific type of dance such as the tango. It also features stories about folk dance ensembles and other aspects of folk culture including food. Although it prints news of the Folk Dance Federation of California, sponsor of the magazine, this title deserves a wider audience than federation members. Folk dance aficionados anywhere will enjoy its articles.

676. **JOPERD: The Journal of Physical Education, Recreation, & Dance**. Reston, Va.: American Alliance for Health, Physical Education, Recreation, and Dance, 1930- . 9/year. 0730-3084.

Because it covers all the interests of the American Alliance for Health, Physical Education, Recreation, and Dance, *JOPERD* devotes only a fraction of its publishing to dance. Aimed at educators, it features dance once or twice a year by clustering a group of articles around a theme. "Dance Marketplace," for example, examined the impact of the proliferation of dance education on the field. Another issue looked at the connections between dance and sport. This title will be most useful to those who teach dance either in secondary schools or colleges. Dancers and dance academy teachers will find *Dance Magazine* (entry 668) more helpful.

676. **Kinesiology and Medicine for Dance**. Princeton, N.J.: Princeton Periodicals, 1977- . 2/year. ISSN 1058-7438.

Dancers and the physicians who look after them should welcome this refereed periodical devoted to the sports medicine of dance. Health, nutrition, proper movement techniques, and injury prevention all contribute to a dancer's long and successful career, and all have been discussed in this forum. Reports on dance medicine conferences are included. This title should be preferred to *Dance Medicine Health Newsletter* (entry 669), which is not as scholarly.

677. **Movement and Dance: Magazine of the Laban Guild**. Tadworth, England: Laban Guild, 1948- . Annual. No ISSN.

The British *Movement and Dance* reports on the activities of the Laban Guild and prints the Laban Lecture, given at the annual conference. The Guild continues the work of dance teacher Rudolf von Laban who pioneered a system of dance notation called Labanotation. The journal reviews books and publishes articles of interest to dance teachers. Beginning in 1991, *Movement and Dance* has included a section describing various dance groups in Britain and their activities.

678. **Movement Theatre Quarterly**. Portsmouth, N.H.: National Movement Theatre Association, 1983- . Quarterly. ISSN 1065-1519.

A journal for mimes, dancers, and other movement specialists, this features several short articles, news notes, and book and video reviews. It fulfills its primary purpose of keeping its readers current in the field of movement studies and performance.

679. **The New Dance Review**. New York: Anita Finkel, 1988- . Quarterly. ISSN 1040-8908.

A relatively new, low-budget journal, *The New Dance Review* publishes "performance oriented critical writing on dance." Articles focus a discerning eye on dancers, choreographers, and companies. Recent writers have reviewed Peter Martins' *Sleeping Beauty* performed by the New York City Ballet; compared several versions of *Romeo and Juliet*; and discussed the Royal Ballet's July 1991 visit to New York. With its stapled pages, nonglossy cover, and lack of advertising, this review does not look substantial, but its writing lifts it above its humble appearance.

680. **Studies in Dance History**. Pennington, N.J.: Society of Dance History Scholars, 1989- . 2/year. ISSN 1043-7592.

Important names in dance scholarship, such as Genevieve Oswald and Selma Jeanne Cohen, are associated editorially with this new journal, which has attracted leading dance historians as authors. It seeks to publish "scholarly research writing on the history of dance and related disciplines." Each issue is devoted to a single work or a collection of works on a single topic. The material may be a discussion of new research, a reprint of an out-of-print source, or the first publication of an important primary source. Early issues included a set of biographical materials about modern dancer and choreographer Helen Tameris; a reprint of an 1831 monograph; and an analysis of Martha Graham's technique. If it maintains its quality, *Studies in Dance History* should become the most important journal for the history of dance in all forms.

681. **UCLA Journal of Dance Ethnology**. Los Angeles: Department of Dance and Graduate Student Association, University of California Los Angeles, 1977- . Annual. ISSN 0884-3198.

Written by dance ethnology professors and students, this annual publishes papers from the previous year's Forum on Dance Ethnology. Articles describe, analyze, and interpret dance and movement in many different cultures. Recent research has included a study of the Inuit drum dance from Canada and the use of "oriental" dance in Hollywood films. This title reminds readers that dance traditions run deep in all cultures, and dance itself encompasses more than ballet and modern dance.

Chapter 13

Libraries and Archives

This chapter describes a representative selection of libraries and archives that contain significant holdings of materials in the performing arts. Besides those listed here, many public and some academic libraries collect playbills and other materials related to local performing groups. Readers interested in British library and archival collections should consult Howard's *Directory of Theatre Resources: A Guide to Research Collections and Information Services* (entry 493). *Performing Arts Libraries and Museums of the World* (entry 503) lists important repositories worldwide.

682. **American Museum of Magic**. 107 E. Michigan Ave., Marshall, MI 49068. 616/781-7666. Hours: By appointment only.

The museum's 11,000-volume library contains monographs, manuscripts, films, scrapbooks, and videos relating to magic and magicians. The museum itself exhibits posters, equipment, memorabilia, and other objects used by Houdini, Blackstone, and other magicians.

683. **Batchelder-McPharlin Collection**. University of New Mexico, Fine Arts Library, University of New Mexico Library, Albuquerque, NM 87131. 505/277-2357; FAX 505/277-6019. Hours: 8 a.m.—10 p.m. Monday—Thursday; 8 a.m.—6 p.m. Friday; 10 a.m.—9 p.m. Saturday; Noon—10 p.m. Sunday during the academic term. Call for summer and holiday hours.

After puppet historian and expert Paul McPharlin died, his widow, Marjorie Batchelder McPharlin, kept her collection of puppetry materials and some of his collection for a number of years. She eventually sold them to the University of New Mexico. The library includes books, journals, pamphlets, puppets, and other materials associated with the history of puppetry. *Puppetry Library* (entry 175) describes the book collection, lists journals in the collection and indicates the number of uncataloged items. The rest of the Paul McPharlin collection may be consulted at the Detroit Institute of Arts (entry 708).

684. **Brigham Young University. Theodore Fuchs Collection**. Harold B. Lee Library, Brigham Young University, University Hill, Provo, UT 84602. 801/378-2905. Hours: 8 a.m.—5 p.m. Monday—Friday.

Theodore Fuchs was a pioneer in the field of theatrical lighting design and author of *Stage Lighting*, the "first major book ever published dealing in depth with theatrical lighting." Although he spent most of his career at Northwestern University, where he chaired the theatre department for many years, Mr. Fuchs donated his papers to Brigham Young University. They reflect not only his academic career but also his work as a designer and consultant on over 275 theatres and auditoriums. The holdings are described in a register available from the library.

198 / 13—Libraries and Archives

685. **California Polytechnic State University. Special Collections**. University Library, California Polytechnic State University. San Luis Obispo, CA 93407. 805/756-2305; FAX 805/756-1415. Hours: 10 a.m.—2 p.m. Monday—Friday.

The result of a gift, the California Polytechnic State University at San Luis Obispo holds a collection of about 100 monographs on puppets and puppetry. A small number of issues of puppetry journals are also available. Readers may access the collection through the library's online catalog.

686. **Chicago Public Library Special Collections**. Harold Washington Library Center, Floor 9-N, 400 South State St., Chicago, IL 60605. 312/747-4960. Hours: Noon—4 p.m. Monday—Friday and by appointment.

Concentrating on local theatre, the Chicago Public Library holds records of nineteenth-century Chicago performances, including some programs antedating the Great Fire of 1871. More than 2,000 programs record theatre productions from 1875 to 1936, and theatre-goers' scrapbooks document the years 1891 to 1956. The library also serves as the repository for the archives of several of Chicago's contemporary theatres including the Goodman Theatre, Body Politic, and Steppenwolf.

687. **Detroit Public Library. E. Azalia Hackley Collections**. 5201 Woodward Ave., Detroit, MI 48202-4093. 313/833-1460. Hours: 9:30 a.m.—5:30 p.m. Tuesday, Thursday—Saturday; 1 p.m.—9 p.m. Wednesday.

One of the most important collections of materials documenting African-American performing arts, the Hackley Collection holds records of musicians, actors, dancers, and other Black performers. Materials collected include books, photographs, prints, manuscripts and personal archives, sheet music, and recordings. The pamphlet file holds over 250,000 clippings and other ephemera relating to "the history and achievements of black people in the performing arts." The collection is described in the library's published catalog (entry 162).

688. **Folger Shakespeare Library**. 201 E. Capitol St., SE, Washington, DC 20003-1094. 202/544-4600; FAX 202/544-4823. Hours: 8:45 a.m.—4:45 p.m. Monday—Friday; 8:45 a.m.—Noon and 1:00—4:30 Saturday.

The most important collection of Shakespeare and Renaissance materials in the country, the Folger holds books, manuscripts, prints, engravings, and other materials related to Shakespeare and his contemporaries. It also collects materials on theatre generally and Shakespeare production specifically. Its holdings have been described in its *Catalog of Printed Books* (entry 165), *Catalog of Manuscripts* (entry 164), and *Catalog of Prints and Engravings* (entry 166).

689. **Free Library of Philadelphia. Theatre Collection**. Logan Square, Philadelphia, PA 19103. 215/686-5427; FAX 215/563-3628. Hours: 9 a.m.—5 p.m. Monday—Friday.

The second largest theatre collection in an American public library (New York's is the largest), the Theatre Collection of the Free Library tries to collect "everything available on theatre and other forms of entertainment in Philadelphia and Pennsylvania." Books, periodicals, and all types of nonbook materials are available, over 1 million items in all. Besides legitimate theatre, the collection emphasizes the circus, minstrel shows, vaudeville, and burlesque. Reflecting Philadelphia's early importance in the history of American theatre, the Free Library's collection serves historians with its large collection of playbills, posters, and pictures dating back to 1803. Programs represent productions in New York, San Francisco, London, Paris, and many other, smaller, cities as well as Philadelphia.

690. **George Mason University. Special Collections and Archives**. Fenwick Library, George Mason University, Fairfax, VA 22030-4444. 703/993-2220; FAX 703/993-2229. Hours: 12:30 p.m.—4:30 p.m. Monday—Friday and by appointment.

George Mason University holds on permanent loan the archives of the Federal Theatre Project, the nation's first large-scale government program for the arts. The project brought theatre to scores of small towns throughout Depression-era America between 1935 and 1939 and provided jobs for actors and other theatrical workers. The large collection has been described in *The Federal Theatre Project: A Catalog-Calendar of Productions* (entry 550). George Mason also holds part of the papers of actor Robert Breen, executive secretary of the American National Theatre and Academy during the 1940s and 1950s. (The rest of Breen's papers are housed at the Jerome Lawrence and Robert E. Lee Theatre Research Institute of The Ohio State University [entry 698]). Together, the two collections provide source material important to the history of American theatre during the middle of the twentieth century.

691. **Hampden-Booth Theatre Library**. The Players, 16 Gramercy Park, New York, NY 10003. 212/228-7610. Hours: By appointment only.

Begun with the personal library of Edwin Booth, the Hampden-Booth Theatre Library collects in the areas of nineteenth-century American and British theatre and twentieth-century theatres operated in the actor-manager tradition. Four principal collections are the Edwin Booth Collection including the actor's papers, account books, and other business archives as well as his collection of theatre books; the Walter Hampden Collection, which documents this actor-manager's career; the Union Square Theatre Collection, records of the theatre 1872-1883; and the William Henderson Collection of English Playbills, approximately 4,000 bills for plays produced between the years 1747 and 1888. The library also houses smaller collections, including the personal papers of many actors. In addition, many paintings, drawings, and other works of art related to the theatre may be viewed on the walls of The Players. Researchers must call for an appointment to use the library.

692. **Harvard Theatre Collection**. Harvard College Library, Harvard University, Cambridge, MA 02138. 617/495-2445; FAX 617/495-1376. Hours: 9 a.m.—5 p.m. Monday—Friday.

Founded in 1901, Harvard's collection is the nation's oldest performing arts research library. It holds more than 5 million items on the history of theatre, dance, and popular entertainment. It contains over 3 million playbills and programs alone, half a million photographs, 250,000 engravings, and countless other items. Dance materials include books, librettos, prints, and drawings on the history of ballet. In 1991 the library received a bequest of valuable materials documenting the Ballets Russes, the company that featured Nijinsky and Diaghilev. See Hall (entry 168) for a catalog of the library's engravings.

693. **The Hertzberg Circus Collection & Museum**. 210 Market Street, San Antonio, TX 78205-2826. 512/299-7810; FAX 512/271-9497. Hours: 9 a.m.—5 p.m. Monday—Saturday; 1 p.m.—5 p.m. Sundays and holidays during May—September only.

13—Libraries and Archives

The oldest public collection of circus materials was assembled by San Antonio lawyer Harry Hertzberg who bequeathed it to the San Antonio Public Library in 1940. The library contains an extensive collection of books, periodicals, posters, photographs, and manuscripts. A particularly important source is the unpublished manuscript of Colonel C. G. Sturtevant's *Who's Who in the American Circus*. The 16,800 entries provide an extremely large file of circus people and acts. The Hertzberg staff has indexed many circus periodicals and scrapbooks, and the card catalog describes all the books in the collection, including the many rare books. The Hertzberg is one of the finest circus collections in the United States, together with the Robert L. Parkinson Library at the Circus World Museum (entry 712) and the circus collection at Illinois State University (entry 695).

694. **Howard University. Founders Graduate Library. Channing Pollock Theatre Collection**. 103 Founders Library, 500 Howard Place, NW, Washington, DC 20059. 202/806-7259. Hours: 8:30 a.m.—5:00 p.m. Monday—Friday.

Centered around the manuscripts, correspondence and rare books of the late Channing Pollock, American playwright and critic, the Howard collections contain diaries, scrapbooks, playbills, portraits, and other materials associated with many periods of theatrical history. The growing collection currently holds more than 19,000 volumes and 170,000 nonbook items. The catalog may be consulted at the library.

695. **Illinois State University. Circus Collection**. Department of Special Collections, Milner Library, Normal, IL 61761-0900. 309/438-7450. Hours: 10 a.m.—Noon and 1 p.m.—4:30 p.m. Monday—Friday and by appointment.

One of the best circus collections in the world has been assembled by Illinois State University, in part because neighboring Bloomington, Illinois was once the winter home of many circus performers. The collection's monographs have been described in Sokan's work (entry 185), but the large files of clippings, programs, route books, correspondence, and pamphlets can be accessed only through files at the library. The circus art collection is accessible through OCLC. The library holds more than 100,000 ephemeral items as well as over 5,000 book titles.

696. **The Institute of the American Musical**. 121 N. Detroit St., Los Angeles, CA 90036. Hours: By appointment only to serious scholars.

Founded in 1972, the Institute's collection emphasizes recordings of theatre, film, and popular music from the 1890s to the present. However, it also houses books, sheet music, playbills, and scripts related to musical productions. The Institute opens its collection to researchers only, but it often lends materials for exhibitions held by museums and other institutions.

697. **International Theatre Institute of the United States, Inc. Library**. 220 W. 42nd Street, Suite 1710, New York, NY 10036. 212/944-1490; FAX 212/944-1506. Hours: 1 p.m.—5 p.m. Monday—Friday.

The United States branch of the International Theatre Institute maintains a library that documents contemporary theatre in 145 countries. Books, periodicals, playbills, and papers are arranged by country and deal with all aspects of theatre including puppets, mime, and minstrelsy. The collections are described in Lee Ash's *Subject Collections* (6th ed. New York: R. R. Bowker, 1985) and in *Theatre & Performing Arts Collections* (entry 9).

698. **Jerome Lawrence and Robert E. Lee Theatre Research Institute.** The Ohio State University, 1430 Lincoln Tower, Columbus, OH 43210-1230. 614/292-6614; FAX 614/292-3061. Hours: 9 a.m.—noon and 1 p.m.—4 p.m. Monday—Friday during the academic year. Call for summer and holiday hours.

Named for native Ohioans and playwrights Jerome Lawrence and Robert E. Lee, the collection at Ohio State University includes Lawrence and Lee's own collections of autographed plays published during the past fifty years, major critical works, posters, photographs, and the memorabilia of long careers. The repository also houses a 450,000-frame microfilm archive of theatre history of the Western world. Starting in 1951, this resource was created by microfilming documents, promptbooks, playbills, and other materials in more than 100 European libraries at the instigation of OSU Theatre Collection founder John McDowell. The Institute also houses the growing archives of dancer and choreographer Twyla Tharp.

699. **Keith/Albee Vaudeville Collection.** Special Collections, University of Iowa Libraries, Iowa City, IA 52242-1098. 319/335-5867; FAX 319/335-5830. Hours: 9 a.m.—Noon, 1 p.m.—5 p.m. Monday—Friday.

Saved from destruction and donated to the University of Iowa, the records of the Keith/Albee chain's theatres make up a valuable record of vaudeville life during its heyday. Comprising about 50 linear feet, the records fall into two major categories. The first is a set of report books from 1902 to 1923 in which Keith/Albee managers across the United States reported on their currently booked acts, their reactions, and the audiences' reactions. The second series is a series of books of clippings for the Keith/Albee theatres in and around Providence, Rhode Island. Both reviews of vaudeville acts and advertisements were clipped and saved. The collection is accessible through an inventory.

700. **Library of Congress. Manuscript Division.** James Madison Memorial Bldg., Rooms 101-102, Washington, DC 20540. 202/707-5383. Hours: 8:30 a.m.—5 p.m. Monday—Saturday.

The Manuscript Division of the Library of Congress holds large numbers of collections related to performing arts. The personal papers of a great number of actors including Charlotte Cushman, Minnie Maddern Fiske, Ruth Gordon, Hume Cronyn, Jessica Tandy, Laura Keene, and Groucho Marx are found here. Playwrights represented by scripts include Lillian Hellman, Garson Kanin, Henry Denker, and Maxwell Anderson. From the business side of the arts, the papers of theatrical agent Lucy Kroll and public relations expert Edward L. Bernays form just two of many collections. William Zorach and the Provincetown Players are represented by 14,000 items. The copyright drama collection includes about 450,000 plays written between 1900 and 1978. (Since 1978, plays are available in the copyright department on microfilm.) Because the division's holdings are so vast, researchers should inquire by letter or telephone to ascertain whether the library holds any material of interest.

701. **Library of Congress. Rare Book and Special Collection Division.** Thomas Jefferson Bldg., Room 256, Washington, DC 20540. 202/287-5434; FAX 202/707-5844. Hours: 8:30 a.m.—5 p.m. Monday—Friday.

The rare book and special collections division of the Library of Congress holds a large collection of theatre playbills and a collection on the subject of magic. The personal library of Harry Houdini is housed here. Library staff will answer questions by correspondence or telephone.

702. **Library of Congress and the John F. Kennedy Center for the Performing Arts. The Performing Arts Library**. John F. Kennedy Center for the Performing Arts, Washington, DC 20566. 202/707-6245. Hours: 11 a.m.—8:30 p.m. Tuesday—Friday; 10 a.m.—6 p.m. Saturday.

A joint project of the Library of Congress and the Kennedy Center, this library "serves the research and information needs of the public, artists, and staff of the Center." A large reference collection includes 5,000 books, 450 periodicals, and over 6,000 recordings and videotapes. Both dance and theatre are emphasized, and the librarians operate a telephone and mail reference service for the public. The library is linked to the rest of the Library of Congress by computer and audio links.

703. **Los Angeles Public Library. Literature and Fiction Department**. 630 W. Fifth St., Los Angeles, CA 90071-2097. 213/612-3287; FAX 213/612-0408. Hours: Noon—8 p.m. Monday-Tuesday; 10 a.m.—5:30 p.m. Wednesday—Saturday.

The Los Angeles Public Library has been collecting both printed plays and playbills for local productions for a long time. The playbill collection extends from the 1920s up to the present. The collection of published plays is extensive, and the library also holds local authors' plays in manuscript form.

704. **McGill University. Rosalynde Stearn Puppet Collection**. Rare Books and Special Collections Department, McLennan Library, 3459 McTavish Street, Montreal, H3A 1Y1, Canada. 514/398-4711; FAX 514/398-7184. Hours: 9 a.m.—5 p.m. Monday—Friday.

The result of a 1952 gift by Rosalynde Osborne Stearn, once "Canada's foremost puppet theatre director," this collection includes more than 600 books as well as puppets, toy theatres, theatrical portraits, and puppet-related prints, posters, and drawings. Most of the books date from the late nineteenth and early twentieth centuries and are written in many European languages. They include both puppet plays and books about puppetry. Mrs. Stearn collected the puppets to represent different times and countries, and they encompass string marionettes, glove puppets, Chinese shadow puppets, and Javanese rod puppets. The collection's catalog (entry 183) describes its various holdings briefly. When the catalog was published in 1961, the Stearn Collection was believed to be second in size only to the Paul McPharlin Collection at the Detroit Institute of Arts (entry 708). A third large collection is the Marjorie Batchelder McPharlin collection now housed at the University of New Mexico (see entry 175).

705. **Metropolitan Toronto Reference Library. Arts Department**. 789 Yonge Street, Toronto, M4W 2G8, Canada. 416/393-7707; FAX 416/393-7229. Hours: 9 a.m.—9 p.m. Monday—Thursday; 9 a.m.—6 p.m. Friday; 9 a.m.—5 p.m. Saturday; 1:30 p.m.—5 p.m. Sunday mid-October—April.

The Arts Department of the Metropolitan Toronto Reference Library collects books, periodicals, and nonbook material related to the performing arts in Canada and elsewhere. Over 100,000 books on theatre, drama, dance, and popular entertainment are augmented by extensive files of newspaper clippings, pamphlets, and publicity materials. The library holds more than 40,000 programs for theatre productions across Canada and from foreign countries as well. The special collections room houses engravings, manuscript collections, posters, photographs, and a large collection of stage and costume designs.

706. **National Endowment for the Arts Library**. 1100 Pennsylvania Avenue, NW, Room 213, Washington, DC 20506. 202/682-5485. Hours: By appointment only.

A working library for the staff of the National Endowment for the Arts, this collection includes a small reference collection, 7,000 books, and 125 periodical titles on topics such as the arts, arts management, preservation, and arts finance. Unique to the library are the reports and other documents generated by the NEA staff, its fellows, and its consultants. Members of the public must call for an appointment to use this library.

707. **New York Public Library for the Performing Arts. Billy Rose Theatre Collection**. 40 Lincoln Center Plaza, New York, NY 10023-7498. 212/870-1639. Hours: Noon—7:45 p.m. Monday, Thursday; Noon—5:45 Wednesday, Friday; 10 a.m.—5:45 p.m. Saturday.

The premiere theatre collection in the United States and perhaps the world is housed at the New York Public Library. Begun in 1931 with a bequest from playwright and producer David Belasco, the collection offers more than 5 million items for study encompassing all areas of theatre—drama, musical theatre, film, television, radio, circus, magic, vaudeville, and puppetry—and all parts of the world. The largest part of the collection is nonbook material including scripts, promptbooks, programs, personal archives, clippings, photographs, and production designs. Sooner or later, any serious theatre researcher will end up at the NYPL's collection. The *Catalog of the Theatre and Drama Collections* and its supplements (entries 179, 178) act as finding aids for the riches of the collection.

708. **Paul McPharlin Memorial Puppet Library and Collection**. Detroit Institute of Arts Research Library, 5200 Woodward Ave., Detroit, MI 48202. 313/833-7929; FAX 313/833-2357. Call for hours.

Given to the Detroit Institute of Arts after his death in 1948, the Paul McPharlin Collection reflects his wide-ranging interests in the field of theatre. More than 400 books relate to puppetry, the field in which McPharlin was an acknowledged expert and an author. Another 900 volumes deal with theatre, dance, film, circus, and magic. Ranging from the eighteenth century to the mid-twentieth century, the books include many rare items. The puppet books encompass "practically every title in print in all languages" at that time including puppet plays. The books are integrated into the Institute library's collection and may be accessed through its catalog. The library also holds McPharlin's correspondence.

709. **Pennsylvania State University. Special Collections Department**. Fred Lewis Pattee Library, Pennsylvania State University, University Park, PA 16802. 814/865-1794. Hours: 8 a.m.—5 p.m. Monday—Friday.

Readers interested in theatre lighting may find the Century Lighting collection at Pennsylvania State University to be of interest. It contains about 10,000 drawings for lighting systems installed in theatres and auditoriums throughout the United States and abroad between 1950 and 1970. Penn State also houses the Cutler Theater Collection of 1,000 programs and 6,000 photographs related to theatre, dance, and opera. Most of the materials date from the 1880s to the 1970s. They document primarily British and American performance but also include some European operas and ballets.

13—Libraries and Archives

710. Princeton University. Visual Materials Division. Department of Rare Books and Special Collections. Princeton University Library, 1 Washington Rd., Princeton, NJ 08544. 609/258-3223. Hours: 9 a.m.—5 p.m. Monday—Friday during the academic year. 8:30 a.m.—4:30 p.m. during the summer.

Princeton holds large collections of books and other materials related to theatre, dance, and entertainment. Collections include playbills from the eighteenth century to the present, posters, and set and costume designs. Princeton owns the extensive archives of actor-manager William Seymour. The working papers of the Barnum & Bailey Circus up to 1909 are held by Princeton and are augmented by other circus materials. The library also holds the papers of producer Max Gordon and financier and arts patron Otto Kahn. The Tams-Witmark Archives contains scores, promptbooks, and other materials related to American musical comedies and operettas of the early twentieth century and is complemented by the Ashton Sly Collection of English musical comedies. Because the holdings are large, researchers are advised to inquire about needed resources before visiting the library.

711. Robert F. Wagner Labor Archives. Elmer Holmes Bobst Library, New York University, 70 Washington Square South, New York, NY 10011. 212/998-2440; FAX 212/995-4070. Hours: 10 a.m.—9 p.m. Monday, Thursday; 10 a.m.—5:45 p.m. Tuesday, Wednesday, Friday; 10 a.m.—5 p.m. Saturday during the academic term. Call for summer and holiday hours.

Founded in 1977, the Wagner Archives collects materials on the history of organized labor. It holds records of the Actors' Equity Association, the American Guild of Variety Artists, the Actors' Fund of America, and the United Scenic Artists. It has also microfilmed records of many unions that deal with the performing arts. Containing a large amount of production material from 1913 to the present, the records document performances not just of New York City theatres, but also of regional and touring companies, tent shows, variety acts, and other entertainment troupes.

712. Robert L. Parkinson Library and Research Center, Circus World Museum (owned by the State Historical Society of Wisconsin). 426 Water Street, Baraboo, WI 53913. 608/356-8341, ext. 282. Hours: 8 a.m.—Noon, 1 p.m.—5 p.m. Monday—Friday.

Hometown of the Ringling Brothers, who founded "The Greatest Show on Earth," Baraboo, Wisconsin was for many years the winter home of the Ringling Brothers Circus. Now housed in many of the original buildings is the largest circus museum in the world. As part of the Circus World Museum complex, the library holds a large collection of materials dealing with all aspects of the American circus. These include the advance agents' advertising tools (posters, newspaper ads, and advertising booklets); route books that list the circus' season route on a daily basis; circus movies; programs; photographs; books; periodicals; and archives of circuses and individuals. The library also includes extensive files on American wild west shows. The staff will answer specific questions by telephone or correspondence and will advise researchers on the availability of materials before a trip to the library is planned.

713. The Shubert Archive. 149 West 45th Street, New York, NY 10036. 212/944-3895; FAX 212/944-3767. Hours: Open by appointment only to qualified researchers. Contact the Archive for more information.

Based on the records of The Shubert Organization, at one time "America's largest producing and theatre owning operation," The Shubert Archive contains more than 4 million documents relating to the history of Broadway theatre. Correspondence, scripts, costume designs, architectural plans, and press clippings are some of the types of materials available to researchers. Most of the documents date from the early decades of this century. The Archive actively acquires materials by gift such as the recent donation of twentieth-century playbills from The Players theatrical club. Its newsletter, *The Passing Show* (entry 625) describes new acquisitions, and its collections may be accessed through finding aids available at the repository.

714. **University of California, Davis. Shields Library. Department of Special Collections**. Davis, CA 95616. 916/752-1621; FAX 916/752-3148. Hours: Noon—4 p.m. Monday—Friday.

The Davis collection contains papers of many theatre personalities, theatre programs, and archives of several experimental theatre groups. The largest of these is the archives of the San Francisco Mime Troupe, but the collection also holds those of the Living Theatre and the Bread and Puppet Theatre. In addition it contains the papers of collector William G. Powell and theatre professor Glenn M. Loney. The collection's catalog may be consulted at the library.

715. **The University of Florida Belknap Collection for the Performing Arts**. University of Florida Libraries, 204 Library Way, Gainesville, FL 32611. 904/392-0322; FAX 904/392-7251. Hours: 8 a.m.—5 p.m. Monday—Friday and by appointment.

The best performing arts collection in the southeastern United States was developed by librarian and bibliographer Sarah Yancey Belknap, also known for her *Guide to the Performing Arts* series (entry 203). Among the many holdings are papers of dancers Ted Shawn and Ruth St. Denis; turn-of-the-century programs of the Ringling Circus; scripts, scores and rare short films of vaudeville acts from around 1900; American and British playbills and broadsides dating back to 1790; and many photographs of actors and actresses. Costume designer John Ridge is represented by 1,500 of his designs.

716. **University of Georgia Libraries. Hargrett Rare Book and Manuscript Library**. Athens, GA 30602. 706/542-7123; FAX 706/542-6522. Hours: 8 a.m.—5 p.m. Monday—Friday; 9 a.m.—5 p.m. Saturday during the school year; call for holiday hours.

The University of Georgia's growing performing arts collection emphasizes theatrical costume. It includes the Paris Music Hall Collection of thousands of original costume renderings by such artists as Erté, Freddy Wittop, and George Barbier. The Freddy Wittop Collection includes the archives of Wittop, winner of the Tony Award for Outstanding Costume Design for his work on *Hello, Dolly!*. The library also holds the library and personal papers of actor Charles Coburn.

717. **University of Michigan Library. Theatre Collection**. The Special Collections Library, 711 Harlan Hatcher Graduate Library, University of Michigan, Ann Arbor, MI 48109-1205. 313/764-9377; FAX 313/764-0259. Hours: 10 a.m.—Noon and 1 p.m.—5 p.m. Monday—Friday; 10 a.m.—Noon Saturday.

The University of Michigan holds materials of interest to both dance and theatre scholars. The theatre collection includes correspondence of Alfred Lunt, Lynn Fontanne, playwright Arthur Wing Pinero, Dion Boucicault, Ben Greet, and others. The Sanders

Theatre Collection contains 16,000 nineteenth-century playbills as well as posters, scrapbooks, and photographs. Michigan's book collection contains a large collection of Shakespeare works, many of Dryden's plays, a large collection of pre-1850 English drama, and many American nineteenth-century plays. The "Ballet Alphabet A to Z" is a collection of photographs of 400 ballet dancers on display at the School of Dance and the Performing Arts.

718. **University of Southern California. Cinema—Television Library and Archives of Performing Arts**. Room 206 Doheny Library, Los Angeles, CA 90089-0182. 213/740-8906; FAX 213/747-3301. Hours: 9 a.m.—4:45 p.m. Monday—Friday; 9 a.m.—1 p.m. Saturday during the academic term.

Although the USC collection concentrates on film and television, it contains much material related to theatre personalities, mainly actors who worked both on stage and in front of the camera. Scrapbooks, photographs, and other materials are available for actors Edward G. Robinson, Billie Burke, and Brian Aherne, producer Albert Lewis, and playwright William DeMille, for example. USC also holds a good collection of materials relating to Ole Olsen of Olsen and Johnson vaudeville fame. Playbills for productions in Los Angeles, Chicago, and New York form another part of the collection. The library's collections of MGM, Twentieth Century-Fox, and Warner Brothers archives contain many scripts of plays, some rare, which were the basis for later film scripts. USC's collections are described in Linda Harris Mehr's *Motion Pictures, Television and Radio: A Union Catalogue of Manuscript and Special Collections in the Western United States* (Boston: G. K. Hall, 1977).

719. **University of Texas at Austin. Theatre History and Dramatic Literature Collections, Harry Ransom Humanities Research Center**. 2114 Harry Ransom Center, Austin, TX 78713. 512/471-9122; FAX 512/471-9646. Hours: 8 a.m.—5 p.m. Monday—Friday and by appointment.

The University of Texas maintains many collections of theatre materials, some of which have been described in Frederick Hunter's book (entry 170). They include a large group of playbills and programs from eighteenth- and nineteenth-century London; the B. J. Simmons Collection of 29,000 costume designs; the Garden Conway Collection of designs for Paris music hall and British film productions; several groups of photographs and engraved portraits; posters; and prompt scripts. Because Hunter's book is now twenty-five years old, researchers should contact the library for additional information about its holdings.

720. **University of Washington Libraries. Drama Library**. Hutchinson Hall, DX-20, Seattle, WA 98195-0001. 206/543-5148; FAX 206/543-8512. Hours: 9 a.m.—6 p.m. Monday, Wednesday; 9 a.m.—7 p.m. Tuesday, Thursday; 9 a.m.—5 p.m. Friday; 1 p.m.—5 p.m. Sunday during the academic year; call for summer and holiday hours.

This library's strength lies in its collection of more than 14,000 twentieth-century acting editions and over 2,000 nineteenth-century British and American acting editions of plays. It also collects costume material in a variety of formats such as books, serials, slides, clipping files, and patterns. In addition, press releases and brochures of major theatre companies in the United States are housed in file cabinets and accessed through the catalog.

721. **Wisconsin Center for Film and Theater Research.** 816 State St., Madison, WI 53706. 608/262-0585. 1 p.m.—5 p.m. Monday—Friday.

A joint project of the State Historical Society of Wisconsin and the University of Wisconsin, the Center collects "primary material relating to the theater, the motion picture industry, and television documentary and drama programs." Among the hundreds of collections are the papers of Broadway producer Kermit Bloomgarden (*Death of a Salesman*, *The Diary of Anne Frank*); theatrical producer and publisher Daniel L. Blum; playwright Paddy Chayefsky; critic Walter F. Kerr and playwright Jean C. Kerr; and Broadway collaborators Howard Lindsay and Russel Crouse. The holdings are described in *Sources for Mass Communications, Film and Theater Research: A Guide* (Madison: State Historical Society of Wisconsin, 1982).

722. **Yale University. Drama Library.** 222 York St., Box 1903A Yale Station, New Haven, CT 06520. 203/432-1554. Hours: 8:30 a.m.—8:30 p.m. Monday—Friday; 1 p.m.—5 p.m. Saturday during the academic year. Call at other times.

Yale owns one of the largest collections of books and periodicals on drama and theatre in the United States. Intended for the use of its graduate students and faculty but open to other readers, it includes plays and books on the history of theatre, theatre architecture, dramatic criticism, stage and costume design, and many other theatre topics. A large number of theatrical prints and photographs complement the book collection. Another resource is the group of bound production books of Yale School of Drama productions.

Dance Collections

723. **Chicago Dance Collection.** Newberry Library, 60 W. Walton St., Chicago, IL 60610-3394. 312/943-9090. Hours: 10 a.m.—6 p.m. Tuesday—Thursday; 9 a.m.—5 p.m. Friday—Saturday.

The Newberry Library collects "dance-related personal papers, ephemera, and archives of dance studios and dance companies centered in the Chicago area." It also holds materials on Chicago performances by national and international companies. Both Hubbard Street Dance Company and the defunct Chicago City Ballet have deposited their archives here. The library also holds a small group of periodicals and a growing collection of books on dance history.

724. **New York Public Library for the Performing Arts. Dance Collection.** 40 Lincoln Center Plaza, New York, NY 10023-7498. 212/870-1657; FAX 212/787-3852. Hours: Noon—8 p.m. Monday, Thursday; Noon—6 p.m. Wednesday, Friday; 10 a.m.—6 p.m. Saturday.

The New York Public Library's dance collection is the "largest and most comprehensive archive in the world devoted to the documentation of dance." Books, films, photographs, posters, and many manuscripts and archives form this vast collection, which has been described in the *Dictionary Catalog of the Dance Collection* and its supplements (entries 195, 193) and in *Dance on Disc* (entry 194).

725. **University of Pittsburgh. Anna Pavlowa-Karl G. Heinrich Collection**. Hilman Library, University of Pittsburgh, Pittsburgh, PA 15260. 412/648-7710; FAX 412/648-1245. Hours: 8:30 a.m.—5 p.m. Monday—Friday.

Pittsburgh's Pavlowa-Heinrich Collection consists of the personal and business papers of Heinrich, longtime ballet master of the Pittsburgh Civic Ballet and collector of Pavlowa materials. It includes books on dance, scrapbooks, posters, choreographic notes, and photographs. Heinrich also collected materials on Ruth St. Denis and Ted Shawn, on the Ballet Russe de Monte Carlo, and on other dance companies. Of most interest to those researching the Pittsburgh company, this collection contains materials that may be useful to anyone interested in twentieth-century dance.

Chapter 14

Professional Organizations and Societies

Professional associations often provide information, either through publications or directly in answer to queries. The organizations listed in this chapter have been chosen because of their importance in disseminating information both to their members and to the public. Some of them maintain libraries, while others answer questions from their in-house databases. Many publish journals, books, newsletters, and other materials. Readers can find additional organizations by using the *Encyclopedia of Associations* (Detroit: Gale Research, annual).

726. **American Alliance for Theatre & Education**. Department of Theatre, Arizona State University, Tempe, AZ 85287-3411. 602/965-6064.

Working to "provide quality theatre experiences for children and youth" from kindergarten to university age, AATE acts as an advocate for educational theatre, addresses the concerns of its members, and publishes two periodicals. The *Youth Theatre Journal* reports on scholarly research in the field, while *The Drama/Theatre Teacher* provides practical advice to classroom teachers. The organization also publishes monographs on various subjects of interest to children's and educational theatre practitioners. Its archive is housed in Special Collections at the Hayden Library, Arizona State University.

727. **American Association of Community Theatre**. 8209 N. Costa Mesa Dr., Muncie, IN 47303. 317/288-0144.

The organization that represents amateur and community theatre groups, AACT aims to improve the quality and quantity of community theatre productions. Its publications feature practical advice on production, marketing, and fundraising. It also issues an annual membership directory and maintains an information and resource bureau.

728. **American Society for Theatre Research**. Theater Department, University of Rhode Island, Kingston, RI 02881. 401/792-5921.

Established in 1956 to provide an organization for scholars engaged in theatre research, this organization serves the needs of theatre historians. It publishes *Theatre Survey* (entry 651) as well as a newsletter for members. It also publishes monographs and books including the *Index to the Portraits in Odell's Annals of the New York Stage* (entry 567), and it supports the *International Bibliography of Theatre* (entry 51). It also sponsors the electronic discussion list called ASTR-L (entry 588).

729. **ASSITEJ/USA**. Theatre Service, P.O. Box 15282, Evansville, IN 47716. 812/474-0549; FAX 812/476-4168.

The American affiliate of the International Association of Theatre for Children and Young People, ASSITEJ/USA promotes "the development of professional theatre for young audiences." It publishes *TYA Today* (entry 656) and other materials aimed at helping professionals improve children's theatre. It also facilitates international exchange of theatre artists and reports on such exchanges.

730. **Association for Theatre in Higher Education.** c/o Theatre Service, P.O. Box 15282, Evansville, IN 47716-0282. 812/474-0549; FAX 812/476-4168.

Concerned with post-secondary theatre training, production, and scholarship, ATHE exists "to foster interaction and the exchange of information among those engaged in all areas of theatre research, performance, scholarship, and crafts." To that end it publishes *Theatre Journal* (entry 648) and the *Journal of American Drama and Theatre*. Many of its twenty focus groups, based on members' interests, distribute newsletters and facilitate information exchange among themselves. The focus groups reflect the broad scope of this organization, ranging from acting, directing, and design groups to theatre history, Black theatre, and theatre and social change groups.

731. **Association of Performing Arts Presenters.** 1112 16th Street, NW, No. 400, Washington, D.C. 20036. 202/833-2787; FAX 202/833-1542.

A service organization for those who book and present performing artists, usually as part of a season or series, APAP provides information and consultation designed to improve the presenter's efforts. Its database keeps information on programming, audiences, and facilities. It publishes *Inside Arts* (entry 612); *Presenters' Reports*, in which members evaluate performers who appear in their series; and books related to presenting the arts. This organization is the best one to contact when looking for information on presenting as opposed to producing the arts.

732. **Audience Development Committee, Inc.** P.O. Box 30, Manhattanville Station, New York, NY 10027. 212/368-6906.

Established in 1973 "to generate more recognition, understanding and awareness of the arts in black communities," AUDELCO maintains an archives of Black theatre including original scripts, books, pictures, set designs, and files on current theatre groups. It publishes *Overture*, a Black theatre magazine, and a directory of performing arts organizations. AUDELCO also presents annual awards to performers and productions in professional nonprofit Black theatre. Those wishing to use the archives should call for an appointment.

733. **Center for Puppetry Arts.** 1404 Spring St., NW, Atlanta, GA 30309. 404/873-3089.

Founded in 1978, the Center concentrates on performance, education, and museum exhibits. It rightly considers itself "a national resource in the field of puppetry," serving as the headquarters for the American branch of UNIMA (entry 748) and keeping in touch with puppeteers all over the country. The Center houses a puppetry library and a museum of puppets including the famous Muppets of Sesame Street. A recent special exhibit featured puppets of Canadian companies.

734. **Circus Historical Society.** 3477 Vienna Ct., Westerville, OH 43081.

Encompassing circus hobbyists and fans of all types, the Circus Historical Society publishes *Bandwagon* (entry 601) and holds an annual convention.

735. **Institute for Advanced Studies in the Theatre Arts**. 12 West End Ave., Suite 304, New York, NY 10023. 212/581-3133; FAX 800/843-8334.

The nonprofit Institute produces films and publishes books on theatre. Each film "examines a different theatrical style through actual scenes from a classic staging and with regard to its historical significance." Both Western and Asian theatre are covered, and examples include an explanation of the commedia dell'arte, a comparison of the works of Shakespeare and Webster, and a demonstration of Japanese Noh theatre. Books published include translations of plays with the text in the original language facing the English translation.

736. **Institute of Outdoor Drama**. CB 3240 NCNB Plaza, University of North Carolina, Chapel Hill, NC 27599-3240. 919/962-1328.

The Institute "serves as a communications link between operating dramas and as a resource for groups, agencies, or individuals concerned with the production of outdoor historical drama." Among other duties it provides information about outdoor drama and helps theatre companies exchange information. It publishes technical and reference materials and a quarterly newsletter and it maintains archives relating to outdoor historical drama.

737. **International Jugglers Association**. P.O. Box 3707, Akron, OH 44314-3707. 216/745-3552.

Promoting the art of juggling, the organization serves 3,000 members in twenty-one countries. It publishes *Juggler's World* magazine and information brochures designed to introduce juggling to the public. It also answers inquiries from the public regarding juggling, sells videotapes featuring jugglers in performance, and keeps the Ziethen Archives, "the world's most comprehensive source of historical juggling film, video, photographs, and memorabilia."

738. **International Theatre Institute of the United States**. 220 W. 42nd St., Suite 1710, New York, NY 10036. 212/944-1490.

Besides maintaining a first-rate library (see entry 697), the ITI publishes a quarterly newsletter that reports on international theatre activity and reviews books and other publications.

739. **League of American Theatres and Producers**. 226 W. 47th St., New York, NY 10036. 212/764-1122; FAX 212/719-4389.

As the trade association for the theatrical industry, the League "acts as a clearing house of information on past and present Broadway activity in New York and around the nation." The League represents Broadway producers, touring theatrical productions, and presenters of Broadway plays throughout the United States and Canada. Professional nonprofit theatres are represented by the Theatre Communications Group (see entry 745), and amateur theatres by the American Association of Community Theatre (entry 727). The League joins with the American Theatre Wing to present the Antoinette Perry (Tony) Awards, and it manages several audience development programs.

212 / 14—Professional Organizations and Societies

740. **League of Historic American Theatres.** 1511 K St., NW, Suite 923, Washington, DC 20005. 202/783-6966; FAX 202/393-2141.

Dedicated to the preservation, renovation, and active use of historic theatres in the United States, the League organizes conferences and publishes materials that aid those restoring and operating such facilities. Its bimonthy bulletin, its *Directory of Historic American Theatres* (entry 490), and its *Member Profile Book*, which provides data on member theatres, are primary publications. The League also maintains the Chesley Collection, "a unique archive of the nation's historic theatre buildings," which includes manuscripts, playbills, photographs, and other materials.

741. **National Movement Theatre Association.** c/o Pontine, P.O. Box 1437, Portsmouth, NH 03802-1437. 603/436-6660.

Formed to support mimes, clowns, and other movement artists, students, and teachers, the NMTA promotes movement theatre and tries to increase public awareness of this branch of the performing arts. It publishes the journal *Movement Theatre Quarterly* (entry 678), which features reports on the association and articles on the art of movement theatre.

742. **New Dramatists.** 424 W. 44th St., New York, NY 10036. 212/757-6960.

Formed to assist new playwrights, New Dramatists maintains a manuscript library of current and former members' scripts and a collection of theatrical materials. Both are open to the public.

743. **Puppeteers of America.** Five Cricklewood Path, Pasadena, CA 91107. 818/797-5748.

Puppeteers of America publishes *The Puppetry Journal* (entry 635), a membership directory, and a bimonthly newsletter. Its members can use consultant services offered by other members who are experts in various aspects of puppetry and performance. The organization maintains an audiovisual rental library for members and holds national and regional puppetry festivals.

744. **Society of American Fight Directors.** c/o Richard Raether, 1834 Camp Ave., Rockford, IL 61103. 815/962-6579; 800/659-6579.

Dedicated to "training, and improving the quality of stage combat," the Society teaches actors and educators how to safely stage fights and certifies individuals who have passed the requirements set for actor/combatant; teacher; and fight master. It publishes *The Fight Master* in which articles discuss the history and practice of stage combat, and *The Cutting Edge*, a newsletter of SAFD activities and member news.

745. **Theatre Communications Group.** 355 Lexington Ave., New York, NY 10017. 212/697-5230; FAX 212/983-4847.

An important organization, TCG represents the nation's nonprofit professional theatres and provides them with services and programs, including an extensive publishing program. It produces *American Theatre* (entry 596), *Theatre Profiles* (entry 515), *Plays in Process* (entry 633), and *Play Source* (entry 629). It also publishes *TCG Theatre Directory* (entry 513) and a job search bulletin. TCG provides matching funds to its theatres for the purpose of commissioning translations of foreign plays. It has published many books, including both plays and monographs. TCG's importance goes far beyond its member audience and reaches everyone interested in American theatre.

746. **Theatre Historical Society of America**. York Theatre Bldg., Suite 200, 152 N. York Rd., Elmhurst, IL 60126. 708/782-1800; FAX 708/782-1802.

The Society collects information about historic theatres with the aim of encouraging serious study of theatre buildings and preserving the buildings where possible. Although the Society concerns itself mainly with motion picture houses, it also includes legitimate theatres and opera houses. The extensive archive, open to researchers, includes many photographs, negatives, and drawings as well as blueprints, slides, and postcards. The Society publishes *Marquee* (entry 618). The Theatre Historical Society of America concentrates on the history of older buildings while the League of Historic American Theatres (entry 740) concentrates on the operation of extant theatres.

747. **Theatre Library Association**. 111 Amsterdam Ave., Room 513, New York, NY 10023. 212/870-1670.

Founded in 1937, the Theatre Library Association advances "the interests of all those involved in collecting and preserving performing arts materials and in utilizing those materials for purpose of scholarship." It publishes *Performing Arts Resources* (entry 439) and *Broadside* (entry 603), and awards prizes to the best theatre books published each year.

748. **UNIMA-U.S.A.** c/o Center for Puppetry Arts, 1404 Spring St. NW, Atlanta, GA 30309. 404/873-3089.

The American arm of UNIMA serves to link American puppeteers with their colleagues around the world. Open to all puppet enthusiasts, the organization devotes itself to "the cause of international friendship through the art of puppetry." It maintains a calendar of world puppet festivals, publishes a newsletter, and administers a scholarship fund for advanced puppetry training. Its members participate in an international puppet congress and festival every four years. It also serves as an information center in the United States for questions about world puppetry. See also entry 733.

749. **United States Institute for Theatre Technology**. 10 W. 19th St., Suite 5A, New York, NY 10011. 212/924-9088; FAX 212/924-9343.

Composed of design and production professionals, USITT provides services for its members including expositions, symposiums, and conferences. It publishes *TD&T* (entry 640) and many books of interest to technical theatre personnel.

Dance Associations

750. **American Dance Guild**. 31 W. 21st St., 3rd Floor, New York, NY 10010. 212/627-3790.

Founded by dance professionals, the American Dance Guild provides "a forum for the exchange of ideas and methods through its publications, conferences and seminars." It publishes *American Dance* and a newsletter for members. It runs an employment service and sponsors an annual conference around a theme such as women in dance or global issues in dance.

14—Professional Organizations and Societies

751. **Congress on Research in Dance.** Department of Dance, State University of New York College at Brockport, Brockport, NY 14420. 716/395-2590; FAX 716/395-5397.

The Congress on Research in Dance, an organization of dance scholars, publishes *Dance Research Journal* (entry 671), an annual volume (*Dance Research Annual*), and occasional monographs.

752. **Country Dance and Song Society of America.** 17 New South St., Northampton, MA 01060. 413/583-9913.

Although primarily an organization of recreational dancers, the Country Dance and Song Society publishes materials that may be of interest to those who perform traditional and ritual dance for an audience. It publishes *Country Dance and Song* (entry 665) and a bimonthly newsletter for members. Its books and recordings disseminate information about music for all types of country dancing, primarily American and English.

753. **Dance Notation Bureau.** 31 W. 21st St., 3rd Floor, New York, NY 10010. 212/807-7899.

An important organization in the preservation of choreography, the Dance Notation Bureau notates, preserves, and disseminates dance works. Its archive holds hundreds of dance scores, and it helps dance companies restage more than forty works per year. It also trains notators and Labanotation teachers.

754. **Dance/USA.** 777 14th St., NW, Suite 540, Washington, DC 20005-3270. 202/628-0144; FAX 202/628-0375.

As an advocacy and service organization for professional dance, Dance/USA promotes information exchange within the field and with the general public. It publishes *Dance/USA Journal*, a membership directory, and a monthly newsletter. Its information services program provides statistical information on professional dance, and its annual data survey of member companies collects fiscal and operational information on dance company activity. Dance/USA also publishes an annual personnel compensation survey, conducts special projects and surveys as needed, and maintains a library. It is an excellent resource to call on for information about most aspects of professional dance in the United States.

755. **International Council of Kinetography Laban.** 554 S. Sixth Street, Columbus, OH 43206. 614/469-9984.

One of several organizations that carry on Rudolf Laban's work (see also the Laban/Bartenieff Institute of Movement Studies, entry 756), the ICKL promotes research in the Laban "system of movement/dance notation." It sponsors a biennial conference at which members present the results of their studies and publishes the proceedings.

756. **Laban/Bartenieff Institute of Movement Studies.** 31 W. 27th St., New York, NY 10001. 212/689-0740.

The Institute devotes itself to the study of movement according to principles formulated by Rudolf Laban and his student Irmgard Bartenieff. It maintains a library and media resource center that includes published and unpublished materials, films, photographs, and video tapes on the subject of Laban movement analysis. Another organization which carries on Laban's work is the International Council of Kinetography Laban (entry 755).

757. **National Dance Association**. 1900 Association Dr., Reston, VA 22091. 703/476-3436; FAX 703/476-9527.

Part of the American Alliance for Health, Physical Education, Recreation, and Dance, the National Dance Association promotes "the development and implementation of sound philosophies and policies in all forms of dance and in dance education." Particularly interested in education, it publishes both a guide to dance programs in higher education (entry 523), and a scholarship guide. Its publications focus on teaching dance and movement to people of all ages. Association news and concerns are voiced in *JOPERD* (entry 675).

Author-Title Index

This index lists titles of works that are given full annotations, titles of organizations listed in chapters 13 and 14, names of electronic discussion groups described in chapter 11, and authors, editors, compilers, and corporate bodies associated with the publication of the works included. Numbers cited in the index are entry numbers.

ABC of Stage Lighting, 294a
ABI/INFORM, 198
Actors Guide to Monologues: An Index of 700 Monologues from Classical and Modern Plays for Auditions and Classwork, 224
Actors Guide to Scenes, 232
Adamczyk, Alice J., 99
Adelphi Calendar Project 1806-1850. Sans Pareil Theatre, 565
Aesthetics for Dancers: A Selected Annotated Bibliography, 106
Afro-American Poetry and Drama, 1760-1975; A Guide to Information Sources, 15
Afro-American Writers After 1955: Dramatists and Prose Writers, 329
Alfredson, James B., 16
Allen, Beverly, 523
Alternative Press Index, 199
Amateur Magician's Handbook, 406
American Actors, 1861-1910: An Annotated Bibliography of Books Published in the United States in English from 1861 Through 1976, 76
American Actors and Actresses: A Guide to Information Sources, 19
American Alliance for Theatre & Education, 726
American and British Theatrical Biography: A Directory, 364
American and English Popular Entertainment: A Guide to Information Sources, 97
American Association for Health, Physical Education and Recreation. Dance Division, 100
American Association of Community Theatre, 727
American Costume, 1915-1970; A Source Book for the Stage Costumer, 437
American Dance Guild, 750

American Dissertations on the Drama and the Theatre; A Bibliography, 67
American Drama Criticism: Interpretations, 1890-1977, 529
American Drama Criticism: Supplement I to the Second Edition, 530
American Drama Criticism: Supplement II to the Second Edition, 531
American Drama Criticism: Supplement III to the Second Edition, 531a
American Humanities Index, 200
American Literary and Drama Reviews; An Index to Late Nineteenth Century Periodicals, 533
American Museum of Magic, 682
American Musical Theatre; A Chronicle, 547
American Plays Printed 1714-1830; A Bibliographical Record, 128
American Playwrights Since 1945; A Guide to Scholarship, Criticism, and Performance, 335
American Regional Theatre History to 1900: A Bibliography, 64
American Society for Theatre Research, 51, 728
American Song: The Complete Musical Theatre Companion, 384
American/Soviet Playwrights Directory, 333
American Stage to World War I; A Guide to Information Sources, 98
American Theater and Drama Research; An Annotated Guide to Information Sources, 1945-1990, 10
American Theatre Companies, 1749-1887, 391
American Theatre Companies, 1888-1930, 392
American Theatre Companies, 1931-1986, 393
American Theatre History: An Annotated Bibliography, 93a
American Theatre Planning Board, 374
American Theatre: The Monthly Forum for News, Features and Opinion, 596

American Theatrical Arts: A Guide to Manuscripts and Special Collections in the United States and Canada, 522
American Theatrical Periodicals, 1798-1967; A Bibliographical Guide, 88
American Women Dramatists of the Twentieth Century: A Bibliography, 30
American Women Playwrights, 1900-1930; A Checklist, 120
Amsterdam University Library, 150
Anderson, J.J., 568
Angotti, Vincent L., 151
Annals of English Drama 975-1700; An Analytical Record of All Plays, Extant or Lost, Chronologically Arranged and Indexed by Authors, Titles, Dramatic Companies, Etc., 555
Annals of the New York Stage, 566
Annotated Bibliography of Modern Anglo-Irish Drama, 7
Applause/Best Plays Theater Yearbook (formerly The Burns Mantle Theater Yearbook), 375
Applause: New York's Guide to the Performing Arts, 496
Arata, Esther Spring, 17-18
Archer, Stephen M., 19
Arizpe, Victor, 152
Arnold, Janet, 376
Arnott, James Fullarton, 20
Art Index, 201
Arts & Culture Funding Report, 597
Arts & Humanities Citation Index, 202
Arts du spectacle: bibliographie; ouvrages en langue française concernant théâtre, musique, mime, marionettes, variétés, cirque, radio, télévision, cinéma, publiés dans le monde entre 1960 et 1985, 41
Arts in America; A Bibliography, 54
Arts Management, 598
Arts Management: An Annotated Bibliography, 24
Ashcom, B.B., 153
Ashton Sly Collection, 710
Asian Theatre: A Study Guide and Annotated Bibliography, 26
Asian Theatre Journal, 599
ASSITEJ/USA, 729
Association for Theatre in Higher Education, 730
Association of Performing Arts Presenters, 731
ASTR-L, 588

AudArena Stadium...International Guide to Facilities, Supplies & Services, 483
AUDELCO. *See* Audience Development Committee, Inc.
Audience Development Committee, Inc., 732
Auditions and Scenes from Shakespeare, 225
Aversa, Elizabeth, 2
Ayre, Leslie, 256

Babula, William, 21
Back Stage Handbook for Performing Artists, 394
Back Stage Theater Guide, 277
Back Stage: The Performing Arts Weekly, 600
Backscheider, Paula R., 318-20
Bailey, Claudia Jean, 1
Bainton, A.J.C., 154
Baker, Blanche M., 22
Baker's Plays, 186
Balanchine, George, 465-6
Balanchine's New Complete Stories of the Great Ballets, 465
Ball, John, 23
Ballet Annual, 467
Ballet Goer's Guide, 470
Ballet Guide: Background, Listings, Credits, and Descriptions of More Than Five Hundred of the World's Major Ballets, 480
Ballet in England: A Bibliography and Survey, 105
Ballet Plot Index: A Guide to Locating Plots and Descriptions of Ballets and Associated Material, 251
Ballet Review, 660
Ballet Steps: Practice to Performance, 473
Ballett International, 661
Ballett-Journal/Das Tanzarchiv, 662
Baltic Drama: A Handbook and Bibliography, 93
Band-Kuzmany, Karin R. M., 257
Bandwagon, 601
Banham, Martin, 258
Barba, Eugenio, 259
Barnes, Philip, 260
Barranger, Milly S., 357
Barsis, Max, 377
Barton, Lucy, 378
Basic Ballet, 476
Batchelder-McPharlin Collection. University of New Mexico. Fine Arts Library, 683
Baygan, Lee, 379
Beaumont, Cyril W., 101, 307, 468
Belknap, S. Yancey, 203, 219

Bell, Joan Kuder, 225
Bell, Richard O., 225
Bellingham, Susan, 189
Benedict, Stephen, 24
Benford, Harry, 261
Benson, Eugene, 262
Bentley, Gerald Eades, 545
Bergan, Ronald, 380
Berger, Thomas L., 381
Bergeron, David M., 25
Bergman, Hannah E., 155
Bergquist, G. William, 117
Best Church Plays: A Bibliography of Religious Drama, 130
Best Festivals of North America: A Performing Arts Guide, 509
Best Plays. *See* Applause/Best Plays Theater Yearbook
Bibliographic Guide to Dance, 193
Bibliographic Guide to Theatre Arts, 178
Bibliographical Descriptions of Forty Rare Books Relating to the Art of Dancing in the Collection of P.J.S. Richardson, O.B.E., 191
Bibliographical Guide to the Spanish American Theater, 45
Bibliographical List of Plays in the French Language 1700-1789, 119
Bibliography of Books on Conjuring in English from 1580 to 1850, 42
Bibliography of Books on the Circus in English from 1773 to 1964, 94
Bibliography of Canadian Theatre History 1583-1975, 23
Bibliography of Comedias Sueltas in the University of Toronto Library, 176
Bibliography of Conjuring Periodicals in English: 1791-1983, 16
Bibliography of Costume: A Dictionary Catalog of About Eight Thousand Books and Periodicals, 47
Bibliography of Dancing, 101
Bibliography of Dancing: A List of Books and Articles on the Dance and Related Subjects, 107
Bibliography of English Conjuring, 1581-1876, 95
Bibliography of English-Language Theatre and Drama in Canada 1800-1914, 81
Bibliography of English Printed Tragedy, 1565-1900, 135
Bibliography of French Plays on Microcards, 137

Bibliography of German Plays on Microcards, 118
Bibliography of Latin American Theater Criticism 1940-1974, 70
Bibliography of Medieval Drama, 136
Bibliography of Modern Irish Drama, 1899-1970, 72
Bibliography of Spanish Plays on Microcards, 138
Bibliography of the American Theatre, Excluding New York City, 89
Bibliography of the Dance Collection of Doris Niles and Serge Leslie, 192
Bibliography of the English Printed Drama to the Restoration, 123
Bibliography of Theatre Technology: Acoustics and Sound, Lighting, Properties, and Scenery, 49
Billington, Michael, 382
Binger, Norman, 118
Biographical Dictionary of Actors, Actresses, Musicians, Dancers, Managers, & Other Stage Personnel in London, 1660-1800, 331
Biographical Dictionary of Dance, 372
Biographical Dictionary of Scenographers: 500 B.C. to 1900 A.D., 336
Biography Index, 321
Birmingham Public Libraries, 156
Black American Playwrights, 1800 to the Present: A Bibliography, 18
Black Arts Annual, 383
Black Dance: An Annotated Bibliography, 99
Black Image on the American Stage: A Bibliography of Plays and Musicals 1770-1970, 126
Black Masks, 602
Black Newspapers Index, 204
Black Playwrights, 1823-1977: An Annotated Bibliography of Plays, 5
Black Theatre and Performance: A Pan-African Bibliography, 40
Blacks in Blackface: A Source Book on Early Black Musical Shows, 444
Blazek, Ron, 2
Bloom, Ken, 263, 384
Blum, Daniel, 546
Bonin, Jane F., 385
Book of 1000 Plays, 396
Book of Ballet, 474
Book of World-Famous Libretti: The Musical Theater from 1598 to Today, 36
Bordman, Gerald, 264, 547
Boston Public Library, 157

Boulanger, Norman, 287
Bowers, Fredson, 142, 322
Bowman, Ned A., 449
Bowman, Walter Parker, 265
Boyce, Charles, 266
Boyer, Mildred Vinson, 158
Bradford, William C., Jr., 381
Brandon, James R., 26, 300
Brenner, Clarence D., 119
Brigham Young University. Theodore Fuchs Collection., 684
Britain's Theatrical Periodicals, 1720-1967, 90
British Drama League. Library, 159
British Dramatists since World War II, 365
British Humanities Index, 205
British Music Hall, 1840-1923: A Bibliography and Guide to Sources, with a Supplement on European Music-Hall, 82
British Music Hall on Record, 147
British Music Hall: An Illustrated Who's Who from 1850 to the Present Day, 325
British Musical Theatre, 552
British Theatre: A Bibliography, 1901-1985, 28
British Theatre Yearbook, 419
Broadside, 603
Broadway: An Encyclopedic Guide to the History, People and Places of Times Square, 263
Broadway and the Tony Awards: The First Three Decades 1947-1977, 413
Broadway Bound: A Guide to Shows That Died Aborning, 420
Broadway in the West End: An Index of Reviews of American Theatre in London, 1950-1975, 543
Broadway Musicals: Show by Show, 553
Broadway's Prize-Winning Musicals: An Annotated Guide for Libraries and Audio Collectors, 145a
Brock Bibliography of Published Canadian Plays in English, 1766-1978, 140
Bronner, Edwin, 386
Bryan, George B., 323-4
Buerki, F. A., 387
Bull, Robert Hamilton, 265
Burdick, Elizabeth B., 498
Burnim, Kalman A., 331
Burns Mantle Theater Yearbook. *See* Applause/Best Plays Theater Yearbook
Busby, Roy, 325
Business Periodicals Index, 206
Bzowski, Frances Diodato, 120

Caldwell, Harry B., 25
Calendar of English Renaissance Drama 1558-1642, 558
California Polytechnic State University. Special Collections, 685
Cambridge [Records of Early English Drama], 576
Cambridge Guide to American Theatre, 306a
Cambridge Guide to World Theatre, 258
Campbell, Oscar James, 267
Canada's Playwrights: A Biographical Guide, 326
Canadian Theatre Review, 604
Career Opportunities in Theater and the Performing Arts, 395a
Carpenter, Charles A., 27
Casey, Betty, 469
Catalog of Manuscripts of the Folger Shakespeare Library, Washington, D.C., 164
Catalog of Printed Books of the Folger Shakespeare Library, Washington, D.C., 165
Catalog of Prints, Engravings, Photographs, and Original Art Materials/Folger Shakespeare Library, 166
Catalog of the American Musical, 61
Catalog of the E. Azalia Hackley Memorial Collection of Negro Music, Dance, and Drama, 162
Catalog of the Shakespeare Collection, 167
Catalog of the Theatre and Drama Collections, 179
Catalogue of Comedias Sueltas in the Library of the University of North Carolina, 174
Catalogue of Comedias Sueltas in the New York Public Library, 155
Catalogue of Dramatic Portraits in the Theatre Collection of Harvard College Library, 168
Catalogue of Italian Plays, 1500-1700, in the Library of the University of Toronto, 161
Catalogue of the Allen A. Brown Collection of Books Relating to the Stage in the Public Library of the City of Boston, 157
Catalogue of the Dance Collection in The Doris Lewis Rare Book Room, University of Waterloo Library, 189
Catalogue of Theatrical Portraits in London Public Collections, 173
Catalogus van de Circus-Bibliotheek Nagelaten door K. D. Hartmans, 150
Cavanagh, John, 28
Center for Puppetry Arts, 733
Century Lighting Collection, 709

Chambers, Edmund K., 548
Champion, Édouard, 549
Character Catalog: Who's Who in One Hundred Fifty Modern Plays, 440
Charles, Jill, 484
Check List of English Plays 1641-1700, 142
Cheshire, David F., 3, 82
Chester [Records of Early English Drama], 569
Chicago Dance Collection, 723
Chicago Public Library Special Collections, 686
Chicorel Index Series, 226
Chicorel, Marietta, 226
Child Drama: A Selected and Annotated Bibliography 1974-1979, 55
Children's Theatre and Creative Dramatics: An Annotated Bibliography of Critical Works, 35
Chinese Drama: An Annotated Bibliography of Commentary, Criticism, and Plays in English Translation, 69
Choreography and Dance: An International Journal, 663
Chujoy, Anatole, 308
Circus and Allied Arts: A World Bibliography, 96
Circus Historical Society, 734
Circus Report, 605
Circus World Museum. Robert L. Parkinson Library and Research Center, 712
Clarke, Mary, 309, 470
Classical Ballet Technique, 481
Clopper, Lawrence M., 569
Clubb, Louise George, 160
Coe, Linda C., 24
Cohen, Edward M., 121
Cohen-Stratyner, Barbara Naomi, 372
Coleman, Earle J., 4
Collector's Guide to the American Musical Theatre, 145
Collier, Clifford, 524
Comedias Sueltas in Cambridge University Library: A Descriptive Catalog, 154
Comédie Française, 1680-1701: Plays, Actors, Spectators, Finances, 559
Comédie Française, 1er janvier, 1927 à 1937, 549
Comédie-Française de 1680 à 1900: Dictionnaire général des pièces et des auteurs, 557
Comedy on Record: The Complete Critical Discography, 149
Commedia Dell'Arte: A Guide to the Primary and Secondary Literature, 46

Common Man Through the Centuries: A Book of Costume Drawings, 377
Companion to Post-War British Theatre, 260
Companion to the Medieval Theatre, 302
Compilation of Dance Research, 1901-1964, 100
Complete Book of Ballets: A Guide to the Principal Ballets of the Nineteenth and Twentieth Centuries, 468
Complete Book of Puppet Theatre, 389
Complete Catalogue of Plays, 187
Complete Entertainment Discography from the Mid-1890s to 1942, 148
Complete Guide to Modern Dance, 373
Completed Research in Health, Physical Education, Recreation, and Dance, 102
Comtois, M. E., 528
Concise Oxford Dictionary of Ballet, 313
Congress on Research in Dance, 751
Connor, Billie M., 227
Conolly, L. W., 29, 262, 485
Contact Book, 486
Contact Quarterly Dance Journal, A Vehicle for Moving Ideas, 664
Contemporary American Theatre Critics: A Directory and Anthology of Their Works, 528
Contemporary Authors, 327
Contemporary Black American Playwrights and Their Plays: A Biographical Directory and Dramatic Index, 354
Contemporary British Drama 1950-1976: An Annotated Critical Bibliography, 73
Contemporary Dramatists, 334
Contemporary Stage Roles for Women: A Descriptive Catalogue, 407
Contemporary Theatre Architecture: An Illustrated Survey: A Checklist of Publications 1946-1964 by Ned A. Bowman, 449
Contemporary Theatre, Film, and Television, 348
Cook, Dorothy E., 255
Cornyn, Stan, 207
Corrigan, Beatrice, 161
Corson, Richard, 388
Costume Design on Broadway: Designers and Their Credits, 1915-1985, 349
Costume Index: A Subject Index to Plates and Illustrated Text, 255
Costumes for the Stage; A Complete Handbook for Every Kind of Play, 411
Country Dance and Song, 665

222 / Author-Title Index

Country Dance and Song Society of America, 752
Courtney, Richard, 268
Coven, Brenda, 30, 57
Coventry [Records of Early English Drama], 573
Crisp, Clement, 470
Cronologia: opere - balletti - concerti 1778-1977, 587
Cross, Gilbert B., 565
Crothers, J. Frances, 31-2
Crowell's Handbook of Gilbert and Sullivan, 434
Crown Guide to the World's Great Plays; From Ancient Greece to Modern Times, 448
Cumberland, Westmorland, Gloucestershire [Records of Early English Drama], 570
Cumulated Dramatic Index, 1909-1949, 208
Currell, David, 389
Current Biography, 328
Curtain Times: The New York Theatre: 1965-1987, 403
Curtains!!! or A New Life for Old Theatres, 428
Cutler Theater Collection, 709
Cyclopedia of Magic, 281

Daily, George L., 16
Dance: An Annotated Bibliography, 1965-1982, 104
Dance and Dancers, 666
Dance Chronicle: Studies in Dance and the Related Arts, 667
Dance Classics: A Viewer's Guide to the Best-Loved Ballets and Modern Dance, 477
Dance Current Awareness Bulletin, 220
Dance Directory 1990, 523
Dance Encyclopedia, 308
Dance Film and Video Guide, 114
Dance Handbook, 478
Dance in India; An Annotated Guide to Source Materials, 116
Dance in the Musical Theatre: Jerome Robbins and His Peers, 1934-1965: A Guide, 479
Dance Library, A Catalogue, 190
Dance Magazine, 668
Dance Magazine College Guide, 525
Dance Medicine Health Newsletter, 669
Dance Notation Bureau, 753
Dance Notation Bureau Newsletter, 670
Dance on Disc: The Complete Catalog of the Dance Collection of the New York Public Library on CD-ROM, 194

Dance Research Journal, 671
Dance Resource Guide, 13
Dance Resources in Canadian Libraries, 524
Dance Theatre Journal, 672
Dance/USA, 754
Dance World. *See* John Willis' Dance World
DANCE-L, 595
Dancing Times, 673
Davis, Thadious M., 329
Debenham, Warren, 143
Decca Book of Ballet, 472
Delaplaine, A., 487
Derra de Moroda, Friderica, 190
Descriptive and Bibliographic Catalog of the Circus & Related Arts Collection at Illinois State University, Normal, Illinois, 185
Descriptive Catalogue of the Spanish Comedias Sueltas in the Wayne State University Library and the Private Library of Professor B. B. Ashcom, 153
Detroit Public Library, 162
Detroit Public Library. E. Azalia Hackley Collections, 687
Development of Scenic Art and Stage Machinery: A List of References in the New York Public Library, 37
Devine, Mary Elizabeth, 92
Devon [Records of Early English Drama], 576a
Dictionary Catalog of the Dance Collection, 195
Dictionary of Actors and Other Persons Associated with the Public Representation of Plays in England Before 1642, 347
Dictionary of Ballet, 317
Dictionary of Ballet Terms, 312
Dictionary of Developmental Drama: The Use of Terminology in Educational Drama, Theatre Education, Creative Dramatics, Children's Theatre, Drama Therapy, and Related Areas, 268
Dictionary of Modern Ballet, 310
Dictionary of Puppetry, 293
Dictionary of the Black Theatre: Broadway, Off-Broadway, and Selected Harlem Theatre, 462
Dictionary of the Dance, 316
Dictionary of Theatre Anthropology; The Secret Art of the Performer, 259
Dictionnaire des arts du spectacle; français-anglais-allemand, 274
Dictionnaire du théâtre français contemporain, 296

Digests of Great American Plays: Complete Summaries of More than 100 Plays from the Beginnings to the Present, 425
Dillard, Philip H., 33
Dinner Theatre: A Survey and Directory, 496a
Directors Directory; A National Guide to American Stage Directors, 516
Directory of Blacks in the Performing Arts, 339
Directory of British Theatre Research Resources in North America, 485
Directory of Historic American Theatres, 490
Directory of Playwrights, Directors, Designers, 494
Directory of the American Theater 1894-1971, 404
Directory of Theatre Resources: A Guide to Research Collections and Information Services, 493
Directory of Theatre Training Programs, 484
Dixon, Geoffrey, 390
Documents of American Theater History, Volume 1: Famous American Playhouses, 1716-1899, 463
Documents of American Theater History, Volume 2: Famous American Playhouses 1900-1971, 464
Doris Humphrey Collection; An Introduction and Guide, 197
Douglan, Audrey, 570
Drama Bibliography: A Short-Title Guide to Extended Reading in Dramatic Art for the English-Speaking Audience and Students in Theatre, 50
Drama Dictionary, 283
Drama Scholars' Index to Plays and Filmscripts: A Guide to Plays and Filmscripts in Selected Anthologies, Series, and Periodicals, 249
Dramatic List: A Record of the Performances of Living Actors and Actresses of the British Stage, 352
Dramatic Play Lists 1591-1963, 91
Dramatic Re-Visions: An Annotated Bibliography of Feminism and Theatre 1972-1988, 84
Dramatic Texts and Records of Britain: A Chronological Topography to 1558, 62
Dramatics, 606
Dramatist's Bible, 487
Dramatist's Sourcebook, 488
Dramatists Guild Quarterly, 607
Dramatists Play Service, 187
Dressing the Part: A History of Costume for the Theatre, 460

Drew, David, 472
Drewal, Margaret, 14
Drone, Jeanette Marie, 228
Drury's Guide to Best Plays, 79
Dubois, William R., 163
Duffy, Susan, 33a
Dufort, Antony, 473
Dunin, Elsie Ivancich, 103
Dunn, George E., 269
Durham, Weldon B., 391-3

Eagleson, Robert D., 291
Eaker, Sherry, 394
Earl Blackwell's Entertainment Celebrity Register, 330
Early American Plays, 1714-1830: Being a Compilation of the Titles of Plays by American Authors Published and Performed in America Previous to 1830, 141
Early Black American Playwrights and Dramatic Writers: A Biographical Directory and Catalog of Plays, Films, and Broadcasting Scripts, 355
Eddleman, Floyd Eugene, 529-31a
Eighteenth Century British and Irish Promptbooks: A Descriptive Bibliography, 63
Elizabethan Dramatists, 322
Elizabethan Stage, 548
Ellis, James, 122
Emerson, Robert, 229-30, 232
Enciclopedia dello spettacolo, 270
Encyclopedia of Dance and Ballet, 309
Encyclopedia of Magic and Magicians, 303
Encyclopedia of the American Theatre 1900-1975, 386
Encyclopedia of the Musical Theatre, 276
Encyclopedia of the New York Stage, 1920-1930, 560
Encyclopedia of the New York Stage, 1930-1940, 561
Encyclopedia of the New York Stage, 1940-1950, 562
Encyclopedia of World Theater: with 420 Illustrations and an Index of Play Titles, 271
English and American Stage Productions: An Annotated Checklist of Prompt Books 1800-1900 from the Nisbet-Snyder Drama Collection, Northern Illinois University Libraries, 163
English Drama, 1660-1800: A Guide to Information Sources, 66
English Drama, 1900-1950: A Guide to Information Sources, 74

English Drama and Theatre, 1800-1900: A Guide to the Information Sources, 29
English Drama of the Nineteenth Century: An Index and Finding Guide, 122
English Drama to 1660, Excluding Shakespeare: A Guide to Information Sources, 77
English Renaissance Theatre History: A Reference Guide, 85
English Theatrical Literature, 1559-1900: A Bibliography: Incorporating Robert W. Lowe's A Bibliographical Account of English Theatrical Literature Published in 1888, 20
Epstein, Lawrence S., 489
Essay and General Literature Index, 209
Essays in Theatre/Études théâtrales, 608
Esslin, Martin, 271
Estreno, 609
Ethnic Theatre in the United States, 445
European Drama Criticism 1900-1975, 536
Everyman Companion to the Theatre, 457
Ewen, David, 395

Facts on File Dictionary of the Theatre, 292
Famous Actors & Actresses on the American Stage: Documents of American Theater History, 371
Federal Theatre Project: A Catalog-Calendar of Productions, 550
Festivals Sourcebook, 517
Festivals U.S.A., 492
Field, Shelly, 395a
Fifty Years of German Drama: A Bibliography of Modern German Drama, 1880-1930. Based on the Loewenberg Collection in the Johns Hopkins University Library, 171
Film, Television and Stage Music on Phonograph Records: A Discography, 144
Fireside Companion to the Theatre, 290
Firkins, Ina, 231
Fitzsimmons, Linda, 551
Fleshman, Bob, 34
Fletcher, Ifan Kyrle, 191
Fletcher, Steve, 396
Folger Shakespeare Library, 164-7, 688
Folk Dance Scene, 674
Forbes, Fred R., 104
Fordyce, Rachel, 35
Forrester, F.S., 105
Franks, Don, 397
Free Library of Philadelphia. Theatre Collection, 689

French Court Dance and Dance Music: A Guide to Primary Source Writings 1643-1789, 111
French-English Dictionary of Technical Terms Used in Classical Ballet, 307
Frick, John W., 490
Fuld, James J., 36
Funny Women: American Comediennes, 1860-1985, 361
Furtado, Ken, 122a

Gadan-Pamard, Francis, 310
Galloway, David, 571
Gamble, William Burt, 37
Gänzl, Kurt, 398, 552
Gänzl's Book of the Musical Theatre, 398
Gassner, John, 272
Gay and Lesbian American Plays: An Annotated Bibliography, 122a
Gay Theatre Alliance Directory of Gay Plays, 127
Geisinger, Marion, 273
Genii: The International Conjurors' Magazine, 610
George, David, 572
George Mason University. Special Collections and Archives, 690
German Stage, 1767-1890: A Directory of Playwrights and Plays, 442
Ghost Walks: A Chronological History of Blacks in Show Business, 1865-1910, 578
Gilbert & Sullivan Dictionary, 269
Gilbert and Sullivan Concordance: A Word Index to W. S. Gilbert's Libretti for the Fourteen Savoy Operas, 390
Gilbert and Sullivan Companion, 256
Gilbert and Sullivan Lexicon in Which Is Gilded the Philosophic Pill, 261
Gill, Robert, 38
Giteau, Cecile, 274
Glazer, Irvin R., 399
Glossary of the Theatre. In English, French, Italian and German, 257
Gohdes, Clarence, 39
Gordon, Gilbert, 400
Gould, Robert B., 490a
Grant, Gail, 311
Granville, Wilfred, 275
Gray, John, 40
Great Jews on Stage and Screen, 337
Great Stage Stars: Distinguished Theatrical Careers of the Past and Present, 344

Great Theatres of London: An Illustrated Companion, 380
Great Writers of the English Language: Dramatists, 363
Green, Stanley, 276, 401, 553
Greenfield, Peter, 570
Greg, Walter W., 123-4
Griffiths, Trevor R., 277
Grumbach, Jane, 229-30, 232
Gruver, Elbert A., 402
Guernsey, Otis L., Jr., 403
Guide to Chinese Poetry and Drama, 71
Guide to Critical Reviews. Part I, American Drama, 1909-1982, 537
Guide to Critical Reviews. Part II, The Musical, 1909-1989, 538
Guide to Critical Reviews. Part III, Foreign Drama, 1909-1979, 539
Guide to Dance in Film: A Catalog of U.S. Productions Including Dance Sequences, with Names of Dancers, Choreographers, Directors, and Other Details, 108
Guide to Dance Periodicals, 219
Guide to Fairs and Festivals in the United States, 507
Guide to Japanese Drama, 8
Guide to Monologues: Men; An Index of Over 800 Monologues from Classical and Modern Plays, 229
Guide to Monologues: Women; An Index of Over 800 Monologues from Classical and Modern Plays, 230
Guide to Opera & Dance on Videocassette, 65
Guide to Play Selection: A Selective Bibliography for Production and Study of Modern Plays, 125
Guide to Reference and Bibliography for Theatre Research, 1
Guide to the Baltimore Stage in the Eighteenth Century: A History and Day Book Calendar, 577
Guide to the Performing Arts, 203
Guide to the Theatre and Drama Collections at the University of Texas, 170
Guide to Theatre in America, 489
Guillot, Genevieve, 474
Guilmette, Pierre, 524
Guinness Book of Theatre Facts and Feats, 382

Hainaux, René, 41
Halford, Aubrey S., 405
Halford, Giovanna M., 405
Hall, Lillian A., 168
Hall, Trevor H., 42-3

Halliday, F. E., 278
Hamilton, David A., 251
Hammer, Kalsu, 301
Hampden-Booth Theatre Library, 691
Handbook of American Popular Culture, 6
Handbook of Costume, 376
Handel, Beatrice, 491
Handel's National Directory for the Performing Arts, 491
Hannaford, WIlliam E., 175
Hanson, Patricia King, 508
Hanson, Stephen L., 508
Hara, Arnold, 554
Harbage, Alfred, 555
Harlem Renaissance; A Historical Dictionary for the Era, 284
Harris, Janet S., 175
Harris, Richard H., 44
Harris, Steve, 144
Harris, Trudier, 329
Hartnoll, Phyllis, 279
Harvard Theatre Collection. Harvard College Library, 692
Hatch, James V., 5, 126
Hawkins-Dady, Mark, 280
Hay, Henry, 281, 406
Hebblethwaite, Frank P., 45
Heck, Thomas F., 46
Helbing, Terry, 127
Hellner, Nancy, 122a
Hennessee, Don A., 129
Herbert, Miranda C., 342
Herefordshire and Worcestershire [Records of Early English Drama], 575
Herrick, Marvin T., 169
Hertzberg Circus Collection & Museum, 693
Heys, Sandra, 407
High Performance, 611
Highfill, Philip H., 331
Hiler, Hilaire, 47
Hiler, Meyer, 47
Hill, Frank Pierce, 128
Hill, Kathleen Thompson, 492
Hischak, Thomas S., 281a
Historic Costume for the Stage, 378
Historical Guide to Children's Theatre in America, 432
History of English Drama, 1660-1900, 131
History of the Pulitzer Prize Plays, 458
Hixon, Don L., 129
Hochman, Stanley, 282
Hodgson, Terry, 283
Hoffman, Herbert H., 233
Hoggett, Chris, 408

Holden, Michael, 409
Hotaling, Edward R., 48
How Quaint the Ways of Paradox!; An Annotated Gilbert & Sullivan Bibliography, 33
How to Locate Reviews of Plays and Films: A Bibliography of Criticism from the Beginnings to the Present, 540
Howard, Diana, 410, 493
Howard, John T., Jr., 49
Howard, Thomas E., 413
Howard University. Founders Graduate Library. Channing Pollock Theatre Collection, 694
Humanities; A Selective Guide to Information Sources, 2
Humanities Index, 210
Hume, Robert D., 75
Hummel, David, 145
Hunter, Frederick J., 50, 170
Hutera, Donald, 478

Illinois State University. Circus Collection., 695
Illustrated Magic Dictionary, 285
Index of Characters in English Printed Drama to the Restoration, 381
Index to Characters in the Performing Arts, 446
Index to Children's Plays in Collections, 237-8
Index to Children's Plays in Collections, 1975-1984, 239
Index to Dance Periodicals, 221
Index to Folk Dances and Singing Games, 246
Index to Full Length Plays 1895 to 1925, 252
Index to Full Length Plays 1926 to 1944, 253
Index to Full Length Plays 1944 to 1964, 254
Index to One-Act Plays, 240
Index to One-Act Plays. Supplement 1924-1931., 241
Index to One-Act Plays. Second Supplement 1932-1940, 242
Index to One-Act Plays for Stage and Radio. Third Supplement 1941-1948, 243
Index to One-Act Plays for Stage, Radio, and Television. Fourth Supplement 1948-1957, 244
Index to One-Act Plays for Stage, Radio, and Television. Fifth Supplement 1956-1964, 245
Index to Opera, Operetta, and Musical Comedy Synopses in Collections and Periodicals, 228
Index to Plays, 1800-1926, 231
Index to Plays in Periodicals, 235

Index to Plays in Periodicals, 1977-1987, 236
Index to the Portraits in Odell's Annals of the New York Stage, 567
Inge, M. Thomas, 6
Ingram, R.W., 573
Inside Arts, 612
Institute for Advanced Studies in the Theatre Arts, 735
Institute of Outdoor Drama, 736
Institute of the American Musical, 696
International Association of Libraries and Museums of the Performing Arts, 51
International Bibliography of Theatre, 51
International Council of Kinetography Laban, 755
International Dictionary of Theatre, 280
International Dictionary of Theatre Language, 300
International Directory of Theatre, Dance and Folklore Festivals, 498
International Federation for Theatre Research, 51
International Folk Dancing U.S.A., 469
International Guide to Children's Theatre and Educational Theatre: A Historical and Geographical Source Book, 455
International Jugglers Association, 737
International Mimes & Pantomimists Directory 1974/1975, 52
International Theatre Institute of the United States, Inc., 697, 738
International Vocabulary of Technical Theatre Terms, in Eight Languages: American, Dutch, English, French, German, Italian, Spanish, Swedish, 294
Ireland, Joseph N., 556
Ireland, Norma Olin, 254
Italian Plays (1500-1700) in the Folger Library: A Bibliography with Introduction, 160
Italian Plays, 1500-1700, in the University of Illinois Library, 169
Itzin, Catherine, 494

Jackson, Sheila, 411
Jacobean and Caroline Stage, 545
James, Thurston, 412
Jerome Lawrence and Robert E. Lee Theatre Research Institute, 698
Jewell, James C., 413
Joannidès, A., 557
John Willis' Dance World, 471
Johns Hopkins University Library, 171
Johnson, Albert, 130

Johnson, Caludia D., 53
Johnson, Vernon E., 53
Johnston, Alexandra F., 574
Jones, Mabel Barrett, 174
JOPERD; The Journal of Physical Education, Recreation, and Dance, 675
Jopling, Norman, 396
Joseph Papp and the New York Shakespeare Festival: An Annotated Bibliography, 57
Journal of Arts Management, Law, and Society, 613
Journal of Dramatic Theory and Criticism, 614

Kabel, Rolf, 301
Kabuki Costume, 447
Kabuki Encyclopedia: An English-Language Adaptation of Kabuki Jiten, 286
Kabuki Handbook: A Guide to Understanding and Appreciation, with Summaries of Favorite Plays, Explanatory Notes, and Illustrations, 405
Kaminsky, Laura J., 172
Kaplan, Mike, 332, 414
Kaprelian, Mary H., 106
Karp, Rashelle S., 234
Karpel, Bernard, 54
Kawachi, Yoshiko, 558
Kaye, Phyllis Johnson, 333
Keith/Albee Vaudeville Collection, 699
Keller, Dean H., 235-6
Kellner, Bruce, 284
Kennedy, Carol Jean, 55
Kerslake, J. F., 173
Kersley, Leo, 312
Kesler, Jackson, 56
Kienzle, Siegfried, 415
Kimball, Robert, 61
Kinesiology and Medicine for Dance, 676
King, Christine E., 57
King, Kimball, 58-60
Kirkpatrick, D.L., 334
Klausner, David. 575
Koegler, Horst, 313
Kolin, Philip C., 335
Krasker, Tommy, 61
Kreider, Barbara A., 237-8
Kullman, Colby H., 416

Laban/Bartenieff Institute of Movement Studies, 756
Lacy, Robin Thurlow, 336
Lamb, Andrew, 398
Lamb, Geoffrey, 285
Lancashire, Ian, 62

Lancashire [Records of Early English Drama], 572
Lancaster, H. Carrington, 559
Langhans, Edward A., 63, 300, 331
Langley, Stephen, 417
Language of American Popular Entertainment: A Glossary of Argot, Slang, and Terminology, 306
Language of Ballet: An Informal Dictionary, 315
Language of Show Biz: A Dictionary, 295
Language of Show Dancing, 475
Larson, Carl F.W., 64
Later American Plays, 1831-1900; Being A Compilation of the Titles of Plays by American Authors Published and Performed in America Since 1831, 133
Latin American Play Index, 233
Latin American Theatre Review: A Journal Devoted to the Theatre and Drama of Spanish and Portuguese America, 615
Laughter on Record: A Comedy Discography, 143
Lawliss, Chuck, 418
Lawrence, Jerome, 698
League of American Theatres and Producers, 739
League of Historic American Theatres, 740
Lee, Robert E., 698
Lee, Susan E., 490a
Leiter, Samuel L., 286, 560-2
Lemmon, David, 419
Leon, Ruth, 496
Leonard, William Torbert, 420-2
Leslie, Serge, 192
Levine, Robert, 65
Lewine, Richard, 423
Leyson, Peter, 424
Library of Congress and the John F. Kennedy Center for the Performing Arts. The Performing Arts Library, 702
Library of Congress. Manuscript Division, 700
Library of Congress. Rare Book and Special Collection Division, 701
Lighting Design Handbook, 461
Lighting Design on Broadway: Designers and Their Credits, 1915-1990, 350
Lighting Dimensions, 616
Lim, Virginia, 519
Link, Frederick M., 66
List of Masques, Pageants, etc.: Supplementary to a List of English Plays, 124

228 / Author-Title Index

Literature and Theater of the States and Regions of the U.S.A.: An Historic Bibliography, 39
Litto, Fredric M., 67
Lively Arts Information Directory: A Guide to the Fields of Music, Dance, Theatre, Film, Radio and Television, in the United States and Canada, 518
Lloyd Evans, Barbara, 532
Lloyd Evans, Gareth, 532
Loewenberg, Alfred, 68
Logasa, Hannah, 240-5
London Stage 1660-1800: A Calendar of Plays, Entertainments & Afterpieces, Together with Casts, Box-receipts and Contemporary Comment, 563
London Stage, 1890-1899: A Calendar of Plays and Players, 580
London Stage, 1900-1909: A Calendar of Plays and Players, 581
London Stage, 1910-1919: A Calendar of Plays and Players, 582
London Stage, 1920-1929: A Calendar of Plays and Players, 583
London Stage, 1930-1939: A Calendar of Plays and Players, 584
London Stage, 1940-1949: A Calendar of Plays and Players, 585
London Stage, 1950-1959: A Calendar of Plays and Players, 585a
London Theatre Record. *See* Theatre Record
London Theatres and Music Halls 1850-1950, 410
London Theatres; A Short History and Guide, 424
Loney, Glenn, 564
Lopez, Manuel D., 69
Los Angeles Public Library. Literature and Fiction Department, 703
Lost Broadway Theatres, 459
Lost Plays and Masques 1500-1642, 134
Lost Theatres of London, 429
Lounsbury, Warren C., 287
Love, Paul, 314
Lovell, John, Jr., 425
Lowe, Jacqueline, 475
Lucha-Burns, Carol, 426
Lyday, Leon F., 70
Lyman, Darryl, 337
Lynch, Richard Chigley, 427
Lynk, William M., 496a
Lynn, Richard John, 71

Mackie, Joyce, 476
Mackintosh, Iain, 428
MacNicholas, John, 338
Magazine and the Drama: An Index, 247
Magic: A Reference Guide, 4
Magic as a Performing Art: A Bibliography of Conjuring, 38
MAGIC: An Independent Magazine for Magicians, 617
Magriel, Paul David, 107
Mailard, Robert, 310
Makeup for Theatre, Film & Television, 379
Manchester, Phyllis Winifred, 308
Mander, Raymond, 429-30
Mapp, Edward, 339
Mara, Thalia, 315
Marks, Patricia, 533
Marquee: The Journal of the Theatre Historical Society of America, 618
Martin, Linda, 340
Maske und Kothurn; Internationale Beiträge zur Theaterwissenschaft, 619
Mason, Francis, 465-6
Matlaw, Myron, 288
May, Robin, 431
McCallum, Heather, 497
McCaslin, Nellie, 432
McDonagh, Don, 373
McDonald, Arthur W., 551
McGill, Raymond D., 341
McGill University. Rosalynde Stearn Puppet Collection, 183, 704
McGraw-Hill Encyclopedia of World Drama, 282
McKnight, William A., 174
McManaway, James G., 142
McNeil, Barbara, 342
McPharlin, Marjorie Batchelder, 433
McPharlin, Paul, 433
Medieval English Theatre, 620
Merin, Jennifer, 498
Meserve, Mollie Ann, 499
Metropolitan Toronto Reference Library. Arts Department, 705
Mikhail, E. H., 7, 72-4
Mikotowicz, Thomas J., 343
Miletich, Leo N., 145a
Milhous, Judith, 75
Miller, George B., Jr., 175
Miller, Lynn F., 528
Miller, Tice L., 306a
Minneapolis. Public Library. Music Department, 246

Mitchenson, Joe, 429-30
MLA International Bibliography of Books and Articles on the Modern Languages and Literatures, 211
Mobley, Jonnie Patricia, 289
Mochedlover, Helene G., 227
Modern British Dramatists, 1900-1945, 366
Modern Dance Terminology, 314
Modern Drama, 621
Modern Drama in America and England, 1950-1970: A Guide to Information Sources, 44
Modern Drama Scholarship and Criticism 1966-1980: An International Bibliography, 27
Modern International Drama: Magazine for Contemporary International Drama in Translation, 622
Modern World Drama: An Encyclopedia, 288
Modern World Theater: A Guide to Productions in Europe and the United States Since 1945, 415
Molinaro, J.A., 176
Money for Performing Artists, 501
Monro, Isabel, 255
Moore, Frank Ledlie, 434
Mordden, Ethan, 290
More Black American Playwrights: A Bilbiography, 17
Morley, Sheridan, 344
Morrow, Lee Alan, 435
Movement and Dance: Magazine of the Laban Guild, 677
Movement Theatre Quarterly, 678
Moyer, Ronald Lee, 76
Mullin, Donald, 345
Mullin, Michael, 177
Muriello, Karen Morris, 177
Music and Dance in Puerto Rico from the Age of Columbus to Modern Times: An Annotated Bibliography, 113
Music and Dance Periodicals: An International Directory & Guidebook, 110
Music Index, 222
Musical Notes: A Practical Guide to Staffing and Staging Standards of the American Musical Theatre, 426
Musicals No One Came to See: A Guidebook to Four Decades of Musical-Comedy Casualties on Broadway, Off-Broadway and in Out-of-Town Tryout, 1943-1983, 450

Musicals! A Directory of Musical Properties Available for Production, 427

National Dance Association, 757
National Endowment for the Arts Library, 706
National Movement Theatre Association, 741
National Newspaper Index, 212
Neal-Schuman Index to Performing and Creative Artists in Collective Biographies, 356
Nelson, Alan H., 576
Nelson, Alfred L., 565
New Complete Book of the American Musical Theater, 395
New Dance Review, 679
New Dramatists, 742
New Theatre Handbook and Digest of Plays, 297
New Theatre Quarterly, 623
New York Public Library for the Performing Arts. Billy Rose Theatre Collection, 707
New York Public Library for the Performing Arts. Dance Collection, 193, 724
New York Public Library. Performing Arts Research Center, 194
New York Public Library. The Research Libraries, 178-9, 195
New York Theatre Critics Reviews, 534
New York Theatre Sourcebook, 418
New York Theatrical Sourcebook, 500
New York Times Biographical File, 346
New York Times Index, 213
New York Times Theater Reviews, 535
Newcastle upon Tyne [Records of Early English Drama], 568
Newsbank Review of the Arts: Performing Arts, 214
Nicoll, Allardyce, 131
Niemeyer, Suzanne, 501
Nineteenth and Twentieth Century Drama: A Selective Bibliography of English Language Works: Numbers 1-3029, 135
Nineteenth-Century American Drama: A Finding Guide, 129
Nineteenth Century Theatre, 624
Nineteenth-Century Theatrical Memoirs, 53
Nonprofit Repertory Theatre in North America, 1958-1975: A Bibliography and Index to the Playbill Collection of the Theatre Communications Group, 172
Norwich, 1540-1642 [Records of Early English Drama], 571

Notable Names in the American Theatre, 341
Notable Women in the American Theatre; A Biographical Dictionary, 357
NTC's Dictionary of Theatre and Drama Terms, 289
Nungezer, Edwin, 347

O'Brien, Jacqueline Wasserman, 518
O'Brien, Robert, 132
O'Donnell, Monica M., 348
O'Donnol, Shirley Miles, 437
Odell, George C. D., 566-7
Ohio State University. Jerome Lawrence and Robert E. Lee Theatre Research Institute, 698
Old Conjuring Books: A Bibliographical and Historical Study with a Supplementary Check-list, 43
Omanii, Abdullah, 5
Once Was Enough, 421
101 Stories of the Great Ballets, 466
Onions, C. T., 291
Opera Plot Index: A Guide to Locating Plots and Descriptions of Operas, Operettas, and Other Works of the Musical Theater, and Associated Material, 250
Original British Theatre Directory, 502
Ottemiller's Index to Plays in Collections; An Author and Title Index to Plays Appearing in Collections Published Between 1900 and 1985, 227
Owen, Bobbi, 349-51
Oxford Companion to Canadian Theatre, 262
Oxford Companion to the American Theatre, 264
Oxford Companion to the Theatre, 279

Packard, William, 292
Palmer, Eileen C., 239
Palmer, Helen H., 536
Parisian Stage: Alphabetical Indexes of Plays and Authors, 586
Parker, David L., 108
Parker, J. H., 176
Pascoe, Charles Eyre, 352
Passing Show, 625
Paul McPharlin Memorial Puppet Library and Collection, 708
Pence, James Harry, 247
Penguin Dictionary of the Theater, 298
Penninger, Frieda Elaine, 77
Pennsylvania State University. Special Collections Department., 709
PERFORM, 589

PERFORM-L, 590
Performance, 626
Performing Arts & Entertainment in Canada, 627
Performing Arts Annual, 438
Performing Arts Biography Master Index, 342
Performing Arts Books, 1876-1981: Including an International Index of Current Serial Publications, 78
Performing Arts/Books in Print: An Annotated Bibliography, 80
Performing Arts Journal, 628
Performing Arts Libraries and Museums of the World, 503
Performing Arts Research: A Guide to Information Sources, 11
Performing Arts Resources, 439
Perry, Jeb H., 353
Peterson, Bernard L., Jr., 354-5
Peterson, Richard, 440
Philadelphia Theatres, A-Z: A Comprehensive, Descriptive Record of 813 Theatres Constructed Since 1724, 399
Philpott, Alexis Robert, 293
Physical Education Index, 223
Pickering, David, 292
Pictorial History of the American Theatre, 1860-1985, 546
Plant, Richard, 23
Play Index, 248
Play Source, 629
Player's Library: The Catalogue of the Library of the British Drama League, 159
Players Guide: The Annual Pictorial Directory for Stage, Screen, Radio, and Television, 504
Playhouse America! A Directory of Theatres and Theatre Companies in the U.S.A., 505
Plays & Masques at Court During the Reigns of Elizabeth, James, and Charles, 579
Plays and Players, 632
Plays for Children and Young Adults: An Evaluative Index and Guide, 234
Plays in Process, 633
Plays in Reviews 1956-1985: British Drama and the Critics, 532
Plays International, 634
Plays of Jewish Interest, 121
Plays, Players, & Playwrights: An Illustrated History of the Theatre, 273
Plays: The Drama Magazine for Young People, 631

Playwright's Companion: A Submission Guide to Theatres & Contests in the U.S.A., 499
Political Left in the American Theatre of the 1930's: A Bibliographic Sourcebook, 33a
Poorman, Susan, 356
Princeton University. Visual Materials Division. Department of Rare Books and Special Collections, 710
Prisk, Berneice, 441
Prize-Winning American Drama: A Bibliographical and Descriptive Guide, 385
Pronko, Leonard C., 8
Prudhommeau, Germaine, 474
Puppet Theatre in America: A History, 1524-1948. With a Supplement Puppets in America Since 1948 by Marjorie Batchelder McPharlin, 433
Puppeteer's Library Guide. The Bibliographic Index to the Literature of the World Puppet Theatre, 31-2
Puppeteers of America, 743
Puppetry Journal, 635
Puppetry Library: An Annotated Bibliography Based on the Batchelder-McPharlin Collection at the University of New Mexico, 175

Quinn, Edward, 272

Rachow, Louis A., 9
Rae, Kenneth, 294
Raffe, W.G., 316
Raymond, Jack, 146
Reader's Encyclopedia of Shakespeare, 267
Reader's Encyclopedia of World Drama, 272
Readers' Guide to Periodical Literature, 215
Records of Early English Drama, 568-576a
Records of the New York Stage from 1750 to 1860, 556
REED-L: Records of Early English Drama, 591
Regional Theatre Directory, 506
Register: Directory of Designers, Artists, and Craftspeople, 519
Register of English Theatrical Documents 1660-1737, 75
Regueiro, José M., 180-1
Reichenberger, A.G., 183
Reid, Francis, 294a
Reimer-Torn, Susan, 477

Research Collections in Canadian Libraries. Pt. 2. Special Studies. Sect. 1. Theatre Resources in Canadian Collections, 497
Research in Dance, 109
Resources in Sacred Dance: Annotated Bibliography from Christian and Jewish Traditions, 115
Restoration & Eighteenth Century Theatre Research, 636
Restoration and Eighteenth-Century Dramatists, 318-20
Restoration and Eighteenth Century Theatre Research: A Bibliographical Guide, 1900-1968, 92
Reynolds, Nancy, 477
Richel, Veronica C., 442
Ritchey, David, 577
Robert F. Wagner Labor Archives, 711
Robert L. Parkinson Library and Research Center, Circus World Museum, 712
Roberts, Vera Mowry, 357
Robertson, Allen, 478
Robinson, Alice M., 357
Robinson, Doris, 110
Robinson, John William, 20
Roden, Robert F., 133
Rodgers and Hammerstein Fact Book: A Record of Their Works Together and with Other Collaborators, 401
Rogers, Paul P., 182
Rogerson, Margaret, 574
Rosalynde Stearn Puppet Collection, 183, 704
Rotoli, Nicholas John, 18
Rowse, A. L., 443
Rugg, Evelyn, 176
Rust, Brian A. L., 147-8
Ruyter, Nancy Lee Chalfa, 103

Salem, James M., 79, 537-9
Salgado, Gamini, 457
Samples, Gordon, 249, 540
Sampson, Henry T., 444, 578
Samuel French's Basic Catalog of Plays and Musicals, 188
Savarese, Nicola, 259
Savidge, Charlotte, 292
Scenic Design on Broadway: Designers and Their Credits, 1915-1990, 351
Schlessinger, June H., 234
Schlundt, Christena L., 111, 479
Schneider, Ulrich, 82
Schoolcraft, Ralph Newman, 80

Schwartz, Judith L., 111
Sedgwick, Dorothy, 81
Segrave, Kerry, 340
Seigel, Esther, 108
Selber, Charles, 475
Selected Theatre Criticism, 541
Selected Vaudeville Criticism, 542
Selective Index to Theatre Magazine, 207
Seller, Maxine Schwartz, 445
Senelick, Laurence, 82
Sergel, Sherman Louis, 295
Shakespeare A to Z; The Essential Reference to His Plays, His Poems, His Life and Times, and More, 266
Shakespeare: An Illustrated Dictionary, 305
Shakespeare and the Musical Stage: A Guide to Sources, Studies, and First Performances, 48
Shakespeare at Stratford upon Avon; The Libraries of the Royal Shakespeare Theatre and the Shakespeare Birthplace Trust, 184
Shakespeare Bibliography: The Catalogue of the Birmingham Shakespeare Library, 156
Shakespeare Companion, 1564-1954, 278
SHAKESPEARE ELECTRONIC CONFERENCE, 592
Shakespeare Glossary, 291
Shakespeare in Production, 1935-1978: A Selective Catalogue, 21
Shakespeare Promptbooks: A Descriptive Catalogue, 83
Shakespeare Survey, 445a
Shakespeare's Characters: A Complete Guide, 443
Shaland, Irene, 10
Sharp, Harold S., 446
Sharp, Marjorie Z., 446
Shattuck, Charles H., 83
Shaver, Ruth M., 447
Shemanski, Frances, 507
Shipley, Joseph T., 448
Show Music on Record: The First 100 Years, 146
Show Tunes, 1905-1991: The Songs, Shows, and Careers of Broadway's Major Composers, 454
Shubert Archive, 713
Sibley, Gertrude Marian, 134
Silverman, Maxwell, 449
Simas, Rick, 450
Simon, Alfred, 296, 423
Sinclair, Janet, 312

Slide, Anthony, 358, 508, 541-2
Smith, Ronald L., 149, 359
Sobel, Bernard, 297
Society of American Fight Directors, 744
Sokan, Robert, 185
Somerset, J. Alan B., 451
Songs of the Theater, 423
Source Materials in the Field of Theatre: An Annotated Bibliography and Subject Index to the Microfilm Collection, 151
Sourcebook for the Peforming Arts: A Directory of Collections, Resources, Scholars, and Critics in Theatre, Film, and Television, 508
Sources on African and African-Related Dance, 14
Southern, Richard, 294
Southern Theatre, 637
Spanish Drama Collection at the Ohio State University Library: A Descriptive Catalog, 152
Spanish Drama Collection in the Oberlin College Library: A Descriptive Catalog, 182
Spanish Drama of the Golden Age: A Catalogue of the Comedia Collection in the University of Pennsylvania Libraries, 180
Spanish Drama of the Golden Age: A Catalogue of the Manuscript Collection at the Hispanic Society of America, 181
Spanish Plays in English Translation: An Annotated Bibliography, 132
Spencer, David G., 92
Spivack, Carol, 509
Stage Costume Handbook, 441
Stage Crafts, 408
Stage Deaths: A Biographical Guide to International Theatrical Obituaries, 1850 to 1990, 323
Stage Fights: A Simple Handbook of Techniques, 400
Stage Guide: Technical Information on British Theatres, 409
Stage It with Music: An Encyclopedia Guide to the American Musical Theatre, 281a
Stage Lives: A Bibliography and Index to Theatrical Biographies in English, 324
Stage Makeup, 388
Stage Management: A Guidebook of Practical Techniques, 452
Stage Manager's Handbook, 402
Stage Managers Directory, 510

Stage Scenery, Machinery, and Lighting: A Guide to Information Sources, 86
Stage Specs: A Guide to Legit Theatres, 490a
Stagecraft for Nonprofessionals, 387
STAGECRAFT, 593
Stages: The National Theatre Magazine, 638
Stanley, William T., 543
Stars of Stand-up Comedy: A Biographical Encyclopedia, 359
Steadman, Susan M., 84
Stearn's Performing Arts Directory, 526
Steele, Mary Susan, 579
Stern, Lawrence, 452
Stevens, David, 85
Stevenson, Isabelle, 453
Stoddard, Richard, 86-7
Stratford Festival Story: A Catalogue-Index to the Stratford, Ontario, Festival 1953-1990, 451
Stratman, Carl J., 88-92, 135-6
Straumanis, Alfreds, 93
Studies in Dance History, 680
Studwell, William E., 250-1
Sturtevant, C. G., 693
Summer Theatre Directory, 511
Survey of Arts Administration Training, 512
Suskin, Steven, 454
Swortzell, Lowell, 455
Szmuk, Szilvia E., 155

Tams-Witmark Archives, 710
Taylor, John Russell, 298
Taylor, Thomas J., 93a
TCG Theatre Directory, 513
TCI (formerly Theatre Crafts), 639
TD&T: The Journal for Design & Production Professionals in the Performing Arts, 640
TDR: The Drama Review: A Journal of Performance Studies, 641
Teaterord [Theatre Words]. 299
Technical Manual and Dictionary of Classical Ballet, 311
Ten Modern American Playwrights: An Annotated Bibliography, 58
Ten Modern Irish Playwrights: A Comprehensive Annotated Bibliography, 59
Ten Years of Films on Ballet and Classical Dance 1956-1965, 112
Terry, Walter, 480
Texas Collection of Comedias Sueltas: A Descriptive Bibliography, 158
Text and Performance Quarterly, 642
Theater, 643

Theater Dictionary: British and American Terms in the Drama, Opera, and Ballet, 275
Theater Lexikon, 301
Theater Props Handbook: A Comprehensive Guide to Theater Properties, Materials, and Construction, 412
Theatre and Allied Arts: A Guide to Books Dealing with the History, Criticism, and Technic of the Drama and Theatre and Related Arts and Crafts, 22
Theatre and Cinema Architecture: A Guide to Information Sources, 87
Theatre and Performing Arts Collections, 9
Theatre at Stratford-upon-Avon: A Catalogue-Index to Productions of the Shakespeare Memorial/Royal Shakespeare Theatre, 1879-1978, 177
Theatre Backstage from A to Z, 287
Theatre Check List; A Guide to the Planning and Construction of Proscenium and Open Stage Theatres, 374
Theatre Communications Group, 745
Theatre Companies of the World, 416
Theatre Crafts Directory: Manufacturers, Suppliers, & Consultants for the Entertainment Technology Industry, 514
Theatre Historical Society of America, 746
Theatre History in Canada/Histoire du théâtre au Canada, 644
Theatre History Studies, 645
Theatre Information Bulletin, 646
Theatre Ireland, 647
Theatre Journal, 648
Theatre Language: A Dictionary of Terms in English of the Drama and Stage from Medieval to Modern Times, 265
Theatre Library Association, 747
Theatre Lighting: An Illustrated Glossary, 304
Theatre Management and Production in America: Commercial, Stock, Resident, College, Community, and Presenting Organizations, 417
Theatre Notebook, 649
Theatre of the British Isles, Excluding London: A Bibliography, 68
Theatre Profiles: The Illustrated Reference Guide to America's Nonprofit Professional Theatre, 515
Theatre Quarterly. See New Theatre Quarterly
Theatre Record, 544
Theatre Research International, 650

Theatre Royal, Bath: A Calendar of Performances at the Orchard Street Theatre, 1750-1805, 554
Theatre Survey, 651
Theatre Topics, 652
Theatre World, 456
Theatre: History, Criticism and Reference, 3
Theatre: Stage to Screen to Television, 422
THEATRE: The Theatre Discussion List, 594
Theatres of London, 430
Theatrical Calendar, 653
Theatrical Costume: A Guide to Information Sources, 56
Theatrical Designers: An International Biographical Dictionary, 343
Theatrical Index, 654
Theatrical Movement: A Bibliographical Anthology, 34
Themes in Drama, 655
Thomas, James W., 516
Thompson, Annie F., 113
Thompson, Donald, 113
Thompson, Glorianne Jackson, 14
Thompson, Lawrence S., 137-9
Thomson, Peter, 457
Thomson, Ruth Gibbons, 252-3
Three Centuries of English and American Plays: A Checklist. England: 1500-1800: United States: 1714-1830, 117
Times Index, 216
Tintori, Giampiero, 587
Tony Award: A Complete Listing, with a History of the American Theatre Wing, 453
Tony Award Book: Four Decades of Great American Theater, 435
Tony, Grammy, Emmy, Country: A Broadway, Television and Records Awards Reference, 397
Toohey, John L., 458
Toole-Stott, Raymond, 94-6
Towers, Deirdre, 114
Trapido, Joel, 300
Trefny, Beverly Robin, 239
Trilse, Christoph, 301
Troxell, Kay, ed., 115
Twentieth-Century American Dramatists, 338
Twentieth-Century Criticism of English Masques, Pageants, and Entertainments: 1558-1642: With a Suplement on the Folk-Play and Related Forms by Harry B. Caldwell, 25
20th Century Drama, 360
20th Century Theatre, 564

Twenty Modern British Playwrights: A Bibliography, 1956 to 1976, 60
TYA Today (Theatre for Young Audiences Today), 656

UCLA Journal of Dance Ethnology, 681
UNIMA-U.S.A., 748
United States Institute for Theatre Technology, 749
University of California, Davis. Shields Library. Department of Special Collections, 714
University of Florida Belknap Collection for the Performing Arts, 715
University of Georgia Libraries. Hargrett Rare Book and Manuscript Library, 716
University of Michigan Library. Theatre Collection, 717
University of Pittsburgh. Anna Pavlowa—Karl G. Heinrich Collection, 725
University of Southern California. Cinema—Television Library and Archives of Performing Arts, 718
University of Texas at Austin. Theatre History and Dramatic Literature Collections. Harry Ransom Humanities Research Center, 719
University of Washington Libraries. Drama Library, 720
Unterbrink, Mary, 361

Van Hoogstraten, Nicholas, 459
Van Zile, Judy, 116
Variety: The International Entertainment Weekly, 657
Variety Entertainment and Outdoor Amusements: A Reference Guide, 12
Variety International Show Business Reference, 1983, 414
Variety Obits: An Index to Obituaries in Variety (1905-1978), 353
Variety Obituaries 1905- , 362
Variety's Who's Who in Show Business, 332
Vaudevillians: A Dictionary of Vaudeville Performers, 358
Vaughan, David, 309
Vaughan Williams Memorial Library Catalogue of the English Folk Dance and Song Society, 196
Ver Nooy, Winifred, 240-2
Victorian Actors and Actresses in Review: A Dictionary of Contemporary Views of Representative British and American Actors and Actresses, 1837-1901, 345

Victorian Plays: A Record of Significant Productions on the London Stage, 1837-1901, 436
Vince, Ronald W., 302
Vinson, James, 363

Wagner, Anton, 140
Wagner, Robert F., 711
Wagonheim, Sylvia Stoler, 555
Walkup, Fairfax Proudfit, 460
Wall Street Journal Index, 217
Ward, Carlton, 490
Warren, Gretchen Ward, 481
Washington Post Index, 218
Wasserman, Paul, 517
Wasserman, Steven R., 518
Waters, T. A., 303
Watson, Lee, 461
Wearing, J. P., 29, 364, 580-585a
Webb, Elmon, 519
Wegelin, Oscar, 141
Wehlburg, Albert F. C., 304
Weinstock, Richard A., 509
Weintraub, Stanley, 365-6
Wells, Stanley, 305
Wemyss, Francis Courtney, 367
Wemyss' Chronology of the American Stage from 1752 to 1852, 367
Wentink, Andrew Mark, 197
Wesson, John M., 576a
Whalon, Marion K., 11
White Tops: Devoted Exclusively to the Circus, 658
Who Was Who in the Theatre: 1912-1976: A Biographical Dictionary of Actors, Actresses, Directors, Playwrights, and Producers of the English-Speaking Theatre, 368

Who's Where in the American Theatre: A Directory of Affiliated Theatre Artists in the U.S.A., 520
Who's Who in Entertainment, 369
Who's Who in Shakespeare, 431
Who's Who in the American Circus, 693
Who's Who in the Theatre, 370
Wichmann, Elizabeth, 26
Wicks, Charles Beaumont, 586
Wilmeth, Don B., 12, 97-8, 306-06a
Wilson, G.B.L., 317
Wisconsin Center for Film and Theater Research, 721
Woddis, Carole, 277
Woll, Allen L., 462
Women & Performance: A Journal of Feminist Theory, 659
Women in Comedy, 340
Woodward, Gertrude L., 142
Woodyard, George F., 70
Working Actor's Guide, L.A., 521
World Ballet and Dance, 482

Yale University. Drama Library, 722
York [Records of Early English Drama], 574
Yorkshire Stage 1766-1803: A Calendar of Plays, Together with Cast Lists for the Wilkinson's Circuit of Theatres (Doncaster, Hull, Leeds, Pontefract, Wakefield, and York) and the Yorkshire Company's Engagements in Beverly, Halifax, Newcastle, Sheffield, and Edinburgh, 551
Young, William C., 371, 416, 463-4, 522
Yugoslav Dance: An Introduction and List of Sources Available in United States Libraries, 103

Subject Index

This index covers entries for all books, periodicals, organizations, electronic discussion groups, and library collections in this guide. Numbers cited in the index are entry numbers.

Acoustics
  bibliographies, 49
  dictionaries and encyclopedias, 287
Actors and actresses. *See also* Women performers
  bibliographies, 19, 53, 76
  biographies, 321, 323-4, 328, 330, 339, 341, 344-5, 347-8, 367-8, 370-1
  directories, 504, 520
  library collections, 700, 715, 718
Actors and actresses, Jewish. *See* Jewish actors and actresses
Actors' Equity Association—library collections, 711
Actors' Fund of America—library collections, 711
Adelphi Theatre (London), 565
Africa
  dance—bibliographies, 14
  theatre—
    bibliographies, 40
    catalogs, 162
African-American dance
  bibliographies, 99
  catalogs, 162
  library collections, 687
  periodical indexes, 204
  yearbooks, 383
African-American plays—bibliographies, 126
African-American playwrights
  bibliographies, 5, 17-18, 26
  biographies, 354-5
African-American theatre
  bibliographies, 15
  biographies, 339
  chronologies, 578
  dictionaries and encyclopedias, 284
  handbooks, 444, 462
  library collections, 687
  organizations, 732
  periodical indexes, 204
  periodicals, 602
  yearbooks, 383

American Guild of Variety Artists—library collections, 711
American National Theatre and Academy—library collections, 690
Architecture, theatre. *See also* Theatres; subheading theatres under names of cities and countries
  bibliographies, 87, 449
  handbooks, 374, 449
Arts—management. *See* Performing arts—management
Asia. *See also* China; Japan; India
  theatre
    bibliographies, 26
    periodicals, 599

Ballet. *See also* Dance
  bibliographies, 105
  characters—handbooks, 446
  dictionaries and encyclopedias, 307-13, 315-17
  handbooks, 465-66, 468, 470, 472, 474, 477-78, 480
  periodicals, 660-63, 666-68, 671, 673, 679
  synopses—indexes, 251
  technique—handbooks, 473, 476, 481
  yearbooks, 467, 482
Baltimore—theatre—chronologies, 577
Berlin, Irving—bibliographies, 61
Bitnet lists. *See* Dance—electronic discussion groups; Theatre—electronic discussion groups
Black dance. *See* African-American dance
Black plays. *See* African-American plays
Black playwrights. *See* African-American playwrights
Black theatre. *See* African-American theatre
Booth, Edwin—library collections, 691
Boston Public Library, Allen A. Brown Collection, 157
Breen, Robert—library collections, 690
British Drama League—catalogs, 159

238 / **Subject Index**

Broadway (New York City)—dictionaries and encyclopedias, 263
Burlesque-bibliographies, 12, 97

Canada
 performing arts—library collections, 705, 784
 plays—bibliographies, 140
 playwrights—biographies, 326
 theatre
  bibliographies, 23, 81
  dictionaries and encyclopedias, 262
  periodicals, 604, 627, 644
  theatres—directories, 483, 490a
Carnivals
 bibliographies, 12, 97
 dictionaries and encyclopedias, 306
Characters. *See* Ballet—characters—handbooks; Musical theatre—characters—handbooks; Plays —characters—handbooks
Chicago
 performing arts—library collections, 686, 723
Children's plays
 indexes, 234, 237-39
 periodicals, 631
Children's theatre. *See also* children's plays
 bibliographies, 35, 55
 dictionaries and encyclopedias, 268
 handbooks, 432, 455
 organizations, 729
 periodicals, 656
China. *See also* Asia
 theatre—bibliographies, 69, 71
Choreographers. *See* Dance—biographies; Modern dance—biographies
Choreography *See also* Ballet; Dance; Modern dance
 periodicals, 663
Church plays. *See* Plays, religious
Circus
 bibliographies, 6, 12, 94, 96-97
 biographies, 693
 catalogs, 150, 178-79, 185
 dictionaries and encyclopedias, 306
 library collections, 693, 695, 707, 710, 712
 organizations, 734
 periodicals, 601, 605, 658
Combat, stage. *See* Fighting, stage
Comedians—biographies, 340, 359, 361
Comedias sueltas. *See* Spain—plays

Comédie Française (Paris)—chronologies, 549, 557, 559
Comedy. *See also* Comedians—biographies
 discographies, 143, 148, 149
Commedia dell'arte—bibliographies, 46
Community theatre—organizations, 727
Conjuring. *See* Magic
Costume
 bibliographies, 47, 56
 handbooks, 376-78, 411, 437, 441, 447, 460
 indexes, 255
 library collections, 715-16, 719
 periodicals, 639-40
Costume designers
 biographies, 349
 directories, 519
Critics. *See* Great Britain—theatre—reviews; Europe—theatre—reviews; Theatre-Reviews; United States—theatre-reviews

Dance. *See also* African-American dance; Ballet; Folk dance; Modern dance
 bibliographies, 6, 13, 34, 54, 99-116
 biographies, 321, 323-24, 328, 372-73
 indexes, 364
 careers—handbooks, 395a
 catalogs, 189-97
 dictionaries and encyclopedias, 307-17
 dictionaries, multilingual, 307, 311-12, 315
 directories, 523-26
 education—directories, 395a, 523, 525
 electronic discussion groups, 595
 filmographies and videographies, 65, 108, 112, 114
 handbooks, 465-82
 library collections, 692, 698, 715, 717, 723-25
 library resources—directories, 524
 medical aspects—periodicals, 669, 676
 organizations, 750-57
 periodicals, 660-81
  bibliographies, 110
  indexes, 203, 219-23
 sources—bibliographies, 111
 videographies. *See* Dance—filmographies and videographies
 yearbooks, 471, 482
Dance, folk. *See* Folk dance
Dance history—periodicals, 667, 680
Dance management. *See* Performing arts—management
Dance, modern. *See* Modern dance

Dance notation
 organizations, 753, 755-56
 periodicals, 670-71
Dance, religious—bibliography, 115
Derra de Moroda, Friderica, 190
Designers, theatrical
 biographies, 336, 343, 349-51
 directories, 494, 519
Detroit—performing arts—library collections, 687
Detroit Public Library, E. Azalia Hackley Memorial Collection of Negro Music, Dance, and Drama—catalogs, 162
Dinner theatre—directories, 496a
Directors. *See* Play directors
Dramatists. *See* Playwrights

Educational theatre. *See* Children's theatre
Electronic discussion groups. *See* Dance—electronic discussion groups; Theatre—electronic discussion groups
England. *See* Great Britain
Estonia—theatre—bibliographies, 93
Ethnic theatre. *See* United States—ethnic theatre—handbooks
Europe. *See also* names of individual countries
 theatre—reviews, 536, 539

Federal Theatre Project, 550, 690
Festivals—directories, 492, 498, 507, 509, 517
Fighting, stage
 handbooks, 400
 organizations, 744
Folger Shakespeare Library—catalogs, 164-167
Folk dance
 catalogs, 196
 dictionaries and encyclopedias, 316
 handbooks, 469
 indexes, 246
 organizations, 752
 periodicals, 665, 674, 681
France
 Dance—sources—bibliographies, 111
 plays—bibliographies, 119, 137
 theatre
  chronologies, 549, 557, 559, 586
  dictionaries and encyclopedias, 296
Fuchs, Theodore, 684

Gays—plays. *See* Plays, gay and lesbian
Germany
 plays
  bibliographies, 118
  catalogs, 171
 theatre—handbooks, 442
Gershwin, George, 61
Gershwin, Ira, 61
Gilbert and Sullivan
 bibliographies, 33
 dictionaries and encyclopedias, 256, 261, 269
 concordances, 390
 handbooks, 434
Gilbert, William Schenck. *See* Gilbert and Sullivan
Great Britain
 plays—bibliographies, 117, 122-24, 131, 134-35, 139, 142
 theatre
  bibliographies, 20, 62, 68, 91
  biographies, 331, 345, 347, 352, 364
  catalogs, 159
  chronologies, 545, 548, 551, 554-55, 558, 564, 568-76a, 579
  dictionaries and encyclopedias, 260, 275
  directories, 494, 502
  library resources, 485
  periodicals, 620, 632, 636, 649
   bibliographies, 90
   indexes, 205, 216
  reviews, 532, 536, 539, 543-44
  sources, 62
  yearbooks, 419
 theatre, medieval—bibliographies, 62, 77
 theatre, sixteenth century—bibliographies, 25, 77, 85
 theatre, seventeenth century
  bibliographies, 25, 66, 75, 77
  sources, 75, 92
 theatre, eighteenth century
  bibliographies, 63, 66, 75, 92
  sources, 75
 theatre, nineteenth century
  bibliographies, 29, 53
  handbooks, 436
 theatre, twentieth century—bibliographies, 28, 60, 73-74
Great Britain—theatres, 409, 428. *See also* London—theatres

Hairstyles. *See* Costume; Makeup
Hammerstein, Oscar, II—handbooks, 401
Hampden, Walter—library collections, 691
Harlem (New York City)—dictionaries and encyclopedias, 284
Hart, Lorenz
  bibliographies, 61
  handbooks, 401
Heinrich, Karl G.—library collections, 725
Homosexuals—plays. *See* Plays, gay and lesbian
Houdini, Harry—library collections, 701
Hubbard Street Dance Company—library collections, 723
Humphrey, Doris, 197

Illinois State University Circus and Related Arts Collection—catalog, 185
India—dance—bibliography, 116
Internet lists. *See* Dance—electronic discussion groups; Theatre—electronic discussion groups
Ireland—theatre
  bibliographies, 7, 59, 63, 72
  periodicals, 647
Italy
  plays—catalogs, 160-61, 169
  theatre. *See* Commedia dell'arte
  theatres. *See* Scala Theatre (Milan)—chronologies

Japan. *See also* Asia, Kabuki
  theatre
    bibliographies, 8
    dictionaries and encyclopedias, 286
    handbooks, 405, 447
Jewish actors and actresses—biographies, 337
Jewish plays—bibliographies, 121
Johns Hopkins University Loewenberg Collection—catalog, 171
Juggling—organizations, 737

Kabuki
  dictionaries and encyclopedias, 286
  handbooks, 405, 447
Keith/Albee Theatres—library collections, 699

La Scala. *See* Scala (Milan)
Latin America
  plays—indexes, 233
  theatre
    bibliographies, 45, 70, 233
    periodicals, 615
Latvia—theatre—bibliographies, 93
Lesbians—plays. *See* Plays, gay and lesbian
Leslie, Serge, 192
Library of Congress—performing arts—yearbooks, 438
Lighting designers—biographies, 350
Listservs. *See* Dance—electronic discussion groups; Theatre—electronic discussion groups
Lithuania—theatre—bibliographies, 93
London
  theatre
    chronologies, 563, 565, 580-85a
    portraits—collections, 173
    theatres, 380, 409-10, 424, 429-30
Los Angeles
  performing arts—library collections, 703
  theatre-directories, 521

Magic
  bibliographies, 4, 6, 12, 38, 42-43, 95, 97, 178-79
  biographies, 281, 406
  dictionaries and encyclopedias, 281, 285, 303
  handbooks, 406
  library collections, 682, 701, 707
  periodicals, 610, 617
  bibliographies, 16
Makeup—handbooks, 379, 388
Masques
  bibliographies, 25, 124, 134
  chronologies, 579
McGill University Library Rosalynde Stearn Puppet Collection—catalogs, 183
McPharlin, Marjorie Batchelder—library collections, 683
McPharlin, Paul—library collections, 683, 708
Medicine shows
  bibliographies, 12
  dictionaries and encyclopedias, 306
Medieval plays. *See* Plays, medieval

Subject Index / 241

Mime
 bibliographies, 34, 51-52
 organizations, 741
 periodicals, 678
Minstrel shows—bibliographies, 12, 97
Modern dance. *See also* Dance
 biographies, 373
 dictionaries and encyclopedias, 314
 handbooks, 477-78
Monologues and scenes—indexes, 224-25, 229-30, 232
Music hall
 bibliographies, 82, 97
 biographies, 325
 discographies, 147
Musical theatre. *See also* Gershwin, George; Gershwin, Ira; Gilbert and Sullivan; Rodgers, Richard
 bibliographies, 6, 12, 36, 48, 51, 61, 97
 characters—handbooks, 446
 chronologies, 547, 552, 553
 dance—handbooks, 475, 479
 dictionaries and encyclopedias, 276, 281a
 discographies, 144-48
 handbooks, 384, 395, 398, 401, 423, 426-27, 444, 450, 454
 library collections, 696, 707, 710
 synopses—indexes, 228, 250
 videographies, 65

New York City. *See also* Broadway (New York City)—dictionaries and encyclopedias; Harlem (New York City)—dictionaries and encyclopedias
 performing arts—directories, 496, 500
 theatre—chronologies, 556, 560-62, 566-67
 theatres, 418, 459
New York Public Library—catalogs, 178-79, 193-95
New York Shakespeare Festival—bibliographies, 57
Niles, Doris, 192

One-act plays—indexes, 240-245
Opera. *See* Musical theatre
Operetta. *See* Gilbert and Sullivan; Musical theatre
Outdoor theatre—organizations, 736

Papp, Joseph—bibliographies, 57
Paris—theatre—chronologies, 549, 557, 559

Pavlova, Anna—library collections, 725
Performance art—periodicals, 611
Performing arts. *See also* Ballet; Circus; Dance; Magic; Modern dance; Musical theatre; Puppet theatre; Theatre
 bibliographies, 2, 11, 22, 41, 54, 78, 80
 biographies, 324, 328, 330, 332, 339, 346, 348, 369
 indexes, 321, 342, 356, 364
 careers—handbooks, 395a
 characters—handbooks, 446
 directories, 489, 491
 education—directories, 395a
 library resources—bibliographies, 9, 439
 management, 24, 198, 206
  handbooks, 417
  periodicals, 598, 612-13, 646, 653-54
 obituaries, 362
 indexes, 323
 periodicals—indexes, 198-223
Philadelphia
 performing arts—library collections, 689
 theatres, 399
Play directors—directories, 494, 516
Playbills
 catalogs, 172
 library collections, 686, 689, 692, 697, 701, 703, 707, 713, 715, 717, 719
Playhouses. *See* London—theatres; New York City—theatres; Philadelphia—theatres; United States—theatres; and names of individual theatres
Plays. *See also* subheading plays under names individual countries
 bibliographies, 79, 117-42
 catalogs, commercial, 186-88
 characters—handbooks, 381, 440, 443, 446
 handbooks, 396, 415, 420-22, 448
 in periodicals—indexes, 235-36
 indexes, 226-27, 231, 233-45, 248-49, 252-54
 prizes, 385, 397, 413, 435, 453, 458
  directories, 488, 499
 synopses, 396, 415, 425
Plays, African-American. *See* African-American plays
Plays, gay and lesbian—bibliographies, 122a, 127
Plays, Jewish. *See* Jewish plays
Plays, medieval-bibliographies, 136
Plays, religious—bibliographies, 130

Playwrights
  bibliographies, 5, 17-18, 44, 58-60
  biographies, 318-20, 322, 326-27, 329, 333-35, 338, 357, 360, 363, 365-66, 368
  directories, 494
  organizations, 742
  periodicals, 607
Pollack, Channing—library collections, 694
Porter, Cole—bibliographies, 61
Portraits, theatrical
  catalogs, 168, 173
  indexes, 567
Prizes. See Plays—prizes
Prompt books
  bibliographies, 63, 83
  catalogs, 163
Properties, theatrical
  bibliographies, 49
  handbooks, 412
Puerto Rico—dance—bibliographies, 113
Puppet theatre
  bibliographies, 31-32, 51, 97
  catalogs, 175, 178-79, 183
  dictionaries and encyclopedias, 293
  handbooks, 389, 433
  library collections, 683, 685, 704, 707, 708
  organizations, 733, 743, 748
  periodicals, 635

Religious dance. See Dance, religious
Religious plays. See Plays, religious
Richardson, P. J. S., 191
Ridge, John, 715
Robbins, Jerome, 479
Rodgers, Richard
  bibliographies, 61
  handbooks, 401
Royal Shakespeare Theatre—catalogs, 177, 184
Russia—theatre—dictionaries and encyclopedias, 273

Sacred dance. See Dance, religious
Sacred plays. See Plays, religious
San Francisco Mime Troupe—library collections, 714
Sans Pareil Theatre (London), 565
Scala Theatre (Milan)—chronologies, 587
Scenes—indexes. See Monologues and scenes—indexes
Scenographers. See Designers, theatrical
Set designers. See Designers, theatrical
Seymour, William—library collections, 710

Shakespeare, William
  catalogs, 156, 164-67
  characters—handbooks, 443
  dictionaries and encyclopedias, 266-67, 278, 291, 305
  electronic discussion groups, 592
  library collections, 688
  stage history
    bibliographies, 21, 48, 57, 83
    catalogs, 177, 184
    handbooks, 451
    reviews, 527
    yearbooks, 445a
Shakespeare Memorial Theatre—catalogs. See Royal Shakespeare Theatre—catalogs
Shawn, Ted—library collections, 715, 725
Show dancing. See Musical theatre—dance—handbooks
Showboats—bibliographies, 97
Shubert Archive—periodicals, 625
Shubert Organization
  library collections, 713
  periodicals, 625
Songs—handbooks, 384, 423, 454
Sound. See Acoustics
Spain
  plays
    bibliographies, 132, 138
    catalogs, 152-55, 158, 174, 176, 180-82
  theatre—periodicals, 609
Stage fighting. See Fighting, stage
Stage lighting
  bibliographies, 49, 86
  dictionaries and encyclopedias, 287, 294, 304
  directories, 500, 514
  handbooks, 294a, 387, 408, 461
  library collections, 684, 709
  periodicals, 616, 639-40
Stage Management
  directories, 510
  handbooks, 402, 452
  periodicals, 639-40
Stage properties. See Properties, theatrical
Stage-setting and scenery
  bibliographies, 37, 49, 86
  dictionaries and encyclopedias, 287, 294
  directories, 500, 514
  electronic discussion groups, 593
  handbooks, 387, 408
  organizations, 749
  periodicals, 639-40

St. Denis, Ruth—library collections, 715, 725
Stearn, Rosalynde—library collections, 704
Stratford, Ontario Shakespeare Festival, 451
Striptease—bibliographies. *See* Burlesque—bibliographies
Sullivan, Sir Arthur. *See* Gilbert and Sullivan

Tams-Witmark Archives, 710
Tent shows—dictionaries and encyclopedias, 306
Tharp, Twyla—library collections, 698
Theatre. *See also* Children's theatre; Masques; Musical theatre; Subheading theatre under names of individual countries and cities
  acoustics. *See* Acoustics
  architecture. *See* Architecture, theatre
  bibliographies, 1, 3, 22, 34, 50-51, 54, 67, 178-79
  biographies, 323-24, 328, 330, 332, 339, 344, 346, 348, 368, 370, 508
    indexes, 321, 342, 356, 364
  careers—handbooks, 395a
  catalogs, 151, 157, 159, 178, 179
  designers. *See* Designers, theatrical
  dictionaries and encyclopedias, 256-275, 277, 279-80, 282-83, 288-90, 292, 295, 297-301
  dictionaries, multilingual, 257, 274, 294, 299
  dinner. *See* Dinner theatre
  directories, 486, 489, 501, 508, 514, 520
  education—directories, 395a, 484, 512
  electronic discussion groups, 588-94
  finance—periodicals, 597
  handbooks, 382, 414, 415, 457
  library collections, 682-722
  library resources
    bibliographies, 439
    directories, 485, 493, 497, 503, 508, 522
    periodicals, 603
  management. *See* Performing arts—management
  medieval—dictionaries and encyclopedias, 302
  nineteenth century—bibliographies, 53
  obituaries, 362
    bibliographies, 323
    indexes, 353
  organizations, 726-749
  periodicals, 596-659
    indexes, 198-218, 247
  reviews, 527-544. *See also* reviews under Europe—theatre; Great Britain—theatre; United States—theatre
  twentieth century—bibliographies, 27, 41, 44
Theatre Communications Group—catalogs, 172
Theatre companies
  directories, 505
  handbooks, 391-393, 416
Theatre Magazine—indexes, 207
Theatres
  directories, 483, 487-88, 490, 505
  organizations, 740, 746
  periodicals, 664, 672, 678
Tony Award. *See* Plays—prizes

United Kingdom. *See* Great Britain
United Scenic Artists—library collections, 711
United States
  dance—bibliographies, 54
  ethnic theatre—handbooks, 445
  performing arts—yearbooks, 383, 438
  plays
    bibliographies, 117, 120, 126, 128-29, 133, 139, 141
    handbooks, 375, 386, 404, 425
    prizes. *See* Plays—prizes
  theatre
    bibliographies, 10, 39, 54, 64, 89, 93a, 98
    biographies, 341, 357, 364, 367, 371
    chronologies, 546, 550, 564
    dictionaries and encyclopedias, 264, 273, 275, 281a, 284, 306a
    directories, 520. *See also* United States—theatre companies—directories; United States—theatres—directories
    handbooks, 386, 394, 445
    periodicals, 596, 637
      bibliographies, 88
    pictorial works, 546
    reviews, 528-31, 533-35, 537-38, 541
    yearbooks, 375, 383, 403-04, 456
  theatre, eighteenth century—bibliographies, 64, 98
  theatre, nineteenth century—bibliographies, 53, 64, 76, 98
  theatre, twentieth century
    bibliographies, 33a, 58
    catalogs, 172
  theatre companies, 391-393
    directories, 499, 505-506, 511, 513, 515

United States (*continued*)
  theatres
    directories, 483, 490, 490a, 499, 505-506, 511, 513, 515
    handbooks, 449, 463-64
University of New Mexico Batchelder—McPharlin Puppetry Collection—catalogs, 175
University of Texas—catalogs, 170
University of Waterloo Library Dance Collection—catalogs, 189

Variety (newspaper)
  indexes, 353
  obituaries, 362
    indexes, 353
Vaudeville
  bibliographies, 12, 178-79
  biographies, 358
  dictionaries and encyclopedias, 306
  indexes, 364
  library collections, 699, 707, 715
  reviews, 542

Vaughan Williams Memorial Library—catalogs, 196

Wild west shows
  bibliographies, 12
  library collections, 712
Williams, Vaughan, Memorial Library—catalogs. *See* Vaughan Williams Memorial Library—catalogs
Wittop, Freddy—library collections, 716
Women and theatre
  bibliographies, 84
  roles, 407
Women performers
  biographies, 340, 357, 361
  periodicals, 659
Women playwrights
  bibliographies, 30, 120
  biographies, 357

Yugoslavia—dance—bibliographies, 103

LIBRARY USE ONLY
DOES NOT CIRCULATE